State and Society in 21st-century China

This book shows how China's economic "Mandate of Mammon" cannot fully replace the legitimist "Mandate of Heaven." The ex-Communist state dispossesses its proletariat and arrests strike leaders but not ordinary strikers. Tax evasions, moral deviances, local uses of election laws against officials, and other half-institutionalized forms of social politics are richly documented here. The chapters mix fresh research with bold new interpretations. Most of these authors show China's regime type as incoherent, neither residual-revolutionary nor transitional-liberal. The editors have thus unified the book around a theme that contributes to comparative politics. Everyone who is interested in contemporary China needs to read this book. I will certainly use it in courses.

> Lynn T. White III, Professor of Politics and International Affairs,
> Woodrow Wilson School, Princeton University

Written by a team of leading China scholars, this book explores the dynamics of state power and legitimation in 21st-century China, and the implications of changing state–society relations for the future viability of the People's Republic. Subjects covered include:

- the legitimacy of the Communist Party;
- state–society relations;
- ethnic and religious resistance;
- rural and urban contention;
- nationalism;
- popular and youth culture;
- prospects for democracy.

Broad in sweep and rich in empirical detail, this timely volume will appeal to students and scholars of contemporary China, as well as those interested in the dynamics of political and social change.

Peter Hays Gries is Assistant Professor of Political Science at the University of Colorado, Boulder and Co-Director of the Sino-American Security Dialogue. He is author of *China's New Nationalism: Pride, Politics and Diplomacy.*

Stanley Rosen is Professor in the Department of Political Science at the University of Southern California. He has published widely on China and his books include *Red Guard Factionalism and the Cultural Revolution in Guangzhou* and *Policy Conflicts in Post-Mao China: A Documentary Survey with Analysis* (co-edited with John P. Burns).

Asia's Transformations
Edited by Mark Selden, Binghamton University
and Cornell University, USA

The books in this series explore the political, social, economic, and cultural consequences of Asia's transformations in the 20th and 21st centuries. The series emphasizes the tumultuous interplay of local, national, regional, and global forces as Asia bids to become the hub of the world economy. While focusing on the contemporary, it also looks back to analyze the antecedents of Asia's contested rise.

This series comprises several strands:

Asia's Transformations aims to address the needs of students and teachers, and the titles will be published in hardback and paperback. Titles include:

State and Society in 21st-century China
Crisis, contention, and legitimation
Edited by Peter Hays Gries and Stanley Rosen

The Battle for Asia
From decolonization to globalization
Mark T. Berger

Ethnicity in Asia
Edited by Colin Mackerras

Chinese Society
Change, conflict and resistance (2nd edition)
Edited by Elizabeth J. Perry and Mark Selden

The Resurgence of East Asia
500, 150 and 50 year perspectives
Edited by Giovanni Arrighi, Takeshi Hamashita, and Mark Selden

The Making of Modern Korea
Adrian Buzo

Korean Society
Civil society, democracy and the state
Edited by Charles K. Armstrong

Remaking the Chinese State
Strategies, society and security
Edited by Chien-min Chao and Bruce J. Dickson

Mao's Children in the New China
Voices from the Red Guard generation
Yarong Jiang and David Ashley

Chinese Society
Change, conflict and resistance
Edited by Elizabeth J. Perry and Mark Selden

Opium, Empire and the Global Political Economy
Carl A. Trocki

Japan's Comfort Women
Sexual slavery and prostitution during World War II and the US occupation
Yuki Tanaka

Hong Kong's History
State and society under colonial rule
Edited by Tak-Wing Ngo

Debating Human Rights
Critical essays from the United States and Asia
Edited by Peter Van Ness

Asia's Great Cities Each volume aims to capture the heartbeat of the contemporary city from multiple perspectives emblematic of the author's own deep familiarity with the distinctive faces of the city, its history, society, culture, politics, and economics, and its evolving position in national, regional, and global frameworks. While most volumes emphasize urban developments since the Second World War, some pay close attention to the legacy of the *longue durée* in shaping the contemporary. Thematic and comparative volumes address such themes as urbanization, economic and financial linkages, architecture and space, wealth and power, gendered relationships, planning and anarchy, and ethnographies in national and regional perspective. Titles include:

Hong Kong
Global city
Stephen Chiu and Tai-Lok Lui

Shanghai
Global city
Jeff Wasserstrom

Singapore
Carl Trocki

Beijing in the Modern World
David Strand and Madeline Yue Dong

Bangkok
Place, practice and representation
Marc Askew

Asia.com is a series which focuses on the ways in which new information and communication technologies are influencing politics, society, and culture in Asia. Titles include:

Asia.com
Asia encounters the Internet
Edited by K.C. Ho, Randolph Kluver, and Kenneth C.C. Yang

Japanese Cybercultures
Edited by Mark McLelland and Nanette Gottlieb

Literature and Society is a series that seeks to demonstrate the ways in which Asian Literature is influenced by the politics, society, and culture in which it is produced. Titles include:

Chinese Women Writers and the Feminist Imagination (1905–1945)
Haiping Yan

The Body in Postwar Japanese Fiction
Edited by Douglas N. Slaymaker

RoutledgeCurzon Studies in Asia's Transformations is a forum for innovative new research intended for a high-level specialist readership, and the titles will be available in hardback only. Titles include:

1. **Chinese Media, Global Contexts**
   Edited by Chin-Chuan Lee

2. **Imperialism in South East Asia**
   'A fleeting, passing phase'
   Nicholas Tarling

3. **Internationalizing the Pacific**
   The United States, Japan and the Institute of Pacific Relations in War and Peace, 1919–1945
   Tomoko Akami

4. **Koreans in Japan**
   Critical voices from the margin
   Edited by Sonia Ryang

5. **The American Occupation of Japan and Okinawa**
   Literature and memory (now available in paperback)
   Michael Molasky

Critical Asian Scholarship is a series intended to showcase the most important individual contributions to scholarship in Asian studies. Each of the volumes presents a leading Asian scholar addressing themes that are central to his or her most significant and lasting contribution to Asian studies. The series is committed to the rich variety of research and writing on Asia, and is not restricted to any particular discipline, theoretical approach, or geographical expertise.

China's Past, China's Future
Energy, food, environment
Vaclav Smil

China Unbound
Evolving perspectives on the Chinese past
Paul A. Cohen

Women and the Family in Chinese History
Patricia Buckley Ebrey

Southeast Asia
A testament
George McT. Kahin

State and Society in 21st-century China

Crisis, contention, and legitimation

Edited by
Peter Hays Gries
and Stanley Rosen

RoutledgeCurzon
Taylor & Francis Group

NEW YORK AND LONDON

First published 2004
by RoutledgeCurzon
29 West 35th Street, New York, NY 10001

Simultaneously published in the UK
by RoutledgeCurzon
11 New Fetter Lane, London EC4P 4EE

RoutledgeCurzon is an imprint of the Taylor & Francis Group

Typeset in Times by Taylor & Francis Books Ltd
Printed and bound in Great Britain by TJ International Ltd, Padstow,
Cornwall

Library of Congress Cataloging in Publication Data
State and society in 21st century China: crisis, contention, and
legitimation / Edited by Peter Hays Gries and Stanley Rosen.
p. cm. – (Asia's transformations)
1. China – Social conditions – 1976– 2. China – Politics and
government – 1976– 3. Popular culture – China. I. Gries, Peter Hays,
1967– II. Rosen, Stanley, 1942– III. Series.
HN733.5.S74 2004
306'.0951–dc22

2003023895

British Library Cataloguing in Publication Data
A catalogue record for this book is available from the British Library

ISBN 0–415–33204–4 (hbk)
ISBN 0–415–33205–2 (pbk)

For Mônica and Zeus

For Sheila, Dorothy, Debbie, and Melanie

Contents

Contributors

Harley Balzer, Associate Professor of Government and International Affairs and former Director of the Center for Eurasian, Russian, and East European Studies, Georgetown University.

Bruce J. Dickson, Associate Professor of Political Science and International Affairs, The George Washington University.

Peter Hays Gries, Assistant Professor of Political Science, University of Colorado, Boulder.

Richard Kraus, Professor of Political Science, University of Oregon.

Colin Mackerras, Foundation Professor, Department of International Business and Asian Studies, Griffith University, Brisbane.

Kevin J. O'Brien, Professor of Political Science, University of California, Berkeley.

Stanley Rosen, Professor of Political Science, University of Southern California.

Vivienne Shue, Leverhulme Professor of Contemporary Chinese Studies, Oxford University.

Dorothy J. Solinger, Professor of Political Science, University of California, Irvine.

Patricia Thornton, Assistant Professor of Political Science, Trinity College.

Timothy B. Weston, Associate Professor of History, University of Colorado, Boulder.

Teresa Wright, Associate Professor of Political Science, California State University, Long Beach.

Acknowledgments

The idea for this volume began at a panel held at the 2001 annual meeting of the American Political Science Association in San Francisco, California. Entitled "Contested Claims: Popular Opinion and Regime Legitimacy in 21st Century China," the panel stimulated talk of a more comprehensive collaborative volume, which took shape after panel chair Peter Gries asked Stanley Rosen to contribute a chapter and co-edit the volume with him. With funding from the East Asian Studies Center, USC, and the USC-UCLA Joint Center for East Asia, Rosen then hosted a follow-up conference at the University of Southern California in April 2002 and the volume was born.

Peter Gries would like to acknowledge financial support provided by a postdoctoral fellowship at the Mershon Center for Security Studies at Ohio State University and research funds provided by the University of Colorado. His intellectual debts are longer. The early work of Stanley Rosen, Anita Chan, and Jon Unger on the Cultural Revolution inspired his interest in pursuing an academic career in Chinese politics. Working with Stan on this project, therefore, has been particularly rewarding. At the University of Michigan, Martin Powers inspired him to rethink the question of "Chinese popular opinion," and directed him toward Lin Yutang's neglected 1936 gem *A History of the Press and Public Opinion in China*. At Berkeley, a reading of Max Weber's seminal work on authority and his much maligned 1922 *Religion of China* further inspired a desire to re-examine the dynamics of state legitimation in China.

Stanley Rosen would like to acknowledge financial support from the Center for International Business Education and Research (CIBEAR), the College of Letters, Arts and Sciences, and the Center for International Studies, all at the University of Southern California. In addition, an earlier grant from the Smith Richardson Foundation provided valuable funds for travel and data-gathering. The library facilities and warm reception on his frequent visits provided at the Universities Service Centre for China Studies at the Chinese University of Hong Kong, under the wonderful leadership of H.C. Kuan and Jean Xiong Jingming, were invaluable. The Centre's staff, most especially Karen Ho (responsible for periodicals) and Betty Kam (responsible for newspapers), deserve particular thanks. While there are too many people and institutions to thank in mainland China, he would like to mention the staff of the Foreign Affairs Office at Beijing Normal University for their support during his frequent stays there.

Gries and Rosen would like to collectively thank the efforts of the many people at Taylor & Francis who have greatly improved the final manuscript. Thanks in particular go to acquisitions editor Craig Fowlie, series editor Mark Selden, production editor Alfred Symons, editorial assistants Zoe Botterill and Laura Sacha, and copy-editor Mark Ralph. They would also like to thank Arianne Gaetano and each of the contributors to the volume, with whom collaboration has been a pleasure.

Introduction

Popular protest and state legitimation in 21st-century China

Peter Hays Gries and Stanley Rosen

After a quarter century of "reform and opening," early 21st-century China appears to differ from Mao's China not merely in degree, but also in kind. Having outgrown the planned economy, Deng Xiaoping's decentralization of economic authority and limited embrace of the market mechanism has paid off. China's economy has grown at or near double-digit rates for most of the past two decades. China is now third, behind only the United States and Japan, in the overall size of its economy, and will soon surpass Japan and move into second place. Contrary to the expectations of many analysts who witnessed the massive street demonstrations of Beijing Spring and the brutal military crackdown of 4 June 1989, the Chinese Party-state has not only survived, but seemingly prospered.

But economic growth has been uneven, benefiting cities over the country-side and coastal areas over the hinterland. The growth of inequality has been both rapid and startling. According to a Chinese press report, in 2001 80 per cent of China's wealth was in the hands of less than 20 per cent of the population. Moreover, of the fifty richest Chinese as designated by *Forbes*, only four paid personal income taxes.[1] Not surprisingly, a survey conducted by China's People's University found that only 5.3 per cent of the public felt that China's rich had gotten their wealth through proper means.[2] Party cadres in the countryside live in multi-storey brick houses while peasants live in shacks. Rural migrants work as virtual slaves in urban factory compounds with no job security and none of the welfare benefits that were formerly the pride of the state sector. Free unions are outlawed, and work-place conditions are questionable. In the first six months of 2002, over 53,000 Chinese workers were killed in workplace accidents.[3] Capitalist exploitation in China today arguably rivals the days of the Robber Barons in the US a century ago.

As a result, a baffling array of disorderly social protests has appeared. In the countryside, corrupt village elections have sparked peasant ire – some protestors even taking their complaints all the way to Beijing. Tax protests are also on the rise in rural China, as peasants suffer from the "scissors effect" of rising national taxes and inflation on the one hand, and local levies and cadre extortion on the other. Beijing has responded to such peasant grievances with a mixture of co-optation and suppression. The central – and thus far highly successful – strategy is divide and rule: allowing individual protests at enterprises or villages while sharply cracking down on any attempts to generalize them across space or organization.

In the cities, meanwhile, labor unrest is increasing. In March 2002, desperate workers organized massive labor protests that rocked the streets of north-east rustbelt cities like the Daqing oil capital and Liaoyang. The state responded with divide-and-conquer tactics, arresting labor leaders and accommodating the rank and file's demands for back pay. Since China's entry to the World Trade Organization (WTO) in 2001, urban unemployment and protests have increased. Indeed, the People's Armed Police has been instructed to prepare for "sudden incidents," and blue-collar megacities like Chongqing have doubled the size of their public security forces. With millions laid off from state-owned enterprises (SOEs), urban workers, once the pride of Mao's China, have become a specter haunting early 21st-century China.

But labor unrest is not the only urban concern of the Chinese Communist Party (CCP). In 1999, Beijing witnessed major religious and nationalist protests. In April of that year, over 10,000 Falun Gong practitioners staged a silent protest outside the leadership compound Zhongnanhai in central Beijing. Their peaceful appeal to the government to cease religious persecution backfired: the Party elite initiated a Mao-style mass campaign seeking to discredit leader Li Hongzhi and suppress his "heretical sect." The Falun Gong has fought back, however, both staging continued protests within China and conducting Internet and telecommunications offensives against the CCP from overseas.

The next month, following the American bombing of the Chinese Embassy in Belgrade and the death of three government employees, Chinese across the country poured out into the streets for nationalist demonstrations. In Chengdu, protestors set fire to the American consulate. In Beijing, students threw bricks at American embassy buildings as People's Liberation Army (PLA) soldiers looked on. Then Vice-President Hu Jintao was forced to go on national television to plead with popular nationalists for calm.

After two decades of dramatic economic and social change, the political system in China is under increasing pressure to change. Founded by a small number of activists, in 1998 the fledgling China Democracy Party (CDP) – the first true opposition party in the history of the People's Republic – emerged in 24 of China's 30 provinces, autonomous regions, and municipalities. The next year, the CCP's response to the emergent CDP shifted from tolerance to suppression: all major CDP activists were either jailed or exiled. At the fall 2001 6th Plenum of the 15th Central Committee of the Chinese Communist Party, however, the CCP sought to adjust to the times: "To realize its goals of uniting and leading the Chinese people ... to further promote modernization ... the Party should represent the development requirements of China's advanced social productive forces."[4] Where Mao's generation of communist leaders had denounced capitalists as "running dogs," today's "fourth generation" leadership is now co-opting them into the Party.

Rethinking state–society relations in China

What can we make of this diverse array of political actors and practices? Are state–society relations in early 21st-century China qualitatively different from those that marked the 20th century? Or do the Confucian and Maoist legacies constrain the shape of political contention in China today?

And what are the implications of these new state–society dynamics for the *legitimacy* of the CCP? Is China destined to democratize? Or will the Communist Party maintain its rule for the foreseeable future? What issues and actors are the most likely to threaten the stability of the regime, and how will Beijing respond to them?

Until the most recent wave of scholarship, the frameworks that Western scholars traditionally used to address such questions had become far less helpful in understanding the dynamics of post-Tiananmen China. Influenced by a Liberal fear of the state, it had long been common among Western observers to depict Chinese politics as a simple matter of coercion: the "butchers of Beijing" – to borrow a line former president Bill Clinton used during his election campaign in 1992 – imposing their will upon a submissive people. Europeans fighting absolutism first constructed the foil of "Oriental despotism" to preach the virtues of liberty to their compatriots. Montesquieu, for instance, depicted Asia – in contradistinction to Liberal England – as the natural home of slavery.[5] To extol the virtues of liberty, Westerners largely depicted the Oriental state as omnipotent, while Asian societies were impotent.

This Western view of Asian state dominance over society continued in the post-war period, only China was fitted into a "totalitarian" rather than "Oriental" template. During the Cold War, Mao's China – like Stalin's Russia – was depicted as a land of total state control of the individual. In the American imagination, the "Red Menace" of communism represented everything Americans had fought against in the War of Independence: the loss of freedom to tyranny.

With the end of the Cold War, the 1990s witnessed the emergence of new "civil society" and "public sphere" approaches to Chinese politics. New public spaces like private bookstores and cafes came under intense scrutiny. Was China witnessing the emergence of the civil society so essential to the emergence of democracy in the West? Elizabeth Perry has argued that this new approach propelled Western research on Chinese politics out of the grasp of the earlier totalitarian view.[6] While writings informed by this new approach have significantly advanced our understanding of China, some of the key assumptions from the earlier Oriental despotism and totalitarian paradigms persist. Many state–society writings continue to take the form of top-down "strong state, weak society" arguments.[7] Moreover, in the aftermath of the collapse of the Soviet Union and the Eastern Bloc, and the 1989 military crackdown in Tiananmen Square, Beijing has become – in the eyes of many Americans inside and outside the scholarly community – the last major bastion of Communist Tyranny against which to depict America as the Land of the Free. Indeed, the 1989 image of a solitary Chinese man blocking an advancing PLA tank in Tiananmen Square has revitalized this "state dominates society" view of Chinese politics. As Richard Madsen has noted, Americans continue to construct their "Liberal Myth" in opposition to perceived Chinese tyranny.[8]

These past approaches to Chinese state–society relations – Oriental despotism, totalitarianism, and civil society/public sphere – shared two problems. First and foremost, each suffered from a Liberal bias that fated them to tell us more about ourselves than they did about China. China largely served as a mirror within which we could see that which we most treasure about ourselves: our liberty. Secondly, these approaches were largely procrustean, foisting Western categories and concepts onto Chinese realities. Like the mythical Greek monster Procrustes, who made his captives fit his bed – whether that required stretching or cutting off their limbs – Western China scholars frequently took theories derived from the Euro-American experience and forced China to fit them. In the recent heated debate over whether or not a civil society/public sphere exists in China, for instance, both sides largely assumed that for China to successfully democratize, there must be a Western-style autonomous space for public political activity. Optimists would examine a Starbucks in Shanghai, find two intellectuals having a conversation, and proclaim, "Eureka! They're following our road to democracy!" Pessimists, by contrast, would lament: "They're discussing the best way to make money in China's new economy – not politics. China will never democratize!" Notably, both sides of this civil society debate often shared the assumption that political change in China must resemble that experienced in the West, dismissing the possibility that China may take a very different road to political development.

The reform period that officially began with the decisions of the 3rd Plenum of the 11th Central Committee in December 1978 set China on a new path to development, with economic modernization made the central task. However, it was only in the aftermath of the events of 1989 and the Party-state's recognition that its previous sources of legitimacy – based upon both moral and economic performance – had been effectively shattered that a new relationship between state and society began to be forged.[9] While continuities persist, the Party-state has in important ways created both a new society and a new style of politics.

Building upon recent scholarship, this volume seeks to re-conceptualize the dynamics of early 21st-century Chinese politics.[10] If we are to understand state–society relations in China, we will need to be careful about using

Western concepts and deductive theories to understand Chinese realities. We thus argue for an inductive, bottom-up interrogation of political contestation in China.

What does it mean to speak of *"the"* Chinese state? The Communist Party, for instance, is frequently anthropomorphized (made human) as a unitary actor capable of strategic choice and coordinated behavior. Does such a monolith exist in China today? We argue that it does not. As Deng Xiaoping decentralized the structures of Chinese governance in the 1980s and 1990s, he was seeking to strengthen the Party – not to democratize it. As a result, however, the number of Party and state actors involved in political contestation has proliferated rapidly. And local Party and state actors are not the passive puppets of higher-ups. As Kevin O'Brien relates in his chapter (Chapter 5): "when I was traveling with a Ministry bureau chief in a Fujian village, and we encountered a village cadre who refused to release some election results, the Ministry official said: 'I'm your bosses' bosses' bosses' boss, so turn over the results.' And the lowly village leader responded: 'Because you're my bosses' bosses' bosses' boss, go to hell.'" In its dealings with the provinces, Beijing is frequently all thumbs. The Chinese state today is no unitary actor – if it ever was.

Even more importantly, the chapters of this volume seek to "bring society back in." Where Western studies of Chinese politics have generally taken a top-down approach, highlighting state dominance, we seek to recover the voices and roles that the common Chinese people play in Chinese politics. China is not a formal democracy, but "Chinese popular opinion" is not an oxymoron. The Chinese people – peasants, workers, students – are increasingly contesting the legitimacy of the current regime; analysts would be wise not to ignore them.

We thus seek to deconstruct and reconstruct our understandings of both "state" and "society." Our conceptual move is deceptively simple: adding an "s." Speaking in the plural of "state*s*" and "societie*s*" liberates us from the beguiling but decidedly Liberal notion of a David society fighting valiantly against a Goliath state. State and social actors in China, we find, are not always unitary and antagonistic; they can and often do form alliances with each other and against other political groups. Conversely, there can be conflict *within* segments of both "state" and "society." For instance, the peasants in neighboring villages may have very different attitudes toward the local tax collector.

Central to the analysis of such diverse forms of political contention is the interrogation of the *dynamics of interaction* between political actors. Following Max Weber, we maintain that power and authority are not static attributes or things that particular actors possess.[11] Instead, power and authority exist *in relationship*. We customarily say that "John is powerful" or "John has power"; what we really mean, however, is that "John has power *over* Jim and Jill." Power and authority are relational, negotiated through a continuous process of claims and responses.[12] Thus, a local cadre may successfully claim authority before one group of peasants, but not before another group. As Neil Diamant has noted in a recent discussion of Mao's China, "Different institutions were afforded different degrees of legitimacy by different classes, at different times and in different regions of the country."[13] Legitimacy, in Mao's China and today, is never a state *possession*; instead, state and social actors continuously contest it. "State" and "society" are mutually constituted in the process.

In addition to being relational, power can be thought of as a continuum, with coercive forms of power at one end, and more legitimate or authoritative forms of power at the other.[14] When the state's claims to legitimacy are not affirmed, or when protestors openly defy its authority, the state can resort to force. This is indeed what the CCP did so dramatically during the Tiananmen Massacre of 1989. But resorting to violence only undermines the legitimacy of the state before the people – and no state can survive for long by force alone.

Mao Zedong knew this. He is well known in the West for saying that "Power grows out of the barrel of a gun."[15] Less well known, but, we argue, equally important, was Mao's argument at the onset of the Cultural Revolution that "When you make revolution, you must first manage public opinion."[16] Mao understood the need to deploy both coercive and legitimate forms of power.

What combination of coercive and legitimate forms of power is the Chinese state currently deploying? In which direction along the coercive–legitimate continuum of power is the 21st-century Chinese polity heading? If social actors increasingly reject the legitimacy of state power, will the state progressively resort to force? A People's Republic relying on coercive and not legitimate power is not likely to last very long. Conversely, if the state's various claims to legitimacy are successful, the regime will not need to rely on coercion, and will likely remain stable well into the 21st century.

Between Heaven and Earth

Legitimacy is central to politics everywhere. The specific rules that govern its contestation, however, vary across both time and space. In traditional China, it was the literati who legitimated or de-legitimated the regime by conferring positive or negative status upon it. As interpreters of the political classics and custodians of the "Mandate of Heaven," the literati could and often did challenge the emperor's legitimacy claims. Proponents of the "Oriental despotism" and "totalitarian" views of Chinese politics fail to grasp this crucial ruler–literati dynamic. For instance, Western scholars often point to the examination system as evidence of the literati's *dependence* on the imperial state: co-opted into the state system, they are seen as lacking the autonomy so essential to pluralist politics.[17] However, if we step back from Eurocentric assumptions about the public sphere to think about politics from a Chinese perspective, the examination system can be seen as evidence of the literati's *independence*. In his 1921 *Religion of China*, Max Weber rightly argues that the examinations were a basis of the literati's own authority. In imperial China, especially after the Han Dynasty, "literary education was the yardstick of social prestige." Weber stresses the "magico-charismatic meaning" of the examinations in the eyes of the people: the successful examination candidate was "by no means a mere applicant for office qualified by knowledge. He was a proved holder of magical qualities."[18] As historian Mark Edward Lewis has recently argued, by elevating the idealized past of the Zhou Dynasty above contemporary dynasties, the literati were able to claim "independence vis-à-vis the state."[19] Where appeals to the past are generally seen as "conservative" in the West, they are frequently "progressive" in the Chinese context. Again we see how Western assumptions can blind us to the realities of Chinese politics.

In addition to possessing their own charismatic and legal-rational authority, the literati also played a vital role in checking the emperor's legitimacy claims. Emperors that sought legitimate forms of power were forced to respond to the charismatic claims of the literati custodians of sacred texts. Traditional norms and the requirement of proof for his charismatic claims limited the emperor's charismatic-traditional authority. Chinese cosmology, which held that the worlds of man and nature were united in a *yin/yang* balance, was the basis of political rule. A deviation from orthodox Confucianism in the world of politics was seen as leading to natural disasters. The literati, Weber notes, were an independent status group responsible for this orthodoxy. Thus, "every generally threatening event at once placed power in the hands of the literati. For such events were considered the result of a breach of tradition and a desertion of the classic way of life, which the literati guarded."[20] The literati thus "limited the power of the chief by making him dependent on a definite social group."[21] Historian Wang Aihe has recently explored the Han Dynasty competition "between scholar-officials, who defined and confined emperorship by systemizing cosmology and monopolizing moral authority, and the emperor and his hired religious specialists, who resisted the constraints of moral authority." The Chinese character for king (*wang*, 王) visually depicts the terms of this contest: the three horizontal strokes represent the three realms of Heaven, Man, and Earth, while the central vertical stroke connecting the three signifies the sovereign. The emperor, Wang Aihe forcefully argues, did not "possess" power, but was the "pivot" responsible for keeping the three realms aligned: "emperorship in Han China was culturally and symbolically produced and reproduced, constantly being contested within cosmological discourse."[22] In imperial China, in short, rulers needed the approval of the literati if they were to wield legitimate power.

In the post-revolutionary period, intellectuals carried on the functions of the traditional literati. Recognizing that intellectuals checked his power, Mao persistently attacked them, demoting them from "literati" (*shidaifu*) to the "stinking ninth class" (*choujiuceng*). At the same time, however, Mao often *needed* intellectuals, and was able to make astute use of groups of literati throughout his career. This was perhaps particularly the case during the Cultural Revolution, when his opponents occupied the highest rungs of the Communist Party. Thus, he ensured that some of the key members of the Cultural Revolution Small Group, responsible for promoting Mao's revolutionary agenda during that political movement, were intellectuals. These radical intellectuals, in turn, were supported by student Red Guards. If the use of force to silence intellectuals during periods like the Anti-rightist Movement of the late 1950s signaled reversions to coercive forms of power, they did not fundamentally alter the role of Chinese intellectuals as the custodians of the "Mandate of Heaven." As with Mao, Deng Xiaoping, Li Peng, and the Party elders' 1989 decision to use force against the students in Tiananmen marked a resort to coercion.[23] Their earlier agreement to meet with Wuer Kaixi and other student leaders during the Beijing Spring, however, demonstrates that they also recognized the continuing role of intellectuals in legitimizing the regime.

Although the continuities outweigh the changes, the communications revolution and Deng Xiaoping's policy of "reform and opening" (*gaige kaifang*) have had a significant impact on the nature of legitimation in China today. Specifically, the language of legitimacy is evolving, and audiences of popular opinion have better views of the political stage.

First, the language of Chinese politics is undergoing what we call "deformalization." This is changing both the nature and the role of popular opinion in China. By "formalizing" or restricting the political code, propagandists under Mao Zedong and Deng Xiaoping were able to control political discourse.[24] In the 1990s, Jiang Zemin and his culture czar Ding Guan'gen attempted to continue in this tradition. Today, the Party still seeks to control politics by "setting the tone" (*ding diaozi*) for everything from key political events to whether music DJs can say "Hello" in English or discuss Christmas on their radio shows.

However, while China's elites were never able to attain their goal of completely monopolizing political discourse (*yiyantang*), that goal is now farther away than ever. Economic reform has led to the proliferation of media at the local level. While Jiang and Ding's "Rectification of the Press Campaigns" were somewhat successful in reducing the numbers of non-Party publications, decentralization made the media more difficult for the Party to control. Unofficial publications, distributed through the "second channel" (*erqudao*), are proliferating. And financial autonomy has further reduced the media's dependency on the state.[25] The communications revolution, meanwhile, has greatly increased the number of voices participating in political discourse. Politics is a frequent topic in Chinese chatrooms, e-mail networks, and Internet websites. These developments have led to a deformalization in the language of politics. Political rhetoric from Hong Kong and Taiwan, for instance, has had a noticeable impact on political discourse in the mainland.[26] An expanded political vocabulary allows a greater number of actors to appear on the political stage, gives them greater latitude in their performances, and makes them harder to control.

A second notable change in state legitimation today is that audiences of popular opinion have a better view of the political stage. Although officially prohibited, books and magazines on elite politics, and even the personal lives of the elite, are bestsellers. Jurgen Habermas's account of the historical function that the "public sphere" played in Europe is pertinent here: with the open discussion of elite politics, the secrecy and mystery underpinning traditional authority are stripped away.[27] Similarly, popular opinion arguably regulates Chinese society and politics today. Zhou Yi of Nanjing University Press has argued that the fear of losing *face* constrains behavior, leading to sincerity in social relations.[28] Concern for maintaining *face* has the same disciplining impact on politics. Political elites, increasingly "in the people's gaze" (*zhongmu kuikui*) with the telecommunications revolution, are not always very comfortable. As a Chinese friend told *Time* correspondent Jaime FlorCruz, "The Chinese emperor is now wearing a bikini."[29]

In sum, the information revolution and China's two decades of "reform and opening" have significantly altered the nature of political contention in China today. The number and variety of political actors has proliferated dramatically, deformalizing political discourse and making it harder for the state to control. And the audience watching political dramas has also expanded, increasingly disciplining the political actors on stage and delimiting their freedom of movement.

Contested claims

The twelve chapters of this volume interrogate the dynamics of political contention in China at the turn of the 21st century. We begin with an exploration of the logics or grammars underlying the Chinese state's claims to legitimacy. Vivienne Shue (Chapter 1) argues that "embedded in the very logic of legitimation advanced by a system of domination we can find the grammar that may be used most effectively by citizens and subjects … in resistance to that system." Specifically, Truth, Benevolence, and Glory are three of the key logics of legitimation in China today. Focusing on Truth, Shue explores why the Chinese state views a seemingly harmless sect of mystics like the Falun Gong as a threat. Citizens and subjects almost never swallow whole the legitimacy claims of their rulers. Even at the most totalizing of authoritarian political moments, popular dissent and disbelief are commonly expressed as people negotiate the precise terms on which they will give their obedience to the state. Employing a multi-stranded and multi-layered conceptualization of the dynamics of political authority in China today, Shue argues that the Chinese state clearly interpreted the Falun Gong as a dire challenge to its claim to possess the moral Truth.

Shue's opening chapter goes far beyond the limited subject of popular religion. Where other chapters focus on discrete threats to Party legitimacy – tax protestors, independent labor unions, popular nationalists, etc. – Shue explores the Falun Gong as a *comprehensive* threat undermining the very foundations of communist rule. She also challenges the conventional wisdom – both in scholarly and in journalistic writing on China – that the state's main claim to legitimacy rests on its economic achievements, "in an improving standard of living, in 'growth' or in 'development.' " A regime basing its legitimacy on performance alone is intrinsically unstable; Shue suggests that regime legitimacy depends upon the maintenance of *stability*. It is not the regime's *technical* capacity to develop the economy that is important, but the *political* capacity to preserve a peaceful and stable order under which the economy can grow.

Shue's discussion of the sources of legitimacy is also important because it leads us directly toward an assessment of the new relationship between central and local authorities, a theme that is common in several of our chapters. Jae Ho Chung has criticized studies which analyze central–local relations primarily in fiscal terms, suggesting that the Center has encouraged local entrepreneurship, and is willing to accept local deviations so long as they are growth oriented. The Center is not, however, willing to tolerate deviations in political or organizational matters.[30] In a telling anecdote from one of his field trips, Tony Saich makes the same point about basic contradictions inherent in central–local relations. A Party secretary from an industrial town told Saich that he had privatized virtually all of his local industry. Saich responded that the secretary appeared to be in breach of a central Party policy that ruled out the use of the word "privatization." The official in turn upbraided Saich for exhibiting such a limited understanding of CCP principles. He explained that the basic principle of Party work was to rally around Comrade Jiang Zemin to ensure social stability. If he did not privatize the SOEs under his jurisdiction, he would be faced with a financial crisis that would lead to social unrest. Thus, "far from contradicting Party policy, his privatization policy was perfectly attuned to it."[31]

This strategy of decentralizing decision-making power on economic issues while retaining political and organizational control has arguably succeeded in altering the central state's relationship with society and in refurbishing some of its lost legitimacy after Tiananmen. As Zhao Dingxin and others have argued, the state has attempted to insulate itself from many grievances of the urban population; such grievances are now aimed at the leaders of particular factories or firms. Unlike the 1980s, when most economic grievances were state centered, in the 1990s and into the new millennium in many local economic conflicts, the state frequently positions itself as a mediator rather than the target of aggrieved citizens. Where the state is able to handle such grievances carefully, it increases its legitimacy.[32]

Several of our chapters suggest the complexity of state–society relations and regime legitimacy in present-day China. Describing the recent fall of workers from masters to near mendicants, Dorothy Solinger (Chapter 2) is pessimistic about the new relationship between the state, enterprise administrators, and workers. Deploying the trope of "the crowd," she explores the radically altered status of the old proletariat of today and its totally reshaped relationship to the state in the wake of the economic reforms. With the sudden surge in dismissals of state workers after 1995, the key component of the relationship between the state and labor is *fear*, "a searing dread on both sides." Moreover, plant officials – especially those in failing firms – are no longer "custodians"; they have taken on the role of "embezzler," serving neither the central state nor their original worker-wards. The three parties – state, administrator, and worker – "once supposed allies, have become mutually antagonistic."

Timothy B. Weston (Chapter 3) also examines the struggle of urban workers to survive in a China that has become part of the global economy. He explores the implications of China's accession to the WTO in a context of rising urban unemployment and official corruption. Charges of corruption are particularly potent, as they challenge the state's claims to what Shue calls Benevolence and thus legitimacy. Weston argues that it is unlikely that these workers will seek to or successfully topple the present regime on their own, but suggests that their protests are forcing the Communist Party to shift its rhetorical position on the meaning of socialism and to seek a new basis of legitimacy. The millions of laid-off workers are therefore *contesting* the Communist Party's core ideological claims and are threatening its ability to out-maneuver challengers from the Left, "the critical location on the political spectrum from which the Party has laid claim to power since the revolution in 1949." Whether unemployed workers will be able to merge with other social groups to threaten the Party-state remains an open question.

Patricia Thornton (Chapter 4) turns our attention to tax protest and evasion. She argues that tax resisters, particularly those who have not benefited as rapidly from market reforms, often develop collective strategies that rely upon organizational and ideological resources that originate in Maoist China. In one of her key findings, Thornton argues that regardless of regional, organizational, or discursive variations in protest repertoires, the state appears increasingly fractured, with local cadres finding new grounds for solidarity with the workers and farmers with whom they interact on a daily basis, and against the Center. Thornton suggests that this lowest tier of the Party and state bureaucracy – finding itself at the mercy of an increasingly restive population below and an increasingly remote and extractive state above – may indeed prove instrumental in deciding the fate of both state and social forces. Thornton and Solinger thus paint very different pictures of the relations between state and social actors, again pointing to the diversity of political practices in China today.

In an exploration of the grammars of resistance in the Chinese countryside, Kevin O'Brien (Chapter 5) examines what he calls "boundary-spanning contention": popular pressure that is arguably legal, permissible in some eyes but not in others. In particular, he looks at rigged local elections in rural China. O'Brien argues that examining episodes of contention between official politics and politics by other means can help locate the Chinese regime across a number of dimensions: what is institutionalized and what is not, what is participation and what is resistance, who is a challenger and who is a polity member, what citizenship entails and who enjoys it. O'Brien depicts Chinese state power as both fragmented and divided against itself. In common with several other contributors, what emerges in his chapter is a multi-layered state that has grand aspirations but formidable principal–agent problems. In other words, lacking complete information about local conditions, officials in Beijing have difficulty controlling the behavior of local cadres whose interests may diverge from Beijing's. Thus, those contemplating collective action can take advantage of China's limited institutionalization to "venue shop," uncovering supporters in various bureaucracies and at different levels of the political system who have a stake in seeing their appeals addressed. Furthermore, because they use the regime's own policies and legitimating myths to justify their actions, their "rightful resistance" is difficult to dismiss.

In her comparison of the China Democracy Party (CDP) and the China Labour Bulletin (CLB), Teresa Wright (Chapter 6) uses interviews and documentary research to explore the contested nature of state legitimacy and the fragmented nature of state power in China today. The initial CCP response to the formation of the CDP was confused and inconsistent, with CDP activists – not unlike the "rightful resisters" O'Brien discussed – consciously playing on openings created by the lack of clear central direction. While the CCP has asserted its legitimacy based on a claim to represent "the masses," the CDP founders used a more procedural definition of legitimate rule, emphasizing the creation of a government established through the conscious approval of the public through free, impartial, and direct democratic elections. Moreover, in a roughly similar way to the workers in Weston's chapter, who contested the CCP's core ideological claims, the CDP's new conception of political legitimacy challenged the symbolic power of the CCP to unilaterally define "right and wrong." The CLB, by contrast, challenges not only the state's claims to truth, but also its claims to benevolent care for the Chinese worker. Wright demonstrates how China's continuing market transition and immersion in the global economy have changed the form and method of intellectual dissent in striking ways.

While the role of the CCP is discussed in virtually every chapter in this book, only Bruce Dickson's contribution (Chapter 7) directly assesses the Party's strategies for adapting to the varied challenges confronting them at the onset of the 21st century. Dickson discovers a Party that has embraced "inclusion," drawing in a wider range of social groups while reducing its emphasis on its traditional bases of support.

A 2002 Chinese Academy of Social Sciences (CASS) survey offers empirical data that strongly supports Dickson's conclusions, but also suggests the unbalanced nature of these trends. The CASS study, citing official statistics, notes that the percentage of Party members among private enterprise owners climbed from 13.1 per cent in 1993 to 17.1 per cent in 1995, and 19.8 per cent in 2000. Even more striking is the comparison of Party members among private enterprise owners and industrial workers in the four cities and county seats that the survey examined in detail. These figures vary significantly, depending on a number of factors, particularly local government policies toward private entrepreneurs.[33] What is clear, however, is the differential pattern of CCP recruitment, with highly modernized areas actively recruiting the "winners" of economic reform – such as private enterprise owners – while more "backward" and largely rural locations continue to recruit from the worker and peasant classes.[34] Indeed, according to an authoritative source, by the end of 2002, 30.2 per cent of private enterprise owners had become Party members.[35] Again, we see a China – and a Communist Party – fragmented and in transition.

This new pattern of Party recruitment, as the chapters by Shue and Wright document, has not affected the Party's reluctance to surrender its monopoly on political organization. More specifically, as Dickson shows, the CCP's new policy has two basic planks. First, the policy of inclusion accepts the need to create new institutional links with society, with new social organizations existing in a "corporatist" relationship to the state. Secondly, the policy of inclusion requires the reaching out to and co-opting of newly emerging social elites, in particular the professional and technical elites and private entrepreneurs. Given these striking changes, Dickson asks: "Who does the Party represent?" The answer to this question is of course contested, both inside and outside the Party, and is crucial to the larger issue of legitimacy. While some argue that inclusion and adaptation are necessary to preserve the Party's right to rule and promote its economic program, others argue that it is a betrayal of the Party's traditions and will undermine rather than boost the Party's legitimacy.

Issues of Party recruitment are also addressed by Stanley Rosen (Chapter 8), albeit from the perspective of those being recruited. Drawing on survey and public opinion data, debates in youth journals, and interviews in China, Rosen investigates the seemingly paradoxical and contradictory behavior of China's current youth cohort, discussed extensively in the Chinese media as the "fifth generation" or "the new mankind" (*xinxin renlei*). Born between 1976 and 1985, this generation has been inundated with cues from the globalized culture and has set out in pursuit of the "cool" (*ku*), often defined by pop culture icons and other phenomena from beyond mainland China's borders. Examining youth attitudes toward CCP membership, the effects of new stratification patterns on friendship, and the rising importance of money as a determinant of an individual's value, he finds that in the sphere of social relations, upwardly mobile youth are reluctant to interact with those from lower strata, for fear that such contact will tarnish their image. Moreover, money has become essential for success across generations, by way of an increasingly commercialized educational system where access to schooling has become increasingly dependent on one's family wealth. Strikingly, the regime is openly encouraging, or at least not discouraging, these changes. In common with Dickson, Rosen finds growing numbers of young people applying for Party membership and the Party still holding appeal as an effective patronage machine, providing opportunities for youth entering the job market. He also offers corroborative data to Wright's analysis on why young adults in their twenties, who have been the most active participants in most of the major political movements in the post-Mao period and in demonstrations in other countries, have not been particularly active in the CDP. But neither have people in any other age group, given the tiny appeal that the Party had.

Nationalism is often discussed as a primary source of legitimacy for a Party-state with a discredited ideology, and the chapters by Peter Hays Gries and Richard Kraus (Chapters 9 and 10 respectively) speak directly to that issue. Focusing on the "fourth generation" of thirty-something nationalists in China, Gries argues that although the anti-foreign substance of popular nationalism today is largely congruent with that of official or state nationalism, it is challenging the state's hegemony over nationalist discourse. Interrogating three separate waves of nationalism in late 1990s China – the Diaoyu Islands protests of 1996, the *China Can Say No* sensation of 1996–97, and the Belgrade bombing protests of May 1999 – Gries argues that the CCP responded to each with a different combination of suppression and co-optation, largely suppressing Diaoyu protestors, seeking to co-opt and utilize the *China Can Say No* fever, and striving just to respond to the demands of angry Belgrade bombing demonstrators. This movement away from suppression and towards co-optation suggests the emergence of a popular nationalism that is increasingly challenging the CCP's claims to nationalist legitimacy.

Through the power of nationalism, legitimacy often attaches itself to specific cultural phenomena or even objects. Working at the intersection of politics and culture, Richard Kraus explores the Chinese state's response to popular pressures to recover art looted by imperialists in the 19th century, thereby erasing the shame of national humiliation. The episode of the Looted Zodiac Animal Heads pitted the Chinese army against the Western fine arts establishment, and raised questions about China's position in the global cultural economy. Kraus argues that political legitimacy must be won on two fronts. Domestic populations must believe in their rulers' right to occupy office, but foreign states must also diplomatically recognize these same leaders' right to rule. Kraus suggests that this "two front" battle for legitimacy presents a basic contradiction. The search for domestic legitimacy through repatriating lost art may hinder China's efforts at gaining greater international acceptance. In this sense, those in the West who view China as a difficult rising power in economic and military affairs may also see the

Chinese politics of art repatriation as a "high art" example of revisionist behavior toward the existing international aesthetic order.

Examining the complicated issue of Han-minority relations, Colin Mackerras (Chapter 11) uncovers patterns familiar from the previous chapters. For example, market forces and modernization have exerted a profound impact on all ethnic groups in China, weakening the pull of traditional cultures and offering opportunities to those who accept the legitimacy of the Chinese state. Minority youth, seeking a rising standard of living, see their interests inextricably linked to cooperation with the Han, even if feelings of ethnic identity point in the opposite direction. Mackerras, of course, makes important distinctions among the fifty-five state-recognized minority ethnic groups, noting for example that ethnicity counts far more in determining how Tibetans and Uygurs feel about the legitimacy of the CCP than it does among such groups as the Koreans or Zhuang, because the sense of identity of the former is stronger and based more solidly on historical resentments.

Can these different modes of political contention in China today be better grasped in comparative perspective? Harley Balzer (Chapter 12) concludes the volume with an exploration of how the experience of the communist "extrication" in the former Soviet Union and Eastern Europe can inform our understanding of the evolution of state–society relations in China today. He argues that it is "civic society" – not civil society – that best captures the *interdependence* of state and social actors in both Russia and China today. Both are "managed pluralist" regimes that both encourage and limit political and cultural diversity in a common attempt to maintain their monopolies of political power.

The twelve chapters of the volume thus explore the many different kinds of claims that state actors today make to legitimacy, the various responses that social actors make to those claims, and their own counterclaims. What can this teach us about the future of Chinese politics? Are the CCP's days numbered? Or will it adapt and endure well into the 21st century?

State legitimation in 21st-century China

In June 1989, the CCP elite chose to deploy coercive power. In the aftermath of the Tiananmen Massacre, therefore, the regime faced the daunting task of not just polishing its image, but restoring its legitimacy. It did so by emphasizing performance, both economic and moral, and de-emphasizing communist ideology. Regime legitimacy was to be restored by persuading the populace that the CCP was the best – indeed the only – viable force that could make Chinese citizens rich (the economic component) and the country powerful (the moral component), able to assume what is widely perceived domestically as its rightful place among the world's great powers.

Following Deng Xiaoping's 1992 "Southern Tour" to jumpstart the market economy, the CCP focused on raising the standard of living of the urban population, particularly those in the coastal cities who were best situated to take advantage of the state's new economic initiatives. Along with rising incomes, the state relaxed certain social controls so that, for example, parents could choose primary and secondary schools for their children, university graduates could choose their own jobs rather than be compelled to accept a state job allocation, and strict residential requirements (the *hukou* system) were relaxed, so that individuals could migrate in search of employment or a better life.[36]

In addition to offering them a degree of social and economic freedom, the People's Republic offered its citizens a more varied cultural life. China in the 1990s witnessed an explosion of tabloid newspapers and sensationalistic magazines. The elimination of state subsidies and the necessity for all cultural organizations to adjust to market demands has brought forth television programs and newspapers – such as "Focal Point Inquiry" ("*Jiaodian fangtan*") and *Southern Weekend* (*Nanfang zhoumo*) – that have won broad popular approval by emphasizing investigative journalism and the exposure of corruption. Evening entertainment was enhanced with the increase in the number of discos and karaoke bars, and the import of ten "blockbuster" movies per year, beginning with *The Fugitive* in October 1994 and including *Titanic*, with a box-office take of over US$44 million, the most financially successful movie ever shown in China.[37] The increasing penetration of cosmetics, toiletries, and other such Western wares spearheaded a virtual revolution in consumer goods. Indeed, cadres of neighborhood watch committees, long responsible for regulating and reporting on most aspects of residents' daily lives, are now serving foreign corporations by delivering product samples door to door and selling cable television subscriptions.

In this new environment, traditional ideological appeals to implement Marxism–Leninism–Mao Zedong Thought and build a socialist China find little resonance among the public. However, the state has been very successful in promoting "patriotism" (read: nationalism) to supplant the discredited system of political virtue that had been so important a part of the socialization process for all Chinese prior to the reforms.

We find, then, some formidable sources of regime legitimation to buttress the Party-state in the face of the types of protest described in the chapters to follow. The future of the Chinese state may be far from clear, but there is little evidence that it is in imminent peril.

The Chinese regime has not succumbed to the fate of the former Soviet Union and its erstwhile Eastern European allies, and yet it faces protests from a wide variety of social groups. A lively literature has thus emerged, debating the future of the Chinese Party-state. "Pessimists" argue for the almost inevitable collapse of the regime, while "optimists" predict China's equally inevitable rise to superpower status by the mid-21st century.[38]

One frequent topic in the scholarly literature is the likelihood of Chinese democratization. When the *Journal of Democracy* invited contributions in late 2002, following the 16th Party Congress, for a special issue on China's future, even the editors of the journal were surprised by the divergence of opinion that surfaced. Their contributors, like ours, were divided over how to reconcile the regime's successes, including rapid economic growth, massive social transformations, and relative political stability, with the obvious challenges to the sustainability of this success. These challenges include structural weaknesses in the economy, a marked increase in income inequality, and a closed political system that is increasingly incongruent with an economy more and more oriented toward the market.[39]

Some contributors argued over how institutionalized and regularized the political and legal systems had become, and whether institutional reform – including the development of "input institutions" such as village elections, which help the regime respond to public needs more quickly and effectively – had contributed to elite unity and government effectiveness, and thereby enhanced regime legitimacy.[40] Other contributors disagreed over whether the inclusion of new social elites – such as the middle class and private enterprise owners – will contribute to the successful growth of democratization, or will merely aid the CCP in defending its authoritarian rule.[41] Finally, there was contention over China's "state capacity," with leading specialists divided over whether the regime had "reinvigorated" its governing institutions, or is facing a "governance crisis."[42] Two Chinese contributors were particularly pessimistic. Chen An, focusing on ever-widening inequalities and social cleavages, suggests that the CCP faces an impossible dilemma. It cannot recover support from its traditional base among the workers and peasants through the redistribution of wealth without alienating the newly rich groups it has so assiduously co-opted in recent years.[43] But the bleakest view comes from He Qinglian, the author of the 1997 Chinese best-seller *The Pitfalls of Modernization*. Writing after her move to the West in 2002, she characterizes Chinese politics as "volcanic," suggesting that current stability masks the likelihood of a sudden and dramatic regime collapse.[44]

These debates took on added urgency when the SARS (Severe Acute Respiratory Syndrome) epidemic emerged in Guangdong province in the fall of 2002 and quickly spread to Beijing and beyond China's borders. The Chinese leadership's reaction to SARS presents a fascinating case study of what has and has not changed in state–society relations, and the imperatives – both domestic and foreign – that constrain a country which has become integrated into the global community.

Although SARS erupted as early as November 2002, it was not reported to central authorities until February 2003. The Chinese news media was under a continuing ban not to report on the outbreak. In addition to being state secrets, epidemics are bad for business. Official statements and press reporting repeatedly emphasized China's success in controlling SARS, with a reassuring, and soon to prove embarrassing, 28-page pamphlet entitled *SARS Is Not Terrible* quickly becoming a best-seller in mainland bookstores.[45] Meanwhile, alternative sources of information were providing a far more alarming picture, mixing the known facts with a host of wild rumors.

The new leadership under President Hu Jintao and Premier Wen Jiabao, in office only since their ratification by the National People's Congress on 19 March 2003, faced an immediate credibility crisis. On 17 April, at an unscheduled but carefully planned meeting of China's leading policy-making body, the Politburo of the CCP, Hu acknowledged previous government misinformation on the severity of the disease and committed the Party to full mobilization against the epidemic. The mayor of Beijing and the minister of public health were summarily fired for covering up the seriousness of SARS. "Iron Lady" Wu Yi and other respected officials associated with Zhu Rongji, the reformist former premier, were put in charge of containing the disease. Detailed data on the illness began to be released daily, and inspectors from the World Health Organization (WHO) were granted unprecedented access. Altering the previous ban on publicity, the Chinese media were now given more freedom to report on the crisis, and public opinion agencies, initially constrained from revealing their survey results on popular knowledge about SARS, were now allowed to share their findings with the media, so long as the results were "truthful and objective." In a successful effort to restore lost credibility, the Hu–Wen leadership team moved visibly around the country and filled the airwaves with exhortations to defeat the epidemic. After this dramatic reverse course, opinion polls showed a rising confidence in the new leadership.[46]

Such a striking *volte-face* caused a jolt not only in China, but among China-watching analysts as well. Once again, optimists and pessimists diverged in their interpretations of the new leadership's performance. Many began to ask whether SARS could become "China's Chernobyl," in reference to the explosion of a nuclear reactor in that Soviet city in April 1986. Coming only a year after Mikhail Gorbachev came to power, Chernobyl has generally been regarded as an important accelerator for his programs of *glasnost* ("openness") and *perestroika* ("restructuring"), and ultimately for the fall of the Soviet Union, its Communist Party, and the Soviet empire.[47]

Optimists pointed to Beijing's dramatic policy reversal as a harbinger of bolder steps toward political openness in the future. Pessimists, by contrast, noted that SARS was slowing China's economic growth, threatening the regime's performance legitimacy. Furthermore, despite the rhetoric of candor, the government maintained tight control over how the campaign against SARS was to be reported. While little if any public criticism of the earlier cover-up was tolerated, the official media cast the CCP as the driving force defending the populace against the disease. Hundreds were arrested for spreading "rumors" through the text-messaging system used on mobile phones. The CCP, in an effort to hunt down possible SARS cases apartment by apartment, resurrected its network of community activists, suggesting at least a temporary return to Mao-style mass campaigns – not progress towards democratization.[48]

However, as John Pomfret has argued in the *Washington Post*, the *reasons* for the dramatic policy reversal reveal the immense domestic and international pressures the leadership faced, and suggest, at a minimum, the difficulties of controlling information and stonewalling in early 21st-century China. In the SARS case, the WHO and the foreign media clamored for accountability. A retired surgeon at a military hospital reported government lies about the outbreak to the Chinese media. While taking no action themselves, the information was leaked to *Time* magazine, setting in motion a process of dissemination that led, indirectly by way of e-mail, back to China. The Chinese public – including government officials themselves – demanded access to such information. New technologies allowed the unfolding drama to be chronicled in real time on the Internet and through short text messages sent to mobile phones.[49] In short, having in effect lost control over the dissemination of information to popular domestic sources and foreigners, the new Chinese leadership was virtually compelled, both by frightened ordinary citizens and by its own officials, to act to increase its credibility before the society from whom it claims legitimacy.[50] As for the whistleblower who exposed the public deception, Doctor Jiang Yanyong enjoyed a brief run as a "hero" in the Chinese media, with exaggerated official reports on the preferential treatment the government was giving him as a valued "expert." In reality, he was quickly "gagged" and ordered not to give interviews to foreign media. Even interviews with Chinese media had to be approved not just by his hospital, but by the Chinese military. As his daughter noted, "China does not want anyone to imitate him."[51]

While the long-term impact of the SARS epidemic on state–society relations and political legitimacy remains to be seen, it is our hope that the chapters in this volume can provide a context for understanding such events, and can offer some guideposts for critically assessing the evolving relationship between the Chinese state and its citizenry in an epoch of rapid economic and social change.

Notes

1 Lu Si, "Can the money taken from the pockets of the rich be put into the pockets of the poor?" *Zhongguo shehui daokan* (*Chinese Society*), No. 1, January 2003, p. 9.

2 Li Jingyu, "Some rich people are feeling uneasy," *Xinwen zhoukan* (*Chinese Newsweek*), No. 8, 10 March 2003, p. 24.

3 Wang Shaoguang, "The problem of state weakness," *Journal of Democracy*, Vol. 14, No. 1, January 2003, p. 40.

4 "Communiqué of the 6th Plenum of the 15th Central Committee of the Chinese Communist Party," Xinhua English, 26 September 2001. Our thanks to Lyman Miller for this reference.

5 To be sure, Enlightenment intellectuals like Voltaire admired China – but to the same ends of criticizing European absolutisms and extolling the new Liberalism.

6 Elizabeth J. Perry, "Trends in the study of Chinese politics: state–society relations," *China Quarterly* 139 (1994): 704–14.

7 Western scholars examining Chinese workers, peasants, and intellectuals have emphasized the dependency of these social groups on the state. On *workers*, see, e.g., Andrew Walder, *Communist Neotraditionalism: Work and Authority in*

Chinese Industry (Berkeley: University of California Press, 1986). On *peasants*, Jean Oi takes a similar top-down approach to patron–client relations in the countryside: see *State and Peasant in Contemporary China: The Political Economy of Village Government* (Berkeley: University of California Press, 1989). On *intellectuals*, Timothy Cheek and Carol Hamrin's discussion of "establishment intellectuals" also highlights the dependency of intellectuals on their political patrons: see "Introduction: collaboration and conflict in the search for a new order" in their co-edited volume, *China's Establishment Intellectuals* (Armonk, NY: M.E. Sharpe, 1986).

8 Richard Madsen, *China and the American Dream: A Moral Inquiry* (Berkeley: University of California Press, 1995).

9 Zhao Dingxin defines legal-electoral, ideological, and performance legitimacy as the three basic sources of state legitimation during 1980s China. The state was authoritarian, society was poorly organized, and state legitimation was based on moral and economic performance. This particular state–society relationship, in conjunction with the great uncertainties brought about by state-led economic reform, led to the rise and shaped the development of the 1989 movement. See Dingxin Zhao, *The Power of Tiananmen: State–Society Relations and the 1989 Beijing Student Movement* (Chicago: University of Chicago Press, 2001), pp. 1–35.

10 Three recent edited volumes also examine state–society relations in China. In *Popular Protest and Political Culture in Modern China* (Boulder: Westview Press, 1994), editors Jeffrey Wasserstrom and Elizabeth Perry had broader aims than ours, with protest tied to larger issues of Chinese political culture. In *Chinese Society: Change, Conflict and Resistance* (London and New York: Routledge, 2000), editors Elizabeth Perry and Mark Selden note that although an extensive literature has been created on China's remarkable economic achievements, there has been rather less scholarly concern devoted to its social and political consequences – "the externalities of the reform agenda." The Perry/Selden volume introduces Chinese society through an examination of the conflicts and "dominant modes of resistance" engendered by the reforms. Such resistance is also one of the themes we explore. However, *Chinese Society* contains little explicit discussion of legitimacy – the core of our volume – although their emphasis on resistance implies that state legitimacy is under contestation. In *Remaking the Chinese State: Strategies, Society, and Security* (London and New York: Routledge, 2001), editors Chien-min Chao and Bruce Dickson begin by noting the partial success of the Party-state's post-Tiananmen strategy. By surrendering some of its control over the economy and society, and allowing more economic growth and a more lively cultural life to emerge, the Communist Party has sought to increase its legitimacy and strengthen its authority.

11 See Max Weber, *The Theory of Social and Economic Organization* (New York: The Free Press, 1964).

12 On the "conflicting imperatives" of Weberian authority, see Reinhard Bendix, *Nation-building and Citizenship: Studies of our Changing Social Order* (Berkeley: University of California Press, 1977).

13 Neil J. Diamant, *Revolutionizing the Family: Politics, Love, and Divorce in Urban and Rural China, 1949–1968* (Berkeley: University of California Press, 2000), p. 319.

14 Legitimacy is here understood as the political type or subset of the broader concept of authority.

15 Mao Zedong, "Problems of strategy in China's revolutionary war" (December 1936), *Quotations From Chairman Mao Tse-Tung* (the "Little Red Book") (Peking: Foreign Languages Press, 1966), p. 61. The resonance of this Mao quote in the West loudly bespeaks Liberal fears of "totalitarianism" and state coercion.

16 Mao Zedong, "Talk to the Central Committee Cultural Revolution Group" (February 1970). Cited in Michel Oksenberg, "The political leader," in Dick Wilson (ed.) *Mao Tse-tung in the Scales of History* (New York: Cambridge University Press, 1977), p. 84.

17 See, e.g., Elizabeth Perry, "Casting a Chinese 'democracy' movement: the roles of students, workers, and entrepreneurs," in Wasserstrom and Perry (eds) *Popular Protest*, p. 148.

18 Max Weber, *Religion of China: Confucianism and Taoism* (New York: Free Press, 1968; originally published in 1921), pp. 107, 128.

19 Lewis argues that "Writing created a literary double of the actual world, and this invented world became the highest reality." The literati were the custodians of that higher reality. See Mark Edward Lewis, *Writing and Authority in Early China* (Albany: State University of New York Press, 1999), pp. 109, 363.

20 Max Weber, *Religion of China*, pp. 117, 139.

21 Max Weber, *The Theory of Social and Economic Organization*, p. 345.

22 Wang Aihe, *Cosmology and Political Culture in Early China* (New York: Cambridge University Press, 2000), pp. 22, 190, 206.

23 See Zhang Liang (compiler), Andrew Nathan and Perry Link (eds), *The Tiananmen Papers* (New York: Public Affairs Press, 2000).

24 See Michael Schoenhals, *Doing Things with Words in Chinese Politics: Five Studies* (Berkeley: Institute of East Asian Studies, University of California, 1992).

25 See Zhao Yuezhi, *Media, Market, and Democracy in China: Between the Party Line and the Bottom Line* (Urbana: University of Illinois Press, 1998), and Daniel Lynch, *After the Propaganda State: Media, Politics, and "Thought Work" in Reformed China* (Stanford, CA: Stanford University Press, 1999).

26 Chen Guanglei, "Changes in the Chinese vocabulary under reform and opening," *Yuyan jiaoxue yu yanjiu* (*Language Teaching and Linguistic Studies*) 2 (1997): 15–23.

27 "Public sphere" is in many ways a misleading translation of the German *oeffentlichkeit*. Habermas described the rise of the public "sphere" as involving, conversely, the *collapse* of traditional boundaries between ruler and ruled. The walls of the metaphoric castle that separates Sovereign from Subject are symbolically torn down, *not* built up. See Jurgen Habermas, *The Structural Transformation of the Public Sphere: An Inquiry into a Category of Bourgeois Society* (Cambridge, MA: MIT Press, 1989).

28 Zhai Xuewei, "The faces of 'face,' " *Dongfang wenhua zhoukan* (*Oriental Culture Weekly*) 12 (1997): 8–9.

29 Jaime FlorCruz, personal communication, September 2003.

30 Jae Ho Chung, "Reappraising central–local relations in Deng's China: decentralization, dilemmas of control, and diluted effects of reform," in Chao and Dickson (eds) *Remaking the Chinese State*, pp. 46–75.

31 Tony Saich, *Governance and Politics of China* (New York: Palgrave, 2001), p. 20.

32 Zhao Dingxin, *The Power of Tiananmen*, p. 341.

33 Kellee Tsai and Susan Whiting have recently noted the varying impacts that local governments can have on the private sector. See Kellee S. Tsai, *Back-alley Banking: Private Entrepreneurs in China* (Ithaca: Cornell University Press, 2002), and Susan H. Whiting, *Power and Wealth in Rural China: The Political Economy of Institutional Change* (New York: Cambridge University Press, 2001).

34 The most extreme case of those examined was Shenzhen, the highly modernized special economic zone (SEZ) on the Hong Kong border, where 22.2 per cent of private enterprise owners were Party members while 0 per cent of industrial workers were Party members. In the least developed location, Zhenning County in Guizhou Province, where 64.6 per cent of the population was made up of

rural laborers and only 3.6 per cent were industrial workers, over 10 per cent of industrial workers were Party members, but the equivalent figure for private enterprise owners was 0 per cent, primarily because only 0.2 per cent of the population fit this latter category. Only 5.2 per cent of the large number of rural laborers were Party members, however, reflecting both the smaller overall number of Party members in less developed areas of the country as well as the declining number of Party members in rural China. See Lu Xueyi (general ed.), *Dangdai zhongguo shehui jieceng yanjiu baogao* (*Research Report on the Social Stratification of Contemporary China*) (Beijing: Shehui kexue wenxian chubanshe, 2002), pp. 10–37.

35   *Lingdao juece xinxi* (*Information for Leadership Decision-making*), No. 8, March 2003, p. 29.

36   This relaxation did not, however, mean that rural residents were permitted to move permanently to the urban areas and become entitled to such urban benefits as education and health care.

37   Stanley Rosen, "The wolf at the door: Hollywood and the film market in China," in Eric J. Heikkila and Rafael Pizarro (eds) *Southern California and the World* (Westport, CT: Praeger, 2002), pp. 49–77.

38   For a pessimistic view, see Gordon C. Chang, *The Coming Collapse of China* (New York: Random House, 2001). For an optimistic view, see Daniel Burstein and Arne de Keijzer, *Big Dragon: China's Future: What It Means for Business, the Economy, and the Global Order* (New York: Simon & Schuster, 1998).

39   Pei Minxin, "Contradictory trends and confusing signals," *Journal of Democracy*, Vol. 14, No. 1, January 2003, pp. 73–81.

40   For the positive view of institutional reform, see Andrew J. Nathan, "Authoritarian resilience," *ibid.*, pp. 6–17. For the negative view, see Bruce Gilley, "The limits of authoritarian resilience," *ibid.*, pp. 18–26. Ironically, Nathan and Gilley had recently co-authored a book entitled *China's New Rulers: The Secret Files* (New York: New York Review of Books, 2002).

41   For the positive view of the role of new social elites, see Xiao Gongqin, "The rise of the technocrats," *Journal of Democracy*, January 2003, pp. 60–65. For the negative view, see Bruce J. Dickson, "Threats to Party supremacy," *ibid.*, pp. 27–35.

42   For the positive view of the PRC's state capacity, see Yang Dali L., "State capacity on the rebound," *ibid.*, pp. 43–50. For the negative view, see Wang Shaoguang, "The problem of state weakness," *ibid.*, pp. 36–42.

43   Chen An, "The new inequality," *ibid.*, pp. 51–56.

44   He Qinglian, "A volcanic stability," *ibid.*, pp. 66–72.

45   "SARS isn't terrible, according to a new booklet," *South China Morning Post*, 7 April 2003 (online edition).

46   John Pomfret, "Outbreak gave China's Hu an opening," *Washington Post*, 13 May 2003, p. A01; Pei Minxin, "Don't hold your breath for openness in China," *Financial Times*, 7 May 2003 (online edition); Erik Eckholm, "Rude awakening: SARS shakes complacent mood of China and spotlights shortcomings in its system," *New York Times*, 13 May 2003, pp. A1, 12; Charles Hutzler, "SARS spurs unity in China leaders," *Asian Wall Street Journal*, 16 May 2003, p. A1; Ching-Ching Ni, "SARS crisis forces China to open up," *Los Angeles Times*, 9 May 2003, p. A10.

47   See the cover story in the *Economist*, 26 April–2 May 2003, pp. 9–10, entitled "The SARS virus: could it become China's Chernobyl?" See also "China's Chernobyl," *The London Times*, 21 April 2003 (online), and "A great leap forward in China," *The Japan Times*, 12 May 2003 (online).

48   For examples of pessimistic views, see Pei, "Don't hold your breath"; Liu Baopu, "Five myths about China and SARS," *Asian Wall Street Journal*, 13 May 2003, p.

A11; and Laurie Garrett, "SARS forces change in China," *Newsday*, 18 May 2003 (online). Despite government censorship on media reporting, some newspapers and magazines were boldly taking risks. For example, the managing editor of *Caijing* (*Finance and Economics*) published special issues and weekly editions on SARS. Reported in Nailene Chou Wiest, "On the case," *South China Morning Post*, 19 May 2003 (online). The *21st Century Economic Herald* (*Ershiyi shiji jingji baodao*) also published hard-hitting editorials on the need to "transform governance" in China (as on 14 May 2003, online).

49 Pomfret, "Outbreak gave China's Hu an opening." About 60 million Chinese surf the Internet and some 90 million send regular text messages, suggesting the daunting task the government faces in controlling information.

50 On the other hand, the SARS crisis has led to very little structural change, particularly in the workings of the Chinese bureaucracies and their clients. Short-term economic imperatives still appear routinely to trump public health issues. Thus, as of August 2003, while scientists were combing southern China for the source of the SARS virus, exotic wild animals – considered among the most likely sources – have reappeared for sale in public markets. Agricultural authorities, concerned with increasing rural incomes, have long encouraged farmers to move into such high-value areas as wild-animal breeding. Health officials, likely to bear the blame if SARS were to return, have lost out, once again, in this bureaucratic struggle. See Ben Dolvin, "China's failures," *Far Eastern Economic Review*, 21 August 2003, pp. 32–33.

51 Reuters, 22 May 2003. As a further example of the use of Doctor Jiang for propaganda purposes, roadside display cases juxtaposed Chinese press reports on his truthful revelations to the activities of Jayson Blair, the former *New York Times* reporter who "made his name overnight with fabrications and lies." We are grateful to David Kelly for this information.

1   Legitimacy crisis in China?[1]

Vivienne Shue

> Stability, no less than revolution, may have its own kind of Terror.
>
> E.P. Thompson[2]

At the turn of the 21st century, the strenuous conditions of social existence in China offered up plenty of cause for popular protest. The further dismantling of the old socialist system, the deepening marketization of economic relations, and the startling *de facto* redistributions of property rights were all contributing to social change and disruptions on a grand scale. Tens of thousands of state-sector workers were being laid off from their jobs without adequate benefits and without much prospect of re-employment. Tens of millions of poor migrant laborers, many of them still children, were streaming into the cities from rural areas to compete for jobs, but were left more or less entirely to fend for themselves, and could survive, often, only by enduring appalling living and working conditions. Those who opted to stay on the land, and they amounted still to a majority of the total population, were frequently denied a fair price for their crops even as they were too often subject to brutally inequitable tax assessments and other arbitrary levies by local officials. The poverty became so desperate in some rural areas that medical investigators sent back reports about whole villages full of people, many dying of AIDS, who had become infected with HIV when they had resorted to selling their own blood to survive. Women of childbearing age all over the country lived under relentless, sometimes vicious, official insistence that they limit their pregnancies even as they had to endure, for all that, painful family pressures to produce more sons. Artists and intellectuals, becoming ever more enmeshed in corrosively commodified relations of creative work and production, were at the same time still denied full freedom of expression, and remained subject to the rigors of a system of state censorship which, though it was clearly eroding, could nonetheless exert itself in ways that ranged from risibly obtuse to odiously oppressive. Ethnic minority groups with grievances against the Party and the state were subject to wary official surveillance and were still denied meaningful opportunities to express their views in public. Thus, nearly voiceless, minority peoples in the western regions of the country looked on in mounting anger and frustration as incoming waves of Han migrant settlers threatened to engulf them in their own homelands. Meanwhile, massive damage to China's natural environment – to the air, to the water, to the forests, and to the land – the effects of pesticide mismanagement and of over-rapid and under-regulated processes of industrialization and urbanization, literally sickened the brains and bodies of many unwitting victims and threatened the health and safety of millions more.

There is abundant evidence that, throughout the decade of the 1990s, numerous episodes of popular protest against such conditions of life did in fact take place in China – protests often directly aimed against state policies, state practices, and state officials.[3] Work stoppages, sit-ins, tax refusals, complaint petitions, public demonstrations, suicides meant to shame officials into action, riots, terror bombings, and an even richer repertoire, licit and illicit, of more covert measures of resistance and evasion have all been reported over recent years and on up to the present. Most of these actions have remained local or otherwise limited in scope, however. The police, the secret police, the military, and the civil official hierarchies, ever watchful, have all worked hard to contain such incidents, defusing crises when necessary with some measured concessions, and decapitating in embryo as many groups or units as they deemed might develop into the organizational skeletons for larger-scale collective actions. Thus, in China since that paroxysm of state violence on 4 June 1989, we have seen many popular protests, some limited protest "waves" perhaps, but no major social movements – no sustained movement of popular opposition from workers, migrants, poor farmers, women, students, intellectuals, ethnic minorities, or environmentalists. No opposition movement, that is, until (of all things) Falun Gong.

Falun Gong: history and heresy

In the spring of 1999 near Zhongnanhai,[4] a throng (estimated at something over 10,000 – not a tremendously large number in the Chinese context) of *qigong* meditation practitioners staged a mostly silent and composed, cross-legged, one-day sit-in. They were protesting having been slandered and harassed for their beliefs by a few secular-science activist intellectuals and publicists and some municipal government officials in Tianjin who were apparently trying to dissuade young people from the practice of *qigong*.[5] This dramatically resolute, peaceful "appeal" to the government for a redress of grievances apparently so shocked and surprised state leaders that they hurriedly launched an intensive investigation of the Falun Gong group and its leader, Li Hongzhi. Less than two months later, after the investigation was completed, top officials declared Falun Gong to be an "heretical sect," and its believers and their activities to constitute nothing less than a fearful and profound threat to China's social peace and stability. They banned the group, then ordered and relentlessly carried out a nationwide campaign to dissolve its network of teachers and disciples and to discredit Li Hongzhi and his followers. The official assertion that this previously nearly unheard-of group of non-violent, mystic popular religionists, who liked to gather in public parks to practice their meditation exercises, posed a threat of the gravest kind to social order, peace, and political stability in the country seemed incongruous to many.[6] Yet precisely that claim formed the ultimate basis and the justification for the reign of terror that ensued. And the state's campaign of suppression – which still goes on – has been so intense, so embittered, and so harsh as to have shocked and surprised, in its turn, numerous observers in the West.[7] With so many other structural reform crises and plausibly pressing causes for protest on the social agenda in China these days, few of us working in the field would have been likely to predict ahead of time that the first serious social protest movement to challenge the authority of the state since Tiananmen would crystallize around issues of spirituality, *qigong* meditation, and mystic syncretism.[8] But should we all have been taken quite so much by surprise?

As the Falun Gong events unfolded, students of modern Chinese history naturally pointed to some of the more obvious past parallels. Syncretic popular religious sects and secret societies have been implicated more than once before in challenging state power and provoking political crises in China. White Lotus rebels shook the last dynasty at the end of the 18th century; the armies of the Taiping Heavenly Kingdom nearly brought the sagging dynasty down in the middle of the 19th; and the bloody violence of the Boxers contributed both directly and indirectly to the final collapse of the Qing at the beginning of the 20th.[9] The implication that was meant to be drawn by those who reacted to the Falun Gong phenomenon first of all by pointing out the historical parallels was plain enough. Contemporary Chinese leaders, it can be presumed, know their own history; or at least they have been taught some version of it. When, to their horrified astonishment, in the closing hours of the 20th century, they discover budding in their very midst what appears to them to be a cult-like sect of popular religionists who practice curious healing exercises, who meditate with the aim of acquiring certain supernormal powers, and who use millennial-sounding language, a sect complete with a charismatic teacher for a leader whose actual organizational base may be rudimentary but who claims to have millions of followers – well, the historical resonances in all of that are just too rich to be ignored. Such a group, however much it may insist that its motives are benignly apolitical, must, by these facts alone, be counted as a political threat, because groups like it have effectively threatened sitting states in China before and have brought chaos and instability in their wake.[10] Everyone who has been taught even a little bit about China's modern history knows what such groups have been capable of in the past. Thus, the chilling warning to people in power contained in that single Falun Gong demonstration, the insinuation of the possibility of potentially devastating social insubordination, was palpably and directly intelligible to any Chinese, however meekly it may have been delivered by middle-aged ladies milling around in padded jackets.

Still, pointing in this fashion to historical parallels, however correctly drawn and symbolically potent they may be, can take us only part of the way toward understanding. History does not, as we know, simply repeat itself. An association with what was powerful once in the past need not prove powerful today. The governing apparatus in China has changed profoundly since late-imperial times, for one thing. It has far greater organizational capacity and control over domestic affairs than could possibly have been commanded by the precariously overextended late-Qing civil and military hierarchies that were so badly rocked by sectarian rebellion in earlier times. And Chinese society has changed profoundly as well. People in China who are attracted, for their health and general well-being, to *qigong* meditation regimens and the like nowadays get their lessons from cassette tapes and videos or from the Internet, and they schedule their meetings with one another via cell phones. Though in some ways their beliefs and actions may be plainly reminiscent of past social protest movements, the mental and the material worlds that today's Falun Gong practitioners inhabit are not by any means the same as those of the Boxers or the White Lotus rebels. Comprehending the symbolic politics of the present in light of what is known and remembered about the past, thinking as Charles Tilly has taught us, in terms of an only-very-slowly-evolving repertoire of protest,[11] can indeed help us to understand why certain distinctive political modes and tactics keep seeming to reappear within a society, even as they are also updated to meet the needs of changing times. Yet there would seem to be, even beyond this important insight, a still more fundamental issue waiting to be considered. Why was it that China was prone to produce precisely this form of popular protest in the first place? And why is it that rather than appearing merely as a quaint anachronism, this form of protest can be made so salient in the present moment? What is it about popular transcendental spiritual sects that makes them such a good mode for the expression of oppositionist sentiment in Chinese politics? Or, to turn the question around, what has it been about the systems of authority and domination that have arisen in China that provokes opposition in the form of mystic religious sects and movements?

The logic of legitimation (and opposition)

As Max Weber observed, different systems of domination deploy different logics for the legitimation of their rule. And the specific logics of legitimation that are advanced have consequences for the concrete forms of compliance that are required of citizens and subjects, as well as for the forms of political contention that arise in different societies. As Weber succinctly summarized this basic insight,

> every ... system [of domination] attempts to establish and to cultivate the belief in its legitimacy. But according to the kind of legitimacy

which is claimed, the type of obedience, the kind of administrative staff developed to guarantee it, and the mode of exercising authority, will all differ fundamentally.[12]

And as more contemporary students of political authority and contention, such as E.P. Thompson and Jim Scott, have further made clear, the very bases on which claims to legitimacy are advanced provide "the raw material for contradictions and conflict" in a society.[13] Scott, for example, has argued that

> the very process of attempting to legitimate a social order by idealizing it … provides its subjects with the means, the symbolic tools, the very ideas for a critique … For most purposes, then, it is not at all necessary for subordinate classes to set foot outside the confines of the ruling ideals in order to formulate a critique of power.[14]

Or, to put it another way, embedded in the very logic of legitimation advanced by a system of domination we can find the grammar that may be used most effectively by citizens and subjects in making statements in opposition and in resistance to that system.[15] As Gries and Rosen note in the Introduction to the present volume, the legitimacy of most systems of domination is subject to continuous contestation. This is a point to which we will return. For the moment, I wish to argue only that by examining closely the specific grounds on which the legitimacy of a system is alleged, we will better appreciate why it is that certain kinds of counter-allegations – particular forms of opposition and protest – are the ones that can be used most potently against that system. Let us consider, then, what have been the main claims made in Chinese logics of legitimation.

Looking at the present regime, many analysts would surely be tempted to offer the opinion that the Chinese state's main claims to legitimacy rest in its economic achievements, in an improving standard of living, in "growth" or in "development." Some such working assumption about state legitimation is frequently made in both journalistic and scholarly writing on China these days. The pressing question that starting from just such an assumption inevitably leads analysts to pose then becomes: "What if the Chinese economy cannot keep on growing at its recent unprecedented rates? What legitimacy would the government in power then have left?" But this approach to the matter, in my view, is seriously flawed. For while recognizing that steady economic growth or the lack of it may well act as an important conditioning factor influencing the popularity of a government, we also know beyond doubt that economic success alone is neither a necessary nor a sufficient condition for political legitimacy.

In China, furthermore, it is important to note that now, more than ever in recent memory, central state authorities are ill-positioned to claim direct credit for whatever economic advances are in fact taking place. The heart of the post-Mao reform project, after all, has been to pry away what is figured as the "dead hand" of central state planning from its stranglehold on the economy. Since the reforms first got underway in earnest in 1978, much of the responsibility for economic development has been reallocated away from central power-holders. It has settled in two quite different quarters. First, economic responsibility now resides much more in communities, localities, and at lower levels of the governing apparatus, since these units have been given far greater resources and broader discretion with which to craft and pursue localized strategies of growth and development, or not.[16] And secondly of course, under the post-Mao reforms, much more power has been granted to (or is now exerted through) the workings of markets. The vaunted magic and the notorious vagaries of markets now account for much more of the actual economic growth and change that takes place in China than was the case before. And this new reality serves even further to obscure the question of who might rightly take the credit for growth – or take the blame for economic failure. As legitimate responsibility for the economy has been dispersed and, to some extent, obfuscated in this way, so we have seen that popular protests arising out of the economic and social pain of the transition in China have likewise been dispersed. Suffering state-sector workers and peasants have been prone to frame their protests in localized and limited ways, taking as their protest targets not the architects of central reform policy but local "bad" officials, "incompetent" firm managers, and "heartless" employers. The combined effects of decentralization and marketization have worked to the advantage of the central state, then, making it somewhat easier for the center to contain and quell those protests that have arisen while simultaneously sustaining its own appearance of legitimacy.[17]

This is not to say that central authorities either can or would even want to wash their hands entirely of responsibility for economic performance. Official trumpeting of glowing statistics remains a part of the trappings of rule in China now, as it was under Mao. But central state responsibility for the economy has now become once-removed from what used to be called "the production front." Beijing authorities claim a kind of credit only for their excellent and enlightened general policies (*zhengce*) today – policies that permit and encourage the economy to flourish. *The maintenance of the conditions in which the economy does develop and the people do enjoy more prosperity* – this, I believe, comes much closer to capturing the actual core of the contemporary Chinese state's claims to rule legitimately. What, then, are held to be the general conditions the maintenance of which will most likely produce such happy effects? Those conditions are, in a word, the conditions of *stability* – the conditions of social peace and order. The present regime stakes its legitimacy, as I read it, not on its technical capacity to steer and to grow the economy, but on its political capacity to preserve a peaceful and stable social order under which, among other good things, the economy can be expected to grow.

Deconstructing stability: the ideals of Truth, Benevolence, and Glory

The idea that good government is about taking responsibility for maintaining harmony with the natural cosmos and peace in the social order has an ancient genealogy in China – a genealogy far too long and too subtle to be traced to its earliest sources here.[18] Fortunately, however, the work of H. Lyman Miller, on the later imperial era, can provide us with a more manageable historical starting point for considering the role that ideas about order and stability had, by that time, come to play in Chinese political thought:

> China in the late imperial period was governed by a bureaucratic monarchy. The seat of political authority resided in the person of the emperor. The emperor's purview was in principle comprehensive, and so his pronouncements were authoritative in every arena of human thought and action ... His authority was legitimated by a Confucian cosmology that placed him at the pivot between the cosmic natural order and the human social order – the "Son of Heaven" ... [T]he emperor's character and behavior – particularly his observance of proper rituals and ceremonies – and by extension the ethical conduct of the officials of his regime ensured harmony between and within the natural and social orders. If the emperor's character was upright, if he performed the proper rites, and if his administration was just, then peace and order would prevail ... By the same token, deficiencies of the emperor and his government in any of these respects could be expected to bring disorder in the natural and social worlds: floods, droughts, earthquakes ... in the former, and social disorder and rebellion in the latter. In hindsight, the collapse of a dynastic house and its replacement by another could be understood and so legitimated in terms of this moralistic cosmology.[19]

In the long tradition of Chinese statecraft that endured into the early part of the 20th century, the legitimacy of a sitting government was linked to the preservation of social order and this, in turn, was linked to the emperor's and his bureaucrats' true knowledge of and participation in a moralistic cosmology, an ethical science of the universe encompassing both its human and its natural elements. Rule was legitimated first and foremost by the ruler's claim to possess this true knowledge, as this knowledge was revealed through study and learning, through divination, and through the perfection of certain arts and sciences such as music and astronomy. Governance that was legitimate was also conceived as suffused with ethical goodness which expressed itself in the magnanimity of the emperor and his officials. Good government was characterized by benevolence – by taking responsibility for the welfare of the people and showing a degree of compassionate care for them. Good government – legitimate rule that was based on true knowledge of the universe and characterized by humane benevolence – was, furthermore, itself taken to be the embodiment and the exemplification of the very superiority and glory of the Sinic culture. The best rulers and officials, those who governed in accord with universal truths and manifested the proper benevolence toward their subjects, might hope and expect to preside over a stable and harmonious order, and the very florescence of economy, the arts, and of philosophy that would emanate from such an enviable order would, in turn, engender awe on the part of all those who beheld it, and would thereby further glorify the Sinic civilization and all the lands and peoples under the sway of the empire.

Thus, three of the key components in the logic of legitimation and the pursuit of harmony and stability were Truth, Benevolence, and Glory. These three do not constitute an "exhaustive list" of all the possible elements of state legitimation in imperial times. They were, I think it safe to say, however, certainly among the very most important constitutive concepts in the complex constellation of Chinese thought relating to state power and to legitimacy.[20] China's imperial rulers diligently made great display of their own and their court's earnest pursuit of these very high ideals. Emperors maintained whole academies of learned scholars and scientists, for example, dedicated to searching out the natural and the ethical truths embedded in the way of the cosmos. Armed with the moral truths discovered through study and self-cultivation, the entire apparatus of the Chinese state went on to take "moral instruction as a basic aspect of rule," and "aimed to shape the education of both elites and common people."[21] The goal of the imperial state was not merely to discover and to act itself in accord with the truth, but to spread the truth throughout society, to "shape popular beliefs and reduce the appeal of heterodox thought."[22]

In pursuit of the ideal of benevolence in its rule, also, the late imperial state made enormous commitments of effort and wealth. On the premise that good government required "supporting the people and regulating their livelihoods,"[23] state officials intervened extensively in what R. Bin Wong refers to as "ecological and economic matters." As he recounts,

> The search for social order led to state policies designed to stabilize the supply of various goods, especially food … During the Qing dynasty, a sophisticated system of food-supply management was created in which the central government gathered information on grain prices, weather, and rainfall from local officials in order to predict when and where in the empire serious food shortages might occur and to react to difficulties when they did appear. The centerpiece of state efforts at intervening in food-supply conditions in both routine and extraordinary ways was a granary system which stored several million tons of grain. Located mainly in county seats and small market towns, granaries represented official commitments to material welfare beyond anything imaginable, let alone achieved, in Europe.[24]

Grain shortages and famines could not always be averted, of course. The state's efforts to ensure and promote the popular welfare often failed, however much more precociously this value appeared as part of the logic of legitimate rule in China than it did in the West. Still, legitimation for local officials and members of the elite may have depended more, at times, on the display of benevolent concern itself, rather than on the actual saving of lives.[25] Through the granary system and through a whole array of formally and informally state-and-local-elite-supported orphanages, widow homes, and public relief projects, the late imperial system of domination made a point of displaying the virtue of charitability.[26]

As for the goal of enhancing the glory of Sinic culture and civilization, Qing emperors pursued a policy of territorial expansion, subduing militarily a number of regions and peoples in Inner Asia. They vigorously sought to expand and reproduce their conception of civilization and their vision of social order through space whenever possible. And when their military forces were inadequate for further conquest, which was the case a good deal of the time, they relied instead on the tribute system as a means to assert their cultural superiority and to project the glory of China outward into the rest of the world. According to Wong again,

> Despite [military] weaknesses, or perhaps in part as a response to them, the Chinese state succeeded in creating a framework for its international relations that placed other countries in a tributary status, a ritual position confirmed by the presentation of tribute, the presentation of gifts by the Chinese to the emissaries, and various agreements on a set schedule of visits every several years ... From the Chinese point of view, the tribute system met the challenge of ordering the Chinese world with the Chinese state at the center ... Foreign governments generally allowed the Chinese to promote this view without necessarily accepting it themselves.[27]

In the imperial logic of legitimation, securing the domestic order and stability came first. From a stable order at home might follow the necessary revenues and the other means for making further territorial conquests. But if not by conquest, then by cultural splendor and the projection of a confident superiority itself, the empire could still manage to command the respect of those powers on its periphery and beyond that might otherwise pose a threat, and literally awe them into cautious symbolic subordination.

By the mid- to late 19th century, however, China's military and technological weaknesses made this older vision of a world order centered on Sinic civilization very difficult to sustain. China's cultural superiority became harder and harder simply to assume, and her national glory came to be measured not in its radiant splendor, but in painful comparisons with other rising empires and competitor states. By the end of the century, the legitimating ideal of national "glory" had been redefined by Chinese philosophers and statesmen. Glory came to be understood no longer primarily in terms of civilized behavior and cultural florescence, but in the more vulgarly material terms of "wealth and power." Tributes and other polite forms of ritualized respect from foreign powers would remain sensitive issues, extremely important to 20th- and 21st-century Chinese rulers. But by the time the last dynasty fell, the ideal entailed in projecting the glory of Sinic civilization out into the rest of the world had been infused with more modern meanings – military might, advanced technology, industrialization, and (to return to an earlier point) more modern-day conceptions of economic "growth" and "development." The old values of Truth, Benevolence and Glory were never conceded. They were, rather, stretched by modernity to encompass some new contents and meanings – new knowledges, new social projects, and new measures of grandeur.

Possession of a special knowledge of transcendent truth, benevolent care for the common people, and the conscious glorification of the Chinese nation were each to exhibit remarkable endurance as ideals of good government, however, despite the 19th century's deep shocks to the last dynasty and even long after the final ruin of the imperial system. Most of the key realities of government and politics in China were to be radically altered, as we know, during the turbulent course of the 20th century. Yet these three basic themes in the rhetoric of state legitimation were not, by any means, to vanish from the scene. Far from becoming simply outmoded or being erased by newer ideas, in fact, these three legitimating norms have been revived again and again, in new and different guises. The specific content of their meanings has been continually adjusted and altered to suit the needs of changing times. But the ideals of Truth, Benevolence, and Glory have been constantly renewed in Chinese discussions around the subject of good governance and in China's modern politics of state legitimation and opposition. These three were plainly visible as governmental claims to authority under Mao.[28] And it is one of the chief contentions of this essay that they remain central themes in the state legitimation project of the post-Mao era.

The doctrines of Truth nowadays professed by Chinese leaders are no longer those of Confucian learning and Daoist cosmology, of course. The official standards for judging what knowledge is "true" knowledge now are those of modern scientific rationalism and pragmatic empiricism. "Seek truth from facts," as Deng Xiaoping so memorably put it. Scientific knowledge and technological know-how are presented by the state not only as exhibiting and belonging to a universal set of established, non-falsifiable truths; they are figured also as morally sound and good because, through science and technology, modernization will be achieved. The transcendently positive ethical value attached to the teleology of attaining modernity suffuses the scientific empiricism accepted and promoted as the only allowable epistemology by the Chinese state today.[29]

The state today also continues to base its legitimacy in part on its claim to practice humane Benevolence toward its subjects. The requisite governmental care and concern for the poor and for those at risk are no longer expressed in what were some of the more paternalist policies associated with the Maoist past. But they now take many other new and interesting forms, ranging from numerous small acts of patronage undertaken individually by sitting officials, to massive government-led efforts at mobilizing charitable relief through nationwide foundations and emergency funds.[30] It remains imperative in the contemporary logic of governmental legitimacy that both national-level officials and local office-holders be seen to take the lead in mobilizing the charitable provision of social support for those in dire need. Helping to underwrite orphanages and old-age homes has once again become a prominent vehicle for the expression of official benevolence. But the repertoire of magnanimous gestures has been updated, too, to include such modern "good causes" as providing scholarships for needy students and organ donations for the sick, and for the sake of science.[31]

As for the enhancement of the nation's Glory, the present government, as we have all had occasion to note, associates itself most vigorously with the vision of a newly "rising China," a China that will no longer tolerate the bullying or the disdain of other nations, a China that will one day definitely outstrip the accomplishments of all other competitors.[32] Assertively nationalistic official posturing about the glories of Han culture have been so pronounced since the 1989 debacle, in fact, that some observers have been tempted into believing (incorrectly, in my view) that patriotic sentiment has become the only popular value on which the contemporary state now bases its appeals for legitimacy. As with promoting the nation's economic growth and development, protecting and enhancing China's international prestige and military prowess should not be supposed to be an independently or comprehensively legitimating value in itself. The alternating expressions of pride and anxiety we find in China concerning these two grand ambitions are better understood, rather, as continuing sub-themes within a larger saga – the saga of upholding the Glory of the Sinic civilization. It is important to appreciate that the state's logic of legitimation today is not a reductionist or a singular one; it remains, much as it was in imperial times, multifaceted and composed of intricately interlaced assertions about cosmological truth, humane benevolence, and the glories of China's past and China's future.

Reading the logic of legitimation backwards

To return to our earlier analytic hypothesis, then, in any system of domination's own logic of legitimation we should be able to find encoded the basic grammar for protest, the "raw material" that is available to be used most powerfully in opposition to that system. If legitimate authority is claimed on the basis of bloodlines and royal descent, opposition politics can be expected to revolve heavily around family genealogies, cloak-and-dagger plots and counter-plots inside the court, and the real or imagined *bona fides* of pretenders to the throne. If a state's legitimate authority is claimed on the basis of holy writ, opposition political movements will likely coalesce around alternative versions of the sacred texts and canons, and differing interpretations of the heavenly will revealed in them. If a state's legitimate authority is claimed on the basis of democratic elections, charges of vote tampering, election fraud, and illegal or unwholesome campaign finance practices will be likely to figure prominently in the politics of opposition. If, as argued in the preceding section, in China some of the most central claims to legitimacy have rested on the combined ideals and values of Truth, Benevolence, and Glory, then what sorts of counterclaims would serve most powerfully to contest that legitimacy and galvanize political opposition?

The assertion that state actions are enhancing the national glory may be countered in several powerful ways. Charges of traitorousness at top levels, of selling out the nation and the people can be made, as indeed they were so devastatingly against the "alien" Manchus during the closing decades of the Qing, and against the warlord government that signed the Versailles Treaty in 1919. Popular movements and demonstrations arising out of incensed national pride have been a common and highly effective form for the expression of political opposition in China for well over a century. The 1980s and 1990s witnessed many national-cultural patriotic outbursts in Chinese cities, and the politics of national pride remains a highly sensitive area for state legitimation and de-legitimation today, as the essays by Gries and Kraus in this volume (Chapters 9 and 10 respectively) both show very well. Chinese leaders can never afford to be outflanked by social forces that manage to portray themselves as more ardently patriotic than the government. Yet the government's own intense official nationalism, projected through the media and other forms of propaganda, often only serves to raise the ante where the passionate defense of national glory is concerned. This is a potentially dangerous political syndrome, a somewhat volatile dimension along which we can expect to continue to see the legitimacy of the contemporary Chinese state called into question by opponents of the system.

The assertion that the state behaves benevolently toward the people is also open to challenge on several grounds. Most prominent among these perhaps, rampaging popular discourses on the subject of official corruption in China have served, time and again, to galvanize political opposition and give the lie to the officially cultivated mystique of benevolent governance. Official claims to be carrying out the business of the state in the spirit of humane and magnanimous charity have almost always been contested in the Chinese people's critiques of their rulers, where cynical reference is so readily made to the corruption, the venality, and the self-serving behavior of sitting officials. That officialdom can and must be expected to be shot through with nepotism and corruption is, in fact, an axiom of Chinese popular political culture. But when ordinary people in China allege, as they so frequently do, that corruption is rampant, they are not merely pointing the finger at some particular guilty officials; they are challenging the authority of the entire state system that stakes a claim to legitimacy on the basis of official selflessness and benevolence. Popular disgust and protest over corrupt practices were factors leading to the collapse of many a former dynasty and regime, not least visibly in the dramatic withdrawal of public support that led to the expulsion of the Guomindang government and the victory of the Communist Party on the mainland. In the vigor and the unrelenting din of popular discourse on corruption in China today, then, we hear again the ruled speaking back to the rulers on the subject of benevolence. The critique of power being leveled at the contemporary Chinese state along this dimension (as the essays in this volume by Thornton (Chapter 4), Weston (Chapter 3), and Solinger (Chapter 2) all serve to illustrate) undeniably constitutes another one of the most salient and powerful challenges to its legitimacy and to its capacity to rule authoritatively.[33]

If in the angry and bitter popular discourses on official corruption we find oppositionist challenges to the legitimacy of the state's claims to be governing humanely and benevolently, and if in the melodramatic indignation of popular discourses on national strength and national humiliation we find oppositionist challenges to the legitimacy of the state's claims to be upholding and advancing the glory of China, where then do we find popular challenges to the state's claims to be acting in accord with the highest of moral truths to be found in the way of the cosmos? We find these most powerfully, I would suggest, in the discourses and practices of popular religion. Contemporary popular religious sects, with their syncretic systems of thought and action, posit an even higher, more all-encompassing, and more potent ethical and epistemological order than the one embraced by the state. They insist on a mystical moral order that transcends the modern-rational scientific mode of knowing what is true. Chinese popular religious beliefs and practices invoke a universe of ghosts and deities, of animal spirits and immortals, whose positive power to affect the human condition cannot be explained by modern science, and whose ethically based motives for action and inaction do not fit comfortably with the norms and values intended to guide human choices that are put forward for the edification of the people by the Chinese state. In this lies the special potency of sectarian religion as a vehicle for denying the authority of the state and for mobilizing protest against it.

The state's claim to "truth" and the challenge of popular religion

In imperial China, unlike medieval and early modern Europe, there was no autonomous system of church schools taking care of the basic education and the moral training of the social and political elite. There was no separate organization of the guardian faith to conduct inquisitions and suppress heterodox popular religious beliefs and practices. Moral training for the elite and the suppression of popular religious heresies were the affair of the state in China. As James Watson has argued,[34] the imperial state maintained its own approved pantheon of recognized deities, and it attempted to "standardize the gods" throughout the realm by encouraging the worship only of those spirits admitted to the official pantheon. It promoted its own preferred deities, encouraging their worship by ever-wider circles of the populace. But the state also at times co-opted into its official pantheon pre-existing popular deities who had acquired important followings, taking advantage for itself of their prestige and presumed potency while, at the same time, avoiding a stand-off between official and non-official religion, and blurring the lines between the two.[35] The state maintained the final word on what did and did not constitute true belief. But in practice, different deities symbolized different (and sometimes competing) values to different groups in society, and the state exercised only a loose control over the actual content of belief. It exerted its authority in social life through what Prasenjit Duara has conceived of as a broad "cultural nexus," an interlacing of official and non-official roles in local society which included the participation of state bureaucrats in the life of religious temples and shrines.[36] In this complexly multi-stranded cultural nexus linking state and society, much productive ambiguity about the bases of temporal and supernatural "power" was deliberately sustained. The state, on the one hand, authorized the worship of certain deities. And yet, the mystical power these local gods and spirits were already believed by the people to possess also adhered, in a way, to the state's own officials as they acted out their leading roles in the rituals and ceremonies of village and small-town life. State officials had the power to validate popular deities, and popular deities had the power to validate the state.

As Duara has argued, the productive ambiguities of ruling through the cultural nexus were relentlessly broken down in China by the processes of modern state-making that took place after the Qing collapse. Facing up to the challenges posed by imperialism – the confusing and terrifying jolts delivered by foreign military and technological superiority, alien religious and secular philosophies, and Western conceptions of modernity and power – the educated classes of Chinese gradually turned their backs on the resources for rule that were embedded in popular religious god and ghost worship. Both the Guomindang and the Communist Party-states launched repeated campaigns to try to get people to give up popular religious beliefs and ritual practices. These came to be labeled as mere "superstition," something shameful to be eradicated and not eligible to be incorporated in the modes of modern governance. If peasants and petty urbanites continued, well on into the 20th century, to venerate gods and ghosts, to propitiate spirits with offerings, to make pilgrimages to holy mountains, and to consult geomancers and shamans, these practices could be comprehended by state officials and by members of the Chinese intelligentsia alike only as the lamentable markers of continuing Chinese backwardness. And as Duara has further pointed out, contrasting some of the choices made by 20th-century Indian intellectuals with those made by their Chinese counterparts, the consuming commitment of Chinese intellectuals to the narrative of modernity ... has obscured the vitality of popular culture, religion, and their associational life and delegitimated the critique of modern ideologies originating outside of modern discourses. Despite the repeated persecution of the intelligentsia by the Chinese state, it is this shared narrative [of modernity] which has thrown so many of them repeatedly into the arms of the state and at the same time alienated both from the living cultures of the "masses" and of "tradition." While the state has made effective use of the narrative of modernity to expand its own powers, the Chinese intelligentsia has robbed itself of alternative sources of moral authority which it might have found in history and popular culture.[37]

After 1949, secular-scientific Marxism and Mao Thought ascended to become the new official cosmological "truths" upheld and purveyed by the state. Marx's universalist teleology of progress, leavened by the moral sensibilities of proletarian class struggle and the Maoist ideals of revolutionary virtue, were relentlessly pressed upon the people. Alternative popular histories, cosmologies, virtues, and beliefs were denounced and driven underground. Shrines and temples were destroyed. Shamans were put through forced re-education. State suppression of popular heterodoxies was, for a generation or so, extremely intense. In recent years, a state-orchestrated public re-evaluation of Mao Thought and of the Marxian theory of history has taken place in China. Some of the older interpretations given to Marxist verities have had to be dropped or, anyway, very sharply bent in order to accommodate the present government's new guiding theory of "socialism with Chinese characteristics." But the post-Mao period has seen no official backing down from the secular-rational empiricist-modernist values embedded in Marxism. Popular religious belief and practice remains, according to the state's truth, mere superstition. Insofar as people still believe in gods and immortals, make offerings to appease the ghosts of the departed, or think about their moral choices in terms of karma and the transmigration of souls, the state has failed in its pedagogic project of building "spiritual civilization" and in its modernizing effort to civilize the subaltern.[38] In the state's view, and in the view of most of China's intelligentsia, widespread popular religious practice can be evidence only that the "quality" (*suzhi*) of a large proportion of the population still remains deplorably "low."[39]

Yet, in the various social spaces opened up by the post-Mao reforms, there has emerged nothing short of a vigorous popular religious revival in China, one that embraces Buddhism, Daoism, and a host of syncretic sects. Kenneth Dean has characterized this revival as "an extraordinary renaissance of reinvented traditional forms of ritual activity":

Hundreds of thousands of temples have been restored, rebuilt, and reconsecrated. Millions of people have taken part in ritual events which have become more frequent each year as well as more complex and multifaceted. This activity has been most intense in southeast China, particularly in Fujian, Guangdong, and Zhejiang, but there is increasing evidence that local religious practices are spreading all across China.[40]

Some of these reinvented traditions, including the ones that Dean has studied, are tied closely to localities. They are spiritual expressions, often, of community-based collaborations and competitions.[41] In sects of this type, popular religion can be "the pivot for a complex network of forms of local social organization that counterbalance state interventions from above: family, lineages, village, regional alliances of villages." Their ritual practices may work to "interrupt the downward flow of state signification aimed at reforming the individual."[42] They can, as Dean argues, be regarded as a somewhat contained form of resistance or opposition to state domination and an expression of the ongoing human effort to "achieve autonomy and self-definition."[43] Even so, state officials, and especially local state officials, may find it expedient to tolerate and even encourage their activities. Their performances and gatherings, their shrines and processions, can be good for local business. They can even attract tourists from Taiwan, Southeast Asia, and Hong Kong, bringing in with them foreign currency, donations, and investments.[44] These local religious activities can have "picturesque" and "exotic" qualities that fold well into the commodification of certain Chinese cultural performances and artifacts that also forms part of the contemporary state's agenda for dealing with social diversity.[45] For reasons such as these, some localized popular religious sects may be able to find official shelter and support in the ambiguities of the local "cultural nexus" of state and society now being reconstructed in some parts of the country.

The Falun Gong phenomenon, however, does not fit this more tolerable type of religious sect. Not localized at all, it has proven to be eminently transportable, spreading throughout China and, via the Internet, around the world.[46] Falun Gong's leader, Li Hongzhi, has cultivated a charismatic image and, in the wake of the state's campaign against him, has adopted a combative demeanor toward the government in Beijing and toward China's high officials. Falun Gong websites have referred to those who arrest and suppress believers inside China as "monsters" and "demons," and have carried cartoons lampooning Jiang Zemin himself. Nor does Li's ethical philosophy fit well with the consumerist values of the commodity culture that the Beijing government broadcasts. Master Li teaches his followers to try to let go of all earthly attachments, and he castigates as demonically evil the corrosive values of the market place.[47] Li not only rejects the ideals of the socialist market economy which the Chinese state now seeks to foster; he also rejects the claims to cosmological truth that are accorded by the state to the demystified rationality of modern science. Li claims knowledge of a higher science, one that is not yet comprehended on earth. He utilizes the language of modern science and medicine in his teachings at times, speaking of tumors, of time-space dimensions, and the like. But this, as he explains, is simply because these terms and categories are the only ones that will be widely understood by people on earth at this time. Li's cosmology is, his disciples are given to understand, much greater than the scientistic official cosmology. It features a host of paranormal possibilities, from predatory fox spirits that can inhabit human bodies, to contacts with extraterrestrials. Li's standards of morality are also far more demanding than the official ones. His followers must cultivate goodness for its own sake. They must turn away from all desires for fame and fortune, or they will not be saved.

The challenge posed by popular religious beliefs and practices like those of Falun Gong cuts right to the heart of the Chinese state's own logic of legitimation. Falun Gong teaches people to disdain, as rigid but patently imperfect, the whole modernist, secular-scientific understanding of the cosmos in which the state roots its governing authority. And Falun Gong teaches people to regard as pitiably misguided the poor conception of morality and goodness that has come to characterize Chinese society under the state's own program of market socialist reform. The teachings of Li Hongzhi thus stand in the profoundest possible opposition to the present political order. They assail the ethical truths on which the entire political construct is meant to rest. However peacefully they practice their meditation exercises and however much they may regard "politics" as being beneath them, those swept up in the Falun Gong phenomenon never had a chance of remaining "apolitical" in China.[48] With its slogan, *"Zhen, Shan, Ren"* – "Truth, Goodness, and Forbearance" – Falun Gong makes almost a perfect counter-hegemony. Truth! – but not the state's narrow empiricist truths. Goodness! – but not the state's dubious versions of benevolence. Forbearance! – but not the state's vulgarly assertive "wealth and power" concept of what it means to attain real glory.

Precisely because Falun Gong does represent such an absolute challenge – a challenge to the very foundations of the state's authority and legitimacy – government officials insist on complete extermination of the threat. It is one thing to demonstrate for lower taxes or better benefits. These are goods the state can, if it will, (benevolently) confer upon those who can show they have righteous claims to consideration. The people's demand itself implies the power and the authority of the state to satisfy the need. It is quite another thing, however, to demonstrate for Truth, Goodness, and Forbearance. The demand itself implies the lack. An assault like Falun Gong's, on the legitimating foundations of state authority, is thus perceived as a threat to the entire existing system of domination – a threat to order and stability. And the enormity of the threat itself is, in turn, used to justify the draconian severity of the repression. Intimidations, arrests, tortures – the crackdown has been a hard one, carried out by "a hard lot of men."[49] This is the apt phrase used by E.P. Thompson (in the passage from which the quotation that begins this essay is drawn) to characterize Walpole and the Hanoverian Whigs of the 1720s and 1730s, as they pushed through the cruel punishments of the "Black Act" to crack down on hunters, whom a nervous state, fearing armed sedition, wished now to classify as "poachers." As Thompson strives to remind us, it has been in the name of safeguarding "stability" that some of history's nastiest political terrors have been excused.

The logic of state legitimation in China makes popular religious practice and belief a challenge to authority – because it celebrates a higher truth. It is the state's own logic of rule that endows popular religious movements with their political salience and makes them potent vehicles for the expression of opposition and protest. When such popular religious sects and movements are content to operate furtively and on the margins, or when they remain explicitly locally bounded in their activities and scope, or when they seek and secure protections from local officials who hope to gain something from their existence, the heresies and the other dangers entailed in their beliefs are often, somehow, found to be tolerable. But when, as in the case of Falun Gong, such a sect goes overtly "national," making a bid for broader public sympathy and staging its rituals and demonstrations in nationally/symbolically sacred spaces such as Zhongnanhai and Tiananmen, then syncretism will be officially equated with sabotage. The legitimacy of the entire system, which rests on the preservation of a stable public order, will then be seen to depend utterly on the obliteration of heretical beliefs among the people.[50] Until and unless the Chinese state moves on to a newer repertoire of legitimation claims – one that does not include official knowledge of ultimate ethical truths – we can expect popular religious belief and practice to continue to be perceived *always as a potential*, and *sometimes as an active*, counter-hegemonic danger to stability and order. And we can expect the high value accorded to stability, by the great majority of the rulers and the ruled alike, to contribute to the sanctioning of Inquisition-like trials and terrors to suppress China's new-style old believers.

A crisis of legitimacy or two cheers for ambivalence?

I have argued here against giving in to reductionist conceptions of what is entailed in having, and in holding onto, political legitimacy in contemporary China. In China, as in other modern political systems which have grown gradually out of older and prior forms of polity, the legitimacy claims of the state are layered deep historically, multi-stranded, and complex. I have also suggested that, in the patterns of contentious politics that surround state legitimation and de-legitimation in the Chinese context, it is the government's capacity to sustain stability and social order that is generally held up as the touchstone value. The very goodness that is imagined to be attendant on social order is, further, closely related to certain very particular high ideals – ideals of seeking and promoting the epistemological and moral Truth, of governing with a degree of humane Benevolence, and of protecting and enhancing the national Glory. The state's antagonists in society, those who doubt or deny its legitimacy, I have further argued, "speak back" to power with charges and counterclaims that tend to be constructed along these very same dimensions of value. State claims to be advancing the national Glory are met by popular counterclaims of leadership weakness, vacillation, or betrayal. State claims to be governing with Benevolence are met by popular counterclaims of callousness, corruption, and venality. And state claims to be promoting the demonstrable empirical and moral Truth are met by powerful alternative epistemologies, popular counter-truths, and counter-moralities such as those of Falun Gong.

Each one of these three hallmark patterns of contentious politics – so clearly related to the processes of state legitimation and de-legitimation in China – is broadly and prominently in evidence today. And this has no doubt contributed to the penchant of many observers these days to speculate, somewhat loosely, about an ongoing "crisis of legitimacy" in China. The arguments that have typically been advanced along these lines, often simplistic ones, are surely already familiar, so they may be summarized very briefly. Belief in Maoism and Marxism are said to be "dead" in China today, killed off by the market reforms and the transparently self-serving behavior of power-holders at all levels of the system. The resultant sudden crisis of faith is so severe among the people of China, who are supposed previously to have lived in thrall to the official ideology, that the state has had to scurry to find some other doctrine to fill the void. By most such accounts, official nationalism is that chosen new doctrine, and patriotism has thus been pumped up by the state to take the place of the old ideological commitment in the minds of China's hapless masses.[51] On this view of things, one whole coherent set of relatively uncomplicated beliefs about the state's legitimacy is imagined to have been pulled out of people's heads, while another whole set of even more uncomplicated principles has been plugged in to fill the empty slot. Functionalist analyses like these, in my view, grossly misread the complexity of the lived world of belief most human beings encounter. Such approaches to questions of legitimacy downplay human agency and creativity and ignore the multiplicity of the worlds of value we all inhabit.

Citizens and subjects, as students of popular resistance and protest have taught us, almost never swallow whole the legitimacy claims of their rulers. Even at the most totalizing of authoritarian political moments, popular dissent and disbelief are commonly expressed as people negotiate the precise terms on which they will give their obedience to the state. As Karen Petrone has concluded in her noteworthy study of official holidays and mass celebrations during the high-Stalinist era, "While citizens within reach of Soviet discourse were bombarded with carefully censored messages, they interpreted these messages in a wide variety of ways and used the discourse of the state to create alternative visions of their worlds."[52] Likewise, during the most radical of radical moments in China, the Cultural Revolution, we clearly witnessed people calculatedly and creatively deploying the state's own rhetoric of "class struggle" to pursue interests, values, and identities of their own. On closer inspection, then, ordinary people rarely turn out to be the gullible true believers that states (and some social scientists) may imagine. Or, to quote E.P. Thompson once again, this time making reference to the sartorial habits of the British court system, "people are not as stupid as some structuralist philosophers suppose them to be. They will not be mystified by the first man who puts on a wig."[53] They will, much more commonly, take the raw material that state logics of legitimation offer them and do their best to bend these to ends and visions of their own.

Yet I submit that while citizens and subjects may, most often, not be mystified by the prevailing legitimacy claims of states, neither are they always consciously and systematically engaged in countering the state's hegemony – as some of the literature on "everyday forms of resistance" might lead us to expect. Most people, most of the time, I would suggest, are quite appropriately ambivalent about the legitimacy of the system in which they find themselves. They know – through their own experiences, through the trusty testimony of others, through rumor, and through humor – of plenty of good reasons to accept and plenty of good reasons not to accept their state's authority. Their multi-stranded knowledge and experience of living in society teaches them that some officials are, after all, honest, well-meaning, or efficient; that some claims made by governments do, in the end, prove out. They know these things to be true even as they also know that numerous other officials are venally abusing their trust and that governments frequently lie. The inhabitants of complex societies sustain correspondingly complex and highly inflected understandings of their own social reality and of social possibility. This is true even of those who are scarcely literate and who live in remote regions.[54] The very experience of domination most often marries objection with acceptance. It is bivalent, and so people are ambivalent.

The state in China today strives continuously, agonistically, as all states must strive, more or less perpetually, against antagonists, to validate and revalidate their authority. In China, no doubt due to the very breadth and magnitude of the grand social and economic transformations that are currently underway, the pressures being brought to bear in this contest and the stakes of the game may seem higher than usual. The level of contention over authority is elevated throughout society. And so, not unexpectedly, is the expressed level of popular doubts and ambivalences about power. This palpable heightening in the expression of mixed feelings on the part of the people has contributed, I think, to the view some hold that the state in China now faces "a crisis of legitimacy." But the condition of human ambivalence experienced amid a swirl of claims and counterclaims about the legitimacy of power should not in itself, in my view, be taken as evidence of crisis. Living in a state of acute ambivalence might be considered, rather, quite the most common fate for citizens and subjects everywhere who must confront what Max Weber called "the generally observable need of any power, or even of any advantage of life, to justify itself."[55]

Notes

1 My thanks to the American Council of Learned Societies for generous research support and to four indulgent colleagues, Marc Blecher, Kenneth Foster, Dorothy Solinger, and Sidney Tarrow, for reading and offering challenging comments and criticisms on an earlier draft of this essay. I wish it were possible to respond adequately to each one.

2 E.P. Thompson, *Whigs and Hunters: The Origins of the Black Act* (New York: Pantheon, 1975), p. 258.

3 For some recent scholarly discussions of worker protest, see Ching Kwan Lee, "Pathways of labor insurgency," in Elizabeth Perry and Mark Selden (eds) *Chinese Society: Change, Conflict and Resistance* (London: Routledge, 2000), pp. 41–61, and Ching Kwan Lee, "Lost between histories: labor insurgency and subjectivity in reform China," paper presented at the 53rd Annual Meeting of the Association for Asian Studies, 22–25 March 2001. See also Wang Zheng, "Gender, employment and women's resistance," in Perry and Selden, *Chinese Society*, pp. 62–82. On migrants, see Dorothy Solinger, *Contesting Citizenship in Urban China* (Berkeley: University of California Press, 1999); Michael Dutton, *Streetlife China* (Cambridge: Cambridge University Press, 1998); Hein Mallee, "Migration, hukou and resistance in reform China," in Perry and Selden, *Chinese Society*, pp. 83–101; and Li Zhang, "Migration and privatization of space and power in late socialist China," *American Ethnologist* 28(1) (2000): 179–205. On peasant protest, see Thomas Bernstein, "Instability in rural China," in David Shambaugh (ed.) *Is China Unstable?* (Armonk, NY: M.E. Sharpe, 2000), pp. 95–111, and Thomas Bernstein and Xiaobo Lü, *Taxation Without Representation in Contemporary Rural China: State Capacity, Peasant Resistance, and Democratization, 1985–2000* (New York: Cambridge University Press, 2003). See also Lianjiang Li and Kevin O'Brien, "Villagers and popular resistance," *Modern China* 22(1) (1996): 28–61; Kevin O'Brien, "Rightful resistance," *World Politics* 49(1) (1996): 31–55; and Jonathan Unger, "Power, patronage and protest in rural China," in Tyrene White (ed.) *China Briefing 2000* (Armonk, NY: M.E. Sharpe 2000), pp. 71–94. On artists and intellectuals, see Merle Goldman, "The potential for instability among alienated intellectuals and students in post-Mao China," in Shambaugh, *Is China Unstable?*, pp. 112–124; Gérémie Barmé, "The revolution of resistance," in Perry and Selden, *Chinese Society*, pp. 198–220; and Robert Efird, "Rock in a hard place: music and the market in nineties Beijing," in Nancy Chen, Constance Clark, Suzanne Gottschang, and Lyn Jeffery (eds) *China Urban* (Durham, NC: Duke University Press, 2001), pp. 67–86. On women's issues, see Zheng, "Gender, employment and women's resistance"; Tyrene White, "Domination, resistance and accommodation in China's one-child campaign," in Perry and Selden, *Chinese Society*, pp. 102–119; and Cecilia Milwertz, "Control as care: interaction between urban women and birth planning workers," in Kjeld Brødsgaard and David Strand (eds) *Reconstructing Twentieth-century China* (Oxford: Clarendon Press, 1998), pp. 92–112. On ethnic minorities, see June Dreyer, "The potential for instability in minority regions," in Shambaugh, *Is China Unstable?*, pp. 125–142, and Uradyn Bulag, "Ethnic resistance with socialist characteristics," in Perry and Selden, *Chinese Society*, pp. 178–197. And finally, on environmental protests, see Jun Jing, "Environmental protests in rural China," in Perry and Selden, *Chinese Society*, pp. 143–160.

4 This is the office and residential compound used by high Party-state officials, adjacent to Tiananmen Square, in the heart of Beijing.

5 The general term *qigong* refers to regimens of breath and body exercises that may be studied and practiced, individually and in groups, by those in pursuit of greater physical, mental, and spiritual self-control and well-being. The initial

article assailing the Falun Gong group of *qigong* practitioners, which appeared in a teen science and technology journal published in Tianjin, was written by He Zuoxiu, a leading physicist and member of the Chinese Academy of Sciences. See Danny Schechter, *Falun Gong's Challenge to China: Spiritual Practice or "Evil Cult"* (New York: Akashic Books, 2000), Ch. 6, for an account of the events leading up to the protest demonstration at Zhongnanhai.

6 As Elizabeth Perry has noted in *Challenging the Mandate of Heaven: Social Protest and State Power in China* (Armonk, NY: M.E. Sharpe, 2002), p. xix, "The [Falun Gong] gatherings were nonviolent and remarkably disciplined. While the government insisted that these demonstrations were the most serious political threat since the 1989 student uprising, it was hard to see why."

7 As Patsy Rahn points out in "The Falun Gong: beyond the headlines," "Most people in the West see the campaign as unnecessarily exaggerated and harsh, similar to political campaigns waged during the Mao era." And many inside China clearly joined in with this view. As Perry, *Challenging the Mandate of Heaven*, p. xix, reports, "judging from discussions with people in China at the time, this particular campaign was not a resounding success ... The draconian nature of the campaign was suggestive of a deeply frightened and insecure central leadership. People wondered out loud: Had crimes so serious as to warrant the arrest of thousands really occurred?" See www.let.leidenuniv.nl.bth/FalunRAHN.htm (2000, p. 1), accessed 9 July 2001.

8 Some anthropologists were on to these issues earlier than the rest of us, however. See, e.g., Nancy Chen, "Urban spaces and experiences of *qigong*", in Deborah Davis, Richard Kraus, Barry Naughton, and Elizabeth Perry (eds) *Urban Spaces in Contemporary China* (New York: Cambridge University Press, 1995), pp. 347–361, and Kenneth Dean, *Taoist Ritual and Popular Cults of Southeast China* (Princeton: Princeton University Press, 1993).

9 On the White Lotus, see Susan Naquin, *Shantung Rebellion: The Wang Lun Uprising of 1774* (New Haven: Yale University Press, 1981); on the Taiping, see Franz Michael, *The Taiping Rebellion* (Seattle: University of Washington Press, 1966), and Jonathan Spence, *God's Chinese Son: The Taiping Heavenly Kingdom of Hong Xiuquan* (New York: W.W. Norton, 1996); and on the Boxers, see Joseph Esherick, *The Origins of the Boxer Uprising* (Berkeley: University of California Press, 1987), and Paul Cohen, *History in Three Keys: The Boxers as Event, Experience, and Myth* (New York: Columbia University Press, 1997).

10 For an attempt at a dispassionate summary of some of the content of Master Li's teachings and a consideration of why these particular moral teachings could pose a threat to the state, see Vivienne Shue, "Global imaginings, the state's quest for hegemony, and the pursuit of phantom freedom in China: from *Heshang* to *Falun Gong*," in Catarina Kinnvall and Kristina Jönsson (eds) *Globalization and Democratization in Asia: The Construction of Identity* (New York: Routledge, 2002). The best introduction to Falun Gong philosophy can be found in the Master's own writings: Hongzhi Li, *Zhuan Falun*, 2nd edn, English version (New York: Universe Publishing Co., 1998).

11 Charles Tilly, *The Contentious French* (Cambridge, MA: Harvard University Press, 1986).

12 Max Weber, *Economy and Society: An Outline of Interpretive Sociology* (Berkeley: University of California Press, 1978), p. 213.

13 The phrase comes from James Scott, *Weapons of the Weak: Everyday Forms of Peasant Resistance* (New Haven: Yale University Press, 1985), p. 336.

14 *Ibid.*, p. 338.

15 "Read backwards," as John Sidel puts it, "legitimacy claims specify what exactly, in a given setting, is considered dangerously *illegitimate*." Sidel's insightful analysis goes on, in a manner that Weber would no doubt have well

approved of, to illustrate how several different grammars, or what he calls "languages of legitimation," may be operative within a single system of domination. See John Sidel, "The Philippines: the languages of legitimation," in Muthiah Alagappa (ed.) *Political Legitimacy in Southeast Asia: The Quest for Moral Authority* (Stanford: Stanford University Press, 1995), p. 139.

16 For a discussion of some of the consequences of this new concentration of economic power and dynamism at local levels, see Marc Blecher and Vivienne Shue, "Into leather: state-led development and the private sector in Xinji," *China Quarterly* 166 (2001).

17 I owe this particular insight to some very thoughtful comments made by Sally Sargeson at the workshop entitled "Mapping the local state" convened by Richard Baum and Tony Saich at UCLA, June 2001. For an excellent discussion of the limitations on the framing of recent workers' protests in China, see also Lee, "Lost between histories."

18 Its roots are to be found in the major streams of thought, Confucianism and Daoism, that emerged (after the decline of even more ancient forms of Chinese religion) during the period known as the Eastern Zhou Dynasty, 771–221 bce. On the interplay of these and other strands in very early Chinese political thought, interested readers may consult the magisterial study by Benjamin Schwartz, *The World of Thought in Ancient China* (Cambridge: Belknap Press, 1985).

19 H. Lyman Miller, "The late imperial Chinese state," in David Shambaugh (ed.) *The Modern Chinese State* (Cambridge: Cambridge University Press, 2000), pp. 17–18.

20 For a much deeper consideration of all the issues raised here and more, see the rigorous comparison of European and Chinese patterns of state-making in R. Bin Wong, *China Transformed: Historical Change and the Limits of European Experience* (Ithaca: Cornell University Press, 1997).

21 *Ibid.*, p. 96.

22 *Ibid.* Making the interesting comparison with Europe, Wong here argues that "There is no early modern European government equivalent to the late imperial Chinese state's efforts at dictating moral and intellectual orthodoxy, nor were such efforts particularly important to Europe's state-making agenda, as they were in China. Early modern European states did not share the Chinese state's view that shaping society's moral sensibilities was basic to the logic of rule" (*ibid.*, p. 97).

23 *Ibid.*, p. 93.

24 *Ibid.*, p. 98. For more on the ideas concerning popular welfare that lay behind the imperial state granaries, see Pierre-Etienne Will and R. Bin Wong, *Nourish the People: The State Civilian Granary System in China, 1650–1850* (Ann Arbor: University of Michigan Center for Chinese Studies, 1991).

25 On this point, see, further, Joanna Handlin Smith, "Chinese philanthropy as seen through a case of famine relief in the 1640s," in Warren Ilchman, Stanley Katz, and Edward Queen (eds) *Philanthropy in the World's Traditions* (Bloomington: Indiana University Press, 1998), pp. 133–168.

26 A close and revealing study of these charitable institutions can be found in Angela Leung (Liang Qizi), *Shishan yu Jiaohua: Ming Qing de Cishan Zuzhi* (*Charity and Enlightenment: The Charitable Organizations of the Ming and Qing*) (Taipei: Lianjing, 1997).

27 Wong, *China Transformed*, p. 89.

28 This assertion really requires lengthy supporting elaboration, which I cannot pause to develop here. In brief, I believe it makes sense to see the Maoist Party-state's claims to legitimacy based on its possession of a transcendent universal ethical Truth to have been manifested very clearly in the heavy-duty moral

instruction of the masses that accompanied the propagation of Marxist theory and Mao Thought during that era. The Party-state's claim to Benevolence in those days took such forms as "iron rice bowl" guarantees of livelihood, cradle-to-grave subsistence needs met within the capsulized life of the *danwei*, and repeated fervent expressions and demonstrations of state solidarity with the proletariat and the "poor peasantry." The state's claims to be promoting national Glory then took many interesting forms as well, from the cleansing and militarization of Chinese culture itself, to the obsessions with industrialization, anti-imperialism, and China's pretensions to international leadership within the context of the Third World.

29 On the ethical value accorded by the state to science and to modernity, see Ann Anagnost, *National Past-times: Narrative, Representation, and Power in Modern China* (Durham, NC: Duke University Press, 1997).

30 A discussion and analysis of some of the many contemporary forms of state-led charity can be found in Vivienne Shue, "State power and the philanthropic impulse in China today," in Ilchman *et al.*, *Philanthropy in the World's Traditions*, pp. 332–354. State-led charitable programs and projects such as Project Hope and many others have been ceaselessly, didactically publicized in the Chinese media under Deng and Jiang.

31 On organ donation, see Vivienne Shue, "Donation and the nation: altruism and patriotism in 20th-century China," in Sechin Chien and John Fitzgerald (eds) *The Dignity of Nations: Equality, Competition, and Honor in East Asian Nationalism*, forthcoming.

32 On the official cultural nationalism of the Chinese state, see Gérémie Barmé, *In the Red: On Contemporary Chinese Culture* (New York: Columbia University Press, 1999), Ch. 10; see also Søren Clausen, "Party policy and 'national culture': towards a state-directed cultural nationalism in China," in Brødsgaard and Strand, *Reconstructing Twentieth-century China*, pp. 253–279, and Shue, "Global imaginings." Note in particular the interesting linkage made by Barmé between national-culturalist assertiveness and self-loathing in China. For a different perspective on Chinese national assertiveness and the sense of insecurity, see Fei-Ling Wang, "Self-image and strategic intentions: national confidence and political insecurity," in Yong Deng and Fei-Ling Wang (eds) *In the Eyes of the Dragon: China Views the World* (New York: Rowman and Littlefield, 1999), as well as some of the companion essays collected in that volume.

33 For one major study of corruption and communism in China, see Xiaobo Lü, *Cadres and Corruption: The Organizational Involution of the Chinese Communist Party* (Stanford: Stanford University Press, 2000). The pervasiveness of the oppositionist popular discourse on corruption in China today has been widely noted in journalistic and scholarly accounts. In fact, anyone who lives in China, even for a short time, inevitably hears the angry and sometimes threatening complaints made openly by common people against corruption in government.

34 James Watson, "Standardizing the gods: the promotion of T'ien Hou ('Empress of Heaven') along the South China Coast, 960–1960," in David Johnson, Andrew Nathan, and Evelyn Rawski (eds) *Popular Culture in Late Imperial China* (Berkeley: University of California Press, 1985), pp. 292–324.

35 On these issues, see also the excellent introduction in Meir Shahar and Robert Weller (eds), *Unruly Gods: Divinity and Society in China* (Honolulu: University of Hawaii Press, 1996), Ch. 1.

36 Prasenjit Duara, *Culture, Power, and the State: Rural North China 1900–1942* (Stanford: Stanford University Press, 1988).

37 Prasenjit Duara, *Rescuing History from the Nation* (Chicago: University of Chicago Press, 1995), pp. 226–227.

38 For sensitive analyses of the pedagogic project of the contemporary Chinese state, see Ann Anagnost, "Politics and magic in contemporary China," *Modern China* 13(1) (1987): 41–61, and Anagnost, *National Past-times*.

39 For an analysis of the state's discourse on raising the "quality" of the people, see Anagnost, *National Past-times*, Ch. 5.

40 Kenneth Dean, "Ritual and space: civil society or popular religion?" in Timothy Brook and B. Michael Frolic (eds) *Civil Society in China* (Armonk, NY: M.E. Sharpe, 1998), p. 172.

41 This category of syncretic sect has been most thoroughly explored in *ibid.*, and also in Kenneth Dean, *Lord of the Three in One: The Spread of a Cult in Southeast China* (Princeton: Princeton University Press, 1998).

42 *Ibid.*, p. 289.

43 *Ibid.*, p. 295.

44 For one account of a local government's attempt to turn a shrine into a profit-earning tourist attraction in south China, see Jonathan Unger and Anita Chan, "Inheritors of the boom: private enterprise and the role of local government in a rural south China township," *China Journal* 42 (1999): 45–74.

45 See Anagnost, *National Past-times*, Ch 7. On ethnic tourism and the commodification of minority culture in China, see Louisa Schein, *Minority Rules: The Miao and the Feminine in China's Cultural Politics* (Durham, NC: Duke University Press, 2000), pp. 155–159 and 125–127.

46 For more on the transnational aspect of *qigong* practice and of Falun Gong in particular, see Nancy Chen, *Breathing Spaces: Qigong, Psychiatry, and Healing in China* (New York: Columbia University Press, 2003), esp. Ch. 7.

47 For more on the content of Li's teachings, see Shue, "Global imaginings."

48 Li Hongzhi and other Falun Gong spokespersons have steadfastly maintained that their beliefs and practices are entirely apolitical. Most ordinary Falun Gong practitioners doubtless also share this view of their activities, even, one suspects, many of those who have made the decision to confront state prohibitions directly by continuing their demonstrations.

49 Thompson, *Whigs and Hunters*, p. 258.

50 Or, as Perry, *Challenging the Mandate of Heaven*, p. xx, explains: "Fear of the loss of the Mandate of Heaven was generally seen as the driving force behind the campaign [to suppress Falun Gong]." See here also (pp. xv–xvi) Perry's analysis of the factors of "timing, scale, and composition" of the movement as contributors to the Chinese government's determination to launch a "drastic initiative" to wipe it out – "an initiative so out of step with its [more permissive and conciliatory] attitude toward labor disputes, tax riots or even student … demonstrations."

51 By some of these accounts, however, "not even nationalism could replace the yearning for spiritual fulfillment." So popular religious beliefs and practices such as those of Falun Gong are seen as helping to fill the "vacuum" left by the destruction of "the myth and cult-like image of the late Chairman Mao." John Wong and William Liu, *The Mystery of China's Falun Gong: Its Rise and Its Sociological Implications* (Singapore: East Asian Institute, Singapore University Press, 1999), pp. 47–49.

52 Karen Petrone, *Life Has Become More Joyous, Comrades: Celebrations in the Time of Stalin* (Bloomington: Indiana University Press, 2000), p. 209. And as Petrone further points out (p. 9), "Although it was published much later, Bakhtin's very influential definition of carnival was written in the Soviet Union in the late 1930s and can itself be read as resistance to the Stalinist order. Bakhtin rejected official Soviet celebrations as the 'official truth' and looked to

popular culture for opportunities to overthrow the official discourse, at least temporarily." For more on the recalcitrance of popular culture even during the high-Stalin era, see also Anne Gorsuch, *Youth in Revolutionary Russia: Enthusiasts, Bohemians, Delinquents* (Bloomington: Indiana University Press, 2000).

53 Thompson, *Whigs and Hunters*, p. 262.

54 To this point, see the moving account of the highly intricate and deeply moral understanding of state, society, legitimacy, and responsibility held by the people of a remote community in south-west China in Erik Mueggler, *The Age of Wild Ghosts: Memory, Violence, and Place in Southwest China* (Berkeley: University of California Press, 2001).

55 Weber, *Economy and Society*, p. 953.

2 The new crowd of the dispossessed

The shift of the urban proletariat from master to mendicant

Dorothy J. Solinger

Plainly put, the Chinese state has lost its legitimacy for some tens of millions among its old urban proletariat. In their current guise as informal laborers, these people constitute a largely unstudied component of the transition to capitalism in China, a blight on that rosiness of reform with its supposed rising prosperity that one often hears about.[1] Those constituting this mass consist of that sorry section of the country's manual laborers whose post was snatched from beneath them in the name of efficiency and profits in the course of the reform of the national economy, mostly in the years after 1994.

Although official reports number laid-off workers as low as just a dozen million,[2] internal reports and scholarly papers have put the tally as high as 60 million.[3] And according to a mid-1999 report, some government officials believed at that point that the real number of workers who should be counted as unemployed – including all those currently labeled "as waiting for work" but not included in the unemployed statistics – could be as high as 100 million.[4] Whatever the precise total, even China's own National Bureau of Statistics admits that nearly 31 per cent of those employed in the state sector as of end of year 1997 were cut (from 100.4 million to 76.4 million) within the following four years.[5]

This is a group of mainly unskilled workers who, summarily dismissed from the plants where they had toiled for decades, have had to discover new modes of livelihood from scratch in the midst of middle age. As I have noted elsewhere:

> Along the streets of Chinese inland cities these days, the service sector, starved nearly to death until the early 1980s, seems full of life, packed with business, its practitioners a literal crowd. You can get your shoes shined for two yuan[6] by three different peddlers on just one block, buy what is essentially the same pair of nylons for the same 10 yuan five or six times or the same style ballpoint pen for two or three yuan in the same lane. Or you can choose any one of 10 pedicabs to deliver you as far as a couple of miles away, for as little as a piddling three to five yuan.[7]

Besides such self-employed city folk, others among these millions of state-abandoned, suddenly informal[8] urban laborers work for wages. One of my Wuhan informants was a woman who, first let go by her own firm, had later been dismissed from a private enterprise when its business deteriorated, and was currently dishwashing at a restaurant for 12 hours per day for 300 *yuan* a month, equivalent to about US$3 per day. Another, on her third post-enterprise position, was charged with simply standing at the gates of the idle plant where she had once been employed. A third woman did housework when contacted by the Women's Federation, which could be as rarely as just once a month. She would then be paid by the hour, at the measly rate of 3.2 *yuan*[9] – in slack times, perhaps just US$4 for the entire month.

A trade union study found that 48.7 per cent of the "reemployed" it counted were self-employed, while of the other 51.3 per cent who had been hired, well over half (59 per cent) were engaged in work that was only temporary.[10] As the numbers of those making up the new informal class of furloughed workers mounted steadily, they were described in a set of sobering vignettes that graced the pages of the local newspaper in the central China city of Wuhan in the early summer of 1998:

> Now in a lot of units there's irregular use of labor, obstructing the [laid-off] staff and workers' reemployment ... The textile trade's reemployment service center is entrusted with 10,000 laid-off staff and workers, of whom about 400 have become reemployed ... not one of the 100 units that hired them has taken over social security responsibilities for them or signed a formal contract. Three hired as transport workers for a store's household appliance department were paid only 200 yuan after a month, while the store's regular workers' monthly income averaged more than 1,000 yuan. According to relevant regulations, staff and workers have a three-month probation period, in which wages are rather low. But after the three months a clothing enterprise fired those it had taken on. Of all those placed out of the [reemployment] service center, 44 percent of the total were soon fired for reasons that had nothing to do with their job performance.[11]

Besides having to cope with the psychological shock of losing their jobs, those able to find work – the new informalites – are generally severely strapped financially. In a 1997 investigation in 55 cities across 17 different provinces, 1,300 returned questionnaires revealed that well over half (a full 58 per cent) of the laid-off in the study were obtaining an income under 200 *yuan* per month.[12] In 1999, when the State Statistical Bureau announced that the average national wage of an on-post, urban, state-owned unit worker was 695 *yuan*, only 12.6 per cent of the total laid-off workers (as far as was known to official statisticians) had an income over 500 *yuan*.[13] With the growing numbers of people who have lost their former jobs, it is not surprising that by early 2000, 73 per cent of China's urban population had incomes below the national average, and just 27 per cent were above it, according to a study done in eleven major cities by the Macroeconomic Research Institute of the State Planning Commission.[14]

Their better-educated, more youthful brethren, who can generally more readily retain their jobs or else find a place in the thriving modern sector, or their younger, rural-born cousins migrating into town, fresh from the countryside and prized by employers for their brawn and their grit – and for their readiness to reap the most meager of recompense that assembly line drudgery, construction site exertion, or menial service and market-stall jobs provide – have far less trouble getting work. But these discharged urban-registered people, to the contrary – individuals whose livelihoods and positions were secure and whose spot in society was valued highly for decades – are now often at a loss in getting hired. There are also other workers, demographically similar to those let go, whose firms, doing marginally better, are still sufficiently strapped financially as to be withholding wages and pensions. In the case of those who are the subject of this essay, however, for all practical purposes the tie with their former employers has been sundered irrevocably.[15] The startling thing is that these demeaned menials making up the crowd today are city-born and -registered citizens, members of the once celebrated factory proletariat, turned now into the cohort of the *xiagang*,[16] and not second-class immigrating peasants, who made up the principal set of low-class urban residents just a few years back.[17] In illustration of this crumpling of status hierarchies, the term "*mingong*" – loosely, a label specifying casual labor, which in the recent past was used just to refer to surplus rural workers from the interior – in 1998 sometimes designated the urban laid-off and unemployed as well.[18]

As a writer in the journal of the official trade union bemoaned over the troubles of these workers:

> For a long time, they've been drifting outside the enterprise in a socially marginal situation, especially those in small-scale, scattered, mobile informal departments ... They meet up with many problems and annoyances, but lack any organization's loving care, are without any opportunity to get education or to participate in society.[19]

Another lamented that "some households in special difficulty suffer discrimination in trying to become reemployed." He called attention to the facts that

> Their legal rights and interests are harmed arbitrarily by employers, and they are bearing economic, psychological and social burdens. They feel lost and in a negative mood. Pessimistic and depressed, they're hopeless, lost their confidence ... This is especially so for those who had made a big contribution to their enterprises in the past ... they feel abandoned by society.[20]

As these abuses ground on, it was just a small step from feeling deserted by society to withdrawing faith in the state. For in the twenty-odd years before the restructuring of the economy began in the late 1970s, urban Chinese workers, especially those on the payroll of state-owned firms, could count implicitly upon a kind of covenant with the state that employed them, to provide for the bulk of their basic needs.[21] With the coming of the capitalist market order, that connection workers used to draw between their jobs and their government has now led some to blame the state – which they view as having thrown them aside – for their current jobless plight.[22] Laid-off workers in the city of Wuhan, for instance, told me in the summer of 2002 that

> The furloughed [*xiagang*] workers and those in money-losing enterprises are very dissatisfied with the government. It should take responsibility for our situation, but from the center to the localities all the governments are problematic. The Communist Party, as just one party, can't find a solution. Our government's leadership is poor. What we need is a political solution: our leaders should be elected as they are in the United States. The policies of our government can't be of any help to us.[23]

Such sentiments signal for these people the termination of the legitimacy of officialdom and its governance, as these institutions fail to fulfill the paternalistic role they had always, and seemingly properly, assumed before.

Though separated not just by several centuries but by space and culture as well, the tale of this disenchantment resonates with that of English working people of the 18th century as spun by E.P. Thompson. For those folk too, the coming of capitalism similarly shot down a moral economy which had long sustained an allegiance of laborers to their leaders.[24] As Thompson delineates its predicament upon perceiving that prices would henceforth override sustenance, the "crowd" he describes was likewise confronted with a challenge to its sense of legitimacy:

> By the notion of legitimation I mean that the men and women in the crowd were informed by the belief that they were defending traditional rights or customs ... [their] grievances operated within a popular consensus as to what were legitimate and what were illegitimate practices in marketing, milling, baking, etc. This in its turn was grounded upon a consistent traditional view of social norms and obligations, of the proper economic functions of several parties within the community, which, taken together, can be said to constitute the moral economy of the poor ... this moral economy ... supposed definite, and passionately held, notions of the common weal – notions which, indeed, found some support in the paternalist tradition of the authorities.[25]

In China, these newly informalized, displaced members of the sometime city-based proletariat – with their changed stance with respect to, and their altered treatment by, the state – appear as a powerful symbol of what has shifted and what has not in the posture and behavior of the "people's" government in the PRC today, as compared with its Maoist predecessor. Thompson's image of the legitimacy-challenging "crowd" can serve as a vehicle for presenting this transformation of the workers and of their relational bond with their no longer trustworthy state.

In what follows, I first conjure up continuities and contrasting visions between today's and yesterday's crowds and their respective connections to the state. I then supply some empirical material about the constituent members of this urban crowd, and about how they are affected by current state policies. In the course of this exercise, we will observe the draining away of their loyalty to their leaders and of the legitimacy they once accorded their state. While I borrow from Thompson the concept of crowd, another writer, Elias Canetti, in his book *Crowds and Power*, offers images that help to illustrate the sullying and debilitation of the link that once lay between the Chinese laborer and the state. Canetti's portraits also can summon up a picture of the antitheses between the remnant of the proletariat we see today and its forebear from the socialist past.[26]

The crowd in people's China: continuities and contrasts

Just as the crowd, the masses, in Mao's time inspired awe – by its huge, unfathomable numbers, its eerie internal conformity, and its ostensibly unstoppable vigor – so in the present, untold millions are, once again, all engaging in similar activities, for seemingly endless stretches of time. If the awe felt by the viewer of the crowd of yore was inspired by that crowd's apparent passion, though, the spectator's wonder now is more a result of pathos. For where the earlier crowd, its members unified in collaboration, was allegedly accomplishing miracles, the crowd before us now is composed of people struggling, usually singly, just to stay alive.

According to Elias Canetti, equality is one of the four chief attributes of the generic crowd.[27] And indeed, in both cases, though in disparate ways and for very different reasons (both times having much to do with the posture of the state), the respective crowds' components are indeed equals in some fundamental respects. For those in each are, respectively, more or less homogeneously affected by the state in gross terms and thus react comparably.[28] And the plight of both crowds' members could be seen as the same in another regard: their situations are largely involuntarily constituted, coerced, if to varying degrees and in quite differing ways.

And yet the chasm between the two mammoth hordes is deep, reflecting a sea change in the state's choice of social coalition and its vastly altered ambitions. Under Mao's reign, municipal workers – the urban mass's members – were "masters," in name and in privilege, and the masses of rural peasants (though clearly handled in a far inferior manner) their purported partners. Both the workers and the peasants – when officially mobilized –

constituted the regime's only, or, surely, most legitimate, political actors. In that state, supposedly based upon the lower classes, the formal social status of the crowd's partisans was high, and to be a constituent element within it meant one stood as decidedly *included* within the ranks of the renowned. The legitimacy they accorded the state was, consequently, unquestioned.

As historical actors, when stirred into motion, these Maoist partisans were a rapidly moving and mighty force with fearsome power. For Canetti, this would be the "baiting crowd," which "forms with reference to a quickly attainable goal," toward which it heads "with unique determination." It "has speed, elation, conviction." For the Chinese masses in the days of socialism, though, these traits were increasingly merely feigned, with time. Canetti also notes that "the [baiting] crowd have [*sic*] immense superiority on their side."[29] This in the Mao-era Chinese case was because of the features noted just above. These actors were known to perpetrate such marvels as to spark a prairie fire, stage a revolution, reshape the structure of ownership of agricultural land, appropriate for the state the wealth of the bourgeoisie, forge steel in the fields while surpassing all prior grain growth targets, and surge through the streets in the persons of Red Guards, wantonly deposing and shaming all their superiors.

In stark opposition to that visage of potency, the crowdspeople of today in the cities are the *xiagang*, off-post or laid-off workers. In the year 2000 in a central Chinese city, a man out of work offered his observation, one not wholly without foundation: "Those still at work are very few, about half the workers have been laid off."[30] These folk are perceptibly slowed down today, as against their robust style in the past, and pretty impotent, in the face of the regime's switch of alliance away from the poor, along with its stacking the status hierarchy in favor of those with capital, technical know-how, and the means of easily acquiring more of both of these goods. To be a component of this present crowd, then, is to be among the *excluded*, the abandoned.

Where the old, secure, entitled, full-time proletariat was agent (if without much volition of its own), this set of part-time or overtime informalites is victim; where the former was wound up by the Party, the latter has been unwound, undone by it. These people correspond to Canetti's "flight crowd," which is "created by a threat," in this case the threat of perishing from hunger or from untreated illness. He explains that "the same danger faces them all." Such a crowd could become a panic, should mass flight turn into a "struggle of each against all who stand in its way."[31] While the old crowd was the protagonist in earth-shaking mass movements, the second is the reject in a sort of immobile mass stasis (in Canetti's terms, these are, respectively, the "rhythmic crowd," for which "everything depends on movement," and the "stagnating crowd"),[32] or, at best, the pawn in the leadership's (in league with foreign investors) grand project of global ascent.

Moreover, while the crowd of the past was a united body, an internally relatively uniform aggregation that worked in unison, that mass has been dismantled and disaggregated, atomized in its action first into families by the household responsibility system in the countryside, which cut up the commune after 1980. These family units, in turn, were further carved up into individual actors with the state's permission to migrate, which created a population of "floaters," and by the state's license to launch private businesses just a few years later. As for the urban crowd, from the late 1990s many of its constituents were tossed from their work posts, in their once collective units (*danwei*), one by one.

So as this very brief comparison highlights, the modalities of the crowd in China have both changed and not changed. But what we can say by way of summary is that, in myriad ways, the crowd provides an image, whether of a mob or a herd churned into agitation by political campaigns, or of people in multitudes chased from their workplaces as accounts run dry and plants collapse. Whatever happens, so far the components of the Chinese crowd at any given point (if viewed as a great mass of the population at that particular time and place) greatly resemble each other. At the same time, they reveal in their features, and in their forms and manner of dynamism, the program, the direction, and the aims of the state at each of two respective junctures. Accordingly, as they are switched from benefactor to butt of the state's designs, their own belief in the legitimacy of that state has shifted 180 degrees. We turn now to a closer look at the urban crowd in the age of efficiency and flexible labor.

The urban crowd today: some statistics

Numbers, however debatable, tell a chilling story that confirms furloughed workers' feelings of neglect and their consequent lack of trust in the state. Though official statistics on the "reemployment" of these folk are notoriously slippery, their very collection does suggest that the leadership is well aware of the situation. Unfortunately, the increasing grimness of the data over time indicates that the state's several efforts to help these people have by no means been adequate.

One might be suspicious when even those who compile the figures have to admit, as one did in Wuhan, that "One can't be clear about these statistics; they're relative, not absolute. The situation is dynamic and there's no way to count them" ("... *shuobuqing ... xiangduide ... meibanfa tongji*").[33] According to this official, who cited a figure of about 30 per cent reemployed in Wuhan, it is the numbers of positions known to be newly filled (*renci*), and not the number of people with new jobs, that is counted up once each month, and each year this data is added up, eliminating from the total the jobs that are known to labor administrators to have ended. These figures certainly involve counting the same person – who may have held several very short-term posts in a given year – more than once.

In addition to this vagueness about how to tally the re-employed, there are wide variations in official announcements about their proportions among the laid-off. One article in an internal publication cited a miserable rate of just 27 per cent nationwide who had found new placements as of the end of June 1999.[34] The All-China Federation of Trade Unions reported, on the basis of local labor departments' statistics, that there has been a trend of annual deterioration: in 1998, the re-employment rate was 50 per cent, in 1999, 42 per cent, and in the first eleven months of 2000, down to a mere 16 per cent.[35] According to a 2002 Xinhua release, the rate had dropped to just 9 per cent in the first half of 2002.[36] Moreover, an open official pronouncement asserted that a late 1990s study of 10,000 laid-off workers in ten cities showed that as many as 68 per cent of those with new jobs had held these jobs for just six months or less, including 40 per cent of the total who did so for under three months. A mere 17.26 per cent managed to hold on to their new post for longer than a year.[37]

Another cause for concern about the numbers is the amount of time people are spending out of work: in Hubei province, a September 1997 random sampling of 3,000 laid-off workers in 580 firms in 10 cities and counties revealed that, although 47 per cent were said to be re-employed, as many as another 26 per cent had already been without employment for three years or more, while only 29 per cent had been in that situation for less than a year.[38] Not only were so many languishing laborless, but the occupations they took up if they did find work were most unpromising. According to this same study, 18.6 per cent had turned into odd-job manual workers; 10 per cent did various sorts of hourly work (which usually refers to activities such as picking up others' children from school); 5.2 per cent had seasonal jobs; 60 per cent were individual retailers operating stalls; and a mere 6.8 per cent had obtained formal, contracted employment.

Among the stall-keepers, a worrisome 45 per cent were discovered to be working as vulnerable, mobile peddlers, selling at shifting sites without a license.[39] Other research in 1997 among 360 re-employed staff and workers in Wuhan found that over a third of them (34.54 per cent) had set up a stall, were operating a pedicab, or were driving a taxi; by the autumn of 2000, a pedicab jockey claimed in private conversation that he had a startling 26,000 competitors in his trade in the city![40] If there is any accuracy at all in such a sum, it is not surprising that in the years after 1997, the streets of the city were crammed with a crowd of men pedaling their empty carts, and that their daily take was tiny.[41] As these new informalites see no change in their incomes or their placements year after year, and as they perceive the worthlessness of the niche they have been forced to fill, they increasingly repudiate the state whose policies have put them where they are.

The state abandons its former coalition partner

Despite appearances, the deregulated economic activity adopted by the laid-off does not represent just a straightforward manifestation of the metamorphosis of the Chinese urban economy, some uncomplicated consequence of that system's steadily deepening marketization. Nor do these sellers and service people merely symbolize an instance of the widespread process of privatization[42] that is attending the advance of capitalism on a global scale.[43] It is also inappropriate to view their labor as only the latest incarnation of the secondary sector of China's long-standing "dual market," as if a market, operating according to principles of supply and demand, had merely become bifurcated along some new fault line.[44]

For what is usually billed as the "secondary economy" across the world is a sector comprising marginal and/or denigrated people, usually migrants or minorities, who have been relegated to the least desirable and most unstable work available. No matter how bitter, however, their lives have generally improved significantly in material terms as a result of having joined such markets, as compared with what their existence was like before.[45] But as distinct from the usual secondary-market worker elsewhere, these laid-off Chinese workers are downwardly, not upwardly, mobile.

Furthermore, unlike informalites in other places, the urban people on Chinese streets today are not situated in this niche voluntarily, with dreams of bettering their lot by building businesses or of amassing capital. Rather, they have found themselves in this spot because their former iron rice bowl was snatched away, and for them there is no other means of survival. Since most of these small-time sellers of odd merchandise and manual labor were until recently full-time, life-tenured, completely welfare-entitled and state-employed manufacturing workers, one needs to go beyond the surface signs of their quotidian practices – their superficial appearance as a reborn "private sector" linked to economic "reform" in the urban areas – to get a good grasp of the totality of what is going on.[46]

In understanding their condition, one is also led astray by official formulations aimed at enticing urban residents into the new tertiary or private sectors. In 1999, the National People's Congress amended the state constitution, proclaiming the private sector a "component part" of the national economy. A hopeful sign appeared to be the expanding portion of the national economy occupied by this branch: in the spring of 1999, the State Economic and Trade Commission announced that "private enterprises" were accounting for almost one-fifth of the gross value of industrial output nationally and for a full 37 per cent of the retail trade in consumer goods,[47] figures that are probably much lower than the reality. Despite these promising bits of information, however, a report on the sector admonished – in an analysis which still holds true – that most practitioners in the private sector are seriously constrained by a lack of funding channels.[48] In the especially stricken north-east, people attempting to open their own businesses have often been unable to obtain any government support for their little ventures, and have been heavily taxed.[49]

The predicament of these people is by no means a product of "the market" acting alone. Instead, it derives perhaps primarily from state policies as they have evolved over time and in the recent past.[50] Indeed, in the second half of the 1990s, the Chinese state adopted a set of new policies quite unrestrained by the nature of the social coalition that had formerly buttressed its rule: it abandoned its putative past political partner, the working class, quite callously, in a step it has disingenuously justified as being in labor's own "long-term interest."[51] Just as the sacking campaign was getting underway in force, the 1997 May Day editorial in the Party paper, the *People's Daily*, warned its readers that, "It's possible [that the] benefits of some workers may be temporarily affected. Seen from long-term benefits, the pains are worth enduring."[52]

Ironically enough, in its march toward modernization and economic reform, even as the Chinese leadership has unleashed and encouraged the forces of the market, at the same time it has arrested the full unfolding of some of the chief social processes that generally emerge from marketization elsewhere. Thus, in China, in addition to the advancing affluence, rising levels of education, and embourgeoisement of a section of the working class that took place in many societies along with economic development – and quite markedly so in China's East Asian neighbors, South Korea, Japan, and Taiwan – this informalization of the urban economy in China also represents a regression, not an ascent, for quite a numerous portion of the urban populace. Though one could label these newly jobless members of a lower class in formation, their situation is now defined and shaped as much by their status as *xiagang* workers as it is by some new class category. Indeed, this group of people, chiefly of middle age, has together and all at once fallen into a downward trajectory in their lifestyles and in their prospects.

The overwhelming majority of them were deprived of formal education from having been compelled to quit school and join in the Cultural Revolution (including, for most, a lengthy stint in the countryside) over a decade or so after 1966, and therefore lack any skills beyond those elementary ones connected with the simple factory jobs they have lost. Study after study more or less replicates the findings of sample research done in 1996 nationwide by the State Statistical Bureau. That inquiry discovered that as many as 57 per cent of those laid off had been educated only up to junior-high level; another 14 per cent had received just a primary school education or even less. As many as 70.4 per cent were between the ages of 25 and 44, while another 18.5 per cent were over 45. Women accounted for a total of 64.3 per cent of the sample, though they represented under half the work-force before the sackings started.[53]

True, with the demise of the planned economy, economic forces have played an important role in changing society. For one thing, they have surely infringed on the state institutions' old monopoly on shaping people's fates. And there has certainly been a diminution in the determining power over urbanites' lives of specific institutions such as the *danwei* (work unit).[54] But this move away from the state's planned economy, with its shunting aside of the former urban workforce, has not so far eventuated in any meaningful autonomy for many members of this contingent.[55] For their lives are constricted by the urgent need to scrape up a pittance to keep themselves and their families alive. The meager take of those who work is the result to a large extent of the lack of any true demand-driven economic activity in the emerging labor market, at least insofar as the work done by the furloughed is concerned. This is the case because, given the immense proportions of the official program of enforced dismissals, plus the unspecialized nature of the labor the affected workers have to offer, there cannot be demand sufficient to forge a decent livelihood for the tens of millions made redundant, now struggling to find buyers for their wares and their services.

So the Chinese leadership has fostered a novel style of economic growth and development, one that entails sacrificing and discarding the selfsame working class that once laid the foundation for the present rise to prosperity. In short, in the state's very rush to reform its municipal economy, most of the typical social concomitants of marketization have been suppressed or halted for many. It is these many who now question the current state's right to rule, and who lament the loss of a former day when they stood supreme – at least relative to other social groups – in state rhetoric and in its treatment.[56]

What has become of the old proletariat represents a fundamental and quite sudden reconstruction of the liaison between the state and its former premier workforce. For more than forty years, the Chinese state and its elite laborers, the workers at the urban state-owned enterprises, enjoyed a relationship that was multifaceted, to be sure. But at its core, this tie embodied a strong dose of paternalistic protection, of succor, albeit one laced with surveillance. As is well known, workers labored under a reign of "organized dependency,"[57] in which plant leaders could generally consider themselves to be caretakers – for the employees – but for the state as well, under whose commission managers controlled their charges. In prosaic terms, factory officials were there to administer the daily business of production and workers' welfare. But in a larger sense, they were joined with the Chinese state in enacting a role of benefactor as well as guardian, if a very intrusive one.

All that has changed in the space of just a few short years. Increasingly, as the last century came to a close, the nature of this once often benign connection turned sour. With the sudden surge in the shedding of state workers after the Party's 3rd Plenum of its 14th Party Congress in November 1993, when its heightened commitment to marketization was publicly enunciated – a move that had already seen a start in the late 1980s – the key component of the linkage between state and this laboring segment of society has become fear, a searing dread on both sides. At the same time, many of the one-time intermediaries standing between these two players, the plant officials – especially those in failing firms – have shucked off their pose of custodian and taken on that of embezzler, thereby no longer serving either the central state (except insofar as they obey orders from above to push the workers from their plants) or their original worker-wards.

Thus, the more or less clear line of command and superintendence of old – along which plant management acted toward labor as the agent of the center, which was its principal, directing production and disbursing benefits – has been deflected, such that the three parties (state, enterprise administrators, workers), once supposed allies, have become mutually antagonistic. Now, in the relation between state and this recast lower portion of society, the state's moves are motivated primarily by its fear (though probably also, at least for some among its staffers, by guilt) as it abandons its prior roles, along with its prior protégés. At the same time, the workers, in turn, experience despair mixed with their fear, and, in a growing proportion of cases, embitterment and daring. Their old bestowal of legitimacy upon the state has dissolved along with their prior posts. This is the mid-term inter-echelon and interpersonal dynamic that is developing with the informalization of the urban economy, as the process transforms a crowd of once so-styled "masters" into one of paupers.

The upshot is that the state and its rulers have fallen captive to an increasingly pronounced paradox in the trio of their oft-stated aims – reform, development, and stability: while the leaders strive to develop the economy through market reforms, they must balance a treacherous trade-off between their objectives of development, that is of growth and marketization, which has meant massive discharges and the creation of a new crowd of the dispossessed on the one hand, and a resultant and mounting social instability among these recently disenfranchised on the other. In the process, contestation surely occurs, but this is only one option. More often, intimidation is evident among both parties – the state in its alternately offering (or at least promising) favors and funds to compensate the jobless, or battling and jailing protesters, and the many timorous workers retreating into a crushed quiescence or exhausting themselves with full-time income-seeking.

Conclusion

This material demonstrates that in China today – where rampant economic reforming and enterprise dismantling is decimating a great proportion of the old state sector and the crowd it sustained for decades – unemployment means much more than being out of work on an individual level. Rather, it is serving as the symbol of a collective and sudden informalization of the urban economy, a reforging of a crowd once ennobled and proud into a new crowd, one most commonly cowering and déclassé. Thus, formal Chinese workers, dignified and advantaged for decades, became idle or informal ones in the late 1990s. In the place of the miraculous world of the crowd of yore, we see instead a grim and lackluster one of the undistinguished masses, those let go by their firms. In the altered social status hierarchy in the making in Chinese cities, to be a laborer is lowly, not lordly, as it had been not so long ago. There is, too, quite a transformed tie between the state and its one-time working class, a bond lately characterized much more by mutual fear and shame than by the original socialists' shared and cooperative mission of constructing, with and through their honored crowd, a more fair and egalitarian China.

Notes

1 On the attitudes and protests of the workforce and former workforce, see Ching Kwan Lee, "From organized dependence to disorganized despotism: changing labour regimes in Chinese factories," *China Quarterly* (hereafter *CQ*) 155 (1999): 44–71; Antoine Kernen and Jean-Louis Rocca, "The reform of state-owned enterprises and its social consequences in Shenyang and Liaoning," unpublished ms., 1999; Jean-Louis Rocca, "Old working class, new working class: reforms, labour crisis and the two faces of conflicts in Chinese urban areas," paper presented at the 2nd Annual Conference of the European Union–China Academic Network, 21–22 January 1999, Centro de Estudios de Asia Oriental, Universidad Autonoma de Madrid, Spain; Marc Blecher, "Strategies of Chinese state legitimation among the working class," paper presented to the Workshop on Strategies of State Legitimation in Contemporary China, Center for Chinese Studies, University of California at Berkeley, 7–9 May 1999; and Ching Kwan Lee, "The 'revenge of history': Collective memories and labor protests in north-eastern China," *Ethnography* 1(2) (2000): 217–237.
2 Ministry of Labour and Social Security, National Bureau of Statistics, "The year 2000's statistical report of the developments in labour and social security," *Laodong baozhang tongxun* (*Labor and Social Security Bulletin*) 6 (2001): 36 notes 6.57 million laid-off as of the end of 2000, but Wang Dongjin, deputy minister of labour and social security, referred in February 2001 to "some 20 million laid-off workers" (Reuters, "China to lay off 6.5 million urban workers a month," *Inside China Today*, 16 February 2001).
3 Wang Depei, "'Three people' and 'The second reform,'" *Gaige neican* (*Reform Internal Reference*) (hereafter *GGNC*) 7 (2001): 25. Economist Hu Angang stated that China had laid off 55 million people from 1995 to mid-2002 (China News Digest, 9 July 2002). In late 2001, Tang Jun held that the urban unemployment rate was then between 12 and 15 per cent. See "Social discrimination in the minimum living guarantee system," paper presented at the Conference on Social Exclusion and Marginality in Chinese Societies, sponsored by the Centre for Social Policy Studies of the Department of Applied Social Sciences, the Hong Kong Polytechnic University, and the Social Policy Research Centre, Institute of Sociology, the Chinese Academy of Social Sciences, Hong Kong, 16–17 November 2001, p. 1. See also my article "Why we cannot count the 'unemployed,'" *CQ* 167 (September 2001): 671–88.
4 William H. Overholt, "China in the balance," Nomura Strategy Paper, Hong Kong, 12 May 1999.
5 Dali L. Yang, "China in 2002: leadership transition and the political economy of governance," *Asian Survey* (hereafter *AS*) 43(1) (2003): 34. Hiroshi Imai says that in the 1980s, 99.2 per cent of urban workers were employed in the publicly owned sector, 76.2 per cent of them in state-owned firms and 23 per cent in collectives. Employment in this sector continued increasing through the 1980s and into the first half of the 1990s, when a drop commenced. By 2000, the percentage of total urban workers employed in state firms and collective enterprises had fallen to 38.1 per cent and 7.2 per cent respectively, for a combined total in "public" concerns of 45.3 per cent of the urban workforce. See Special Report, "China's growing unemployment problem," *Pacific Business and Industries RIM* (Tokyo) II(6) (2002): 25.
6 A Chinese *yuan* is equal to about twelve US cents.

7 This paragraph and the several ones succeeding it are taken from my article "Labour market reform and the plight of the laid-off proletariat," *CQ* 170 (June 2002): 304–326. See pp. 308–309.

8 The term "informal" refers to a process whereby employment conditions become more "flexible," entailing elimination of entitlements and benefits, reduction of safety and other humane provisions at the workplace, and denial of job security, where all of these guarantees once existed. These cutbacks in welfare go along with a surge in short-term, temporary jobs having these features, and a marked upswing in very petty projects of brief self-employment.

9 Wuhan street interviews, September 1999.

10 Xue Zhaoyun, "Research, reflections, and suggestions about the reemployment situation of laid-off staff and workers," *Gonghui gongzuo tongxun* (*Bulletin of Trade Union Work*) 7 (2000): 8.

11 *Changjiang ribao* (*Yangzi Daily*), 2 June 1998.

12 Investigation of urban enterprises' laid-off staff and workers' re-employment situation project topic group, "A difficult pass and the way out," from *Shehuixue yanjiu* (*Sociology Research*) 6 (1997) (reprinted in *Xinhua wengao, shehui* 3 (1998): 21).

13 N.a., "Report on 1998–1999 labor insurance statistics," *Laodong baozhang tongxun* (*Labor Insurance Bulletin*) 3 (2000): 36.

14 State Planning Commission, Macroeconomic Research Group, "Establishing a social protection system is the key to our country's social stability," *Neibu canyue* (*Internal Consultations*) (hereafter *NBCY*), 5 May 2000, p. 9.

15 Excellent studies of the entire working class of today include Ching Kwan Lee, "Pathways of labor insurgency," in Elizabeth J. Perry and Mark Selden (eds) *Chinese Society: Change, Conflict and Resistance* (Routledge, 2000), Ch. 2, and "Three patterns of working-class transitions in China," in Francoise Mengin and Jean-Louis Rocca (eds) *Chinese Politics: Moving Frontiers* (New York: Palgrave, 2002), pp. 62–91; Jean-Louis Rocca, "Three at once: the multidimensional scope of labor crisis in China," in Mengin and Rocca, *Chinese Politics*, pp. 3–30; and Feng Chen, "Industrial restructuring and workers' resistance in China," *Modern China* (hereafter *MC*) 29(2) (April 2003): 237–262.

16 Officially, a *xiagang* worker is one who meets all of these conditions: (1) s/he began working before the contract system was instituted in 1986 and had a formal, permanent job in the state sector (plus those contract laborers whose contract term is not yet concluded); (2) because of his/her firm's problems in business and operations, has been let go, but has not yet cut off relations with the original firm; and (3) has not yet found other work in society (see Guo Jun, "What's the difference between laid-off and diverted workers in the state firms?" *Zhongguo gongyun* (*Chinese Workers' Movement*) (hereafter *ZGGY*) 3 (1999): 32.

17 Lora Sabin states that in 1987 Beijing, three-quarters of the employees in the private sector were from the countryside, and by the early 1990s, half the labor force (including owners and employees) held rural household registrations. See "New bosses in the workers' state: the growth of non-state sector employment in China," *CQ* 140 (1994): 944–970. See also Shi Xianmin, "Beijing's privately-owned small businesses: a decade's development," *Social Sciences in China* 14(1) (Spring 1993): 161–162.

18 *Ming Pao* (*Bright Daily*) (Hong Kong), 12 February 1998.

19 Xue Zhaoyun, "Research, reflections," p. 10.

20 Zhang Yuanchao, "We ought to raise our awareness of the livelihood situation of state-owned firms' especially difficult staff and workers," *Zhongguo gongren* (*Chinese Worker*) 7 (2000): 5.

21 The *opus classicus* expounding this idea is Andrew G. Walder, *Communist Neo-traditionalism: Work and Authority in Chinese Industry* (Berkeley: University of California Press, 1986).

22 Typically, in the late 1990s, dissatisfied workers accused their own factory leaders of corruption and mismanagement, and believed it was such behavior that had led to their firm's bankruptcy or collapse. See Feng Chen, "Subsistence crises, managerial corruption and labour protests in China," *China Journal* 44 (July 2000): 41–63.

23 Interview, Wuhan, 19 August 2002.

24 See E.P. Thompson, "The moral economy of the English crowd in the eighteenth century," *Past and Present* 50 (February 1971): 76–136. I got the idea of drawing on this piece from a footnote in Yong-shun Cai, "The silence and resistance of the dislocated: state and laid-off workers in reform China," unpublished ms., Singapore, 2002, p. 4.

25 Thompson, "The moral economy," pp. 78–79.

26 Certainly, there were great discrepancies between the treatment accorded workers in firms of different sizes and degrees of importance under the socialist regime that existed in China between 1949 and 1978. On this, see Andrew G. Walder, "The remaking of the Chinese working class, 1949–1981," *MC* 10(1) (1984): 3–48. But in that time, the working class was acclaimed as the master of the state, and indeed as a unit it was treated better than were the members of any other social group, barring officials, top leaders, and the military.

27 Elias Canetti, *Crowds and Power*, trans. Carol Stewart (New York: Viking, 1963), p. 29. The other three are the desire to grow, its love of density, and its need for direction. Not all of these fit the Chinese crowd so well.

28 On the many disparities within the working class from the 1950s to the 1970s, see Elizabeth J. Perry and Li Xun, *Proletarian Power* (Boulder, CO: Westview Press, 1997).

29 Elias Canetti, *Crowds and Power*, p. 49.

30 Interview at a night market, 12 September 2000.

31 Elias Canetti, *Crowds and Power*, p. 53.

32 *Ibid.*, p. 30.

33 Admission by an official at the Wuhan General Trade Union's Professional Introduction Service Center, 13 September 2000.

34 Yang Yiyong, "An analysis of the employment situation in our country in the year 2000," *NBCY*, 28 January 2000, p. 11.

35 All-China General Trade Union Security Work Department, "Investigation on handling laid-off staff and workers' labour relations and social security continuation issue," *ZGGY* 5 (2001): 14.

36 Terence Tan, "China's jobless can't get new work," *Straits' Times*, 27 September 2002. The date of the Xinhua release was not given.

37 N.a., "1998–1999," p. 35.

38 Hubei Province General Trade Union Livelihood Guarantee Department, "Utilize policy and legal methods, fully promote the reemployment project to develop in depth – an investigation of Hubei's laid-off staff and workers," *Lilun yuekan* (*Theory Monthly*) (Wuhan) 2 (1998): 18.

39 *Ibid.*, pp. 8–9.

40 Interview, Wuhan, 16 September 2000. But on 31 October 2001, informants from the Wuhan branch of the All-China Federation of Trade Unions confirmed that the official figure had gone up to 40,000 as of that date.

41 In the spring of 2003, the city government attempted to clear the streets of these carts by buying the carts from their owners for some 8,000 *yuan* and offering these drivers low-paying, low-status jobs. Communications from Huang Xiangchun, editor of a local Party journal in Wuhan, 11 June and 6 July 2003.

42 At the same time as employment in state units dropped 19.6 per cent between 1995 and 1998, jobs in privately and individually owned urban enterprises increased by 44.8 per cent, according to economist Hu Angang. Cited in the

journal *Jingmao daokan* (*Economic and Trade Guide*), 30 December 1999, in Summary of World Broadcasts (hereafter SWB) FE/3750, G/10, 29 January 2000. Xinhua (hereafter XH) announced in late 1997 that between 1991 and 1995, self-employed and private business provided 40 per cent of the newly created jobs in cities (SWB FE/3098, G/5, 10 December 1997, from XH, 9 December). A 1999 10-city study of 553 re-employed staff and workers laid off from state firms found that 77 per cent of them had switched from state to non-state firms, half of whom went into the private sector (Xue Zhaoyun, "Research, reflections").

43 P. Connolly, "The politics of the informal sector: a critique," in N. Redclift and E. Mingione (eds) *Beyond Employment: Household, Gender and Subsistence* (Oxford: Blackwell, 1985), and Alejandro Portes and John Walton, *Labour Class and the International System* (New York: Academic Press, 1981). Both these works are cited in Michael Pinches, "'All that we have is our muscle and sweat': the rise of wage labour in a Manila squatter community," in M. Pinches and S. Lakha (eds) *Wage Labour and Social Change: The Proletariat in Asia and the Pacific* (Clayton: Centre of Southeast Asian Studies, Monash University, 1987), p. 104.

44 Louis Putterman, "Dualism and reform in China," *Economic Development and Cultural Change* 40 (1992): 467–493, and Flemming Christiansen, "The legacy of the mock dual economy: Chinese labour in transition, 1978–1992," *Economy and Society* 22(4) (1993): 411–436.

45 Michael J. Piore, *Birds of Passage: Migrant Labor and Industrial Societies* (Cambridge: Cambridge University Press, 1979). David Stark, "Bending the bars of the iron cage: bureaucratization and informalization in capitalism and socialism," *Sociological Forum* 4(4) (1989): 637–664 says that the "second economy" is "a broad range of income-gathering activity outside the boundaries of the redistributively coordinated and managed economy."

46 A reborn private sector indeed appeared after the early 1980s. But the current informalites have emerged from a very different social process from the ones that produced the earlier segments of this sector. Those who earlier joined the post-1980 private sector are people who were or hoped to become capitalists, if often just petty ones. They were young people waiting for their first state jobs, migrants from the countryside, ex-convicts, demobilized soldiers, rural cadres, and, especially recently, officials and state enterprise managers. See Susan Young, *Private Business and Economic Reform in China* (Armonk, NY: M.E. Sharpe, 1995); Ole Bruun, *Business and Bureaucracy in a Chinese City: An Ethnography of Private Business Households in Contemporary China*, Research Monograph 43 (Berkeley: Institute for East Asian Studies, University of California, 1993); Ole Odgaard, "Entrepreneurs and elite formation in rural China," *Australian Journal of Chinese Affairs* 28 (1992): 89–108; and David L. Wank, *Commodifying Communism: Business, Trust and Politics in a Chinese City* (New York: Cambridge University Press, 1999).

47 SWB FE/3520, G/11, 27 April 1999, from XH, 26 April 1999.

48 *Ibid.*

49 In *South China Morning Post* (Hong Kong), 7 June 1999.

50 Here I am alluding not just to the years of the planned economy, when state policy and regulations and the incentives these official acts promoted led local managers and leaders to overstaff in the firms and set up unnecessary construction projects. I also mean policies that resulted in massive losses and bankruptcies in recent years, including those that nurtured firms facing competition from newer, non-state firms that operated without welfare responsibilities and which had new equipment. And I refer here also to official credit tightening, as well as to explicit regime calls for downsizing in the enterprises.

51 *Jingji ribao* (*Economic Daily*), 27 April 1998; Deng Baoshan, "Government, enterprise, and laid-off staff and workers' role in reemployment work," *Zhongguo laodong* (*Chinese Labor*) (hereafter *ZGLD*) 3 (1999): 11; see also Zhu Rongji's speech in Tianjin, from *Jingji guanli wenzhai* (*Economic Management Digest*), in *Gongyun cankao ziliao* (*Workers' Movement Reference Materials*) 3 (1998): 5.

52 *Renmin ribao* (*People's Daily*), 1 May 1997, in SWB FE/2908, G/6, 2 May 1997.

53 For one example, see Ma Rong, "Thoughts about state enterprises' staff and workers' layoffs and the question of reemployment," *ZGLD* 2 (1998): 12.

54 Lowell Dittmer and Lü Xiaobo, "Personal politics in the Chinese *danwei* under reform," *AS* 36(3) (1996): 247–249, and Barry Naughton, "*Danwei*: the economic foundations of a unique institution," in Xiaobo Lü and Elizabeth J. Perry (eds) *Danwei: The Changing Chinese Workplace in Historical and Comparative Perspective* (Armonk, NY: M.E. Sharpe, 1997), pp. 169–182.

55 Ming-kwan Lee, "The decline of status in China's transition from socialism," *Hong Kong Journal of Sociology* 1 (2000): 72.

56 On nostalgia for the past, see Ching Kwan Lee, "The labor politics of market socialism: collective inaction and class experiences among state workers in Guangzhou," *MC* 24(1) (January 1998): 3–33.

57 Walder, *Communist Neo-traditionalism*.

3 The Iron Man weeps

Joblessness and political legitimacy in the Chinese rust belt[1]

Timothy B. Weston

In March 2002, tens of thousands of middle-aged former oil industry employees in the city of Daqing, 350 miles north-east of Beijing in Heilongjiang Province, began a massive protest movement that was, in the words of Han Dongfang, a labor rights activist based in Hong Kong, "probably the largest over labor issues since 1949."[2] The protestors were angry about losing their jobs, but only exploded into protest when their factories failed to deliver on promised severance packages. Pointedly, one of the leaflets that the protestors distributed was entitled "Retrenched workers cherish the memory of Mao Zedong"; this leaflet contained the clear political message that many workers want the Communist Party to live up to its earlier promises. By wielding language, slogans, and iconography from what were to them the far brighter days of the 1950s, 1960s, and 1970s, these victims of China's market-oriented reforms challenged the Communist Party on emotionally resonant historical grounds. The Communist Party's grip on power does not appear to be immediately threatened, but protests by retrenched workers have called into question the very basis of its legitimacy.

Despite a crackdown by the local authorities, the demonstrations in China's north-eastern rust belt did not die down quickly. The Daqing protest organizers planned a mass gathering for 4 April 2002 in memory of the Maoist-era model worker "Iron Man" Wang Jinxi. The gathering was to take place in Iron Man Square, which fronts the Daqing petroleum administration headquarters. Wang Jinxi, who died in 1970, became known as the Iron Man in 1960 after he and tens of thousands of workers responded to Chairman Mao's call to free China from its dependence on Soviet oil by moving to the bitterly cold marshlands of Heilongjiang Province to dig for oil. Within a few short years, Daqing was home to China's most important oil-producing facility, and in 1964, the slogan "In industry, learn from Daqing" was sounded across the country. Wang Jinxi was said to epitomize the patriotic spirit and willingness to sacrifice for the collective good that characterized the militant asceticism of the Maoist era. In 1967, he was made a national labor model, and his chiseled visage and powerful figure soon adorned the ubiquitous political posters of the age. The Iron Man has had staying power. As late as the 1980s, young people were encouraged to follow his patriotic example by voluntarily transferring to remote regions to work for China's development.[3]

The date of 4 April 2002 was selected for the mass gathering in Daqing because it was the day of the Qing Ming Festival, the annual occasion when Chinese mourn the dead. The gathering's organizers hoped that 10,000 people would turn out for the occasion, each of them festooned with a white flower in honor of the Iron Man. But honoring Wang Jinxi was to be just one aspect of the day's events, for the gathering was meant to double as a highly pointed political protest, much like the April 1976 movement in Tiananmen Square following the death of Zhou Enlai. Those gathered at the square in Daqing sought to echo the militant determination expressed in a flier handed out a week earlier at Iron Man Square. That flier called on laid-off workers to "follow the Iron Man's example," and argued that "it is better to die twenty years early and struggle with all one's might to the end" than to put up with the injustice being done to them.[4] The demonstrators also planned to resign en masse from the Communist Party in the middle of Iron Man Square and to sign a protest letter against the Daqing Petroleum Administration Bureau, which they accused of unfairly forcing them to sign redundancy agreements that left them without work. The "Three-in-One Day of Action" was thus designed to bring together several related themes to give voice to a powerful cry for justice on the part of people who viewed themselves as victims of the communist government's decision to restructure inefficient state-owned enterprises (SOEs) at the expense of their jobs.[5]

Although clearly expressing disenchantment with the Communist Party, the demonstrators in Daqing nevertheless formulated their protest message out of a vocabulary and symbolic repertoire grounded in the history of Chinese communism. By selecting the venue that they did and choosing to honor the memory of a nationally famous model worker, the protestors sought to turn the Communist Party's own history against it. The protestors' plan to resign from the Communist Party en masse thus should not be viewed as a repudiation of communism, but rather as a rejection of the Party of today in favor of the Party of old. Whereas their employment in SOEs and their membership in the Communist Party at one time was a source of pride and guaranteed them exalted social status, neither now brought them any benefit. For these people, the Party is no longer the paternalistic protector of bygone days.

The Daqing municipal government's efforts to block the protest only deepened the workers' bitterness. The Daqing Public Security Bureau (PSB) issued a "Notice on the Strict Prohibition of Unapproved Burning of Memorial Objects during the Qing Ming Festival" to warn would-be protestors that "trouble-making" would not be tolerated. The PSB's scare tactics worked: on 4 April, only a few hundred showed up at Iron Man Square. In the words of the *China Labour Bulletin*: "As the statue of China's 'Iron Man' model worker, Wang Jinxi, stands in apparent peace and quiet in the Iron Man Square of Daqing, over 80,000 oilfield workers are on the brink of destitution – silenced, and barred from organizing or collective bargaining."[6]

The protesters were foiled on 4 April 2002, yet that turned out to be but one skirmish in a protracted contest between unemployed state workers and various levels of the Chinese government. March and April 2002 also saw massive protests in Liaoyang, capital of Liaoning Province, where thousands of laid-off workers marched through the streets carrying posters of Chairman Mao. The Liaoyang protests in fact turned out to be more protracted than those in Daqing and far more troublesome to the Communist Party. Seeking to gain the attention of delegates then attending the 16th Party Congress in Beijing, in the fall of 2002 thousands of unemployed workers again took to the streets of Liaoyang to state their case, and sporadic smaller-scale protests also occurred during the first half of 2003.[7]

The largest protests by laid-off state workers have taken place in the north-east, home to the greatest concentration of heavy industry in China ever since the Japanese occupation of the 1930s, but a significant number of demonstrations have taken place in other parts of the country as well. In recent years, there have been large-scale protest actions by retrenched SOE workers in Anhui, Gansu, Hebei, Henan, Hubei, Inner Mongolia, Shanxi, Sichuan, and Xinjiang provinces. In a country that has seen some 55 million people laid off since 1995 and in which the total number of unemployed could be as high as 100 million, few places have remained unaffected.[8] Most alarming for China's political leaders is that these demonstrations have been extremely well organized, have spawned independent trade union activities, and have taken place in dialogue with one another in spite of the government's attempt to divide the working class and to impose news blackouts to prevent precisely that kind of linkage from happening. Such developments potentially mean that instead of having to quell disturbances at isolated trouble spots around the country, the powers that be could be faced with a hydra-headed monster able to put forth a strong claim as the legitimate voice of China's working class.

Are we witnessing the emergence of a Polish-style workers' movement that spells the beginning of the end for China's Communist Party? Not in the near term, at least. Experts on China's labor crisis expect the authorities to succeed in preventing such a movement through their multi-pronged strategy of arresting protest leaders, punishing families for the "crimes" of their members, keeping a lid on the free flow of information, displaying and sometimes demonstrating the state's capacity to use force, meeting limited protester demands, constructing a more effective social security system, and assuring the continued growth of the Chinese economy in the hope that laid-off workers will be able to find new employment. Generational and life experience gaps between those formerly or still employed in state-owned factories and migrant workers toiling in private or township and village enterprises also militate against the emergence of a widespread Solidarity-style movement.

Finally, because most of those who are participating in the protests are either laid-off (*xiagang*) or formally unemployed workers, they have little ability to disrupt their factories' production schedules.[9] The protesters in question have lost the ability to strike, in other words, because they have already been shut out of their places of employment. Furthermore, consistent with Andrew Walder's argument that communist China's "neo-traditional" workplace system has succeeded in binding workers to management, few employed workers appear to have gotten involved in their laid-off brothers' and sisters' struggles for justice.[10]

The historical moment

If it is true that the Communist Party has thus far successfully held the "Polish disease" at bay, is it nevertheless the case that the Party is being harmed by the labor protests sweeping the land? Understanding state power to rest both on the ability to wield coercive power *and* on the ability to engender voluntary consent from the governed, the answer to this question is most definitely "Yes." The Party may not be in immediate danger of losing control over society, but in the eyes of many of its once most ardent supporters now belonging to what Dorothy J. Solinger aptly calls the "new crowd of the dispossessed," it has already lost its *raison d'être*. Moreover, the problem is only going to grow worse now that China has acceded to the terms of the World Trade Organization.[11] International competition and the effort to attract foreign investors will force even more of China's inefficient SOEs to streamline or close down, meaning that employees will continue to be shed at a rapid pace.[12] Given that the constituency in question is the core of China's working class, and that the Communist Party has traditionally represented itself as the champion of that class, these developments are highly damaging.

The distinctive threat to the Communist Party posed by angry and impoverished unemployed state workers can best be understood in reference to China's revolutionary history. In practice, workers in SOEs did not always make steady gains under communist rule; during the Cultural Revolution, wages were frozen such that, from 1957 to 1977, their average real value declined by almost 20 per cent, and the shortage of housing meant that employees had to accept cramped and low-quality living space.[13] At various times during that period, workers engaged in militant confrontations with the Party authorities over these and other issues. Nevertheless, since 1949, that same Party has represented itself as the "self-appointed vanguard of a 'worker's state,'" and has valorized workers as the "masters of society."[14] That designation has always been central to the Communist Party's claim that it liberated China from the pre-1949 "feudal" order. Furthermore, during the Mao era, the Party's consistent hostility toward the kinds of people who *were* the masters of society before 1949 – intellectuals, landlords, and managers, for example – as well as the disadvantaged position of the country's vast rural populace, served as a constant reminder to workers of the relative gains that they had made under communist rule. Workers' expanded importance in communist China can be measured in numerical terms. Whereas the working class had some 9 million members at the time of the Communist Revolution, by the early 1980s the number of workers in SOEs alone was close to 30 million; today, China's working class is the largest in the world.[15] Under Chinese communism, labor's exalted status was reflected not so much in high wages, but by the supposedly indestructible "iron rice bowl," the cradle-to-grave benefits provided to SOE employees. This package of benefits – which undoubtedly fostered worker dependency on the state – included permanent employment, essentially free housing and medical care, food and fuel subsidies, travel allowances, pensions, childcare, and education. The iron rice bowl was considered so desirable that its recipients have been called China's "labor aristocracy."[16]

The Communist Party's favorable treatment of workers was in accordance with Marxist theory, which holds that, under capitalism, the proletariat is the most aggrieved class, and that its effort to throw off its chains will lead to a more progressive and just, and therefore higher-order, society. During the Maoist era, that ideological supposition came together with the Party's all-out "war" on behalf of rapid industrialization to create the idea that the working class was akin to a great patriotic army. If China was to survive, let alone advance into the ranks of the world's great powers, it had to rely on the will and fortitude of ordinary workers. The Communist Party could point the way forward, but in the end it needed foot soldiers to do the dirty work, to actually hack at the frozen earth in the marshlands of Heilongjiang and elsewhere. Rugged, honorable, and obedient, Iron Man Wang represented what the Party wanted from those foot soldiers. The Party's constant use of martial language and imagery played on the idea of workers as patriotic soldiers. Few countries willingly send their troops into battle unprepared: if the Communist Party was going to make such heavy demands on Chinese workers, it had to arm them by providing an iron rice bowl. Similarly, it incurred an obligation to take care of its veterans in their old age, after their lifetime of service to the national cause.

The protest discourse

Retrenched workers have made use of this historical legacy and of China's experience under communism more generally in their recent protests. Not only have they proven to be astute students of the radical politics of the Cultural Revolution period (through their demonstrated ability to organize, to make speeches, and to paste up political posters), they have also seized on the idea that they are soldiers who gave their lives to make China modern and strong, and that now, as veterans, the state owes them a livelihood. A banner held aloft at one of the Daqing protests of March 2002 stated: "The *army of industrial workers* wants to live!" Labor rights activist Han Dongfang captured the same sentiment when he wrote that "China's economy was built upon the sweat and toil of tens of thousands of Daqing workers *who left their families and fought on the oil front* to bring China out of oil shortage. The government, with no qualification whatsoever, should make sure that Daqing workers and others live a decent life when they get old, sick and weak."[17] Protestors in Liaoyang, too, blamed the government for turning its back on them. At one rally, labor leader Yao Fuxin stood on a platform in front of the city hall and yelled out: "We devoted our lives to the party, but no one supports us in old age. We gave our youth to the party for nothing." War imagery also came in an open letter that protestors from Liaoyang addressed to Jiang Zemin in March 2002. Speaking of the years – generations even – of service that they and their families had put in at one plant that had recently closed down, the letter-writers stated:

> Liaoyang Ferroalloy Factory was a medium-sized state-owned enterprise with a long history of over fifty years. All the property and assets of the factory were derived from the *hard work, blood and sweat of generations of workers* ... Every year, Ferroalloy contributed billions of *yuan* in tax and profits to the national treasury and the standard of living of the whole workforce rose. This success did not come easily. *It was the result of our pioneering efforts to overcome countless challenges in conditions that were reminiscent of wartime hardships.*[18]

The protestors were particularly angry that their plant had closed down as a result of what they believed was mismanagement, as well as corrupt deal-making between the former director of the factory and the mayor and Party secretary of the City of Liaoyang. There as elsewhere in China, retrenched workers, who are virtually powerless to counteract the corrupt actions that have led to their joblessness, face the added insult of having to watch the wealthy drive luxury cars, dine at fancy restaurants, and shop at high-priced stores. One protestor in Liaoyang delivered a rousing speech that captured this bitterness and his determination to fight on:

> Oil workers know no fear
> The earth brings us oil
> To cast off poverty's hat
> We work all hours in all conditions
> And look forward with hope
> To the red dawn when our work is done.
> Blood, sweat and tears have built these tall buildings
> We toil endlessly while you sit in luxury
> The boss's house is built in a day
> We long for the rainbow of old age
> Though even now we work all hours ...
> The Iron Man shouts for all to hear
> A home and peace for the workers.[19]

At factories across China, rage over mismanagement and corruption has exploded since the restructuring of SOEs was enshrined as official policy at the 15th Party Congress in 1997. That policy assured that growing numbers of enterprises would be forced to shut down, thereby creating an opportunity for unscrupulous managers and Party leaders to help themselves to whatever of value was left at their factories before the inevitable closures took place.

By encouraging market forces while closing down SOEs, China's central government has forced workers to fend for themselves, resulting in a far more fluid and mobile (mostly downwardly) social environment, one over which the Party has far less control than in the past. Indeed, a significant feature of today's labor disputes is that they blur the once sharp lines dividing "society" and "state." The dualistic state–society model is simply inadequate to describe today's complex social and political reality. Multiple actors are involved in these labor conflicts – employed workers, furloughed workers, factory managers, local Communist Party officials, national-level government representatives, officials with the All-China Federation of Trade Unions (ACFTU) – and frequently they do not share interests in common. Under these circumstances, distinct elements of what in the past might have been lumped together in the "state" and "society" categories respectively now find themselves ranged against one another in cross-cutting, shifting alliances.

For example, employed workers with a stake in the maintenance of social and political order have been known to side with management or local Party officials against protestors intent on disrupting the status quo. Likewise, laid-off workers often appeal to their provincial governments or to Beijing to help them in their battles with local Party leaders and corrupt factory managers, many of whom enjoy close ties to powerful figures in the local Communist Party. These furloughed workers are making appeals to the central government precisely because local officials have proven unwilling or unable to attend to their grievances, and because they know that Communist Party leaders are under considerable political pressure to root out corruption. In case after case, managers with strong connections to local government officials have made off like bandits, setting themselves, their families, and their cronies up in fine style, while ordinary workers have been left with nothing. Letter-writers from the Liaoyang Ferroalloy Factory made the following accusations against Fan Yicheng, their plant's Party secretary and director:

> Fan took holidays abroad and gathered up large amounts of foreign exchange to fill his own coffers to the brim. At the factory he bullied and intimidated workers and used hundreds of thousands worth of public funds to refurbish his house and send his two children abroad to study. Fan and his corrupt friends used state funds to eat, drink, gamble, whore, and anything else they felt like doing ... Even more serious was the refusal to pay employees' pension insurance contributions ... As a

result, now that the factory is bankrupt we are unable to draw our pensions and have no way of meeting our livelihood expenses.[20]

The breaking point came in March 2002, when Gong Shangwu, the local delegate to the National People's Congress and former mayor and Party secretary of Liaoyang whom the workers at the Ferroalloy Factory accuse of colluding with Fan Yicheng, stated to a television reporter covering the National People's Congress (then in session in Beijing) that Liaoyang's unemployment problem had been rectified and that the restructuring of industries in the city was going smoothly. Considering that there were over 100,000 unemployed and laid-off workers in Liaoyang when Gong made his statement, this assertion was nothing short of outrageous. In response, thousands of retrenched workers poured into the streets to demand Gong's resignation and, again identifying themselves with China's revolutionary heritage, that Liaoyang be "liberated."[21]

The demonstrators' rhetorical strategy raises the question of who it was, exactly, that was supposed to "liberate" the city, as well as what "liberation" meant to those who put forth the call. One of the most noteworthy features of these protests is that laid-off workers from numerous different factories took part. Some 2,000 former employees of the Ferroalloy Factory were involved, and 15,000 retrenched workers from piston, instruments, leather, and precision tool factories participated.[22] The formation of a cross-factory alliance suggests that the protestors believed that they, the working class, should "liberate" Liaoyang. However, for all that their rhetoric recalls the Maoist period, the protestors were not calling for a return to the ultra-leftist spirit of those days. Rather, in defending their own interests, they were by definition questioning the virtue of the market-oriented change that the Party has embraced in the name of growth and modernization. The social compact of the Maoist past, the protestors were saying, resulted in a more just society than the policies of the reform era that followed. The attachment to Mao and all that he symbolizes was plain to see recently when workers' representatives traveled from Jiamusi in Heilongjiang Province to Beijing to present a petition to the central government: after making their presentation, they "made a pilgrimage to the Mao Mausoleum" and then returned to Heilongjiang. In Chongqing, too, protesting oil workers recently hoisted a banner whose language invoked the past to indict the present – "Iron Man, Iron Man look back, corrupt officials are at your back. Iron Man, Iron Man look ahead, your kids live by begging." After they did so, company leaders felt justified in labeling them reactionaries.[23]

The ambivalent relationship between the authorities and unemployed workers

To view the protestors as reactionaries is to embrace a limited and literal concept of politics that holds that all people who oppose any type of change are enemies of progress. Such a view leaves little room for a discussion of what kind of changes should be supported, or of how positive change can best be brought about. Faced with managers and local officials who show no inclination to address these all-important qualitative issues, retrenched workers have quite naturally looked outside their local environments to the provincial and national governments for assistance. The instinct to turn to Beijing for help in overcoming the abuses and apathy of plant leaders and city officials indicates recognition of the reality that the central government, assuming that it has the will, usually has the power to modify the behavior of local power-holders. But the strategy of appealing to a higher level of the government to discipline a lower level also reveals that the protestors do not view the state in monolithic terms. When protestors from Liaoyang wrote their plea for assistance to Jiang Zemin in March 2002, they used highly respectful language that in no way challenged the dominance of the Communist Party. Instead, they represented themselves as allies of Party central and as guardians of socialism:

> Respected and beloved Secretary General Jiang, we do not oppose the leadership of the Party or the socialist system ... [O]ur efforts [are] aimed to help the country ... eliminate all the corrupt worms boring away at and ruining our socialist economic system ... Since the reforms started, the Chinese working class has been the Party's source of fresh, *combat-ready troops* in the economic *battles* that have faced our country ... [But now] with no other option or way out before us, we hope that you, as our leader, can lead us out of this darkness and put us back on the right track ... We fervently hope that you will read this letter. It is perhaps more than we deserve that you use up your valuable time, but there are genuine reasons for our actions. We had no option but to write directly to you. Finally, we wish you a long and healthy life and offer our deepest respect.[24]

The language of this letter indicates strategic thinking on its authors' part, but it also shows that the demonstrators continue to subscribe to the paternalistic model of politics upheld by the Communist Party. The letter makes clear that its authors are deeply angry with their factory head and with local Party representatives. Conspicuously, however, there is no explicit, larger critique of China's political system here. Rather, the letter-writers are reminding their leader of the Mencian dictum that the little people have a right to rebel when their rulers fail to fulfill their obligations.

For its part, the Communist Party leadership has also displayed ambivalence toward the retrenched workers, and has shown, in Trini Leung's words, "considerable vacillation and a wide divergence of approach, between different government departments and regions, in the official handling of the various workers' protests."[25] Recognizing that it is hemmed in by the legacy of its own historical support for the idea of a workers' state, and wholly cognizant of the risk it would be courting if it entirely ignored the suffering of the millions of unemployed workers, the Party has adopted a carrot-and-stick approach to the demonstrations that aims to mollify the rank and file among the protestors while cracking down on organizers. Time and again in recent years, the Party has offered furloughed workers token payments in order to make their lives more tolerable and to demonstrate that the state does in fact care about their well-being. These monetary awards bring real, if temporary, relief to the protestors. In many instances, the Party has also responded to the demonstrators by promising to investigate the charges of malfeasance that they have leveled at factory heads and local Party bosses. This, too, has sometimes led to meaningful action, even if it has not spurred the Party leadership to alter its fundamental policy of industrial restructuring. For example, in July 2002, Fan Yicheng, the former director of the bankrupt Ferroalloy Factory in Liaoyang, was arrested, and in March 2003 given a thirteen-year prison sentence by the Liaoyang Intermediate People's Court.[26]

In general, however, top Communist Party officials get involved in local labor disputes only after and because they have become explosive. Theoretically, this does not need to be the case, since the Party-run ACFTU – which is the only legal trade union in China – has branch offices in all SOEs. Many cadres who work for the ACFTU genuinely care about the welfare of China's working class and have been outspoken about the desperate need to improve conditions in factories, especially foreign-owned ones that employ rural migrants. Along these lines, in a speech to ACFTU cadres in 2000, Politburo Standing Committee Member and ACFTU Chairman Wei Jianxing complained that "the organization of trade unions in newly established enterprises has simply not happened," and that a 100 million workers in China were not organized. "When there is not even a trade union," Wei asked rhetorically, "what is the point of talking about trade unions upholding the legal rights of workers? Or trade unions being the transmission belt between the Party and the masses? Or trade unions being an important social pillar of state power?"[27] Despite the fact that Jiang Zemin angrily scolded Wei Jianxing for appearing to be "sympathetic" to independent trade unions, workers have little faith in the ACFTU or its chairman.[28] Virtually every time demonstrations have taken place, protestors have reported that they sought help from their local branch of the ACFTU only to be ignored or, worse, reprimanded. Fundamentally, the ACFTU is compromised by the Communist Party's insistence that it promote political and economic stability above all, and that it manage China's labor environment so as to attract foreign investors. Perhaps most telling of the official union's inability to stand up for the interests of workers in SOEs is that the massive protests in Daqing and Liaoyang received no coverage in the pages of the *Workers' Daily*, the official voice of the ACFTU.[29]

The ACFTU's inability to prevent censorship of news on labor unrest is consistent with its refusal to tolerate anything that smacks of independent labor organizing. The *Workers' Daily* and other periodicals regularly report on problems in China's workplaces, including industrial accidents, corruption, and the poor treatment of workers in foreign-owned factories, but the press has remained silent about the protests in the north-east because of their enormous scale and because they have involved the organization of independent trade unions, an activity that is strictly forbidden by the Communist Party.[30] In recent years, Chinese labor law has undergone positive revision, much of it designed to improve work conditions in privately run and foreign-owned factories. While these laws have thus far not been well enforced, they do show that the Party is aware of abuses and seeks to do something about them. On the other hand, Chinese labor law has become increasingly restrictive as regards the right of workers to organize for the defense of their own interests. Between 1975 and 1982, the right to strike was nominally guaranteed by China's constitution, but since 1982, workers have not even had the nominal right to take independent action on their own behalf. Furthermore, China's Trade Union Law leaves no room for doubt as to the ACFTU's obligation to obey the Communist Party leadership: "Trade unions shall observe and safeguard the Constitution, take it as the fundamental criterion for their activities, take economic development as the central task, uphold the socialist road, the people's democratic dictatorship, leadership by the Communist Party of China, and Marxism-Leninism, Mao Zedong Thought and Deng Xiaoping Theory."[31] The Trade Union Law specifically outlaws the formation of trade unions independent of the ACFTU, a phenomenon that occurred in Beijing during the demonstrations of the spring of 1989, and which has occurred sporadically since that time.

The surge in independent trade union activity

Because their pleas to Party leaders generally have not resulted in lasting improvement in their material circumstances, increasing numbers of workers are flouting the Communist Party's authority by turning to independent, worker-led trade unions. In 1999, an organizer of one such union from Gansu Province, Yue Tianxing, was arrested, charged with subverting the government, and given a ten-year prison sentence for publishing a newsletter entitled *Chinese Workers' Monitor* and for organizing thousands of workers who had lost their jobs to demand payment of months' worth of back wages. Hunan labor activist Zhang Shanguang was given a similar sentence for organizing the Shupu County Association for Laid-off Workers and for communicating with foreign reporters. According to human rights organizations tracking his case, Zhang has endured beatings in prison and has been forced to do hard labor for up to sixteen hours a day.[32] Attempts to found independent trade unions occurred in Daqing and Liaoyang in 2002. In Daqing, protestors marched under the banner of the Daqing Petroleum Administration Bureau Retrenched Workers' Provisional Union Committee; in Liaoyang, workers from a variety of different factories joined forces under the banner of an independent organization, the Liaoyang City Unemployed and Bankrupt Workers Provisional Union.

As it had in the earlier cases, the Communist Party responded to these assertions of independence by seeking to "kill the chicken to scare the monkey" – that is by arresting union organizers to frighten rank-and-file protestors away from continued participation. In Liaoyang, the 17 March arrest of labor leader Yao Fuxin resulted in a new, and to the Party highly ominous, development when on 18 March 2002, some 4,000 laid-off Ferroalloy workers joined by upwards of 30,000 supporters from over a dozen other factories marched down Democracy Road to the municipal government building to demand Yao's release. Two days later, three other worker representatives (Pang Qingxiang, Xiao Yunliang, and Wang Zhaoming) were arrested. The detention of these men, who were soon dubbed the "Liaoyang Four," then became the focal point of ongoing protests in Liaoyang. In late September 2002, over 600 Ferroalloy workers unsuccessfully petitioned the municipal government to release the Liaoyang Four before National Day. Timing their actions to coincide with the run-up to the 16th Party Congress, in early November between 3,000 and 4,000 retrenched workers again massed before the government's office to ask "What Crime Have the Liaoyang Four Committed?" and to demand the payment of basic welfare subsidies. Subsequently, when instead of getting a sympathetic hearing from the delegates at the Party Congress, Liaoyang's retrenched workers learned that ACFTU Deputy Chairman Zhang Junjiu stated during a press congress in Beijing that Yao Fuxin "had been detained because he had broken Chinese law by carrying out car-bombings and not because he had organized a workers' campaign," they reacted with outrage and declared that Zhang was inventing things in order to smear the workers' reputation. According to labor activists, such tactics have been employed frequently by authorities seeking to discredit protestors; one of the most common means of doing this is to accuse the demonstrators of having ties to the outlawed Falun Gong spiritual movement. Nevertheless, as already stated, the Party-state is not without its own internal cleavages. Following Zhang's remarks, officials in the Liaoyang government's General Office and from the Liaoyang Federation of Trade Unions, a subset of the ACFTU, stated unequivocally that in fact no car bombings had taken place in Liaoyang, and that Yao was innocent of these charges.[33]

On the lookout for issues around which to mobilize pressure on the Chinese government to uphold the international rights regimes to which it is a party, international labor and human rights organizations openly supported the Liaoyang workers' campaign for the release of the Liaoyang Four as a means of drawing attention to the broad issue of freedom of association in China. Another case that has recently received significant international attention for the same reason is that of Di Tiangui, a former state worker at Taiyuan City Dazhong Machinery Factory in Shanxi Province who is now in prison for writing a series of letters to Jiang Zemin regarding the injustices suffered by workers and for attempting to set up what would be China's first national organization representing retired state workers. In a "call to action" that he distributed to workers in Taiyuan and mailed to people elsewhere in China in May 2002, Di wrote that "our target is indeed the party central committee, Jiang Zemin and the theories of the party and their incorrect policies, but we are not opposing the Communist Party." Despite this disclaimer, Di went on to make assertions that were certain to be interpreted by the Party as subversive, stating that an association of 30 million retirees could have significant political influence, and that "if the Party goes against the will of the workers, the workers must correct the party."[34]

The domestic and international campaigns on behalf of the Liaoyang Four, Di Tiangui, and other imprisoned labor rights activists are highly troubling to a Communist Party already startled by the extent to which information about labor disturbances in one part of the country is finding its way to other parts of the country via "underground" channels. In numerous instances in 2002, retrenched workers elsewhere in China were inspired by the events in the north-east to take to the streets for the defense of their own interests. For example, in May, laid-off oil workers in Hebei Province held demonstrations at which specific mention was made of the events in Daqing and Liaoyang, and in September, Chongqing-based oil workers began to organize themselves to take legal action in defense of their rights to pensions and employment. One of the Chongqing workers acknowledged that he and his colleagues had been receiving information on the Daqing protests and stated: "The workers here view the courage ... of the Daqing workers with great admiration. We think that [they] have earned respect for Chinese workers. Chinese workers are grateful to the workers in Daqing."[35] The massive scale of the unrest in the north-east, added to the fact that the Daqing name carries so much significance for the Chinese working class, no doubt helps to account for this phenomenon.

The Communist Party's balancing act

The Communist Party has reacted aggressively toward organizers of autonomous trade unions. Still, a recent report prepared by Human Rights Watch argues that the Party's response to the unprecedented labor unrest of 2002–03 was relatively restrained:

> In its effort to avoid worker cohesion across occupations, industries, and regions, the Chinese government has tried to avoid fanning worker unrest; it has not, therefore, seized large numbers of labor protestors as soon as they took to the streets. Instead the government has managed protests through a seemingly successful low-key combination of limited force and limited payouts. According to a report, Beijing also instructed officials in the northeastern provinces to avoid coercion whenever possible.

To be sure, local governments have deployed large numbers of armed police in order to intimidate protestors and have resorted to crude measures to restore order, but with the exception of a handful of high-profile figures, few people have been arrested.[36] In general, China's leadership has pursued a divide-and-rule strategy, encouraging employed workers to keep their distance from the protests, and intentionally causing the rank and file among the unemployed to believe that the protests are to blame for the cancellation of payments. Through this sort of skillful management of the situation, the government has thus far successfully prevented a Polish-style movement from taking shape; it recognizes that it must tread lightly, or at least appear to be doing so, in order to avoid further antagonizing the protestors. As the Human Rights Watch report goes on to observe, the Communist Party understands that "a crackdown of the intensity and ferocity that has characterized the Falun Gong campaign" might lead to a backlash from employed workers in addition to those who have lost their jobs, thereby causing serious damage to the Chinese economy.[37]

For their part, the protest leaders have demonstrated an awareness of the growing extent to which China's domestic politics are entangled in a web of international legal and media processes. The Chinese government is wary of these processes and has sought to limit outside involvement in labor disputes by, among other things, expelling foreign reporters who seek to cover them and warning protestors not to speak with foreign journalists.[38] At the same time, it has courted agencies such as the International Labor Organization (ILO), on whose governing body the ACFTU has recently won a seat. This angers Chinese labor activists, who view the development as an ominous sign that the Communist Party's public relations efforts have succeeded in persuading outsiders not to press too hard for the cause of independent trade unions in China.[39] Such setbacks notwithstanding, retrenched workers know that scrutiny by non-governmental organizations, international bodies, and foreign governments is to their advantage in that it produces pressure on the Communist Party to refrain from the use of violence and to follow international rights regimes. With this in mind, protestors have established contacts with foreign journalists who can transmit their stories out of China, and they have blocked trains full of foreigners in hopes of generating media attention to the causes for which they are fighting.[40]

Protestors' attempts to gain international attention reflect a degree of familiarity with rights-based legal discourse and labor norms and the belief that China's membership in the ILO, as well as its ratification of the United Nations-based International Covenants on Economic, Social and Cultural Rights (ICESCR) and on Civil and Political Rights (ICCPR), oblige the Chinese government to allow freedom of association for workers. At the core of the ILO mandate are the following terms: "The ILO formulates international labor standards in the form of Conventions and Recommendations setting minimum standards of basic rights: freedom of association, the right to organize, collective bargaining, abolition of forced labor, equality of opportunity and treatment."[41] In March 2002, the general secretary of the International Confederation of Free Trade Unions (ICFTU), Guy Ryder, wrote to President Jiang Zemin to express concern about the Chinese government's handling of the protests in Daqing. Ryder stated that the use of force to deal with the protestors was not acceptable and, citing China's membership in the ILO, wrote that "the establishment by workers of organizations of their own choosing for the protection of their economic and social interests is an internationally recognized human right, guaranteed by ILO Convention."[42]

The Chinese government has thus far refused to alter its approach to independent trade unions and has trumpeted the recent elevation of the ACFTU representative to the ILO's governing body, but the involvement of foreign watchdogs has forced the Communist Party to take international standards and opinion into account. Thus it is that China's minister of labor and social security, Zhang Zuoji, felt compelled to state in May 2001 that Chinese workers "have freedom of association, in conformity with Chinese conditions," and that there are at present "no people detained or jailed because of legitimate participation in trade union activities."[43] Similarly, the Chinese government's formal response in September 2002 to the ICFTU complaint lodged through the ILO the previous March – that the Liaoyang protest leaders "jointly carried out planned activities of terrorism and sabotage" – can also be understood in this context. In terms of international diplomacy, it was difficult for the Chinese government to justify its detention of the labor leaders with the argument that they had been involved in the formation of an independent trade union.[44] To avoid having to do that, the Party has instead depicted the Liaoyang labor leaders as violent criminals.

While certainly not the outcome that foreign-based human and labor rights organizations desired, they might take some consolation from the fact that their attention to the case of the arrested Liaoyang labor leaders forced the government to worry about their presence and their positions. Furthermore, as protests against the harsh treatment of Yao Fuxin and Xiao Yunliang (the Liaoyang Four became the "Liaoyang Two" in December 2002, when city authorities announced that they were dropping charges against Wang Zhaoming and Pang Qingxiang)[45] by New York-based Human Rights in China and Hong Kong-based *China Labour Bulletin* make clear, the trumped-up charges against the two men have provided supporters of human and labor rights in China with an additional opportunity to attack the Communist Party for failing to uphold its own laws and international covenants to which it has acceded. The two rights groups submitted petitions on Yao and Xiao's behalf to the United Nations Working Group on Arbitrary Detention in November 2002.[46]

Yao Fuxin and Xiao Yunliang finally had their day in the Intermediate People's Court of Liaoyang Municipality on 15 January 2003. Although Yao and Xiao were held in pre-trial custody for ten months, the two men's defenders (Yao had a lawyer, while Xiao was represented by a relative and a friend) were informed of the trial date and given a copy of the prosecution's indictment just hours before the proceedings began. During the trial, several hundred protestors huddled in sub-zero temperatures outside the court-house.[47] Inside, the prosecution never mentioned the terrorism and sabotage charges that government officials had raised in response to complaints from the ILO just months earlier. Instead, Yao and Xiao were "charged with 'subversion' and 'organizing illegal demonstrations,' on the grounds of their alleged 'links with foreign hostile elements' and membership" in the "banned China Democracy Party."[48] Yao and Xiao denied the charges and claimed that their involvement in the demonstrations of March 2002 was motivated simply by their desire to see justice done on behalf of the unemployed workers from the Ferroalloy plant in Liaoyang.

In March 2003, between the trial and the sentencing that took place in May, the ILO's governing body once more appealed to the Chinese govern-ment to release the Liaoyang workers still in detention and to drop all charges against them. The ILO's appeal fell on deaf ears. On 9 May 2003, Liaoyang's judicial authorities found Yao and Xiao guilty of being "'dangerous elements' who posed a severe threat to social 'stability and unity,'" and sentenced them to seven and four years' imprisonment respec-tively. In late June, the two men's appeals were rejected and the case was closed.[49] Following the verdict, *China Labour Bulletin*'s Han Dongfang, who was named as one of the "hostile foreign elements" with whom Yao and Xiao had been in contact, reacted with outrage: "*China Labour Bulletin* is appalled by these lengthy sentences handed down to two men who are guilty of nothing else but attempting to protect and promote the legitimate rights of Liaoyang workers."[50]

Acknowledging that the outcome of Yao and Xiao's cases is devastating to Liaoyang's workers, *China Labour Bulletin* has nevertheless put a brave face on the story by declaring that, while "it remains to be seen whether the harsh and unjust sentences passed on the Liaoyang Two will succeed, as the government clearly hopes, in putting an end to the workers' movement in Liaoyang," it is "clear from the events in Liaoyang over the past year" that "China's workers have at last begun to reclaim for themselves some of the sense of collective power, and autonomy of action, that the Communist Party relieved them of several decades ago when it declared that it alone had the requisite credentials to represent the country's 'labouring masses.'"[51] Unless "the government begins to allow workers some modicum of true independence," a report in *China Labour Bulletin* states threateningly, "it will inevitably face ten, twenty or a hundred Liaoyangs at some point in the not-too-distant future." A dispirited comment by one Liaoyang labor organizer – who would only give the name Tie – made a similar point: "In China, even if you break your head against the wall, it's no use. All we can do is wait for the revolution." Though saying so in different tones, both statements suggest that it is only a matter of time before China contracts the dreaded "Polish disease." [52]

The red sunset

China's rate of unemployment today is the highest since the Communist Party came to power in 1949. The restructuring of SOEs has generated a crisis for millions of workers who were led to believe throughout their careers that they would be able to count on financial security in the late stages of their lives. The abrupt terminating of this social contract in recent years has steadily eroded support for the Communist Party within the working class, a phenomenon that can be measured in the rapid and dramatic drop in the number of workers enrolled in the ACFTU.[53] This chapter has not addressed the often appalling conditions faced by workers employed in township and village enterprises or in foreign-owned factories.[54] The existence of that crisis in addition to the one addressed here indicates that the labor situation in China today is one of the most severe challenges facing the country, and that, for all intents and purposes, the social compact that defined the relationship between the working class and the governing party for over three decades is null and void.

For the time being, the Chinese government is in the driver's seat, and laid-off workers are struggling merely to survive. It is unlikely that these workers will seek to or successfully topple the present regime on their own, but through their claims and protest actions they are nevertheless forcing the Communist Party to shift its rhetorical position on the meaning of socialism and to seek a new basis of legitimacy. In other words, the millions of human casualties of the present attempt to reorient the Chinese economy are contesting the Communist Party's core ideological claims and are threatening its ability to out-maneuver all challengers from the Left – the critical location on the political spectrum from which the Party has laid claim to power since the revolution in 1949. Should the unemployed workers' challenge to the regime's legitimacy merge with similar challenges from elsewhere in society, the threat to the Party could be grave indeed. Short of that, the ongoing labor crisis in the state-owned sector of the Chinese economy promises to accelerate debate over the meaning of socialism and to force the Communist Party to provide disadvantaged members of urban society with new reasons for offering it their political support.

Notes

1 Thanks to Pete Gries, Lee Haiyan, Jeff Wasserstrom, Hanna Weston, and the readers for Routledge for their helpful comments on an earlier draft of this chapter. I alone am responsible for the chapter's contents.
2 Han Dongfang is quoted in Erik Eckholm, "Leaner factories, fewer workers bring more labor unrest to China," *New York Times*, 19 March 2002, p. A8.
3 "Paying the price: worker unrest in northeast China," *Human Rights Watch* 14(6) (C) (August 2002): 29; Roland Lew, "Rebellion in the rust belt," at www.3bh.org.uk/IV/main/IV%20Archive/IV343/IV343%2020.htm. On Maoist asceticism as it pertained to industrial policy, see Andrew Walder, *Communist Neo-traditionalism: Work and Authority in Chinese Industry* (University of

California Press, 1986), Ch. 6. Propaganda art depicting Daqing and Wang Jinxi can be found at www/iisg.nl/~landsberger/dq.html.

4   "Paying the price: worker unrest in northeast China," p. 27.

5   "Model workers for model unemployment," *China Labour Bulletin,* September–October 1997; "Why doesn't the government take steps to resolve its conflicts with the people?" *China Labour Bulletin,* 6 May 2002. (For *China Labour Bulletin,* see www.china-labour.org.hk.) See also Julie Chao, "Thousands of oil workers protest in Chinese city," Cox Washington Bureau, 21 March 2002.

6   *China Labour Bulletin,* E-Bulletin Issue No. 8 (2 July 2002).

7   "Liaoyang workers still fighting," *China Labour Bulletin,* 7 November 2002; Philip P. Pan, "Tactics of Chinese government frustrate labor organizers," *Washington Post,* 30 December 2002. On a protest gathering that took place as late as June 2003, see "Press release: the 'Liaoyang Two': Appeal against 'subversion' charges rejected in a secret hearing," *China Labour Bulletin,* 27 June 2003.

8   The 55 million figure comes from Hu Angang, a leading economist at Qinghua University. See Liu Weimin, "Stop treating state workers favorably: economist," at www.hxwz.org/CND-Global/CND-Global.02–07–11.html.

9   Phone interview with Han Dongfang conducted on 21 March 2002; Ching Kwan Lee, "Pathways of labor insurgency," in Elizabeth J. Perry and Mark Selden (eds) *Chinese Society: Change, Conflict and Resistance* (Routledge, 2000), pp. 41–61; Martin King Whyte, "The changing role of workers," in Merle Goldman and Roderick MacFarquhar (eds) *The Paradox of China's Post-Mao Reforms* (Harvard University Press, 1999), pp. 173–196; and "Paying the price: worker unrest in northeast China," esp. p. 36.

10 Walder, *Communist Neo-traditionalism.*

11 I have written on this issue at greater length in "'Learn from Daqing': more dark clouds for workers in state-owned enterprises," *Journal of Contemporary China* 11(33) (2002): 721–734.

12 Although the state-owned sector's percentage of industrial output value has dropped dramatically since the end of the Mao era, it can "still be considered the backbone of Chinese manufacturing" because it dominates in heavy industry and thus provides "the basic inputs upon which all other sectors depend." Edward Steinfeld, *Forging Reform in China: The Fate of State-owned Industry* (Cambridge University Press, 1998), pp. 13–15.

13 Walder, *Communist Neo-traditionalism,* pp. 193–194, 226.

14 Tim Pringle, "The Chinese working class," *China Rights Forum* 1 (2002): 12–21. For recent work that draws attention to worker unrest since 1949, see Elizabeth J. Perry, *Challenging the Mandate of Heaven: Social Protest and State Power in China* (M.E. Sharpe, 2002), and Jackie Sheehan, *Chinese Workers: A New History* (Routledge, 1998).

15 Whyte, "The changing role of workers," pp. 175–177; Lew, "Rebellion in the rust belt"; Pringle, "The Chinese working class," p. 13.

16 On this, see Walder, *Communist Neo-traditionalism.*

17 Emphasis added. Pan, "Tactics of Chinese government frustrate labor organizers"; Han Dongfang, "50,000 Daqing oilfield workers organize independent trade union," *China Labour Bulletin,* 6 March 2002. On the adoption of lessons learned during the Cultural Revolution, see Pringle, "The Chinese working class," p. 16.

18 Emphasis added. Pan, "Tactics of Chinese government frustrate labor organizers"; "Open letter to the general secretary of the Chinese Communist Party, Jiang Zemin," 5 March 2002; "Paying the price: worker unrest in northeast China," Appendix 1, p. 38.

19 "Conversations with a retrenched oil worker in Daqing (1)," *China Labour Bulletin,* 13 April 2002.

20 *Ibid.*, p. 39.
21 *Ibid.*, pp. 16, 21; "Liaoyang workers still fighting."
22 *Ibid.*, p. 21.
23 Elisabeth Rosenthal, "Workers' plight brings new militancy in China," *New York Times*, 10 March 2003, p. A8; "Better to die fighting than starving to death!", *China Labour Bulletin*, 25 September 2002.
24 Emphasis added. "Open letter to the general secretary of the Chinese Communist Party, Jiang Zemin," pp. 40–41.
25 The quotation is from "The Liaoyang protest movement of 2002–03, and the arrest, trial and sentencing of the 'Liaoyang Two,'" *China Labour Bulletin*, July 2003. That essay is adapted from a chapter by Trini Leung, author of a forthcoming book on labor organizing in China between 1998 and 2003.
26 "Head of Liaoyang Ferroalloy Factory arrested," *China Labour Bulletin*, 2 August 2002; "The Liaoyang protest movement of 2002–03, and the arrest, trial and sentencing of the 'Liaoyang Two.'"
27 Quoted in "Paying the price: worker unrest in northeast China," p. 10.
28 Todd Crowell and David Hsieh, "Court intrigue," *Asiaweek*, 11 February 2000.
29 John Gittings, "Workers gagged by Chinese censorship," *Guardian*, 2 April 2002.
30 On Chinese press coverage of labor problems, see Anita Chan, *China's Workers Under Assault: The Exploitation of Labor in a Globalizing Economy* (M.E. Sharpe, 2001).
31 Quoted in "Paying the price: worker unrest in northeast China," p. 12.
32 "'Learn from Daqing': more dark clouds for workers in state-owned enterprises," p. 728; "Paying the price: worker unrest in northeast China," p. 12; *China Rights Forum*, Summer/Fall 2000, p. 67. For further information about these and other jailed labor activists, see "Profiles of five imprisoned labor activists in China," *China Labour Bulletin*, 21 November 2002.
33 "The Liaoyang Four have been detained for almost seven months – with no formal charges," "Liaoyang workers still fighting," "CLB statement on ACFTU deputy chairman's recent remarks on Yao Fuxin," and "The Liaoyang interviews: CLB follows up accusations of violence against Yao Fuxin by ACFTU leader," *China Labour Bulletin*, 16 October, 7 November, and 12 November 2002 respectively. On accusations that protestors have ties to Falun Gong, see "Paying the price: worker unrest in northeast China," p. 32, and "Retrenched oil workers in Sichuan get organized for legal action," *China Labour Bulletin*, 17 September 2002.
34 "ICFTU lodges complaint with ILO on the detention of labor activist in Shanxi," *China Labour Bulletin*, 27 August 2002; Julie Chao, "Retiree jailed for trying to organize China's pensioners," Cox Washington Bureau, 27 August 2002.
35 See "Hebei Shengli oilfield workers sue employer over retrenchment," *China Labour Bulletin*, 6 May 2002, and "Retrenched oil workers in Sichuan get organized for legal action."
36 "Paying the price: worker unrest in northeast China," pp. 35–36.
37 *Ibid.*, p. 37.
38 *Ibid.*, p. 33.
39 Editor's Note, *China Labor Bulletin*, E-Bulletin Issue No. 8 (7 September 2002).
40 "Paying the price: worker unrest in northeast China," p. 31.
41 "China and the ILO: formalistic cooperation masks rejection of key labor rights," *China Rights Forum* (Spring 2001).
42 "ICFTU on Daqing oilfield workers' protest," *ICFTU OnLine*, 15 March 2002.
43 Erik Eckholm, "China accepts U.N. advice to help ease labor strife," *New York Times*, 20 May 2001.

44 "The Liaoyang protest movement of 2002–03, and the arrest, trial and sentencing of the 'Liaoyang Two.'"
45 *Ibid.*
46 "HRIC and CLB call for immediate release of Yao Fuxin," *China Labour Bulletin*, 25 November 2002.
47 "The Liaoyang protest movement of 2002–03, and the arrest, trial and sentencing of the 'Liaoyang Two.'"
48 *Ibid.*
49 *Ibid.*
50 "The Liaoyang protest movement of 2002–03, and the arrest, trial and sentencing of the 'Liaoyang Two'"; "Yao Fuxin accused of communicating with hostile elements," *China Labour Bulletin*, 15 January 2003.
51 "The Liaoyang protest movement of 2002–03, and the arrest, trial and sentencing of the 'Liaoyang Two.'" Along with the online news service *LabourStart*, which is dedicated to the protection of labor rights around the world, *China Labour Bulletin* has launched a global signature campaign calling for Yao Fuxin and Xiao Yunliang's release. "Press release: the 'Liaoyang Two': appeal against 'subversion' charges rejected in secret hearing."
52 "The Liaoyang protest movement of 2002–03, and the arrest, trial and sentencing of the 'Liaoyang Two'"; Pan, "Tactics of Chinese government frustrate labor organizers."
53 In the 1990s, the ACFTU's membership declined by nearly a third, from 130 to 90 million. Erik Eckholm, "Workers' rights suffer as China goes capitalist," *New York Times*, 22 August 2001.
54 On that crisis, see Anita Chan, *China's Workers Under Assault.*

4 Comrades and collectives in arms

Tax resistance, evasion, and avoidance strategies in post-Mao China

Patricia Thornton

Within months of the February 1997 passing of Deng Xiaoping, the chief architect and symbolic father of the post-Mao reform program, the Chinese countryside was gripped by a rising tide of collective violence. Farmers frustrated by the unrelenting demands of local tax collectors took to the streets in a wave of contentious actions that spilled across the three central provinces of Hubei, Jiangxi, and Sichuan during the summer and fall of 1997. In Jingzhou Prefecture, Hubei Province, rural residents staged parades and demonstrations and filed petitions in more than seventy incidents that accused the authorities of "exploiting and fleecing the peasants." In Tianmen County, a combined force of nearly 3,000 peasants assaulted the Party and government offices, leading to a stand-off with armed police.[1] In Jiangxi's Pengze County, nearly 5,000 peasants from five villages and townships besieged the county government building in hand tractors, shouting "Down with the county lords!" and "Down with the county officials and local despots!" In a separate incident in another Jiangxi county the same month, protesting farmers claimed that they would start an armed rebellion to initiate the third great revolution in modern Chinese history.[2]

Despite the apparent successes of the Dengist reform program in stimulating the market economy, it has also created a milieu ripe for contentious politics. Numerous official, journalistic, and scholarly accounts have pointed to the rising trend in collective violence with growing alarm. One 1993 Chinese government report cited by a Hong Kong periodical noted that over 1.5 million cases of protest had occurred in rural areas that year alone, over 6,000 of which were officially classified as "disturbances" (*naoshi*) by mainland authorities. Of these cases, 830 involved more than one township and more than 500 participants; 78 involved more than one county and over 1,000 participants; and 21 were considered to be "extremely large-scale" (*teda de*) events involving more than 5,000 participants. A surprising number of these confrontations turned violent: during these disturbances, 8,200 casualties resulted among township and county officials, 560 county-level offices were ransacked, and 385 public security personnel were fatally injured. According to the same report, the first four months of 1994 continued the trend of rising violence: collective protests that took place between January and April of 1994 resulted in over 5,000 casualties among county and township government personnel.[3] That same year, the author of the bestselling *China from the Third Eye* argued that by unshackling the peasantry, the Dengist reforms "spelled the beginning of the collapse of the Great Wall [of socialism and Party domination] ... The genie is out of the bottle," and predicted nothing less than a total "social cataclysm" for China in the next decade or so, should current trends continue.[4] More recently, the Taiwanese Mainland Affairs Council reported that the number of public protests and demonstrations on the mainland reached 110,000 in 1999, a jump of 70 per cent over the 60,000 registered in 1998, and that information gleaned during the first half of the 2000 calendar year suggested that collective protests would surpass the record set the previous year.[5]

The restive quality of mass politics in contemporary China stems from a long tradition of collective action, rebellion, and popular contention, insightfully described by Elizabeth Perry, Lucien Bianco, and others.[6] It is therefore hardly surprising that as the post-Mao leadership continues to deepen existing market reforms, both those marginalized and those empowered by such policies have mobilized to press their claims against the regime. This chapter focuses specifically on recent incidents of collective tax protests, and seeks to compare reform-era mass mobilization strategies to those employed by the Maoist regime. Leaving aside acts of violence by individuals and their families against tax collectors and state agents – events which are also on the rise[7] – episodes of collective tax resistance (*kangshui*) in the era of reform clearly demonstrate the capacity of groups, collectives, and even communities to draw upon the organizational resources created by the Mao-era state and to use them to pursue very different aims in the period of reform.

Episodes of tax protest, avoidance, and resistance reflect directly on the larger question of regime legitimacy. Reform-era tax protestors have raised serious questions about the legitimacy of taxes, not only in terms of the types and amounts of tax monies levied, but also in terms of the manner in which they were collected, and then later used, by local governments in the PRC. In the absence of more routinized forms of political expression, rural taxpayers see collective action as a rare opportunity to convey their grievances to those in power. In his work on political contention, Charles Tilly argued that in 19th-century Europe, "most people did not vote, petition, or take positions on national affairs in anything like the contemporary meanings of those terms. Yet they did act together on their interests, broadcasting their demands, complaints, and aspirations in no uncertain terms" through the medium of collective action. Reading the meaning of such events requires careful attention to the particular patterns, or repertoires, that give such episodes shape and form:

> Any population has a limited repertoire of collective action: alternative means of acting together on shared interests. In our time, most people

know how to participate in an electoral campaign, join or form a special-interest association, organize a letter-writing drive, demonstrate, strike, hold a meeting, build an influence network and so on. These varieties of action constitute a repertoire in something like the theatrical or musical sense of the word – but the repertoire in question resembles that of *commedia dell'arte* or jazz more than that of a strictly classical ensemble. People know the general rules of performance more or less well, and vary the performance to meet the purpose at hand.[8]

What can the language of collective action tell us about regime legitimacy in reform-era China? An examination of recent episodes of anti-tax resistance suggests three general repertoires, each of which reflects a different type of fracture within the reform-era polity: protest corresponding to ethnic divides, mobilization that is centered in the vestiges of the Mao-era collective economy, and anti-tax resistance that arises from the new enterprises and social forces that are themselves products of the Dengist reform program.[9] Due to the sensitive nature of Han control over large portions of the west and south-west, both post-1949 and reform-era economic policies have tended to be less rigidly implemented in areas with significant non-Han populations.[10] Perhaps not surprisingly, given the relatively high level of financial support provided for locales in such regions, episodes of collective tax resistance in these areas appear to be relatively rare, and are often conjoined with episodes of ethnic strife and calls for secession and ethnic autonomy. By contrast, reports of tax protests in central China, including those occurring in the north-east rust belt, are far more numerous. Workers and farmers in these areas, whose livelihood is still significantly shaped by the state-imposed institutional structures of the Mao era – the vestiges of the commune in the countryside and the state-controlled industrial work units in the cities – readily draw upon the organizational and discursive legacies of the revolutionary period when they mobilize collectively to protest tax collection. Finally, tax resistance by the reform-era small private businesses and merchants, heavily concentrated in the eastern provinces, but also present in peri-urban areas in central China, often adopt a contract-based language of long-term negotiation and strategic resistance against the demands of local officials.

These three patterns of protest, which appear to be directly related to the deepening of market reforms, offer three different critiques of the current regime's claims to legitimacy. Anti-tax protests that evolve into demands for ethnic autonomy call into question the claims of the Han-dominated Party-state to represent the interests of minority groups, many of which have reacted with alarm to recent influxes of Han settlers to their traditional homelands. Acts of tax resistance by farmers and state enterprise workers that rely heavily upon the class-based language and organizational forms popularized under Mao probe the true depth of the commitment of the current leadership to the interests of the workers and peasants, in whose name the Party still purports to rule. Tax protests spearheaded by the growing class of private entrepreneurs created by the Dengist reform program seek to test the willingness of the current leadership to abide by its own newly stated allegiance to the rule of law in the post-Mao era.

Yet perhaps even more challenging to the legitimacy of the current regime than the size and frequency of such anti-tax protests is the role apparently being played by the lowest tier of the state and Party officials in mobilizing collective action. A close reading of tax protest repertoires suggests that local cadres and enterprise administrators are playing a key role in the transition from episodic waves of protest to sustained social movement. Market reform policies have tied the interests of local cadres, managers, and administrators more firmly to the financial soundness of the collective work unit or local community, and have made them less dependent upon the central state. In recent conflicts over tax remittance, grass-roots cadres and low-level enterprise managers have sometimes sided with local residents and workers, and have on occasion even led resistance efforts against state authorities. Rising tensions between those on the payroll of the central state who "eat imperial rations" and those struggling for survival in the market economy have increasingly erupted into overt violence. Thus, a key finding of this study of tax resistance repertoires in the reform era is that regardless of regional, organizational, or discursive variations, local and state forces appear increasingly fractured, with local grass-roots and enterprise cadres finding new grounds for solidarity with the workers and farmers with whom they interact on a daily basis, against what they see as the insularity of the central state.

Anti-tax resistance and ethnic violence

Tax resistance in largely non-Han western and south-western China is not commonly reported in the Chinese press. Fearing widespread ethnic unrest in such areas, central officials instituted preferential reform policies (*youhui zhengce*) in Xinjiang and other non-Han majority regions, establishing special economic zones "of the same kind as those of the coastal provinces," and in 1992 announced that the tax-sharing arrangements enjoyed by coastal provinces would be applied to nine additional provinces and cities, including Xinjiang. Ethnic minority regions were furthermore entitled to keep 80 per cent of local taxes, as opposed to the usual 50 per cent. Xinjiang has also benefited far more than other provinces from fiscal transfers from the central government.[11]

Yet despite relatively favorable economic arrangements between some areas of "subsistence" China and the central government, reports of rising levels of unrest continue. In these areas, incidents of collective violence initiated by largely non-Han populations propelled by economic dissatisfaction may quickly become large-scale ethnic mobilizations once the Han-majority authorities move to suppress the protest. For example, in 1994, a year marked by significant unrest nationwide in the PRC, Amnesty International noted that acknowledged arrests for pro-separatist or counter-revolutionary activities rose a remarkable 90 per cent in the Tibet Autonomous Region over the previous year. Tibet's Governor Gyaincain Norbu claimed that the "Dalai [Lama] clique took advantage of some social hot spots inland, such as the problems of commodity prices and taxation, to try its utmost to disrupt unity and stability ... in Tibet."[12] Similarly, in 1991, dozens of Tibetan farmers from the Dri region of Qinghai (Amdo) protested outside provincial offices in Xining, with a long banner which proclaimed in Tibetan: "Return our snowlands – Give us back our grasslands – Leave us be – We are dying of hunger."[13] In two separate incidents on 26 and 28 April in Urumqi, 1,000 and 2,000 marchers assembled at various locations around the capital before converging on the People's Square to lodge a collective protest against corruption, inflation, and the failure of the government to "protect the interests of the working class." The autonomous regional Party committee and regional government mobilized nearly the same number of cadres (2,000) to "dissuade" the demonstrators, all the while assuring the protestors that "everything can be discussed and solved." The marchers purportedly chanted "Long Live Xinjiangstan."[14]

According to Amnesty International, a peaceful protest by ethnic Uighurs against a local crackdown on religious groups turned bloody on 5 February 1997 when the police began beating demonstrators. According to official sources, two days of rioting left 10 people dead; but unofficial accounts estimate the fatalities to number 100. Ili Prefecture's governor, Abubsbai Rahim, refused to comment on the diverse reports, but noted with respect to the rioting that the real underlying motives for the protest were economic in nature: "The ethnic issues are core issues tied to the economy. If the economy is going good [*sic*] then everything else is easier to do. If living conditions are improving, then there is less splittism and everyone is happier."[15]

Revolutionary and class-based repertoires

In contrast to the relatively scant information on reform-era collective actions in the western and south-western regions, reports of tax protests in heavily agricultural central China and the north-eastern industrial rust belt have been far more numerous and richly detailed. Workers and farmers in these interior provinces, once the cradle of the centrally planned economy, rely upon their collective resources – both institutional and ideological – to resist the revenue-collection efforts of reform-era officials. Led primarily by farmers protesting tax burdens and the imposition of so-called "miscellaneous fees and levies," such incidents have often included large numbers of participants from many villages or several counties at a time. For example, in May 1997, more than 500,000 peasants assembled, staged parades and demonstrations, and filed petitions in over 50 counties in Hunan, Hubei, Anhui, and Jiangxi provinces. In Hunan and Jiangxi, some of these protests turned into widespread rioting as well. These actions came on the heels of prior mobilizations that involved actions in no fewer than nine provinces, a surge of rural collective action that the April issue of the Hong Kong journal *Dong Xiang* reported as "peasant rebellion." Originally beginning in the winter of 1996 and the spring of 1997, a series of riots, disturbances, and rebellions erupted in 36 mostly rural counties in nine provinces and autonomous regions that involved the participation of nearly 380,000 peasants in demonstrations, parades, and episodes of public petitioning.[16] A few months later, between 28 July and 5 August, nearly 200,000 peasants from 87 townships in 15 counties in Jiangxi Province initiated and participated in a rally and demonstration against "issuing IOU notes," "forcing down grain prices," "increasing taxes and levies," "raising the price of chemical fertilizer," and "setting up government work teams."[17] In early August 1993, another Hong Kong journal reported that some 2,000 peasants from seven villages in southern Anhui rallied against the government's use of IOUs with banners that read "All power to the peasants!" and "Down with the new landlords of the 1990s!"[18]

These large-scale protests in central China have most often been triggered by local government tax-collection policies and practices, including the imposition of the so-called "three arbitraries" (*san luan*) – arbitrary collection of fees (*luan shoufei*), arbitrary levying of fines (*luan fakuan*), and arbitrary apportionments (*luan tanpai*) – that have mushroomed in rural areas during the reform period. In the early 1990s, such strategies were exacerbated by the widespread circulation of "green" and "white" slips in the countryside, IOUs issued to farmers by government officials in charge of mandatory grain procurement in lieu of expected payments.[19] These dire economic pressures on rural taxpayers were further met by steep increases in the prices of agricultural equipment, fertilizer, and other necessities utilized by Chinese farmers, with the prices of some items rising 200 per cent from one year to the next.[20]

In many cases, the requisitioned funds have apparently been used to enrich the local government and its representatives at taxpayer expense. The widespread rioting in Jiangxi and Hubei described above was purportedly caused in large part by misuse of public monies: the local governments in question were believed to have channeled either taxpayer funds or provincial subsidies earmarked for the purchase of agricultural products to build new office buildings for Party and government personnel. Reform-era protesters frequently allege that local government monies have been used to construct lavish villas, purchase imported luxury sedans, and fund sight-seeing tours abroad for ranking cadres. Not surprisingly, targets of recent collective violence include new local government buildings, the vehicles of government personnel, and sometimes the new roads or highways for which levies are often sought.[21]

As the pressures on rural taxpayers have risen in recent years, they have increasingly turned to contentious repertoires of protest that invoke the revolutionary language and class-based oppositions of the Mao era. Large-scale protests have sometimes erupted when rural residents perceive links between the imposition of new fees and levies that have no apparent legal basis and the conspicuous consumption of local cadres. In such cases, extravagant banqueting, foreign tours, and the use of new cars by state officials arouse suspicions that public funds are being misused, and class-based language is used to express the widening socio-economic gap between local bureaucrats and taxpayers. In 1997, such pressures purportedly erupted in widespread rioting involving 100,000 peasants in Jiangxi Province in which rural taxpayers managed to seize the county Party and government buildings, attacked supply and marketing cooperatives, and confiscated chemical fertilizer, cement, and other items in demand by farmers, all the while chanting "Down with the urban bureaucratic exploiting class and share the wealth of new local overlords in the countryside!" and "Establish peasants' own political power!" In Xiushui, Wan'an, and Xingguo counties, protesting taxpayers encircled provincial- and prefectural-level leading Party and government cadres.[22]

In many cases, anti-tax protests in the countryside have given rise to the formation of grass-roots social organizations. In late October 1995, the residents of some townships and villages along the Hubei–Sichuan border established "committees of peasant autonomy," or "peasant autonomous governments," and denounced some local Party cadres as "local tyrants," "swindlers," and "persons driving peasants to rebellion." Rural residents in the Yunxiang and Yunxi regions organized armed self-defense units, broke into state warehouses, and confiscated the fertilizer and farm tools stored there.[23] Between 1990 and 1991, several hundred farmers in Jiangsu's Shuyang County pledged to take "united action" against tax-collection cadres, engaging in a string of three incidents of tax resistance. The Shuyang farmers brandished farm and household implements to repel the tax collectors, destroyed loudspeakers and other tools used by the tax collectors, and paraded in the streets, chanting slogans.[24] A series of such riots occurred in August 2000, when Jiangxi taxpayers in Yuandu, Baitu, Duantang, and Xiaotang protested a steep increase in local land taxes imposed by administrators in nearby Fengcheng Municipality. Following the encirclement of the Yuandu village government offices by over 2,000 angry taxpayers, the unrest spilled over into neighboring villages and townships, ultimately concluding in a series of pitched battles involving some 20,000 rural residents against armed police throughout the area. The Yuandu and Duantang local government offices were destroyed, as were the private homes of ten local Party cadres serving in the Yuandu Party branch.[25]

New enterprises and new social forces in industrializing China

Lü and Bernstein argue that tax burdens – and therefore anti-tax protests – have been less frequent in the more successfully industrialized eastern provinces during the reform era, due to the success in those areas of "township and village enterprises" (TVEs). While it is certainly true that successful TVEs may provide a lucrative source of revenue for local governments, such enterprises in both rural and urban areas were subjected to levels of taxation that one 1989 World Bank report referred to as state-sponsored "fiscal predation."[26] Another report, funded by the central government, found that over 900 types of administrative fees were being collected from private enterprises, on top of which local administrations were also collecting more than 1,000 types of fees and funds. Fees, taxes, and other charges imposed by local cadres on rural enterprises, aside from the rent charged on collective land and property used by such enterprises, include utility fees (for water and electricity); commercial management fees; mandatory life insurance for all employees; security fees (*zhian fei*); sanitation fees; quarantine fees (*jianyi fei*); planned production fees (*jisheng fei*); temporary resident population fees; quality control fees; and flood-prevention fees.[27] In Zhejiang, fully one-third of local government revenues for the 1989 fiscal year was traced back to the fees and surcharges levied against rural enterprises.[28]

Given such financial pressures, it is perhaps not surprising to find small business owners and their employees engaging in collective acts of resistance, evasion, and even violence against tax collectors. This is especially the case among the so-called *getihu*, the employees of which are often members of the same household. A 1998 case in Hunan's Loudi Municipality is typical: a married couple with two storefronts on the same street both selling bamboo goods were ordered to pay two installments of a fixed commercial tax, one for each storefront. The *getihu* owner refused, claiming that the "fixed tax is too high," and that "the two family stores are really one"; after receiving several tax notices, the owner publicly announced that "whoever dares to collect this tax, I will hack to death." After a year, the local tax-collection department attempted to confiscate 300 units of bamboo merchandise in lieu of the overdue taxes. The owner and his wife, along with the store employees, brandished cleavers, shovels, and other tools to fend off the tax collectors. The incident drew a crowd of over 100 sympathetic onlookers who "made it impossible for [the tax collectors] to carry out their duty." Fortunately, the incident concluded without bloodshed.[29]

Other episodes of *getihu* tax resistance, however, have ended in violence. In a similar case in 1995, one Hunan Shuangyuan Village *getihu* was visited by a team of tax collectors and public security officers to collect arrears for the previous two years. Liu Xiazhong, who opened a fiberglass thread-spinning factory in the village in 1993, had never registered the business with either the local commerce or taxation departments, and had purportedly ignored previous notices regarding his arrears. Liu initially pleaded that his production was down and his profits were very low due to local power outages, and so was unable to pay; however, as the Public Security Bureau (PSB) officers on the scene began to arrest Liu, more than ten of his relatives and over 100 employees of the factory surrounded the tax collectors. Liu's grandfather, mother, father, and wife beat the local assistant police commissioner unconscious; some of the factory employees prepared to drag the commissioner's body into the reservoir to drown him, but he came to before this plan could be carried out. In the melee that ensued, one of the tax cadres was seriously hurt, and another police official had his uniform ripped to shreds by the angry crowd.[30]

Similarly, in November 1998, a group of armed inspectors arrived at the Dengjiashan coal mine in Hunan's Jinjiang Township to carry out a major tax investigation. They were met by the mine's two owners, Kuang Xueying and Kuang Yueying, who refused to hand over the account books. The five-member team concluded that the best course of action would be to confiscate the account books and return to the tax offices to conduct the investigation; but upon seeing the legal confiscation order, Kuang Xueying responded: "My family has very strong behind-the-scenes backers in the city and county governments. Public security, procurators, judges, I don't fear any of them: why should I fear your tax-collection department? I could make one phone call and have you all killed!" Thereupon the group was surrounded by a hooting mob of mineworkers. "Sensing danger," the tax collectors prepared to retreat, but Kuang Xueying let loose "a vile stream of invective," followed by a volley of stones, and the amassed mineworkers began hurling mining timbers at the retreating tax cadres, three of whom were savagely beaten when they fell behind their colleagues. Kuang Xueying and Kuang Yueying were arrested soon thereafter, but filed police reports against the tax collectors, claiming that the agents had stolen a purse full of cash and an expensive ring from the sisters during their visit to the mine.[31]

As enterprises and commercial organizations proliferate and diversify, cases of non-family based tax resistance among private businesses have also multiplied in recent years, and local tax collectors are increasingly under attack not merely by business owners, but by employees as well. This appears to be particularly true of tax resistance among collective enterprises now struggling to maintain profitability. For example, in November 1997, six Henan Xinxiang County National Tax Office agents were brutally attacked and badly beaten by employees of the Xinye Collective Company when they visited the enterprise to conduct an on-site audit investigation. The manager of the company's accounting department argued that some of the account books were not "open" for inspection without the prior permission of the local Party branch. However, when the auditors spied the books they required on a nearby table, they decided to simply seize the material on their way out the door. The auditors were chased down by well over a dozen enterprise employees in three cars, who pulled them out of their vehicle and beat them senseless alongside the local highway.[32] In one 1999 case, a small township in Jilin's Lishu County, in which the majority of households were engaged in auto salvaging operations, became the target of an investigation into overdue taxes. When a coterie of county government, tax, and armed police cadres entered the village, one male worker mounted a heap of salvaged scrap metal and repeatedly yelled out "The devils have entered the village!" ("*Guizi jincunle!*") to warn the residents. As the cadres stepped out of the van and prepared their documents, the villagers gathered behind a small hillock, brandishing sickles, spades, and wooden rods, and launched an attack on the party that was quickly quelled by the armed police before any harm was sustained. Months later, with the investigation and charges against them nearing conclusion, one of the residents in arrears commented to a local reporter:

> With respect to tax collection, there is nothing we can say without letting down the government that propped us up for so many years. However, with respect to the tax quotas fixed by the tax department, we have two dissenting opinions. First, it is unreasonable: in one year we can hardly struggle enough to make this little bit of money, and in one instant, they take it away, [the tax] is too high; and the second is that it's unfair: in our village of a few dozen households altogether in a year we fork over 6,000 *yuan*, but other villages pay only 900 *yuan*. If we all handed over the same amount, then we wouldn't have to speak our minds like this.[33]

The dual pinch of reform-era policies designed to decrease central government subsidies and rising tax pressures is not restricted to commercial enterprises. Non-profit, non-production units (*shiye danwei*) also face mounting pressure to open "profit-making windows" and become economically self-sufficient. In many cases, this has resulted in the closure of numerous artistic and cultural institutions, with, for example, one county library closing its reading room to convert it into a lucrative karaoke bar and hotpot restaurant.[34] As a result, collective tax evasion and resistance strategies are increasingly being seen in organizations as varied as entertainment groups, schools, hospitals, and libraries. In one widely reported case in May 1999, a dozen tax-office cadres were dispatched to Huaixiang High School in Hunan's Huarong County. The purpose of their visit was to remediate a case of tax arrears involving the school's snack bar concession. When the owner of the concession informed the party that he was unable to pay his overdue taxes that day, the tax cadres decided to confiscate two of his refrigerated soda cases in lieu of payment. As the team began removing the cases, the concession owner began to scream that he was being robbed by thieves. His cries of distress brought well over 100 of the school's teachers and administrative personnel to the scene, one of whom also placed an emergency call to the local police station to report a crime in progress. Shortly thereafter, the principal arrived at the scene, but not only did he not assist the cadres, he also ordered that the school gates be locked and instructed the teachers to guard all entrances and exits to school grounds. He then announced to all assembled that "taxation does not come to school," and that the school's income could not be appropriated so as "to squeeze taxes out of people." The stand-off between the teachers and the tax collectors was punctuated by intermittent outbreaks of violence instigated by the head of the physical education department. After more than four hours, the local police ordered that the gates of the school be opened and the tax collectors released, one of whom suffered a sprained wrist after repeated tussles with the physical education teacher.[35]

Caught in the cross-hairs: grass-roots cadres and tax resistance

Grass-roots cadres in the countryside and low-level enterprise management personnel are increasingly caught between the cross-cutting demands of local tax departments and the financial health of their enterprises or communities. In rural communities, tax officials attempting to fulfill central directives can quickly run afoul of local authorities and taxpayers alike. In one recent case in Sichuan's restive Pengzhou Municipality, a team of local tax and party cadres set up a hearing one morning to explain the rationale underlying national tax collection. In concluding the presentation, one authority pointed out that the various services provided by the municipality to farmer households, including water, electricity, and property mainte-nance, required funds from the residents. A resident in the audience replied: "Our tax rate is high enough. We demand lower taxes." The official explained that tax rates were set by national authorities, and could not be changed according to local demands. Another resident stood up and announced that "tax laws are instituted by people, and can be revised – the national constitution can be revised too!" Such comments apparently inspired a rising tide of resistance among the meeting participants, including the local leadership: while eating lunch after the hearing, one local village cadre purportedly began yelling to the other assembled residents, "this after-noon come with me to the government to create a disturbance. If you come, I'll give you ten *yuan* apiece; if you don't, I'll fine you ten *yuan* each!" That afternoon, over 100 village residents gathered around the township govern-ment offices, armed with sickles and poles, demanding to have a "discussion" with local authorities regarding the collection of agricultural taxes. In the melee that ensued, four township and tax cadres were beaten.[36]

Some local cadres have also mobilized pre-emptive protests to protect local businesses from demands arising from tax arrears. In one 1995 case in Hunan, Bajiao Township Party Secretary Cao Jingping refused to sign a court order directing a local mine to pay off an overdue loan, in part because the court order mandated that the local government would have to pay off the loan if the mine was unable to come up with the funds. When the municipal Party committee headquarters in nearby Laiyang City attempted to pressure the Bajiao branch into compliance by arresting four residents accused of harassing the mine's supervisors, Party Secretary Cao organized 150 people to participate in a riot in Laiyang which involved pelting the municipal riot police with a volley of stones, and smashing the windows of the municipal courthouse where the Bajiao residents had been sentenced.[37] In one early 1986 report from Hangzhou's Xihu Township, a team of ten tax cadres tried to investigate the merchants of the Fayunlong tea market who had collectively determined not to pay their taxes. The village chief in Lingyin, where the tea market is located, led a mass attack on the tax collectors, which left two of the cadres wounded at the scene.[38]

The organizational impetus behind many reform-era tax resistance cases appears to come from these low-level cadres, who not only suggest strategies for action, but also shape the discursive strategies of the protests as well. According to one classified 1995 report from the State Council (*Guowuyuan*) cited by a Hong Kong periodical, most of the incidents in a wave of rural violence that swept across Shanxi, Henan, and Hunan in recent years were instigated and led by grass-roots cadres, many of them actually organized by township and village Party and state officials. Under their leadership, rural taxpayers, sometimes with the help of "underground organizations," have mobilized under the following slogans: "Return land and property to the peasants!"; "End the exploitation and oppression of the peasant class!"; "Long live the peasant communist party!"; and "Long live the unity of the peasant class!" With the assistance of local cadres, in some rural villages and townships, disgruntled residents have formed "peasant unification committees," "peasant revolution committees," and "peasant rebellion command committees" (*nongmin zaofan zhihui weiyuanhui*).[39] According to an internal reference (*neibu cankao*) report cited by another Hong Kong source, some of the rural Party and government cadres at the township and village levels actively encouraged peasants to demonstrate and personally participated in processions, offering slogans like "Down with the urban bureaucratic exploiting class and divide up the wealth of new local overlords in the countryside!", and "Establish peasants' own political power!" In late July 1995, rural cadres in Lianhua, Tianhe, and other nearby counties organized rallies to "accuse the new despots and landlords of their crimes."[40] In late October 1995, two village cadres in Hunan's Linwu led over 5,000 rural taxpayers to demand the establishment of a "voluntary self-salvation government" (*zidong zijiu zhengfu*) and held a large-scale demonstration. Following the detention of the cadres who led the protest by local public security forces, crowds set fire to public security vehicles, clashed with PSB employees, and confiscated PSB weapons, all the while demanding the release of the detained cadres.[41]

In some cases, the fracturing of political authority at the lower levels appears to be due less to a willingness to lead local taxpayers in defiant protest against government policies than to a lack of clarity over conflicting government mandates. In one 1993 case in Henan's Luyi County, the supervisory municipal postal department, in order to "raise capital to quickly develop the post and communications work unit [*danwei*]," mandated new surcharges on all items mailed through the post office. The Luyi County Party and state cadres concluded that these new charges violated the spirit of the central government's mandate against imposing new miscellaneous fees and taxes, and refused to comply with the directive. Instead, they declared 1993 a "year of no apportionments" (*wu tanpai de nian*) for the residents of Luyi County.[42] In another case in Henan's Ziling Township, over 100 *getihu* established the "Ziling Township, Ziling Village branch *geti* labor alliance" (*Ziling geti laodong xiehui, Zilingcun fenhui*) with the support and cooperation of local officials, who purportedly viewed the alliance as an effective mechanism to secure the timely payment of local taxes. The organization's charter carefully mandated the rights and responsibilities of its members, but stated that "when paying fees and taxes, alliance members must observe the upper limit and heed the common schedule *set by the alliance*." When news of the organization reached the provincial Party committee, the provincial Party secretary dispatched a team to investigate. The organization was promptly declared to be "an illegal popular organization openly boycotting the national tax system," and the organizers were disciplined.[43] In a similar example that took place in Hebei's Dingxing County, a group of Goushen villagers organized a local "poultry farming alliance" under the leadership of one elderly resident, but allegedly with the complicity of local authorities. One November morning, over thirty members of the alliance piled onto seven tractors and surrounded the local tax office in an apparent attempt to intimidate the tax cadres therein. Quick-witted local tax officials set up speakers' platforms at the village's main intersection and proposed an exploratory meeting at which they explained the nationally mandated tax policies to the alliance members. In the meantime, higher-level authorities were notified, and the alliance was declared an "illegal organization" and disbanded with little further resistance.[44] Similar attempts to establish taxpayers' organizations for the purpose of educating taxpayers about national regulations concerning tax and fee collection have met with stiff resistance from local officials who see their activities – " 'demonstrations and parades' and 'hanging big character posters' – as undermining public order."[45]

Another source of Maoist revolutionary language and class-based anti-tax mobilization is retired state and Party cadres. The National Veterans Cadres Bureau noted in 1997 that in the period from 1995 to 1997, retired cadres participated in no fewer than 335 events of collective protest, and submitted at least 125,300 individual petitions protesting state policies. In such cases, it appears that the impetus to collective action among retired cadres stems from withheld pension monies and declining benefits; however, these skilled mass mobilizers trained during the Maoist era have in recent years used their skills to launch repeated attacks on state offices at all levels of government. In one 1997 case, 250 retired cadres from Hebei descended upon the provincial Party committee, denouncing them as "a newly restored Guomindang [Nationalist Party]" and "a newly created bureaucratic class," knocking office supplies from desktops and hurling the cellular phone of one hapless official out of an open window. Six weeks earlier, a group of veteran cadres in Ningxia organized an "anti-corruption and embezzlement team" that used iron bars to destroy seven luxury cars owned by provincial Party cadres. When eleven people were later taken to the hospital as a result of the confrontation, over 500 retired officials rushed the hospital in a gesture of support for the organization. In another incident, the refusal of one Qiqihaer hospital to treat a veteran cadre who was critically ill resulted in a massive demonstration and riot outside the facility, during which armed police fired on the crowd.[46] In 1995, when the Shenyang Municipal government attempted to cut retirement benefits to veteran cadres there, the retirees mobilized a series of highly public protests and had the decision reversed. However, once mobilized, the veteran cadres turned their attention to other cases as well, helping local residents to pen petitions and demonstrate against what they perceived to be the real root of the problem: government corruption. Shenyang authorities apparently found their collective efforts threatening enough to sentence at least one 69-year-old retiree to a labor reform camp for three years.[47]

Conclusion: fissures in the reform-era state

The mounting economic pressures of reform-era policies have been met in recent years by a stunning array of collective efforts to circumvent state demands on individual household and enterprise incomes in the form of taxes, fees, and the seizure of assets. Incidents of collective tax resistance, including strategies of avoidance and evasion, have evolved in response to specific local policies, but have done so in ways that reflect the organizational and discursive legacies of the Mao era. Local protest repertoires reflect the communal resources – both institutional and ideological – within the communities and workplaces from which they arise. In non-Han majority communities in which the central state has continued to subsidize local development projects designed to raise the overall standard of living, tax resistance repertoires appear to be linked to larger issues of ethnic autonomy and separatist goals. In largely agricultural central China, where the financial success of TVEs has yet to make a significant impact, and in the north-eastern rust belt, farmers and workers have borne the brunt of the state's extractive demands, while at the same time also falling prey to steep declines in formerly subsidized social benefits. Strategies of resistance and avoidance in these areas tend to show the hallmarks of the Maoist legacy, preserved, for the most part, in the everyday living and working conditions of the residents. Anti-tax protests involving farmers and workers in these areas frequently invoke the rhetorical repertoires and class-based oppositional language popularized by the Maoist regime, and hearken back to the revolutionary heritage of the "peasant-workers state." In areas marked by greater heterogeneity of socio-economic forms, largely in the capital-rich coastal provinces, collective protests less commonly invoke revolutionary images, but do establish new, or co-opt pre-existing, organizations to press claims against local authorities. In some cases, as economic pressures mount, entire work units have joined together to protect their collective economic interests against the incursions of tax collectors and government authorities; in other cases, new economic forces created by reform-era policies (for example, the *getihu*) have sought to create their own collective alliances, perhaps modeled in part on the institutions propagated by the central government during the Maoist era.

Caught in between this conflagration of state and social forces are low-level local cadres and enterprise managers, many of whom have lent their organizational skills to shape resistance movements against tax-collection efforts. Reports of their participation in such events are clearly a source of alarm for central authorities,[48] who have rightly interpreted this fragmentation of local state power as a challenge to the coherence and efficacy of central state power. Wang Lixiong recently argued that the widening income gap and rising levels of social frustration that have arisen in the transition to market socialism have set the stage for an economic crisis of endemic proportions. According to Wang, the determination of the Deng-era political leadership to end the Party's reliance on Maoist mass mobilization techniques meant the closing off of key channels for voicing popular dissatisfaction, while at the same time creating economic hardship for large numbers of ordinary people. Yet it is precisely the worker- and peasant-heroes raised to believe in the glory of revolt that the current system has marginalized. The net effect of these policies, according to Wang, could easily translate into a Maoist-inspired "economic Cultural Revolution" led by a worker-peasant alliance against the Party and the state.[49]

Bernstein and Lü have suggested that such anxieties motivated central authorities to implement a series of measures designed to empower rural taxpayers by providing them with alternative channels for expression and participation, including village elections. However, they found that even with such measures in place, the key factor in reducing taxpayer burden remained the availability of financial resources at the disposal of local governments.[50] Poorer villages, even those free to elect their local leaders, could still prove fertile ground for the seeds of the type of "economic Cultural Revolution" forecast by Wang Lixiong. Yet, if such an economic crisis is indeed brewing, the critical link may in fact lie at the very lowest tier of the state itself, where the claims to legitimacy of the current regime are tested on a less ideological, and far more quotidian, level. Insofar as market-based reforms have entailed the withdrawal of state subsidies for enterprises and local governments, and therefore created increasing pressures on low-level cadres to develop new sources of revenue, the lowest tier of the Party and state bureaucracy is now finding itself at the mercy of both an increasingly restive population from below and an increasingly remote extractive state from above. As the reforms continue to deepen and take root, it is this tier of the government that may prove instrumental in deciding the fate of both state and social forces alike.

Notes

1 Li Zijing, "A half million peasants rebel in four provinces," *Zheng Ming* (*Contention*) 238 (August 1997): 19–21.

2 Yue Shan, "Five hundred thousand peasants violently rebel in Jiangxi and Hubei," *Zheng Ming* (*Contention*) 239 (September 1997): 21–23.

3 Lu Nong, "Unstable rural situation worsens," *Zheng Ming* (*Contention*) 202 (August 1994): 28–29; also cited by Elizabeth J. Perry in "To rebel is justified: Cultural Revolution influence on contemporary Chinese protest," unpublished paper delivered at Yale University, 1995.

4 Willy Wo-Lap Lam, "Book says peasants are 'active volcano,'" *South China Morning Post*, 10 August 1996, p. 15.

5 Taipei Central News Agency report, 17 August 2000, Foreign Broadcast Information Service (hereafter FBIS), FBIS-CHI-2000-0817.

6 See, in particular, Elizabeth J. Perry, *Rebels and Revolutionaries in North China, 1845–1945* (Stanford: Stanford University Press, 1980), as well as her more recent *Challenging the Mandate of Heaven: Social Protest and State Power in China* (New York: M.E. Sharpe, 2002), and Lucien Bianco, *Peasants Without the Party: Grass-roots movements in Twentieth-century China* (New York: M.E. Sharpe, 2001). Elizabeth J. Perry also discusses Maoist legacies in contemporary protest in her "To rebel is justified." For a valuable comparison of Qing-era and contemporary tax protest, see R. Bin Wong, "Confucian agendas for material and ideological control in modern China," in Theodore Hueters, R. Bin Wong, and Pauline Yu (eds) *Culture and State in Chinese History: Conventions, Accommodations, and Critiques* (Stanford: Stanford University Press, 1997).

7 See, for example, the extensive discussion of individual-level tax resistance in Ch. 5 of Lü Xiaobo and Thomas Bernstein, *Taxation without Representation in Contemporary Rural China* (forthcoming).

8 Charles Tilly, "Speaking your mind without elections, surveys or social movements," *Public Opinion Quarterly* 47(4) (Winter 1983): 462–463.

9 These three trends overlap significantly with the three sub-national environments described (in reverse order) by Thomas Bernstein and Lü Xiaobo in *Taxation Without Representation in Contemporary Rural China*: "industrial rural China, mainly concentrated in the eastern provinces, agricultural China, primarily in the central belt of provinces, and subsistence China, located mostly in the western and southwestern provinces." However, my specific focus on episodes of tax protest suggests a closer correlation between protest repertoires and the particular tax- and fee-collection strategies of local officials than with the broad regions identified by Bernstein and Lü. This correlation is no doubt due in large part to the uneven distribution of institutional forms (both old and new) across the reform-era landscape.

10 Nicholas Becquelin, "Xinjiang in the nineties," *China Journal*, July 2000, pp. 67–68. On the relatively lenient implementation of pre-reform-era economic policies in the south-west, see Guo Xiaolin, "Rice ears and cattle tails: a comparative study of rural economy and society in Yunnan, southwest China," unpublished Ph.D. thesis, University of British Columbia, Vancouver, 1996.

11 Becquelin, "Xinjiang in the nineties," p. 70.

12 Solomon M. Karmel, "Ethnic tension and the struggle for order: China's policies in Tibet," *Pacific Affairs* 68(4) (Winter 1995).

13 Karmel, "Ethnic tension and the struggle for order."

14 Luo Bing and Li Zijing, "The 'enemy's situation' is discovered in seventeen provinces and thirty-three cities," *Zheng Ming* (*Contention*) 200 (June 1994): 10.

15 FBIS, 27 August 2000.

16 Li Zijing, "A half million peasants rebel in four provinces."

17 Yue Shan, "Five hundred thousand peasants violently rebel in Jiangxi and Hubei."

18 FBIS, 10 September 1993; cited by Perry, "To rebel is justified."

19 The problem of mismanaged grain procurement funds peaked in 1992, when the central government distributed IOU notices (called "white slips" by the farmers who received them) in lieu of cash payment for grain. Farmers who received such slips were nonetheless required to pay their taxes, and pay cash for their farming equipment, fertilizers, and pesticides. See Andrew Wedeman, "Stealing from the farmers: institutional corruption and the IOU crisis," *China Quarterly* 152 (December 1997): 802–838.

20 Shi Yong, "An investigation into the rural village burden problem in China," *Jing bao (The Mirror)*, February 1997, p. 33.

21 Yue Shan, "Five hundred thousand peasants violently rebel in Jiangxi and Hubei." Such perceptions are no doubt fueled in part by press reports of the lavish cadre lifestyles, but also by more subtle and subversive reports on the predatory work styles of local tax collectors, such as one that appeared recently in *Hunan shuiwubao (Hunan Taxation News)* that described an incident in which two brothers transporting three pigs one evening were stopped by a tax cadre standing – oddly enough, given the hour – outside the doorway of the brand new tax office building. When they did not heed his demand that they pay a 10 *yuan* livestock slaughtering fee (for the three live pigs), the tax cadre and a colleague hopped on a motorbike and chased the brothers for some distance before catching up with them on a "newly constructed highway" outside the village. Unfortunately, the incident resulted in a violent altercation in which the tax cadre was injured, and the two brothers fled the scene. The manner in which the incident was reported in *Hunan shuiwubao* raises – at least implicitly – questions about the modus operandi of local tax collectors in Hunan's Liuxilong village. See "Resistance over paying a ten *yuan* tax – two tax cadres seriously hurt," *Hunan shuiwubao*, No. 387, 12 May 1998, p. 1.

22 Li Zijing, "A half million peasants rebel in four provinces."

23 Yue Shan, "Five hundred thousand peasants violently rebel in Jiangxi and Hubei."

24 FBIS, 28 October 1991; also cited by Perry, "To rebel is justified."

25 FBIS, 29 August 2000.

26 World Bank, "China – rural industry report," No. 8047-CHA, 1989, cited by Anthony J. Ody, *Rural Enterprise Development in China, 1986–90* (Washington DC: World Bank, 1992), p. 16.

27 Li Peichun, "Fees squeezing out taxes, a weighty topic of conversation," *Jiangsu fazhi bao (Jiangsu Legal Daily)*, 12 August 1997, p. 3.

28 "While regulating rectification, deal correctly with rural enterprises," *Nongcun gongzuo tongxun (Rural Village Work Bulletin)* No. 4, 1989, p. 5.

29 "Senseless tax resistance – a certain Mao and his wife are both taken into custody," *Hunan shuiwubao (Hunan Taxation News)*, No. 404, 10 July 1998, p. 3.

30 "The tremendous gall of ruffians resisting taxes," *Hunan shuiwu bao (Hunan Taxation News)*, No. 214, 31 May 1995, p. 1.

31 "Team of armed inspectors encounter an incident of violent tax resistance," *Hunan shuiwubao (Hunan Taxation News)*, No. 441, 17 November 1998, p. 1.

32 Yan Chunlin, "A vicious and violent case of resistance to tax collection and investigation occurs in Henan," *Zhongguo shuiwu bao (China Taxation News)*, 8 December 1997, p. 1.

33 "How it was that the Jingyou village peasants walked into court," *Zhongguo fazhibao (China Legal News)*, 13 May 1999, p. 1.

34 Lin Hong, "Cultural non-profit enterprises calling out for capital inputs," *Zhongguo shuiwubao (China Taxation News)*, 17 February 1997, p. 1.

35 Bi Yun and Yang Ligang, "Resisting taxes together initiates a lawsuit," *Hunan Shuiwu bao* (*Hunan Taxation News*), No. 548, 30 November 1999, p. 1.

36 Cui Songchun, "The storm over agricultural taxes," *Zhongguo shuiwubao, fazhi zhoukan* (*China Taxation News, Legal Supplement*), No. 46, 2 December 1999, p. 6.

37 FBIS, 24 March 1995; cited by Perry, "To rebel is justified."

38 FBIS, 30 May 1986.

39 Guan Jie, "The situation of large-scale unrest in Shanxi, Henan and Hunan," *Dong Xiang* (*Trend*) 124 (December 1995): 19.

40 Li Zijing, "A half million peasants rebel in four provinces."

41 Guan Jie, "The situation of large-scale unrest in Shanxi, Henan and Hunan."

42 Ma Laiying, "No apportionments in Luyi County," *Jingji shuiwu bao* (*Economic and Taxation News*), 26 September 1993, p. 1.

43 Yan Chunlin, "A behind-the-scenes look at an illegal 'tax resistance organization,'" *Zhongguo shuiwubao* (*China Taxation News*), 27 November 1998, p. 1.

44 Su Chou, "The vicissitudes of a 'tax-resisting village,'" *Zhongguo shuiwu bao* (*China Taxation News*), 25 December 2000, p. 1.

45 Li Xuehui and Wu Ziwu, "Is propagandizing 'burden reduction' still an illegal assembly?" *Hunan shuiwu bao* (*Hunan Taxation News*), 27 February 1998, p. 3.

46 "Veteran cadres are taking to the streets," *China Focus* (Asia Intelligence Wire, 1 March 1998).

47 Elisabeth Rosenthal, "Old-line communists at odds with Party in China," *New York Times*, 2 July 2000. I am grateful to Elizabeth Remick for bringing this source to my attention.

48 Guan Jie, "The situation of large-scale unrest in Shanxi, Henan and Hunan."

49 Wang Lixiong, "Could an 'economic Cultural Revolution' appear?" *Dangdai Zhongguo* (*Contemporary China*) 3 (2000).

50 See Thomas Bernstein and Lü Xiaobo, "Taxation without representation: peasants, the central and the local states in reform China," *China Quarterly* 163 (September 2000): 742–763.

5 Neither transgressive nor contained

Boundary-spanning contention in China[1]

Kevin J. O'Brien

In studies of popular politics, a split exists. Some scholars focus on rather tame and predictable forms of political participation, while others become interested mainly when political action spills out onto the streets. For one set of analysts, attention centers on questions related to voting, lobbying, party activity, and various forms of contacting: how, in other words, the popular classes make use of approved channels of influence. For the other group, how people act up when the authorities are unresponsive and frustration mounts with existing opportunities for expression is of greater concern. Although there are exceptions, inasmuch as some researchers examine a range of institutionalized and uninstitutionalized acts,[2] the two literatures tend to travel along separate tracks: one spotlighting forms of inclusion and legal political behavior, the other, consequences of exclusion and actions that are closer to resistance than to conventional participation.

In their book *Dynamics of Contention*, McAdam, Tarrow, and Tilly take a dim view of such divisions. They argue that many episodes of contention belong in a single definitional universe and that there is no need for wholly distinct literatures on topics such as revolution, social movements, elections, and interest-group politics. For them, so long as popular action entails episodic collective interaction between the makers of claims and their objects, and a government is involved, similar causal processes and mechanisms are at work.[3]

McAdam *et al.* of course recognize differences between what they call transgressive and contained contention. These include whether all the parties are established political actors and whether innovative means of collective action are employed. But then, in short order, they return to the many links between the two sorts of politics, not least because it is difficult to locate where the boundary between transgressive and contained contention lies, and because the two kinds of politics "interact incessantly."[4]

After this bout of provocative claims-making, "for the sake of clarity" in an analysis that already extends from the Mau Mau rebellion to the Montgomery bus boycott, McAdam *et al.* choose to concentrate on episodes involving transgressive contention. Although they note that many transgressive episodes grow out of contained contention, little more is heard about the relationship between transgressive acts and acts not on the transgressive side of the line.[5] The reader is left with a stirring charge to breach the boundary between institutionalized and uninstitutionalized politics and to investigate connections that have often been obscured, neglected, or misunderstood,[6] but with only a sketchy road map for doing so. The relationship of these two forms of contention merits further study. This chapter suggests one way to explore it: namely by focusing on acts that sit near the fuzzy boundary between official, prescribed politics and politics by other means.

Unpacking the state

To examine the links between transgressive and contained contention by looking at episodes that are neither fish nor fowl, some preliminary ground-clearing is called for. For a start, much can be gained by joining the growing corps of scholars who eschew the dichotomies of state-versus-society and us-against-them.[7] In particular, it is important to think about "them" much more systematically by disaggregating the state. This prescription, uncontroversial though it sounds, goes well beyond the familiar injunction to avoid reifying state power. More fundamentally, it involves recognizing that every regime has its own institutional structure and that agents of a government are not always principled agents. Particularly in far-flung, many-layered bureaucracies, officials at different places in the hierarchy often have diverging interests and are subject to different constraints and incentive structures. From the vantage point of people contemplating collective action, this means that states often present attractive, multidimensional targets.[8] Whether a regime is a democracy or anything short of the most repressive dictatorship, the segmentation built into a complex system of power cannot help but produce cracks in the façade of unity. And these openings appear not only because there are regime defectors, minority elites, or elites out of power who seize the role of tribune of the people.[9] At a more basic level, a multi-layered structure itself disorganizes the powerful and can provide opportunities for the disgruntled "to make authorities work for them rather than against them."[10]

Given that states are commonly too fragmented to be treated as unified actors, it is wise to dispense with otherwise useful shorthands like "subordinates" and "superordinates"[11] (at least temporarily) and to remember that collective action often involves more than two parties. Contentious politics is not always a story of neatly divided antagonists, with representatives of the state on one side and members of the popular classes on the other. Sometimes it depends on the discontented locating and exploiting divisions within the government. In these circumstances, setting up subordinates (in society) in opposition to superordinates (in the state) can obscure how people actually go about warding off appropriation and political control. Thinking in terms of challengers pitted against the state can be especially misleading in situations where the aggrieved employ government commitments, legitimating myths, and established values to persuade receptive elites to support their claims. When concerned officials, for instance, champion popular demands to execute laws and policies that have been ignored elsewhere in the hierarchy, unexpected alliances often emerge and simple us-versus-them distinctions break down. On these occasions, contentious politics operates partly within (yet in tension with) official, prescribed politics; it depends on a degree of accommodation with the structure of domination, the deft use of prevailing cultural conventions, and an affirmation – sometimes sincere, sometimes strategic – of existing channels of inclusion.

Once a state is dissected and unpacked into institutionally situated officials with their own interests and preferences, it becomes difficult to classify certain claims-making performances as prescribed, tolerated, or forbidden. The boundary-spanning contention highlighted here is not prescribed or forbidden, but tolerated (even encouraged) by some officials, and not tolerated by others. It is a form of contention that goes on partly within the state and it hinges on the participation of state actors. It exists in a middle ground that is neither clearly transgressive nor clearly contained.

While examples of boundary-spanning contention can be found throughout history and around the globe, it is hardly surprising that contemporary China has been a particularly hospitable incubator. Unlike in many industrialized democracies, where legitimating formulas are well established and the bounds of the permissible tend to be more settled, what is institutionalized and what is not is often hotly contested in newer regimes and in those in the midst of rapid change. In contemporary China, contention over what is contentious reaches deep into the state. Lower and mid-level officials, for instance, are often remarkably hazy about precisely what forms of political expression are acceptable.[12] Much can be learned about the elusive, fluid boundary between unconventional and institutionalized behavior in China (and elsewhere) by exploring popular actions that are arguably legal, permissible in some eyes but not in others.

Boundary-spanning contention in China

In China of late, popular contention has been on the rise. As the chapters by Shue, Weston, Thornton, and Wright in the present volume (Chapters 1, 3, 4, and 6 respectively) demonstrate, since the reforms began in 1978 there have been recurring waves of rural riots, violent urban demonstrations, organized religious protests, and occasional demands to end one-party rule.[13] At the same time, there has been even more contention that (a) operates near the boundary of authorized channels, (b) employs the rhetoric and commitments of the powerful to curb political or economic power, and (c) hinges on locating and exploiting divisions within officialdom. These latter episodes, though not as dramatic as efforts to attack the system of power head-on, occur daily and typically involve the innovative use of laws, policies, and other officially promoted values to defy "disloyal" political elites.[14] They are a form of partly sanctioned, partly institutionalized contention that uses influential advocates and recognized principles to apply pressure on those in power who have failed to live up to some professed ideal or who have not implemented some beneficial measure. The people who engage in this type of contention characteristically combine lawful tactics (e.g. collective petitions, seeking audiences with power-holders) with disruptive but not quite unlawful action (e.g. silently parading with lit candles in broad daylight to symbolize the "dark rule" of local leaders).[15] They always behave in accord with prevailing statutes (or at least not clearly in violation of them), and they use the regimes' own policies and legitimating myths to justify their actions. Their "rightful resistance"[16] is difficult to dismiss because it is based on ethical claims legitimated by official ideologies and because the demands proffered often involve nothing more than the scrupulous enforcement of existing commitments.

Boundary-spanning contention of this sort can appear in many settings; it happens, however, that I am most familiar with it from research on China's countryside. The next section presents evidence from interviews with Chinese grass-roots cadres and officials at higher levels, as well as accounts drawn from government publications and field reports by Chinese researchers. The episodes considered center on clashes involving cadre accountability. Although many other disputes inspire boundary-spanning contention, including conflicts over unapproved fees, contract fulfillment, financial disclosure, land use, and cadre corruption, deploying official discourses and collective action to combat election chicanery has become particularly prominent since the late 1980s. One 1997 study, for instance, reported that two-fifths of the occasions on which rural residents contacted officials concerned elections; another survey showed that as many as 5 per cent of villagers nationwide had lodged complaints over election fraud.[17] Even in regions where grass-roots elections have taken hold most deeply, boundary-spanning contention is climbing. Following the 1997 elections in Fujian, a provincial pacesetter, villagers sent more than 4,000 letters of complaint about voting irregularities to government offices, ten times the number received after the 1993 balloting.[18] And this upward trend shows no signs of abating, most likely owing to a November 1998 revision of the Organic Law of Villagers' Committees (1987), which expressly authorized villagers to combat dishonest elections ("threats, bribes, forged ballots and other improper methods") by lodging reports (*jubao*) with local governments, people's congresses, and other departments (e.g. civil affairs offices). In 1998, when the Organic Law only enjoyed trial status, 17 per cent of all appeals and letters to the Ministry of Civil Affairs concerned elections; in the first half of 1999, this proportion rose to 31 per cent.[19]

In addition to their significance as everyday events, the following incidents were chosen mainly for their ability to shed light on the dynamics of boundary-spanning contention. For Sinologists who are surprised by the proportion of happy endings, it should be noted that uncharacteristically successful cases were selected not because they are typical, but because they are relatively complete and illustrate how an episode of boundary-spanning contention plays out in ideal circumstances.

Pressing for accountability

How to monitor local officials and curb cadre misconduct has become an urgent problem in rural China.[20] One way that the center has attempted to rein in arbitrary and self-serving grass-roots leaders has been by rolling out an ambitious program of village elections. By making the lowest-level cadres more accountable to the people they rule, Party leaders in Beijing hope to shore up the regime, boost their legitimacy, and prevent wayward officials from driving the people to rebellion (*guanbi min fan*).[21] But opposition to free and fair elections has, at times, been fierce. Many mid-level leaders feel that empowering villagers in any way will jeopardize public order and make it more difficult for cadres to complete the many tasks (e.g. birth control, revenue collection) that they are assigned. Some of these officials have acted on their misgivings by blocking or rigging elections, either openly or through subterfuge. Among other tactics, opponents of village self-government have refused to convene elections, monopolized nominations, held snap elections, required that Party members vote for favored candidates, banned unapproved candidates from making campaign speeches, annulled results when the "wrong" candidates won, forced elected cadres from office, and insisted that voting be conducted by a show of hands.[22]

But when local functionaries frustrate efforts to make grass-roots leaders more accountable, some villagers are far from quiescent; instead, they confront power-holders who dare to usurp their right to vote. They stand up for their right to rid themselves of corrupt, unfair, and incompetent cadres by engaging in various forms of protest, a number of which fall into the category of boundary-spanning contention.

In one poor Hebei village, for example, a group of farmers lodged a series of complaints requesting the dismissal of several village cadres. After the township rejected their appeals, the villagers stationed several rotating teams of petitioners in the township to press their case. One day, one of the villagers happened upon a copy of the Organic Law of Villagers' Committees lying on a desk in a township office. He read it, immediately realized its import, and showed it to his fellow complainants. After they studied the Law, they decided to "lodge complaints against the township government for violating the Organic Law by not holding democratic elections." The villagers then devised a plan to increase their leverage and to ensure that their demands would not be brushed aside. They divided themselves into three groups, two of which went to the township government compound and the county civil affairs bureau, while a third composed of village Party members traveled to the county organization department.

Facing a crowd of indignant complainants demanding implementation of a law that had been casually ignored throughout the region, the township government caved in and agreed to hold elections. In the subsequent balloting, the man who had originally discovered the Organic Law was elected director of his villagers' committee.[23]

And it is not just open contempt for the law that leads to boundary-spanning contention. Villagers also act up to protest procedural irregularities that Chinese peasants are often thought to care little about.[24] Organized election boycotts, for instance, have occurred over relatively technical infractions of the Organic Law.[25] In one case, when residents of a Hunan village found themselves facing an illegal snap election, two young men organized their neighbors to plaster seventy-four posters around the village that called on voters to reject hand-picked candidates and to "oppose dictatorial elections." The village's walls were literally covered with oversized characters, all written on white paper (a color that is associated with death and ill-fortune). This threatening display drew the attention of county officials, who investigated the charges and ruled that the balloting should be rescheduled and nominations should be reopened. Although the two organizers were ultimately ordered to cover the posters with replacements written on red paper, their actions delayed an election that violated the Organic Law and other relevant local regulations.[26]

In yet another incident that turned on whether proper procedures were observed, a group of villagers from Hubei Province stopped an election in which nominations were not handled according to law. At the exact moment when the ballots were being distributed, one villager leapt to the platform where the election committee was presiding, grabbed a microphone, and shouted: "Xiong Dachao is a corrupt cadre. Don't vote for him!" Several of his confederates immediately stood up and started shouting words of encouragement, seconding his charges. To further dramatize their dissent, the protesters then tore up their own ballots as well as those of other villagers who were milling about waiting to vote. The balloting was briefly halted, but later resumed. Though township officials at first sought to prosecute the ringleaders for "impeding an election," and the county procurator accepted the case, the Provincial People's Congress, after consultation with the National People's Congress, decided it was "not appropriate to regard their actions as illegal" since the original nominating process had been conducted improperly. The results of the interrupted election were declared null and void and the balloting was rescheduled.[27]

To enhance their bargaining position, resourceful villagers sometimes "skip levels" (*yueji*) in the hope that higher-ranking officials will take their charges more seriously.[28] When defying township leaders who fix elections, villagers often lodge complaints at the county or even higher levels. In one such incident, after a township in Liaoning prohibited several candidates from running for office and did not allow secret balloting, over a dozen villagers traveled at their own expense to the county town, then the provincial capital, and finally Beijing to file complaints. They knew the Organic Law by heart and recited it at every stop along the way while petitioning for a new election.[29]

Some persistent complainants do manage to locate "benefactors" (*enren*) who are willing to give them a sympathetic hearing and investigate their claims. In a notable 1996 case, a group of Hebei villagers went to Beijing to protest a fraudulent vote. When the Ministry of Civil Affairs official responsible for implementing self-government heard that they were in his outer office, he shouted "Bravo!" (*tai haole*). Within a matter of days, the official had dispatched two staff members to look into the charges. In the course of a long investigation that ended with the election being annulled, Ministry officials appeared three times on China's most popular television show devoted to investigative journalism. Immediately following the evening news, in front of a national audience, they openly supported the complainants and warned other local leaders to draw the appropriate lessons.[30]

Sometimes, aggrieved villagers go so far as to contact the media themselves. In a 1998 incident in Shaanxi, some incumbent cadres called an election without forewarning, dispatched roving ballot boxes to collect votes, and hovered over the boxes while prodding villagers to make a choice in their presence. When several voters challenged these strong-arm tactics, the village leadership halted the balloting and announced that all the incumbents had been returned to office. Over 160 villagers then signed a petition protesting this misconduct and sent it to various news outlets. A reporter from *China Business Daily* received their appeal, traveled to the village, and published an account of what happened. Five days after his story appeared, agents of the local public security bureau broke into the home of one of the petitioners, brandishing knives and guns, and cursed the man for contacting the media and the government. After *China Business Daily* published a second story chronicling the latest turn of events, the city government conducted an investigation and its bureau of civil affairs declared the original election invalid.[31]

Boundary-spanning contention can also undermine elected cadres who have engaged in objectionable behavior while in office. In 1996, a township Party secretary outside Harbin barred voters from proposing their own nominees for village director and pre-selected a single candidate. A villager who was familiar with the Organic Law put up a poster denouncing this phony "election" and demanded a new round of balloting. The poster-writer was promptly detained by the township for twenty-four days and nothing came of his complaint.

Over the next few years, the village director enriched himself through land sales that he hid from the public. In late 1998, the lucrative land sales were exposed, under pressure from villagers who cited self-government regulations that promised financial transparency. This also happened to be around the time that the revised Organic Law was enacted. When some villagers saw a TV program trumpeting the Law and learned of their right to recall elected cadres, they contacted the original poster-writer, went to the township, and purchased two copies of the Law and other relevant regulations. The villagers then held ten sessions to review the documents and decided to launch a recall drive. In short order, they gathered 746 signatures (more than twice as many as required) calling for the director's removal. After their petition was rebuffed by the village leadership, they proceeded to the township once again and found a new Party secretary, who sent a team of investigators to verify the signatures and organize a recall meeting. In the ensuing vote, the village director was recalled by nearly a 2:1 margin. Officials from the National People's Congress and the Party secretary of Harbin praised the outcome as evidence of increasing democratic awareness among the rural populace and effective use of the Organic Law to supervise grass-roots cadres and protect villagers' rights.[32]

These episodes suggest that boundary-spanning contention is not merely an example of clever but futile claims-making, of using the language of power deftly but to no avail. Some rural residents have learned how to locate allies within officialdom and to make power-holders prisoners of their own rhetoric by advancing their claims in a particularly effective way – a way that interrogates official claims to legitimacy and questions whether the government can make good on its pledge to rule in the interest of the people. By casting their demands in the language of loyal intentions, these villagers are able to ferret out supporters in various bureaucracies who have a stake in seeing their appeals addressed and in upholding the policies they invoke. They skillfully "venue shop"[33] and take advantage of the limited institutionalization of Chinese politics to press their claims wherever they have the best chance of success. In one place, it might be a civil affairs bureau; in another, it might be a People's Congress complaints office; in a third, it could be a procurator or a discipline inspection committee. These censorious villagers have recognized that state power is both fragmented and divided against itself, and they know that if they search diligently, they can often locate pressure points where elite unity crumbles.

Of course, the odds are stacked against even the most adept complainants, since their targets can almost always point to conflicting norms that make them appear unreasonable and justify obstructing an election.[34] Rules-conscious villagers, for example, may cite clauses in the Organic Law or speak of their right to "reflect problems and expose bad cadres," but their targets can often trump them by invoking "democratic centralism" and the need to maintain "stability above all."[35] Many grassroots leaders are proficient at casting all forms of contention in the ominous light of "rebellion against village cadres," and at countering legal tactics and smothering collective action by winning support from officials at higher levels. The specter of populist cadres who ignore state quotas and other assignments can often be used to de-legitimize even well-grounded boundary-spanning contention. Township and county leaders, in particular, tend to be receptive to pleas that it is impossible to conduct democratic elections while ensuring that village cadres attend to birth control, grain procurement, and revenue collection.[36] Some provincial leaders, too, have been slow to throw their support behind village-level balloting. Elections in large parts of Guangdong, Yunnan, Guangxi, and Hainan, for example, only began in the late 1990s, a decade or more after the original Organic Law was passed.[37]

The media is also unlikely to intervene, as Liu Yawei notes, unless villagers "try something dramatic or when the tension spirals out of control and attracts the attention of provincial or national leaders."[38] Some investigative journalists have been detained, or even roughed up, for championing popular complaints.[39] When all is said and done, mid-level officials often dispatch the police to suppress protesters who disrupt a rigged election or lodge a complaint, or they convince judicial authorities to conduct perfunctory investigations or spend years taking testimony. In today's China, a strong legal case and the use of compelling normative language is merely the ante that gives villagers a seat at the table; in the "politics of signification,"[40] cadres have many more resources than ordinary people to see to it that their understanding of legitimate ways to protest and control protest come out on top.

Still, boundary-spanning claims do not always fall on deaf ears, because some members of the elite believe that offering redress may help placate the discontented and reduce the likelihood of popular unrest while improving policy implementation and cadre oversight. When resourceful villagers cite patently illegal and "undemocratic behavior" or obvious evasion of central intent, their boundary-spanning contention can generate considerable pressure on rural cadres and make it difficult to justify suppressing them as if they were run-of-the-mill protesters.

Pay-offs

What is to be gained by working at the boundary between official, prescribed politics and politics by other means? What can be learned by looking at actions that are simultaneously normative and non-normative – in the eyes of some regime members rule-conforming, and in the eyes of others rule-violating?[41]

First, exploring such acts promises a better understanding of the dynamics of contention because it gets away from the static quality of much research on contentious politics[42] and draws attention to state and movement trajectories. Perhaps most important in this regard, investigating incidents near the contained/transgressive border can offer insights into how the very meaning of contained and transgressive shifts over time. Zeroing in on acts that share some of the advantages of transgression (surprise, uncertainty, and novelty) and some of the benefits of contained contention (accepted, familiar, and easy to employ) can cast light on those critical moments in the evolution of a repertoire of contention when what is forbidden one year, is tolerated the next, and is readily accepted the third. Such research may also help clarify why these junctures are sometimes sudden tipping points and sometimes the product of gradual, incremental experimentation.[43]

Moreover, while it is true that at the extreme, contained contention tends to reproduce a regime,[44] closer to the blurry boundary ambiguity itself can be an engine of change. In systems where the rules themselves are contested and precious few forms of contained contention exist,[45] scrutinizing boundary-spanning acts can provide leverage over questions such as how challengers become polity members and how claims for inclusion come to fruition or not.

In China, for example, people who have become polity members in the eyes of central officials (at least as regards village elections) are fighting to be seen as something more than subjects or challengers by local officials.[46] Certain community members have come to appreciate that unrealized state commitments can be a source of inclusion, and they are busy exploiting the gap between rights promised and rights delivered. To protect themselves and improve their odds of success, these exacting critics tender impeccably reasonable demands and profess little more than a desire to make the system live up to what it is supposed to be. Their claims are usually mindful and circumscribed, local and parochial rather than national and autonomous.[47] The regime has promised them a place in the polity and they expect the system to do justice to its billing.

When villagers come to view state commitments as a source of entitlement, they are acting like citizens before they are citizens.[48] Certain citizenship practices, in other words, are preceding the appearance of citizenship as a secure, universally recognized status. In fact, practice may be creating status, as local struggles perched on the contained/transgressive border start in enclaves of tolerance, spread where conditions are auspicious, and possibly evolve into inclusion in the broader polity. This renegotiating the terms of citizenship, this finding out what the rules of the game are by probing the limits of the permissible, becomes particularly visible when boundary-spanning acts are examined. For this border is a key frontier where concessions are extracted and regime legitimacy is negotiated; and it is here that it becomes clear whether still-contested claims for inclusion are making headway and whether citizenship is becoming less piecemeal and incomplete.

Paying attention to boundary-spanning acts can also help close the gap between the many analysts who study the dynamics of contention and the growing number who are concerned with the consequences of contention (e.g. Does it lead to policy, procedural, cultural, or personal change?). Determining how popular action reshapes a polity's institutional structure has been a characteristic weakness of the social movement literature.[49] Comparatively little is also known about the biographical consequences of contention; in particular, how it affects the values of activists.[50] Many scholars agree that future research should pay more attention to the outcomes of contentious politics.[51] Perhaps by examining boundary-spanning acts a better understanding of the impact of interesting hybrids, like "mildly transgressive" and "proactive contained" contention, could be obtained.

In China, villagers may be struggling to persuade their antagonists that they are engaged in entirely sanctioned behavior, but that is mainly evidence of their tactical good sense.[52] In reality, they are editing and creatively reworking official rights talk, while trying to transcend the strict constructionism that usually constrains them.[53] Consider the practice of dressing up genuinely transgressive claims in contained clothes. This occurs, for example, when community members use vague clauses in the Party constitution or the People's Congress election law to demand election of village Party secretaries – even though the clauses do not strictly apply.[54] Or consider villagers who use out-dated norms, such as the Cultural Revolution-era "four freedoms," to justify putting up big-character posters that expose cadre corruption.[55] Or even more relevant for transforming contested claims into enforceable rights, consider what might be called lateral claims-making. When villagers cite people's congresses as a model for turning village representative assemblies into policy-making bodies,[56] or claim that the principle of mass line democracy entitles them to vote in Party primaries,[57] or quote ambiguous clauses stipulating direct election to demand open nominating procedures, their contention is both loyal and proactive. It is both a way to further their interests within existing limits and a way to assert new rights and pry open clogged channels of participation. It is, in Vivienne Shue's words elsewhere in this volume, an artful means of using the "grammar" embedded in a system of domination to utter statements that raise doubts about that system.

And should these villagers succeed in mounting an effective "critique within the hegemony," their actions can alter outcomes.[58] Illegal levies are sometimes rescinded, rigged elections are overturned, and predatory cadres are reined in. Piercing the hegemony at its weakest point can change life in the village, and it can also affect activists themselves. Protesters undergo a learning experience, become aware of new possibilities, and often end up more inclined to take part in other popular action.[59] (The recent emergence of "peasant leaders"[60] testifies to a heightened willingness to take risks, a sense of empowerment, and other spillover effects on the life course and political consciousness of activists.) Larger-scale structural consequences may be possible, too. How mildly transgressive or contained proactive episodes pan out nationwide may have a bearing on where Chinese politics is heading, at least if there is a bottom-up element to the ongoing transition and not everything originates in the Party leadership compound in Beijing. Among other issues, how boundary-spanning episodes are resolved may offer clues to how pliable the political system is and how likely it is to crumble when faced with future challenges. Analysts would then be better placed to address questions such as: do reform and the "quiet revolution" still have some way to go, or is the motive force for change becoming conventional forms of transgressive contention, like riots, illegal protests, and ultimately revolution?

Studying boundary-spanning acts also promises to bring the relationship between states and popular contention into clearer focus. Commentators have frequently complained that students of social movements overlook the inner workings of government.[61] McAdam *et al.* go so far as to claim that the literature as a whole has been "movement-centered": that "to the extent that it enters at all, the state generally acts as a *diabolus ex machina*, producing opportunities, awaiting mobilization, landing heavily on some actors and facilitating others, but not participating directly in contention."[62] Examining boundary-spanning acts addresses this objection by placing the state at center stage and redirecting our gaze away from those contesting power to their relationships with the powerful. By observing how people work the territory between different levels of government, for example, we can learn why certain sectors of the government regard claims to citizenship to be legitimate while others deny them. Exploring boundary-spanning contention requires unpacking the state, and at the same time it unpacks the state further.

In China, what emerges is a multi-layered state that has grand aspirations but formidable principal–agent problems.[63] The center has structured the implementation environment deftly for some policies, but for others current methods of cadre monitoring are not working as well as they might. China's street-level bureaucrats have many "resources for resistance,"[64] and on some policies (e.g. increased accountability), they see little reason to accede to central plans. Viewing the state from this perspective, it is easy to understand why, when I was traveling with a Ministry bureau chief in a Fujian village, and we encountered a village cadre who refused to release some election results, the Ministry official said: "I'm your bosses' bosses' bosses' boss, so turn over the results." And the lowly village leader responded: "Because you're my bosses' bosses' bosses' boss, go to hell [*jian gui qu ba*]."[65]

Peering under the hood of the state also clarifies why officials at the center might promote village elections and tolerate boundary-spanning contention. In particular, it suggests that empowering ordinary people to serve as watchdogs can make sense even to dyed-in-the-wool Leninists who, like trucking companies that print 800 (freephone) numbers on the backs of their rigs, need on-the-ground sources of information if they are to uncover and stop misconduct by their local agents. Seen in this light, initiating elections and allowing (or even encouraging) boundary-spanning contention are first and foremost solutions to a principal–agent problem: they have less to do with liberal ideology or any newfound affection for pluralism and more to do with preventing local officials from thwarting measures designed to rein them in. Why the center has risked drawing ordinary people into policy implementation becomes evident only when we steer clear of a society-centered approach to contention and spend time discovering why officials at different points in the hierarchy act as they do.

To do this, an "anthropology of the state"[66] is needed. This means studying the state from its lowest administrative legs up to its midriff and its head; it also entails examining relations between different levels of government, and identifying a constellation of state–society interactions that occur in the regions as well as at the center. In the rural Chinese case, this approach leads us to probe various dyads – villagers and village cadres, village cadres and township cadres, township cadres and county officials, villagers and officials at higher levels – to determine why on certain issues central officials tend to be good listeners, counties are sometimes "paper tigers," and townships are predictably unsympathetic. (For, however, local cadres who lead contention aimed at higher levels, see Thornton's chapter in the present volume.) Like many other states, the Chinese state is less a monolith than a hodgepodge of disparate actors, many of whom have conflicting interests and multiple identities. The same central state that discriminates against villagers when they wish to move to urban areas can be a benefactor that acts on their election complaints. The same village cadres who at times protect villagers from overbearing higher-ups can be an enemy when people lodge complaints about rigged elections. Disaggregating the state and inspecting dyads illuminates the cross-pressures under which officials live, and makes sense of behavior that otherwise seems inexplicable; it also enables us to see how strategies of contention adapt to the contours of a given regime as the popular classes discover which openings can be exploited and where their best opportunities lie.

This research strategy has implications beyond China. Boundary-spanning contention probably occurs everywhere, and examining it across time and territory could enhance our understanding of what is transgressive and contained, and what it means for an act to be transgressive or contained. Although homing in on this form of contention might complicate efforts to construct airtight categories, it would also provide an opportunity to triangulate between various intra-state and popular perspectives on what is contained and what is transgressive to produce a nuanced, on-the-ground view of legitimacy dynamics, as well as political and discursive opportunity structures.[67] Much might be learned by examining actions that are normative, non-normative, or something in between, depending on whose perspective one adopts. Such research could, for a start, help locate a polity across a number of dimensions: what is institutionalized and what is not, what is participation and what is resistance, who is a challenger and who is a polity member, what citizenship entails and who enjoys it.

Notes

1 This chapter benefited from the assistance of many Chinese friends and colleagues, most notably my long-term collaborator, Lianjiang Li. Elizabeth Perry, Dorothy Solinger, Peter Gries, and Mark Selden also offered helpful comments. For generous financial support, I thank the Ford Foundation, the Henry Luce Foundation, the Research and Writing Program of the John D. and

Catherine T. MacArthur Foundation, and the Research Grants Council of Hong Kong.

2 Especially inclusive approaches to political participation can be found in Diane Singerman, *Avenues of Participation* (Princeton: Princeton University Press, 1995), and Tianjian Shi, *Political Participation in Beijing* (Cambridge, MA: Harvard University Press, 1997). For analyses of contentious politics that are particularly attuned to relationships with institutionalized politics, see Leslie E. Anderson, *The Political Ecology of the Modern Peasant* (Baltimore: Johns Hopkins University Press, 1994), and Ronald Aminzade, "Between movement and party: the transformation of mid-nineteenth-century French republicanism," in J. Craig Jenkins and Bert Klandermans (eds) *The Politics of Social Protest* (Minneapolis: University of Minnesota Press, 1995).

3 Doug McAdam, Sidney Tarrow, and Charles Tilly, *Dynamics of Contention* (New York: Cambridge University Press, 2001), pp. 4–7, 305.

4 *Ibid.*, p. 7.

5 *Ibid.*, p. 341. Quoted text on p. 8.

6 *Ibid.*, pp. 4–7.

7 On disaggregating the state and recognizing the "blurred and moving boundaries between states and societies," see Joel S. Migdal, Atul Kohli, and Vivienne Shue, *State Power and Social Forces* (New York: Cambridge University Press, 1994), p. 3; see also Elizabeth J. Perry, "Trends in the study of Chinese politics: state–society relations," *China Quarterly* 139 (September 1994): 704–713.

8 Sidney Tarrow, *Power in Movement* (New York: Cambridge University Press, 1994), p. 92.

9 Sidney Tarrow, "States and opportunities: the political structuring of social movements," in Doug McAdam, John D. McCarthy, and Mayer N. Zald (eds) *Comparative Perspectives on Social Movements* (New York: Cambridge University Press, 1996), pp. 55–60.

10 Bert Klandermans, *The Social Psychology of Protest* (Oxford: Blackwell, 1997), p. 194.

11 For a classic definition of popular resistance that uses these terms, see James C. Scott, *Weapons of the Weak* (New Haven: Yale University Press, 1985), p. 290.

12 In one Hebei village I visited, a former Party secretary set up a legal advisory office to help cadres who were regularly being tripped up by villagers who knew more about the law than they did. Interviews, August 1998.

13 See David Shambaugh (ed.), *Is China Unstable?* (Armonk, NY: M.E. Sharpe, 2000); Elizabeth J. Perry and Mark Selden (eds), *Chinese Society* (London: Routledge, 2000); Kevin J. O'Brien, "Collective action in the Chinese countryside," *China Journal* 48 (July 2002): 139–154.

14 For examples, see Lianjiang Li and Kevin J. O'Brien, "Villagers and popular resistance in contemporary China," *Modern China* 22(1) (January 1996): 28–61; Thomas P. Bernstein and Xiaobo Lü, "Taxation without representation: the central and local states in reform China," *China Quarterly* 163 (September 2000): 742–763; David Zweig, "The 'externalities of development': can new political institutions manage rural conflict?" in Perry and Selden, *Chinese Society*, pp. 120–142; M. Kent Jennings, "Political participation in the Chinese countryside," *American Political Science Review* 91(2) (June 1997): 370; and Jude Howell, "Prospects for village self-governance in China," *Journal of Peasant Studies* 25(3) (April 1998): 103–105.

15 This case was a textbook example of boundary-spanning contention because the participants based their claims on two state council regulations, sought to locate allies in the county and provincial government, and engaged in arguably lawful collective action. For details, see Li Renhu and Yu Zhenhai, "*Yangzhao xiang gengming fengbo*" ("The disturbance over changing the name of Yangzhao

Township"), *Banyuetan* (*Fortnightly Chats*) (Neibuban) 6 (March 1993; internal edition): 32–36.

16 Kevin J. O'Brien, "Rightful resistance," *World Politics* 49(1) (October 1996): 31–55.

17 Jennings, "Political participation," p. 366; Tianjian Shi, "Village committee elections in China: institutionalist tactics for democracy," *World Politics* 51(3) (April 1999): 403–404. The figure of 5 per cent seems high. In 1994, the Fujian provincial bureau of civil affairs received 562 election-related complaints and deemed 24 elections invalid. International Republican Institute, "Election observation report: Fujian," Washington DC, May 1997, p. 27.

18 "The Carter Center report on Chinese elections: observation of village elections in Fujian and the conference to revise the national procedures on villager committee elections," Atlanta, GA: The Carter Center, August 2000.

19 Liu Yawei, "Consequences of villager committee elections in China," *China Perspectives* 31 (September–October 2000): 31.

20 See Kevin J. O'Brien and Lianjiang Li, "Selective policy implementation in rural China," *Comparative Politics* 31(2) (January 1999): 167–186; Dali L. Yang, *Calamity and Reform in China* (Stanford: Stanford University Press, 1996), pp. 202–212; Bernstein and Lü, "Taxation without representation"; and Xiaobo Lü, *Cadres and Corruption* (Stanford: Stanford University Press, 2000).

21 There is a large literature on why village elections were introduced and how implementation has fared. For an introduction, see Daniel Kelliher, "The Chinese debate over village self-government," *China Journal* 37 (January 1997): 63–86; Kevin J. O'Brien and Lianjiang Li, "Accommodating 'democracy' in a one-party state," *China Quarterly* 162 (June 2000): 465–489; Shi, "Village committee elections"; Jude Howell, "Prospects for village self-governance"; Xu Wang, "Mutual empowerment of state and peasantry: grassroots democracy in rural China," *World Development* 25(9) (September 1997): 1431–1442; and Robert A. Pastor and Qingshan Tan, "The meaning of China's village elections," *China Quarterly* 162 (June 2000).

22 See Ma Changshan, "*Cunmin zizhi zuzhi jianshe de shidai yiyi jiqi shijian fancha*" ("The epoch-making significance and the imperfect practice of building villagers' self-government organizations"), *Zhengzhi yu Falü* (*Politics and Law*) 2 (April 1994): 19–20; Fan Yu, "*Cunweihui xuanju weifa xu jiuzheng*" ("Law-breaking activities in village elections must be corrected"), *Gaige Neican* (*Internal Reference on Reforms*) 20 (1998): 14–15; Liu, "Consequences of villager committee elections," p. 26.

23 Bao Yonghui, "*Cunmin zizhi fuhe bu fuhe Zhongguo guoqing?*" ("Does villagers' autonomy accord with China's conditions?"), *Xiangzhen Luntan* (*Township Forum*) 6 (December 1991): 11–13. In a similar case, when township officials in Shanxi publicized the Organic Law but refused to carry out an election, farmers from two villages occupied a township office building and would not end their "sit-in" until officials agreed to conduct an honest election. Shao Xingliang, Cui Suozhi, Meng Baolin, and Sun Xueliang, "*Yi min wei tian*" ("Regarding the people as sovereign"), *Xiangzhen Luntan* (*Township Forum*) 4 (April 1994): 10–11.

24 This view is changing. On litigious, rules-conscious Chinese peasants, see Minxin Pei, "Citizens v. mandarins: administrative litigation in China," *China Quarterly* 152 (December 1997): 832–862; "Class action litigation in China," *Harvard Law Review* 111(6) (April 1998): 1523–1541; and Neil J. Diamant, "Conflict and conflict resolution in China: beyond mediation-centered approaches," *Journal of Conflict Resolution* 44(4) (August 2000): 523–546.

25 Whether Chinese with a stronger democratic orientation and a keener sense of internal efficacy are more likely to vote is a matter of some dispute. See Tianjian Shi, "Voting and nonvoting in China: voting behavior in plebiscitary

and limited-choice elections," *Journal of Politics* 61(4) (November 1999): 954–973; and Jie Chen and Yang Zhong, "Why do people vote in semicompetitive elections in China?" *Journal of Politics* 64(1) (February 2002): 178–197. What is not in dispute is that turnout rates are lower than those reported by the government.

26 Zhongguo Nongcun Cunmin Zizhi Zhidu Yanjiu Ketizu, *Study on the Election of Villagers Committees in Rural China* (Beijing: Zhongguo Shehui Chubanshe, 1994), p. 119.

27 *Ibid.*, pp. 164–165.

28 One county procurator reported that up to 60 per cent of collective complainants bypass one or more levels of government. See Fang Guomin, "*Dui dangqian nongcun jiti shangfang qingkuang de diaocha fenxi*" ("Investigation and analysis of the current situation of groups seeking audiences at higher levels"), *Xiangzhen Luntan* (*Township Forum*) 12 (December 1993): 36–37, and Kevin J. O'Brien and Lianjiang Li, "The politics of lodging complaints in rural China," *China Quarterly* 143 (September 1995): 756–783.

29 See Tian Yuan, "*Zhongguo nongcun jiceng de minzhu zhilu*" ("The pathway to grass-roots democracy in rural China"), *Xiangzhen Luntan* (*Township Forum*) 6 (June 1993): 3–4. Needless to say, local officials have a strong incentive to keep villagers uninformed. In a case where complainants demanded to see documents that county leaders claimed restricted their rights and superceded the Organic Law, a county official in Hebei "snorted with contempt and said 'you are not county officials, why would you think you have the right to read county documents.'" See *Nongmin Ribao* (*Farmer's Daily*) (Shehui Wenhua Tekan), Special Issue on Society and Culture, 25 July 1998, p. 1.

30 Interviews, Beijing, July 1994, December 1995. However, a 1997 documentary about villagers petitioning for their electoral rights was abruptly cancelled because of fears it would raise unrealistic expectations. *Far Eastern Economic Review*, 6 November 1997, pp. 56–58.

31 Liu Yawei, "Consequences of villager committee elections," pp. 30–31.

32 *Ibid.*, pp. 32–33.

33 This term was suggested by Sidney Tarrow, personal communication, October 2000.

34 On an unsuccessful complaint, see Xiaolin Guo, "Land expropriation and rural conflicts in China," *China Quarterly* 166 (June 2001): 422–439.

35 Interview with township official, 1993.

36 Liu Yawei, "Consequences of villager committee elections," pp. 25–27, 30–33; Lianjiang Li and Kevin J. O'Brien, "The struggle over village elections," in Merle Goldman and Roderick MacFarquhar (eds) *The Paradox of China's Post-Mao Reforms* (Cambridge, MA: Harvard University Press, 1999), pp. 129–144.

37 On these four provinces "dragging their feet in introducing village self-government," see Sylvia Chan, "Village self-government and civil society," in Joseph Y.S. Cheng (ed.) *China Review 1998* (Hong Kong: Chinese University of Hong Kong Press, 1998), p. 237. Guangdong did not start implementing the Organic Law provincewide until 1999. Jonathan Unger, "Power, patronage, and protest in rural China," in Tyrene White (ed.) *China Briefing 2000* (Armonk, NY: M.E. Sharpe, 2000), pp. 90–91.

38 Liu Yawei, "Consequences of villager committee elections," p. 31.

39 Zhu Kexin, "*Yiqian babai sanshiyi ci gaozhuang*" ("Lodging 1,831 complaints"), *Minzhu yu Fazhi* (*Democracy and Legal System*) 9 (September 1993): 2–6. The magazine sued the local police for illegal detention and subsequently convened a meeting of Beijing journalists and legal scholars to urge better protection of the rights of investigative reporters. See Lu Yunfei, "*Qieshi jiaqiang xinwen yulun jiandu de falü baozhang*" ("Earnestly strengthen legal protection of supervision

through news and public opinion"), *Minzhu yu Fazhi* (*Democracy and Legal System*) 9 (September 1993): 8.

40 For this term, see Donatella della Porta, "Protest, protesters, and protest policing: public discourses in Italy and Germany from the 1960s to the 1980s," in Marco Giugni, Doug McAdam, and Charles Tilly (eds) *How Social Movements Matter* (Minneapolis, MN: University of Minnesota Press, 1999), pp. 69, 92.

41 For these terms, and criticism of those who understate the differences between conventional and protest behavior, see Frances Fox Piven and Richard A. Cloward, "Normalizing collective protest," in Aldon D. Morris and Carol McClurg Mueller (eds) *Frontiers in Social Movement Theory* (New Haven: Yale University Press, 1992), pp. 301–325.

42 McAdam *et al.*, *Dynamics of Contention*, pp. 18, 43, 73.

43 On "repertoires" and gradual versus abrupt change, see Charles Tilly, "Contentious repertoires in Great Britain, 1758–1834," *Social Science History* 17(2) (Summer 1993): 253–280; and William H. Sewell, Jr., "Collective violence and collective loyalties in France: why the French Revolution made a difference," *Politics and Society* 18(4) (December 1990): 527–552. On the advantages of the two forms of contention, see McAdam *et al.*, *Dynamics of Contention*, p. 41.

44 *Ibid.*, p. 8.

45 Some examples of contained contention in China include: petitions to People's Congress deputies, lobbying by women's and environmental groups, collective visits to protest official misconduct under the 1995 Regulations on Letters and Visits, and collective lawsuits.

46 For these terms, see Charles Tilly, *From Mobilization to Revolution* (Reading, MA: Addison-Wesley, 1978), and McAdam *et al.*, *Dynamics of Contention*, p. 12.

47 Charles Tilly, *The Contentious French* (Cambridge, MA: Harvard University Press, 1986), pp. 391–393.

48 Kevin J. O'Brien, "Villagers, elections and citizenship in contemporary China," *Modern China* 27(4) (October 2001): 407–435.

49 For this charge, see Doug McAdam, "Conceptual origins, current problems, future directions," in McAdam *et al.*, *Comparative Perspectives on Social Movements*, p. 36. For exceptions, see Tarrow, *Power in Movement*; William A. Gamson, *The Strategy of Social Protest*, 2nd edn (Belmont, CA: Wadsworth, 1990); and Jenkins and Klandermans, *The Politics of Social Protest*, esp. Part IV.

50 For recent treatments, however, see Michael W. McCann, *Rights at Work* (Chicago: University of Chicago Press, 1994); Lee Ann Banaszak, *Why Movements Succeed or Fail* (Princeton: Princeton University Press, 1996); and Doug McAdam, "The biographical impact of activism," in Giugni *et al.*, *How Social Movements Matter*, pp. 119–146.

51 See, for instance, Paul Burstein, Rachel L. Einwohner, and Jocelyn A. Hollander, "The success of political movements: a bargaining perspective," in Jenkins and Klandermans, *The Politics of Social Protest*, pp. 276, 293, and Marco G. Giugni, "Was it worth the effort? The outcomes and consequences of social movements," *Annual Review of Sociology* 24(1) (1998): 373.

52 See Lucien Bianco, "The weapons of the weak: a critical review," *China Perspectives* 22 (March–April 1999): 6.

53 On "editing" public discourses and appropriating "the discursive trappings of democracy," see Howell, "Prospects for village self-governance," p. 104; see also O'Brien, "Rightful resistance."

54 Interviews, Hebei, October 1993, July 1994.

55 Interviews, Hebei, October 1993.

56 Interviews, Hebei, September–October 1993.

57 Zhou Ziqing and Zhao Zhenji, "*Liangpiaozhi: nongcun dangzuzhi jianshe de youyi changshi*" ("The two-ballot system: a useful experiment in constructing

rural Party organizations"), *Xiangzhen Luntan* (*Township Forum*) 6 (December 1992): 6–7; Lianjiang Li, "The two-ballot system in Shanxi Province: subjecting village Party secretaries to a popular vote," *China Journal* 42 (July 1999): 103–118.

58 For a perceptive discussion of how resistance can originate within a hegemonic discourse, see James C. Scott, *Domination and the Arts of Resistance* (New Haven: Yale University Press, 1990), pp. 90–107.

59 On similar effects elsewhere, see McCann, *Rights at Work*, pp. 230–232, 269, 276; Aristide R. Zolberg, "Moments of madness," *Politics and Society* 2(2) (1972): 206; and Tarrow, *Power in Movement*, pp. 164–169, 174–175.

60 Tan Wen, "*Nongmin yulun lingxiu shi yingxiong haishi diaomin?*" ("Are peasant public opinion leaders heroes or shrewd, unyielding people?"), *Zhongguo Shehui Daokan* (*Guide to Chinese Society*) 4 (2000): 6–9.

61 See Mayer N. Zald, "Looking backward to look forward: reflections on the past and future of the resource mobilization program," in Morris and Mueller, *Frontiers of Social Movement Theory*, p. 339.

62 McAdam *et al.*, *Dynamics of Contention*, p. 74.

63 O'Brien and Li, "Selective policy implementation."

64 On "resources for resistance" and the discretion implementers enjoy, see Michael Lipsky, *Street-level Bureaucracy* (New York: Russell Sage Foundation, 1980), pp. 23–25, and Richard E. Matland, "Synthesizing the implementation literature," *Journal of Public Administration Research and Theory* 5 (July 1995): 148–149.

65 Personal observation, Fujian, July 1992.

66 See Joel S. Migdal, "The state in society: an approach to struggles for domination," in Migdal *et al.*, *State Power and Social Forces*, pp. 15–18. For a discussion of the "anthropology of the state" in a Chinese context, see Neil J. Diamant, "Making love 'legible' in China: politics and society during the enforcement of civil marriage registration, 1950–1966," *Politics and Society* 29(3) (September 2001): 453, 473.

67 For these concepts and applications, see Tarrow, *Power in Movement*, Ch. 5; McAdam *et al.*, *Comparative Perspectives on Social Movements*, Part 1; and Ruud Koopmans and Paul Statham, "Ethnic and civic conceptions of nationhood and the differential success of the extreme Right in Germany and Italy," in Giugni *et al.*, *How Social Movements Matter*, p. 228.

6   Contesting state legitimacy in the 1990s

The China Democracy Party and the China Labor Bulletin

Teresa Wright

In the latter half of the 1990s, many non-Party organizations arose, presenting challenges to official Chinese Communist Party (CCP) articulations of Party-state legitimacy. Two of the most influential and interesting of these groups are the China Democracy Party (CDP) and the China Labor Bulletin (CLB). Reflecting their different foci and purposes, these two associations express notions of legitimacy that call into question the hegemony of the CCP.

The CDP is an overtly political organization; its goal is nothing less than the creation of the first true opposition political party in communist China.[1] As such, it argues that legitimate political power derives from the democratic principle of popular sovereignty, as expressed through free and fair multi-party elections. As noted in Vivienne Shue's chapter in the present volume (Chapter 1), this claim challenges the symbolic power of the CCP to define "right and wrong"; to use Shue's language, it counters official claims that the CCP alone embodies "the truth." Instead, the CDP asserts that what is "right" is simply what the populace decides via procedurally "correct" democratic methods.

The CLB, in contrast, is more concerned with economic matters, seeking the establishment of independent trade unions within China. As such, it argues that legitimate rule rests on the ability of workers to collectively ensure their livelihood, and that this requires autonomous organization on the part of the working class. This definition of legitimacy challenges official claims that the CCP is the only guarantor of both "truth" and "benevolence." In arguing that the current situation in China does not allow workers to enjoy a stable, much less prosperous, livelihood, the CLB charges that official Party-controlled unions are failing to perform their supposedly benevolent duties. Furthermore, the notion that Party-controlled unions do not protect the interests of workers undermines official claims that the CCP alone understands the "true" needs and desires of the working class. As Weston notes in his study of laid-off workers (see Chapter 3), such charges contest the core ideological claims of the CCP, undermining the Party's ability to criticize challenges such as the CLB from the Left. Similarly, such claims on the part of the CLB further validate Shue's assertion that a "system of domination's own logic of legitimation" provides the "'raw material' that is available to be used most powerfully in opposition to that system" (p. 34).

At the same time, the CDP and CLB both consciously play on the CCP's desire for international legitimacy. For example, the CDP timed its initial public announcement to coincide with the visits of important foreign leaders and bodies. Again, this represents an attempt to call the ruling regime on its claims of legitimacy, challenging it to prove that it is indeed worthy of respect and recognition by foreign states. Similarly, both the CDP and CLB appeal to international economic and political norms to justify their actions. Consequently, in responding to the actions of these two groups, CCP elites are forced to consider the possibility that repression might result in an international loss of "*face.*"

The CDP and CLB have utilized somewhat different strategies in working toward their goals. The CDP has focused primarily on ground-level organization and communication, supplemented with electronic communication via the Internet and e-mail. The CLB, in contrast, encourages ground-level organization from its base in Hong Kong, through the dissemination of information and ideas through electronic bulletins and radio broadcasts into the mainland. As such, both groups illustrate how the communications revolution is affecting current debates over legitimation in China. At the same time, it is important to note that both groups couch their goals in moderate language, and consciously emphasize the legality of their actions. Again, this illustrates the ability of oppositional groups to utilize the language and proclamations of the ruling regime to challenge its claims to legitimacy.

How successful have these two groups been in achieving their goals? At its peak, the CDP boasted local party committees in twenty-four provinces and cities, a national preparatory committee, and thousands of members. As the group grew, the authorities responded in a confused and inconsistent fashion. The CDP initially sought official recognition through local appeals to provincial authorities. Although no local CDP group received a positive response, provincial authorities did not react uniformly. Consequently, various local CDP groups probed the receptiveness of individuals in other governmental offices and at different levels. The CDP persisted in this fashion for nearly six months. At that point, however, central party elites made a clear decision to crush the group, ordering the arrest of top CDP leaders. Other major waves of arrests followed, resulting in the virtual extinction of overt CDP activities on the mainland. In marked contrast, the formal organization of the CLB is very small, and has no established base on the mainland. Instead, it compiles its bulletins, and broadcasts its call-in radio show, from its base in Hong Kong. Although most mainland callers represent aggrieved workers, many CCP representatives and officials participate in the show as well. Interestingly, the CLB has been able to operate in this way for nearly ten years virtually free from CCP interference.

Overall, the experiences of the CDP and CLB illustrate that the CCP is far from monolithic, and that autonomous groups can, and do, successfully exploit openings created by decentralized rule and conflicting official interests. Furthermore, these two groups illustrate how the availability of electronic communications methods is aiding the organizational ability of opposition groups. Yet at the same time, differences in the experiences of each group suggest the types of goals and strategies that are most likely to be successful in challenging CCP hegemony.

Political loosening in the 1990s

The CDP and CLB were among the many autonomous associations that arose amid the perceived political, economic, and social loosening of the 1990s. This relaxation began with Deng Xiaoping's famous "Southern Tour" of January–February 1992, which featured official calls for rapid economic liberalization and international opening. Not long thereafter, US representatives traveled to China to discuss China's entry into GATT, and International Olympic Committee (IOC) officials arrived to investigate whether or not they should hold the summer 2000 Olympics in Beijing. In a likely effort to bolster China's prospects on both accounts, the regime granted early parole to a number of prominent political dissidents. Next, in anticipation of the 1998 visits of US President Bill Clinton and UN High Commissioner for Human Rights Mary Robinson, in 1997 the National People's Congress amended the Criminal Law to replace political crimes of "counter-revolution" with a less political designation of offenses regarding "national security." In addition, the 15th Party Congress stressed the need to govern the country by law, and for the first time made reference to human rights. More concretely, Chinese leaders signed the UN Covenant on Economic, Social and Cultural Rights, and declared that they would sign the Covenant on Civil and Political Rights as well.

In this more relaxed atmosphere, dissidents began to renew connections and organize. At first, scattered and small-scale actions appeared. One of the first to engage in public action was Xu Wenli, a veteran activist who was imprisoned from 1982–93 for his participation in the "Democracy Wall" movement of 1978–80. In 1998, shortly following the official announcement regarding the second UN covenant, Xu applied to register a new organization, China Human Rights Watch, in Beijing.[2] Around the same time, Anhui dissidents Mao Guoliang and Wang Donghai applied for permission to register a newsletter entitled *China Human Rights News*.[3] In Hubei, former Democracy Wall activist and political prisoner Qin Yongmin petitioned to publish *Citizen Forum*.[4] In Henan, Xin Yang'an and others used the occasion of the dialogue with the United States to begin publishing *Corruption Watch*.[5] Groups named Labor Watch, Peasant Watch, Religion Watch, and Law Relief Hotline appeared as well.[6] Concurrently, these and other dissidents called for more attention to China's human rights situation in open letters and petitions to China's central government, US President Bill Clinton, and UN Commissioner Mary Robinson.[7]

The rise and fall of the China Democracy Party

The most overtly political group to form during this period was the China Democracy Party.[8] In 1997, once-imprisoned 1989 student leader Wang Youcai began to tentatively work at forming an opposition party. Feeling that the political atmosphere had sufficiently loosened, Wang first broached the idea with some friends in his hometown of Hangzhou, in Zhejiang Province. Around the same time, Wang Bingzhang, an exiled dissident residing in the United States, traveled to China with some companions with the goal of helping dissidents within China form an opposition party. Two weeks later, he was arrested and expelled.[9] Wang and his companions had nonetheless managed to contact domestic dissidents in eight provinces and cities. A number of those with whom he spoke had also been in contact with Wang Youcai.

The Hangzhou group decided to move forward with the formation of a local preparatory party branch. On the eve of Clinton's 1998 visit, group members publicly presented an "Open Declaration of the Establishment of the CDP Zhejiang Preparatory Committee," and a draft of the party constitution. The declaration was posted on the Internet. The purpose of the CDP, it read, was to "establish a constitutional democratic political system, and ... a mechanism of separation of political powers ... the CDP firmly believes that a government must be established through the conscious approval of the public [and must be] established through free, impartial, and direct democratic elections." In order to defuse any potential repressive response, the group stressed that its goals would be sought peacefully:

> the CDP maintains that any political power obtained through the use of violence and violent intimidation is illegal without exception ... The CDP proposes an orderly social transformation, opposes chaos and hitting, smashing and looting, and the use of violence ... The CDP carries out its political goals in a non-violent, peaceful and reasonable fashion, promoting civilized dialogue to solve any disputes and differences. It opposes terrorist activities.[10]

Prior to this announcement, few other dissidents knew of Wang Youcai's activities. Now, those familiar with the Internet could read the news. In addition, the preparatory committee's statement and action were publicized through a key link in Hong Kong: former 1989 activist Lu Siqing. After more than a decade of political activism and official harassment, Lu fled the mainland in 1993 and established a residence in Hong Kong. A computer technician by trade, from 1993–95 Lu collected information from mainland dissidents through e-mail and a personal paging system. In 1996, Lu began to release the news that he gathered to international news agencies. Thus, when the Zhejiang Preparatory Committee made its announcement, Lu quickly passed it on to other mainland dissidents, as well as to international news agencies.[11] This news was then posted on news agency websites and broadcast into China via Voice of America and Radio Free Asia.

Wang Youcai and his friends were eager to build a nationwide party network, yet were well aware of the potential danger involved in such action. As Wang and many others in the Zhejiang group had "blackened" political records, they faced varying degrees of official surveillance. In addition, China's hotels ask for official identification and are required to maintain registration records that are regularly checked by local officials. Members of the Zhejiang committee skirted these limitations in a number of ways. First, they simply made a public appeal for broader support and organization in their declaration, stating: "The CDP calls upon persons of the democracy movement in the various regions nationwide to enter the CDP, to prepare and establish local committees of the CDP in the various provinces and cities, to elect and appoint delegates, to take part in the National Delegates Congress and to organize a nationwide committee."[12] Secondly, a Zhejiang Preparatory Committee member with a relatively clean political record made a sixteen-day tour around the country to encourage the establishment of more preparatory party branches.[13] To avoid detection, Wu did not contact potential members by phone, and did not sleep in hotels.[14] Thirdly, by 1998 many dissidents across the country knew the pager number and e-mail address of Hong Kong-based Lu Siqing, as radio broadcasts on Radio Free Asia and Voice of America had included this information.[15] Lu had their contact information as well. Thus, through him, potential CDP members could relay messages to one another.[16] With all of these varied communication methods working in tandem, preparatory committees began to form in twenty-four cities and provinces.

Aware of the group's precarious position, Wang Youcai and the Hangzhou group consciously emphasized the *preparatory* nature of the committees, and worked hard to follow legal channels. Both China's 1982 Constitution and the UN Covenant on Civil and Political Rights guarantee the right to form political parties. Yet no legal procedures had been encoded in China to allow new political parties to establish a legal status. In this ambiguous situation, CDP leaders decided to test local official responses by having branch preparatory committees attempt to register with their local civil affairs bureaus. The Zhejiang committee tried this tactic on the same day that it published its open declaration, traveling to the Zhejiang Province Civil Affairs Bureau to apply for formal legal status.[17] The authorities accepted the application, but gave no response. Four days later, Wang Youcai was interrogated for eight hours and told to cease his political activities. The next day, Wang returned to the civil affairs bureau to explain his cause, but was told that his appeal dealt with uncharted territory, and thus could not be accepted.[18]

Soon after President Clinton departed the mainland, Wang invited CDP activists to attend a "tea party" to discuss strategy. As they assembled, the authorities made their first repressive response, breaking up the meeting and detaining Wang and fourteen others who had assembled. Most of the others were soon released, but Wang was charged with the political crime of "inciting to overthrow the state." Dissidents within China and overseas petitioned the government, calling for Wang's release. Somewhat amazingly, given that indicted suspects are seldom released from detention, Wang was allowed to return home. He remained under heavy surveillance, though.[19]

Seeing this as a positive sign, other local preparatory branches tested the waters. Interestingly, at least one was encouraged by veteran dissidents now exiled overseas. In August, a group of exiled democracy activists gathered in Boston to discuss the new party. Although they disagreed on tactics, one participant suggested that he contact some Shandong dissidents and encourage them to organize a preparatory party branch. Consequently, he got in touch with Xie Wanjun, a Shandong student leader in 1989 who had never been jailed, but who had been harassed and had encountered difficulty finding a job upon his graduation from university. Xie then contacted some friends in Shandong to begin a preparatory CDP branch.[20] On 10 September, Xie and a friend brought their petition to register the Shandong Province Preparatory Committee to the provincial Civil Affairs Bureau's Office of Social Groups. As an extra precaution, their statement emphasized that the committee "upholds Chairman Jiang Zemin's position as chief of state, and recognizes the CCP as the ruling party during the period of China's political reform."[21] The petitioners were greeted by three officials who read from what appeared to be a prepared statement that presented four conditions for registration: (1) the group must demonstrate assets worth RMB$50,000 (roughly US$6,000); (2) the group must apply for an office space bearing its name; (3) the group must submit the résumés of its chair, vice-chair, and secretary; and (4) the group must submit the names of fifty CDP members. Xie was concerned that the name list was a ploy so that authorities could more effectively repress the party, but he was heartened by the fact that the officials had not rejected the petition outright.[22] In this atmosphere, a third local preparatory committee attempted to register in Hubei Province. Its members were greeted with the same response.[23]

Shortly thereafter, a central Ministry of Civil Affairs official announced that provincial bureaus did not have the power to register political parties.[24] Taking this as a clear sign that efforts at the provincial level would be fruitless, CDP activists from a number of areas attempted to register with the central Ministry of Civil Affairs. With these efforts, though, the limits of official patience wore thin. First, activists from Jilin, Heilongjiang, and Liaoning provinces mailed an application for registration of a "Northeastern Preparatory Committee of the CDP" to the Ministry of Civil Affairs in Beijing.[25] A couple of weeks later, police in Jilin branded the group "an illegal organization," and detained one of its members.[26] Next, four veteran dissidents associated with the Beijing branch who planned a second registration attempt with the central Ministry were interrogated, threatened, or found their homes ransacked. Police clearly warned one, "We're still under the Communist Party's leadership. Setting up political parties is not permitted."[27] Members of the Shanghai branch found their petition for registration returned, and received more stern warnings during a police visit to one of the member's homes. During this exchange, the member reports being told: "You can't go on like this – we'll take you in. This is a directive from above. This is political activity, political thought."[28] On 23 September, the five committees that had been rebuffed issued a joint statement decrying their treatment. The next day, a Shandong committee leader was detained. In October, three more local groups – in Sichuan, Guizhou, and Henan – attempted to register.[29] The Sichuan group's application was refused outright, while the other two received no response.[30]

In early November, apparently without first consulting other local branch members, some CDP members in Beijing upped the stakes. First, along with four fellow Democracy Wall activists, Xu Wenli declared the establishment of the First CDP National Congress Preparatory Work Group, making the first reference to the existence of a national party-related body.[31] Secondly, three of these activists joined a fourth in Tianjin to form a CDP Beijing–Tianjin Regional Party Branch. Importantly, this new group consciously omitted the word "preparatory" from its title, thus implying that the party was already active.[32]

These moves caused confusion within the nascent party, and sparked the wholesale fury of central authorities. Beginning in December, ruling elites harshly cracked down on top CDP members, meting out long prison sentences to dozens. Meanwhile, the fragile democracy party – now lacking its founding members, and also uncertain as to its proper status – entered a new and uncertain phase. In most areas, a second level of leadership assumed control and continued party activities. Some groups followed the lead of the Beijing–Tianjin group and publicly changed their status to "branches," while others felt that this action was too brash, and chose to remain "preparatory committees."[33] The various groups also offered individual declarations and protests against the trials and imprisonment of CDP leaders. Communist Party elites were not amused. A planned meeting of the National Congress Preparatory Work Group in Wuhan was waylaid by official threats against planned participants, and a number of gatherings in Hangzhou were broken up. The only public CDP meeting to come to fruition during this period was on 28 February, when US Secretary of State Madeleine Albright was in Beijing.

In July and October 1999, two more waves of trials and lengthy sentences resulted in the imprisonment of most second-tier CDP leaders. By the end of the year, party members within China had ceased virtually all public activities. Only one – He Depu, a fellow at the Academy of Social Sciences in Beijing – continued to openly proclaim his CDP membership. In

March 2000, he was expelled from the academy and placed under strict surveillance.[34] Nonetheless, He continued to issue occasional statements. In late 2002, he was arrested; he remains in prison. Other known members of the CDP in China have curtailed their public party activities, and are watched closely as well.[35]

Meanwhile, some key CDP founders managed to escape the country, ultimately arriving in the United States. One of them, Shandong Preparatory Committee founder Xie Wanjun, escaped from surveillance and fled to Russia in June 1999. He later was invited to enter the United States.[36] Once in America, Xie quickly connected with CDP members in New York, and worked to maintain and expand the party in this highly repressive atmosphere. Xie decided to work with an already-existing support team in China that had helped public CDP members "behind the scenes," but which had never openly declared an affiliation with the party. These individuals constituted what Xie calls the "second line" of the party. As they were not under surveillance, these secret party members could communicate with overseas party members like Lu Siqing in Hong Kong or Xie in New York without much risk of official notice.[37]

Xie also worked to recruit new members in China. First, he encouraged underground members to contact like-minded relatives or friends. Secondly, Xie established a CDP website with a sign-up page, allowing new members to use an alias to register. Once registered, members are given instructions and informed about general party news.[38] To ensure security, members signing up through the Internet are not given the names of other members; each remains an "independent" party member. Even for those who are recruited in the mainland through ties of kinship or friendship, new members know only the identity of their recruiter. Each recruiter is instructed to bring aboard only two new members, thus forming a series of three-person branches whereby an individual member knows only two others.[39] In this way, the party has followed a strategy of maintaining a public existence, and even continuing to grow on the mainland, although its expansion and actions have been severely curtailed.[40]

The development of the China Labor Bulletin

The China Labor Bulletin developed in a quite different fashion. The CLB was founded in Hong Kong in 1994 by well-known labor activist Han Dongfang. For his attempt to form an independent labor federation in the spring of 1989, Han was imprisoned shortly after the 4 June crackdown. He was set free in 1992, near death with tuberculosis, after being housed in a tiny cell with twenty prisoners infected with the disease.[41] Like other seasoned dissidents, Han's prison time only hardened his resolve to continue the work for which he had been punished. Upon his release, Han quickly renewed his efforts to foster independent labor organization in the mainland. After regaining his health in the United States, in September 1993 Han returned to China. After only one night on the mainland, however, Han was picked up by security officers and sent back to Hong Kong. Han was not prepared to stay in Hong Kong, and was unsure of how to recalibrate his plan to develop autonomous labor unions on the mainland. Before long, though, he decided that his most propitious course of action would be to work toward his goal from Hong Kong.[42]

In 1994, Han founded the CLB. Its stated goal is "to promote independent trade unionism and provide information on the activities of the official All-China Federation of Trade Unions, as well as attempts by workers to organize outside it."[43] In the beginning, the group had only four members. It also had very little in the way of funds. Consequently, it began with very simple activities: the group put together monthly bulletins reporting on labor developments in the mainland, and encouraging workers to stand up for their legal rights. The CLB sent Chinese-language versions of the bulletin to China, and English-language translations to trade unions overseas. As the bulletin's reputation grew, the group was able to attract donations from various overseas trade unions, allowing it to slowly expand its activities and staff. The monthly bulletins became more detailed and frequent, eventually being published every two weeks.[44] In addition, the CLB widened its publications to include petitions to the Chinese government and lists of detained and imprisoned labor activists. It also started a "Solidarity Fund" to raise money to help those who were arrested, as well as their families.

In 1997, the CLB made the leap into radio. In March of that year, Han was interviewed by a reporter for Radio Free Asia (RFA), a private corporation set up in 1996 with US government funding to provide domestic news to persons "denied the benefits of freedom of information by their governments."[45] At the end of the interview, Han asked if the station had anyone to talk about labor issues in China. When the RFA reporter replied that it did not, Han volunteered to do so. The following evening, Han received a phone call from Washington DC inviting him to begin broadcasting as soon as possible. The next week, the show began. Initially, Han's show included official reports on labor activities, as well as his own commentary on the need and best strategies for independent organization. After about three months, Han asked the RFA if he could leave his phone number on the air to solicit calls from the mainland. The RFA agreed, and a call-in portion was added to the show. Soon, Chinese of all stripes were calling in, raising a myriad of issues. After another six months had passed, Han became convinced that the rising number of calls about worker and farmer demonstrations, as well as industrial and other accidents, warranted further investigation. So, Han and his co-workers began to conduct independent investigations of these matters, calling local authorities, victims' families, leaders of demonstrations, etc. Subsequently, Han added a third segment to his show, featuring reports on work-related accidents and demonstrations based on the information gathered by the CLB.[46]

Although the CLB currently has only seven core members, including Han, its impact is notable. Despite the paucity of reliable figures, there is every indication that the radio show's audience is extremely large. Han makes a "conservative guess" that at least 50 million people across China regularly tune in. He bases this estimate on the fact that his callers are so wide ranging – including workers in private, state-owned, and foreign-owned firms; peasants; government and Party officials; professors, teachers and university students; private enterprise bosses; and more. Calls also come in from every province. Consequently, Han believes that there is one listener for every 25–30 persons in China. Buttressing these estimates, in 2002 an official survey was conducted in eight major cities across China. It found at least 8–8.5 million listeners in these cities alone. Given that these were official figures, and imagining their replication across China's other major cities, towns, and villages, Han's estimates appear well founded.[47]

But what actual impact has the group had, aside from attracting radio listeners and readers of its bulletins? Han makes no claim that the CLB has directly caused any labor actions on the mainland. As he states, it is not the case that people "listen, then rebel."[48] At the same time, though, the group's activities do seem to be having a clear indirect impact. First, the information provided by the CLB allows workers across China to learn about their common plight, and become aware that the problems that they face are not isolated or unusual. It also gives them concrete examples of other workers taking action to better their conditions. Furthermore, the strategies propounded by the CLB – namely the use of law to support worker claims and actions, and the selection of worker representatives to speak for demonstrating workers – have been on the rise since the inception of the radio program.[49]

Similarly, official mainland media reports on work-related accidents have significantly increased since the late 1990s, when the CLB's radio show began to broadcast the findings of its investigative work. Han believes that this is connected to the CLB broadcasts, as there is a clear correlation between the stories subject to detailed CLB investigation and those later covered by official sources. For example, following the coal mine explosion of June 2002 in north-eastern China, the CLB extensively investigated the accident, dedicating a number of radio shows and many lengthy bulletins to the topic. About a month later, reporters for the official media began to conduct their own investigations and publish reports. As Han puts it, the CLB "shames the [official] media," revealing that it does not report even basic information about accidents where people are killed.[50] Indeed, since the turn of the millennium, official mainland reports on accidents have been increasingly quick, with basic facts included on the official New China News Agency website only hours after the event. Of course, there are likely a multitude of factors which account for this change, but the correlation in timing between changes in the CLB's radio show and official reporting is notable.

Given that the very goal of the CLB is anathema to the Communist Party, it is surprising that the CLB has been allowed to act unhindered, especially following the handover of Hong Kong to Chinese rule in the summer of 1997. Indeed, Han reports that the group has experienced absolutely no official harassment throughout its existence. In Spring 2003, the group was worried about the effects of the pending passage of the Subversion Bill in Hong Kong – describing it as a "sword hanging above one's head" that can be dropped at any moment.[51] Yet for the time being, the group has been able to engage in its activities without interference.

Contesting CCP legitimacy claims

In different ways, both the CDP and the CLB challenge official articulations of CCP legitimacy. Still, the CDP and the CLB couch their goals in moderate terms, and neither calls for the overthrow of the ruling regime. Similarly, both groups have made a conscious effort to work within the boundaries of the law. At the same time, though, the CLB has been able to maintain its commitment to legal and orderly activities, while the CDP became increasingly characterized by splintering and radicalization.

The CDP's counterclaim: democracy

Although CDP leaders call for gradual reform rather than a rapid transformation or revolution, the very goal of forming an opposition party represents a fundamental challenge to the Communist Party's monopoly on power. Further, the CDP directly confronts official articulations of state legitimacy by espousing the fundamentally Western, liberal notion that legitimate authority derives from the consent of the governed. As noted above, the declaration of the CDP Zhejiang Preparatory Committee maintains that "government must be established through the conscious approval of the public."[52] This liberal notion of legitimacy challenges CCP claims to embody "the truth," instead charging that there is a higher truth in the principles of popular sovereignty and civil rights that can never solely inhere in a single political party. Indeed, it is the very competition among a variety of political parties that allows the "true" voice of the people to be expressed. Moreover, CDP leaders claim that these transcendental rights are embodied in international norms to which all legitimate political organizations must adhere. The CDP argues that "the Universal Declaration of Human Rights [has] specified the inalienable rights which shall not be infringed or violated." In deference to these inalienable rights, "the CDP opposes political monopoly and economic monopoly in any form ... [and] calls for fair competition with the CCP."[53] As CDP leader Xu Wenli argues, legitimate rule rests on the protection of civil rights and the rule of law; "Everyone," he states, "including every party, must obey the Constitution."[54]

Still, the CDP frames its work in non-threatening terms, with early efforts emphasizing the members' continued loyalty to Jiang Zemin and the preparatory nature of their actions. Similarly, CDP activists have sought to attain their goals through peaceful and legal means, and have attempted to work within legal and institutionalized governmental frameworks. Indeed, their actions were largely sparked by new political developments such as China's signing of the UN Covenant on Civil and Political Rights and new pronouncements regarding the rule of law and relaxed definitions of subversion. Throughout the party's existence, CDP documents have referred to this convention, as well as to provisions within China's constitution.[55] Furthermore, especially in the early stages of the party's formation, CDP branch founders repeatedly attempted to follow official procedures for the establishment of social groups, applying for registration and petitioning for recognition.

At the same time, this general emphasis on moderation was somewhat undercut by the increasingly confrontational behavior of some CDP leaders. As early CDP actions were frustrated by government intransigence, some activists felt that it was necessary to raise the stakes and press the authorities for a response. Moreover, those who felt the need for more radical action displayed little concern with negotiating or compromising with other activists who might disagree, instead unilaterally embarking on what they perceived to be the proper next step. In this way, early efforts emphasizing the local, preparatory nature of the emerging party cells transformed into the formation of regional and national groups, as well as actual party "branches." Still, though, even these more bold actions were accompanied by moderate rhetoric; in no case did CDP members on the mainland speak publicly of the need for revolution or the overthrow of the Communist Party.

Along with demonstrating the difficulty involved in autonomous organization on the mainland, the evolution of the CDP illustrates the openings created by decentralized CCP rule. Prior to the decision of central party elites to crush the CDP, local and provincial CCP officials extemporaneously improvised responses to CDP petitions and activities. Although no local or provincial office gave CDP petitioners a favorable reply, each responded in a somewhat different fashion. For example, in Zhejiang, Guizhou, and Henan, authorities accepted CDP petitions, but then ignored them; in Shandong and Hubei, CDP petitioners were presented with a list of conditions for registration; and in Sichuan, a CDP petition was rejected outright. Concurrently, the actions of provincial and local law enforcement officers toward CDP leaders ranged from indifference to warnings, threats, interrogations, searches, and detentions. Aware of these differential responses, CDP activists probed CCP authorities at different levels and in different offices, making entreaties to various departments within different provincial civil affairs bureaus, and later the Ministry of Civil Affairs. Some also suggested appealing to the Standing Committee of the National People's Congress and the Supreme Court.[56]

The CLB: challenging CCP claims to truth and benevolence

The CLB's challenge to CCP legitimacy differs from that of the CDP. As described earlier, the goal of the CLB is to "win the right to establish independent unions and workers' organizations."[57] The CLB suggests that the safest route to achieving this aim is to reform the official All-China Federation of Trade Unions (ACFTU) such that it will be completely autonomous from the CCP.[58] Should that prove to be impossible, the CLB advises workers to form their own independent unions. These goals and activities challenge Communist Party claims to "truth"; the CLB is charging that the Communist Party and the labor unions that it controls are not "true" representatives of the working class. Indeed, CLB leaders state that the desires and interests of workers can only be expressed by unions that are truly autonomous.

In addition, arguing that factory and government officials routinely engage in exploitative and repressive policies that are extremely harmful to the economic and physical security of laborers, the CLB contests the CCP's claim to "benevolence." For example, the CLB exposes and denounces common practices like forced shareholding (*gufenhua*),[59] non-payment of pensions and unemployment stipends, contrived bankruptcies (whereby the factory manager absconds with the factory's assets),[60] and other specific forms of corruption. Furthermore, the CLB publicizes news of industrial and economic accidents that are hidden by local authorities and censored in the official media, thus "shaming" the government, and undermining its claims of benevolence. As noted earlier, this kind of criticism from the Left makes it very difficult for the CCP to uphold its reputation as the "workers' party." To make matters worse for the CCP, the CLB also criticizes the CCP from a liberal standpoint, appealing to international norms such as the right to collectively organize, bargain, and strike.

In pursuit of its goals, the CLB expresses a clear commitment to engaging in law-abiding and orderly actions. Like the CDP, along with appeals to international conventions, the CLB repeatedly refers to provisions within China's own constitution, as well as official laws and regulations. In addition to providing information to workers about collective labor actions across China, the CLB gives them knowledge of the laws and regulations that they may use when engaging in such actions. The CLB also advises disgruntled workers to use specific law-abiding tactics when faced with abuses. For example, to ensure orderly interactions with authorities, the CLB instructs workers to first choose a single leader to represent their interests. Next, the CLB suggests that the leader collect signatures on a petition to present to the local ACFTU official. If the petition is refused, the CLB advises the leader to immediately report back to the workers by holding a mass meeting inside the factory grounds (thereby avoiding the legal need to apply for a permit for a public meeting). Being careful to maintain order and efficiency, the leader should encourage open debate on the matter, followed by a vote on whether or not the group should embark on an effort to recall the union official.[61] Should such an effort fail, workers are advised to consider a public demonstration to pressure officials to attend to their grievances. Even then, however, the CLB emphasizes that public protests should remain orderly and within the boundaries of the law.

Such repeated calls for peaceful and law-abiding labor actions may help to explain why the CLB has managed to remain active for so long without any harassment or repression. As seen in the case of the CDP, a vicious cycle can begin when a group finds itself in confrontation with the authorities. Specifically, government rejection often spurs more radical actions on the part of the group, which then spark even harsher government reactions, which spark only further group radicalization. Thus, by avoiding any direct interaction with the ruling regime (in the form of applying for legal registration, for example), the CLB has avoided the sort of negative government response that might impel it to take more radical actions.

At the same time, the CLB's consistent promotion of legal and orderly worker actions may actually appeal to a ruling regime that is aware of the abysmal working conditions of its laborers, and extremely fearful that these conditions will lead to violent revolt. In other words, it may be that the CCP tolerates the CLB because the group helps to channel worker discontent into relatively orderly and lawful actions, thereby providing workers with a way to voice their dissatisfaction without threatening social stability. In addition, CLB actions may further the ability of central elites to push economic problems onto the shoulders of local political and economic leaders. As scholars such as Zhao and O'Brien have noted, local authorities are placed in the difficult position of losing *face* should they be unable to peaceably resolve conflict within their community, and are thus more likely to work out a settlement. When this is done successfully, the legitimacy of the ruling regime is strengthened.[62]

Still, perhaps the key reason that the CLB has been able to avoid repression is that it operates out of Hong Kong, and not on the mainland. When the group formed in 1994, Hong Kong remained under British rule; consequently, the CLB was entirely free from CCP control. Since the 1997 handover to Chinese rule, Communist Party leaders have been sensitive to international scrutiny of conditions in the former colony, and thus have been exceedingly careful to at least maintain the appearance of tolerance for civil liberties. Of course, in recent years, as the international eye has turned away from Hong Kong, Communist Party leaders have been slowly and covertly clamping down on independent public associations and expression. But they have been loath to engage in outright repression of such groups and activities. As discussed earlier, the selection of Hong Kong as a base was in no way a conscious strategy on the part of CLB founder Han Dongfang, but rather became the default plan when his original intentions were thwarted. Yet ironically, it appears that the CLB has been much more successful at avoiding repression, and thus propagating its message, than it likely would have been had Han been able to establish the group on the mainland.

Conclusion: goals and strategies compared

As these cases show, decentralized CCP control provides openings that may be probed by groups challenging CCP legitimacy. Furthermore, these groups demonstrate how the availability of global communications media has given opposition movements a new resilience in the face of CCP suppression. Through the end of the 1980s, the repression of opposition leaders (through their imprisonment or forced exile) effectively crushed any popular movement that the ruling regime deemed a threat. With the opening of e-mail and the Internet to the general public in the 1990s, this calculus has changed. As shown in the case of the CDP, imprisoning or exiling top movement leaders is no longer sufficient to extinguish a group's activities. Although CDP actions on the mainland have been severely curtailed since the official crackdown, exiled leaders as well as lower-level underground members on the mainland continue to communicate with each other and spread their ideas to others through e-mail and the Internet. Importantly, this also has proven true in the case of the Falun Gong. In the case of the CLB, the group's almost complete reliance on electronic communications methods is a major reason why the organization has been able to avoid CCP interference.

In addition, the experiences of the CDP and CLB demonstrate the importance of maintaining law-abiding actions. In both cases, CCP elites refrained from outright suppression as long as the group engaged in moderate activities that followed legal procedures. In the case of the CDP, it was only when the group became frustrated with official intransigence and began to employ more confrontational tactics (especially announcing the establishment of actual party branches rather than simply "preparatory committees") that the authorities' patience finally snapped. At the same time, the CLB's continuous advocacy of law-abiding actions has made the ruling party elites less likely to feel threatened by the group's existence.

Overall, the relatively successful experience of the CLB suggests strategies that may be usefully employed by other groups seeking social change. As discussed above, the utilization of electronic communications methods and the maintenance of law-abiding activities appear to enhance the longevity of opposition organizations. In addition, the CLB's ability to avoid repression is likely due to the fact that it does not have a grass-roots base on the mainland, but rather contacts its "followers" only indirectly from Hong Kong. Finally, the experience of the CLB indicates that the CCP is much more likely to tolerate popular actions that defuse the potential for more violent public protests and/or push national problems onto the shoulders of local leaders.

Yet, is the avoidance of repression the same as success? Indeed, the very elements that have allowed the CLB to persist also indicate the limited opportunity for effective, long-term opposition movements on the mainland. For, although the actions of the CLB do seem to have had an impact in mainland China, a group that is based outside the mainland and contacts its followers only through radio broadcasts and electronic communications can hardly be called a popular movement with a large grass-roots domestic membership. Furthermore, one may question whether or not the CLB's steadfast commitment to legal activities might undercut its ability to bring about real change in the face of CCP intransigence. Similarly, insofar as the CLB encourages actions that allow national leaders to force the ad hoc resolution of popular grievances through local leaders, the CLB may not address the root causes of public discontent.

Thus, the ultimate lesson of the cases of the CDP and CLB may be a depressing one. At least at present, the political atmosphere on the mainland remains extremely constricted, such that only groups that pose a limited threat to CCP hegemony (such as the CLB) may be allowed to persist. Conversely, domestic grass-roots mobilization that poses a real challenge to CCP rule (such as the CDP) likely will be crushed before it can take root and prosper.

Notes

1 Parties other than the CCP do exist in China, and even have a formal governmental role as part of the Chinese People's Political Consultative Conference. These parties, however, were established in China prior to the communist victory. There were allowed to persist in the communist era due to their alignment with the CCP during the civil war. Despite their formal governmental role, in reality their membership and influence are miniscule.
2 Xu Wenli, "Petition to establish 'China Human Rights Watch,'" printed in *China Spring* 175 (April 1998): 31.
3 Jan van der Made, *Nipped in the Bud: The Suppression of the CDP* (New York: Human Rights Watch, 2000), pp. 5–6.
4 Qin Yongmin, "Petition to publish people's periodical, *Citizen Forum*," printed in *China Spring* 175 (April 1998): 32.
5 Three issues of *Corruption Watch* were published, which are reported to have reached ten provinces. See Qin Yongmin, "Announcement #2: China's human rights situation" (2 November 1998), reprinted in *China Spring* 182 (December 1998): 70.
6 *Ibid.*, pp. 70–71.
7 Van der Made, *Nipped in the Bud*, p. 6. See, for example, Xu Wenli, "Open letter in support of China's entrance into the two UN conventions" (1 February 1998), printed in *China Spring* 174 (March 1998): 36–38.
8 For an extended analysis of the CDP, see Teresa Wright, "The China Democracy Party and the politics of protest in the 1980s–1990s," *China Quarterly* 172 (December 2002): 906–926.
9 More recently, Wang Bingzhang was sentenced to life imprisonment after reportedly being kidnapped from Vietnam.
10 "*Zhongguo Minzhudang Zhejiang Choubei Weiyuanhui Chengli Gongkai Xuanyan*" ("Open Declaration of the Establishment of the CDP Zhejiang Preparatory Committee"), 25 June 1998. Translated in Van der Made, *Nipped in the Bud*, pp. 26–27.
11 *Ibid.*
12 *Ibid.*
13 Hong Kong Alliance for Democracy website, Document 2749 (www.alliance. org.hk/records/2749.htm).

14 Human Rights Watch interview with Yao Zhenxian, 5 April 2000. Cited in Van der Made, *Nipped in the Bud*, p. 8.
15 Interview with Lu Siqing, 28 June 2000; e-mail from Hubei branch, 21 February 2001.
16 Interview with Lu Siqing, 28 June 2000.
17 Van der Made, *Nipped in the Bud*, p. 7. See also Hong Kong Alliance for Democracy website, Record 608 (www.alliance.org.hk/records/608.htm).
18 Hong Kong Alliance for Democracy website, Record 608 (www.alliance.org.hk/records/608.htm).
19 Van der Made, *Nipped in the Bud*, p. 8.
20 Interviews with Zhang Yan, 1 February 2001, and Xie Wanjun, 2 February 2001.
21 Xie Wanjun, Liu Lianjun, and Jiang Fushi, "China Democracy Party Shandong Preparatory Committee registration petition," 6 September 1998, CDP website (http://209.75.88.222/cdp/docs/shandong090698.htm).
22 Interview with Xie Wanjun, 2 February 2001. See also Van der Made, *Nipped in the Bud*, p. 8.
23 *Ibid.*, p. 9.
24 *Ibid.*
25 *Ibid.*
26 *Ibid.*, p. 10.
27 "Chinese police tell dissidents they can't form party," Associated Press, 18 September 1998. Cited in Van der Made, *Nipped in the Bud*, p. 10.
28 Human Rights Watch interview with Zhou Jianhe, 7 April 2000. Cited in Van der Made, *Nipped in the Bud*, p. 10.
29 "Henan branch application for registration," 2 October 1998 (fax to Zhuang Yan).
30 Van der Made, *Nipped in the Bud*, p. 11.
31 Xu Wenli, "China Democracy Party First National Congress Preparatory Work Group announcement," 6 November 1998 (www.freechina.net/cdp/gonggao/gg1.txt). A second statement by the National Congress lists Wu Yilong as the contact person (Van der Made, *Nipped in the Bud*, p. 13, n. 50).
32 Interview with Xie Wanjun, 2 February 2001; interview with Zhuang Yan, 1 February 2001; Van der Made, *Nipped in the Bud*, p. 12.
33 Groups in Shaanxi, Hebei, Henan, Liaoning, and Hunan all became "branches." Van der Made, *Nipped in the Bud*, p. 17.
34 *Ibid.*, p. 22.
35 Interview with Xie Wanjun, 2 February 2001.
36 Interview with Zhuang Yan, 1 February 2001; interview with Xie Wanjun, 2 February 2001; letter from Xie Wanjun to Zhuang Yan via the Russian Consulate, 9 June 1999.
37 Interview with Xie Wanjun, 2 February 2001.
38 *Ibid.*
39 *Ibid.*
40 "Letter from 25 provincial branches"; letter from Wang Xizhe.
41 Interview with Han Dongfang, 7 July 2000.
42 Interview with Han Dongfang, 13 March 2003.
43 *China Labour Bulletin* website, www.china-labour.org.hk/iso/about_us.adp, accessed 31 October 2002.
44 Interview with Han Dongfang, 13 March 2003.
45 Radio Free Asia website, www.rfa.org/front/about, accessed 14 March 2003.
46 Interview with Han Dongfang, 13 March 2003.
47 *Ibid.*
48 *Ibid.*
49 *Ibid.*

50 *Ibid.*
51 *Ibid.*
52 "*Zhongguo Minzhudang Zhejiang Choubei Weiyuanhui Chengli Gongkai Xuanyuan*" ("Open Declaration of the Establishment of the CDP Zhejiang Preparatory Committee").
53 "Urgent call to the international community," Hangzhou, 12 July 1998 (www.freechina.net/cdp; accessed 18 November 1999).
54 Interview with Xu Wenli, *Beijing Spring* 172 (January 1998): 25–26.
55 See, for example, "CDP North-eastern Three-province Preparatory Committee petition," 12 September 1998; "Petition for Social Group registration" (Jilin Preparatory Committee), 5 September 1998; and "Urgent call to the international community."
56 E-mail from Wang Xizhe, 6 August 1999.
57 *China Labour Bulletin* 41 (March–April 1998).
58 *Ibid.*
59 See, for example, *China Labour Bulletin* 37 (July–August 1997), and interview with worker at Nanchang Aluminum Factory, broadcast on RFA 10 and 24 January 1998, reprinted in Han Dongfang, *Reform, Corruption, and Livelihood* (Hong Kong: China Labour Bulletin, 1998), Ch. 10.
60 CLB interview with a laid-off worker, broadcast on RFA 1 November 1997, reprinted in Han Dongfang, *Reform, Corruption, and Livelihood*, Ch. 4.
61 *China Labour Bulletin* 41 (March–April 1998).
62 Dingxin Zhao, *The Power of Tiananmen: State–Society Relations and the 1989 Beijing Student Movement* (Chicago: University of Chicago Press, 2001); Kevin O'Brien, "Rightful resistance," *World Politics* 49(1) (1996): 31–55.

7 Dilemmas of Party adaptation

The CCP's strategies for survival[1]

Bruce J. Dickson

The Chinese Communist Party (CCP) faces a daunting dilemma: how to preserve the Leninist nature of the political system while presiding over the privatization of the economy. It seeks to maintain its monopoly on political organization – a hallmark of Leninism – even while it promotes increased competition in the market. Most observers, in contrast, believe the current conditions in China's political and economic systems are incompatible, and expect political change of some kind will be necessary. Liberal reformers in China, and many outside observers, anticipate that economic liberalization, integration in the global economy, and rising living standards will inevitably lead to China's democratization. The few remaining leftists within the CCP similarly warn that the Party's *gaige kaifang* policies ("reform and opening up") have created economic and social changes that will eventually lead to the Party's collapse. So far, the CCP has stymied these predictions of its demise. In fact, the CCP hopes that these kinds of economic changes will bolster its popularity and legitimate its claim to be China's ruling party, rather than trigger its demise.

The CCP's reform policies have nonetheless exposed severe problems. Some have been generic features of the post-1949 People's Republic; others are unique to the post-Mao era. From the early 1950s to the present, the CCP has debated the question of whom to rely upon for popular support and political and technical skills. Throughout the post-Mao period, the Party has wrestled with the need to open up the economic system without also losing political control. Labor unrest, cadre corruption, and the center's inability to monitor and enforce the local implementation of policy have also been recurrent problems, with varying degrees of intensity, long before the 21st century. In recent years, new problems caused by economic privatization, such as massive lay-offs, unpaid wages, excessive taxation and fees, and rampant corruption, have triggered recurrent and widespread protests, raising questions about the stability of the country and the CCP's ability to maintain control. But as this chapter will show, the CCP has a variety of political and practical advantages that have allowed it to survive, despite these challenges.

On the list of dilemmas facing the CCP, most people would not include ideological consistency as a cause of concern, especially in a time when pragmatism guides the Party's approach to policy, and technocracy defines its style of leadership. But the CCP, or at least some of its leaders, continues to believe that the Party requires an ideological rationale for its continued rule and for the economic, political, and organizational reforms it has undertaken. During the Maoist era, when ideological issues helped determine political survival and even personal well-being, Chinese citizens and outside observers paid careful attention to ideological debates and propaganda formulations. After economic modernization replaced class struggle as the Party's top goal, and communist goals were abandoned in all but name, interest in ideology has waned, and rightfully so. Nevertheless, the Party expends a great deal of effort to publicize ideological innovations, emphasizing how its reform agenda is consistent with its traditional goals and the collective benefit of the country, despite appearances to the contrary. In addition, attention to ideological debates still offers a window on basic conflicts within the Party. As will be shown below, while most in the Party insist that adaptation is necessary for its survival, a small but stubborn fraction insist that such changes are weakening the Party and undermining its legitimate claim to rule.

The CCP finds itself confronted with competing claims for attention. Its response varies, depending on the nature of those claims. On the one hand, the Party has been tolerant of demands that are economic in nature. It has created corporatist-style organizations for various professions, particularly industry and commerce, as a way to integrate itself with individuals and groups who contribute to the economic modernization of the country. In addition to these institutional ties, it has also pursued a co-optive strategy of recruiting new members into the Party. No longer simply a vanguard party of the "three revolutionary classes," that is peasants, workers, and soldiers, the Party now claims to represent advanced productive forces, advanced culture, and the interests of the majority of the Chinese people (the so-called "three represents"). While this effort to re-legitimate itself is often derided as window dressing at best and hypocritical at worst, it reflects the Party's efforts to adapt itself to the changed economic and social environment in China. At the same time, the CCP continues to suppress other demands for political reform and liberalization, such as the formation of new political parties and independent labor unions, that it perceives as threats to its ruling-party status. For the vast majority of Chinese, the political atmosphere is more relaxed and less obtrusive than in the Maoist period, but for political activists who resist the Party's authoritarian rule and challenge restrictions on personal and political freedom, the CCP's hand can still be quite heavy.[2]

In short, the Party's strategy of accommodation reflects what Jowitt described as the phase of "inclusion" for Leninist regimes.[3] Without surrendering its monopoly on legitimate political organization, the Party has attempted to be more inclusive, drawing in a wider range of social groups, reducing its emphasis on its traditional bases of support, and embracing the modernist paradigm while continuing to pay lip service to the goals of socialism. But it is not open to all groups and goals within Chinese society. It continues to exclude and repress those that pose a challenge to its authority and contest its claims to "truth, benevolence, and glory," as noted in Vivienne Shue's contribution to this volume (Chapter 1). As Stepan argued, a state can pursue a combination of inclusive and exclusive policies at the same time, and that certainly has been the case for the CCP.[4]

This multifaceted nature of the CCP's relationship with Chinese society merits better understanding and appreciation. While coercion and repression remain a part of the political reality in contemporary China, it is only a part of the reality. The Party has abandoned its attempt to control all aspects of economic and social life, and with the liberalization of the post-Mao era has also relinquished the tools that would allow it to do so.[5] In its place, it has adopted a more flexible approach, permissive in some respects but still repressive in others. The irony is that its efforts at adaptation may in fact be counter-productive. This is the dilemma that political parties and other organizations face when they contemplate reform: will the changes lead to rejuvenation or further decline?

This chapter begins with a discussion of the factors that have allowed the CCP to endure as the ruling party of China. It will then describe the evolution of the Party's relationship with society. It will look at changes in Party recruitment, which reflect this evolving relationship with society, and its efforts to create new institutional links with certain sectors of society. Following from this, it will then look more closely at the "three represents" slogan, both as a reflection of the Party's strategy and as a guide to its policies. Finally, it will briefly discuss areas where the Party retains its traditional approach to other sectors, excluding them from the Party and repressing their attempts at organized political activity.

Enduring features of Party rule

The CCP's continued status as the ruling party of China is based first and foremost on its monopoly on legitimate political organization. Leninist organizational principles prohibit the formation of competing organizations that could challenge the CCP, and the Party strictly enforces this prohibition. This was seen most vividly in the refusal to recognize autonomous associations for students and workers in 1989, and has been repeated in its suppression of efforts to form autonomous labor unions, the Chinese Democracy Party, and spiritual and religious groups like the Falun Gong and house churches (see the chapters by Teresa Wright (Chapter 6) and Shue (Chapter 1) in this volume). The inability to organize in opposition to the state significantly raises the cost of collective action and lowers the likelihood of a successful challenge.[6]

The Party's survival is not just a result of coercion, however. It has other assets which allow it to remain in power. First of all, its victory in the 1949 revolution still has a residual impact. Whereas ruling communist parties in Eastern Europe were mostly imposed by the Soviet Union, and therefore lacked legitimacy in the eyes of many of the people they governed, the CCP came to power via an indigenous revolution that ousted a discredited and unpopular government. The CCP was not tainted with the image of an outside occupying force, as was the case for Eastern European parties and even the KMT on Taiwan.[7] The result is that it does not have to adapt itself in order to "sink roots" into society, although it is increasingly concerned about the health and viability of its roots. While the Party's policies and practices may not be popular today, it came to power with demonstrable popular support.

In addition to the residual value of its indigenous origins, the CCP also benefits from the apparently widespread belief that it is the best and only safeguard against national disunity and political instability. These are prominent and deeply felt fears among both the state and the society. Political protest and regime change inevitably entail disruption and uncertainty. The CCP can utilize the cultural preference for stability to discredit those who would challenge its monopoly on power. This is one reason why the CCP has stoked nationalistic feelings throughout society. As Peter Gries and Richard Kraus note (in Chapters 9 and 10 respectively), at a time when it no longer promotes class struggle or other communist goals, it can claim to promote nationalistic aspirations, beginning with maintaining national unity and order.

The CCP also enjoys material resources that can engender support. For instance, it is an effective patronage machine. It still controls many key jobs, not just in government but also in the financial and academic worlds as well. With the privatization of the economy, the CCP may not control as many managerial positions in enterprises as it did before, but it is still considerable. Party membership can also smooth access to important resources, such as business and investment opportunities and permission to travel abroad. This is a double-edged sword: while it encourages some people to join to get their slice of the pie, it also contributes to the Party's image as a corrupt and self-serving machine with little regard for collective well-being.

Recognizing that the Party is the only game in town, and that Party membership is beneficial to many career goals, growing numbers of young intellectuals and private entrepreneurs are applying for Party membership. This may seem surprising, because they enjoy the educational and entrepreneurial credentials to succeed on their own. While some are unwilling to join the CCP out of principle or concern that Party membership would constrain their options, others are willing to join for practical reasons because membership still provides important privileges, especially for administrative careers.[8] In recent years, the combination of higher learning or entrepreneurial acumen with a Party card has tangible benefits for many professional and business careers. These kinds of people are not the traditional sources of support for the Party, but the Party recognizes they are necessary partners in its pursuit of economic modernization. The CCP uses the growing number of applications to join the Party and the profiles of those who seek admission as evidence of the Party's continued popularity. While this may be a self-serving misreading of the data, there is no question that the Party continues to grow, from almost 40 million in 1982 to more than 66 million in 2002.

In short, the CCP has remained in power because it enjoys a political monopoly, is an indigenous party, can provide tangible benefits to its members, and successfully attracts new members from the modernizing sectors of the society. These are not static factors, and the CCP has not been passive in remaining relevant. As will be seen in the sections below, the CCP has been transforming its organization and its relations with society to adapt itself to the economic and social environment its reforms are bringing about. Its future prospects largely depend on the success of this transformation.

Corporatism and co-optation: the CCP's policies of inclusion

As the CCP entered the post-Mao period, it abandoned the class-struggle policies and campaigns that characterized the Maoist era, particularly the Cultural Revolution, in favor of promoting economic modernization. With that shift in the basic work of the Party came commensurate changes in the Party's organization and its relationship with society. Whereas Party recruitment and job assignments in the Maoist era had emphasized mobilization skills and political reliability, the new focus on economic modernization put a premium on practical skills and technical know-how for Party members and especially for cadres. Beneficiaries of the Cultural Revolution were removed from their posts, and even the victims of the Cultural Revolution were quickly eased into retirement to make way for younger technocrats.[9]

This shift in the Party's priorities for its members and key personnel had a dramatic impact. The proportion of Party members with a high-school or higher level of education rose from 12.8 per cent in 1978 to 52.5 per cent in 2002. In the CCP's Central Committee, the percentage of those with college degrees rose from 23.8 in 1969 to 55.5 in 1982 and most recently to 98.6 in 2002, and those with technocratic backgrounds (i.e. science, engineering, or management) rose from only 2 per cent in 1982 to 51 per cent in 1997. Among cadres at the county level and above, those with a college education rose from 16.4 per cent in 1981 to 87.9 per cent at the end of 2001.[10]

The most tangible symbol of the Party's transformation is the reduction of peasants and workers among its members. Formerly the mainstay of the Party and the basis for its popular support, they now constitute a minority of Party members. Their numbers dropped from 83 per cent of Party members in 1956 to 63 per cent in 1994 and to only 45 per cent in 2002. This was a drop not only in relative terms, but in absolute numbers as well, from approximately 34 million to less than 30 million in just those few years between 1994 and 2002.[11] New recruitment among peasants and workers is not keeping pace with retirements and deaths among existing members. The CCP no longer gives priority to the subordinate classes for whom it fought the revolution, but instead reaches out to the technological, professional, and entrepreneurial elites that have emerged in the wake of the Party's *gaige kaifang* policies. As a consequence, the CCP has redefined its relationship with society to reflect its current priorities.

By declaring the end of class struggle at the outset of the post-Mao era, the CCP implied that its relationship with society would be more harmonious. Rather than relying on the familiar Maoist instruments of ideological mobilization and coercion, the Party adopted a two-pronged strategy of adaptation: creating new institutions to link state and society, and co-opting new elites into the Party.[12] The Party no longer views society as rife with class enemies determined to overthrow the CCP, but as the source of talent and ambition needed to modernize the economy. While it continues to suppress those it deems as "counter-revolutionaries" or in other ways hostile to its regime, the CCP seeks to cooperate with others who share its economic goals.

The first element of the CCP's new policy of inclusion was the creation of new institutional links with society. Beginning in the 1980s, and accelerating in the 1990s, China experienced the formation of myriad types of social organizations, including chambers of commerce, professional associations, sports and hobby clubs, etc.[13] The growing numbers of these organizations have led some observers to speculate about the potential for civil society emerging in China. However, these organizations for the most part do not enjoy the type of autonomy expected of a civil society. Instead, their relationship to the state is more akin to a corporatist perspective: they are sanctioned by the state, are granted a monopoly on the interest they represent, at least in their locality, and many even have Party or government officials in their leadership. This corporatist strategy was designed not to abandon Party control but to accentuate it with more flexible instruments. As the Party reduced its penetration into the daily life of most of its citizens, these organizations substituted the direct and coercive control over society that characterized the Maoist era for more indirect links.

The second element of the CCP's strategy of adaptation was co-opting newly emerging social elites, in particular professional and technical elites and private entrepreneurs. Given the Party's focus on economic modernization, this was an appropriate strategy. It let the Party be connected directly to the kinds of people who were primarily responsible for the growth and modernization of the Chinese economy. The success at recruiting better-educated members was noted above. Although the Party banned recruiting private entrepreneurs in August 1989, local officials found ways of getting around the ban. In some cases, they claimed the entrepreneurs were managers of individual, collective, or joint stock enterprises and therefore were not, technically speaking, private entrepreneurs. In other cases, local officials simply ignored the ban, arguing that it was unfair to exclude people who were succeeding due to the Party's own policies. Because promoting economic growth was a key criterion for evaluating the work performance of local officials, many were eager to cooperate with the entrepreneurs who could provide that growth. As the private sector grew in importance, the percentage of entrepreneurs who belonged to the Party grew from 13 per cent in 1993 to almost 30 per cent in 2003. Not all of these "red capitalists" were co-opted, however; many Party members, especially Party and government officials, went into business for themselves after joining the Party. Without the ban, the numbers of entrepreneurs seeking to join the Party would have undoubtedly been higher.

After Jiang Zemin proposed lifting the ban in his speech marking the 80th anniversary of the founding of the Party, the rate of recruitment among entrepreneurs was expected to grow. That did not happen immediately, however. Jiang's proposal sparked renewed controversy over the propriety of capitalists within the Communist Party. Even after the 16th Party Congress in November 2002 formally ended the ban, there was no groundswell of entrepreneurs joining the Party. Many entrepreneurs were no longer interested in joining the Party, due to its corrupt image and doubts about the advantages of Party membership. In addition, after the Party Congress, the new leadership of the CCP, especially Hu Jintao and Wen Jiabao, subtly yet significantly shifted the Party's focus away from the new elites that Jiang courted in favor of the traditional base of the Party. How the Party balances the interests of the winners and losers of ongoing economic reforms will be a test of its adaptability and its ability to re-legitimate itself.

This strategy of corporatism and co-optation served to weaken the Party's traditional emphasis on Party-building. It experienced declining recruitment from the "three revolutionary classes" (peasants, workers, and soldiers) and its Party organizations in the cities and countryside atrophied. In the mid-1990s, the Party declared that half its rural organizations were inactive. An estimated 2.5 million Party members joined the "floating population" of migrant workers, further weakening the Party's presence in the countryside. Even though the Party was recruiting the owners of private enterprises, it was less active at recruiting and organizing workers in the private sector. Of the estimated 1.2 million private enterprises in 1998, less than 1 per cent had Party organizations and only 14 per cent had Party members among their workers.[14] In short, the Party's presence was shrinking in the countryside, where roughly 70 per cent of the population still live and work, and virtually non-existent in the private sector, the most dynamic part of the Chinese economy. As the Party shifted its attention toward new professional, technical, and entrepreneurial elites, its ties to the rest of society were allowed to weaken.

As will be seen below, however, this shift in the Party's work and especially in its recruitment priorities was contested by those in the Party who opposed the abandonment of Party traditions. While some in the Party felt adaptation was necessary for the Party's survival and popular legitimacy, others feared that the inclusion of such diverse – and non-proletarian – interests in the Party would destroy the Party's unity and ultimately lead to its dissolution.

Who does the Party represent?

As China's economic reforms have transformed its social structure, leading to the emergence of new elites and potential rivals, the CCP has altered its relationship to society. In the past, the CCP claimed to be the vanguard of the proletariat, but this claim seems quaint amid the rapid marketization of China's economy and the accompanying transformation of its social structure. In order to remain relevant, the CCP has redefined its relationship with society with the so-called "three represents" slogan: the CCP now represents the advanced productive forces (primarily the growing urban middle class of businessmen, professionals, and high-technology specialists), the promotion of advanced culture (as opposed to both "feudalism" and modern materialism), and the interests of the majority of the Chinese people. This concept was first introduced by Jiang Zemin in the spring of 2000, and then propagated through an extensive media campaign. The purpose was to offer a new rationale for the CCP's claim of legitimacy. But it was a contentious claim, met with opposition from some in the Party and with indifference from much of society.

Jiang unveiled the slogan during his spring 2000 inspection tour of several key economic cities in south China. He visited joint ventures, private enterprises, township and village enterprises, as well as state-owned enterprises, and investigated Party-building efforts in these different types of firms. In Zhejiang, he met several private entrepreneurs, all of whom reportedly expressed interest in joining the Party, but were prohibited from doing so by the Party's ban. This experience reportedly helped inspire the "three represents" slogan, because Jiang recognized that the Party could not represent the estimated 130 million workers in the private sector if private firms did not have Party organizations in them.[15] Nearly overlooked when he first used the slogan in February 2000, he re-emphasized and elaborated the concept at a May speech at the Central Party School, after which it was treated to extensive media coverage for months.

Jiang Zemin did not change the definition of the proletariat, as Deng Xiaoping had done in 1978 by adding intellectuals to the working class. Instead, he broadened the definition of the Party's mass character by incorporating new social strata whose interests were equivalent to those of the working class. In his 1 July speech, Jiang said: "The basic components and backbone of the party are those from workers, farmers, intellectuals, soldiers, and cadres. At the same time, it is also necessary to accept those outstanding elements from other sectors of society."[16] The CCP replaced its claim to be the vanguard of the proletariat with a "two vanguards" thesis: it represented the interests of both the working classes (comprising workers, farmers, intellectuals, Party and government officials, and those in the military) and the vast majority of the people, especially entrepreneurs, professionals, and high-tech specialists. While this sleight of hand kept the party's propaganda writers busy for years, the careful parsing of the "three represents" slogan and its implications also served to point up the discrepancy between the ideological needs of the Party and China's dynamic society.

Jiang's efforts to popularize the "three represents" slogan were hampered by the Party's ban on recruiting entrepreneurs into the Party. This ban was enacted in August 1989 out of concern that some entrepreneurs had supported the Tiananmen demonstrators (particularly Wan Runnan, founder of the Stone Corporation) and that the presence of entrepreneurs in the Party was compromising its class character. It was not hard to find an ideological rationale to support the ban. Lin Yanzhi, a member of Jilin's Provincial Party Committee, made a succinct argument against co-opting entrepreneurs:

> If we allow private entrepreneurs [to join the Party], it would create serious conceptual chaos within the party, and destroy the unified foundation of the political thought of the party that is now united, and destroy the baseline of what the party is able to accommodate in terms of its advanced class nature ... A pluralistic political party would certainly fragment ... The party name, the party constitution, and the party platform all would have to be changed ... Therefore, we not only cannot permit private entrepreneurs to join the party, we must encourage those members of the Communist Party who have already become private entrepreneurs to leave.[17]

While the ban on recruiting entrepreneurs made good ideological sense, it was increasingly out of step with the Party's goal of promoting economic development and also with the growing complexity of China's society. If the Party was basing its legitimacy largely on economic growth, it made little sense to exclude the people whose success was the result of following the Party's policies. Traditional class divisions were also being broken down by economic reform, as workers moved between jobs in the state-owned, collective, and private sectors, and as former farmers, intellectuals, and Party and government officials took the chance to "plunge into the sea" (*xiahai*) by opening their own business. As *People's Daily* noted, the new social strata "were originally farmers, intellectuals, managerial personnel of state-owned enterprises, cadres of party and government institutions, scientific and technical personnel, and students who had returned from their studies abroad."[18] As a result, they were said to be different from the capitalists and exploiters of the pre-communist era.[19] Because they were contributing to China's development by following the Party's own policies, excluding such people was clearly not in the Party's long-term interests.

Co-opting entrepreneurs and other new social strata into the Party was not only designed to benefit the Party by tapping new sources of support, it was also intended to pre-empt a potential source of opposition. Jiang Zemin reportedly acknowledged in January 2001 that the Party was considering lifting the ban on entrepreneurs, perhaps to prevent them from aligning themselves with the pro-democracy political activists.[20] Along these same lines, Wang Changjiang of the Central Party School argued that if the Party did not embrace the vast majority of the Chinese people, they will seek to organize themselves outside the political system. Inclusion was intended, at least in part, to prevent organized opposition to the Party, and to maintain political stability and Party leadership.

Finally, Jiang Zemin publicly recommended lifting the ban on entrepreneurs in his 1 July 2001 speech marking the 80th anniversary of the founding of the CCP. In reviewing the consequences of the *gaige kaifang* policies, he noted that private entrepreneurs, freelance professionals, scientific and technical personnel employed by Chinese and foreign firms, and other new social groups had emerged. "Most of these people in the new social strata have contributed to the development of productive forces and … are working for building socialism with Chinese characteristics." While claiming that the workers, farmers, intellectuals, servicemen, and cadres would remain the "basic components and backbone of the party," Jiang claimed that the Party also needed "to accept those outstanding elements from other sectors of the society."[21]

The Party's propaganda machine actively promoted Jiang's "three represents" slogan and his recommendation to incorporate China's new social strata into the Party. Several themes were prominent in this campaign to square the "three represents" with the Party's traditions. First, the Party claimed that its class nature was not determined solely by the economic class of its members: "The practical experience of our party shows that the structure of the party membership is related to and to a certain degree influences the party's character. However, it is not the decisive factor affecting the party's character."[22] Historically, workers were never the majority of Party members, but rather peasants, intellectuals, soldiers, and students. Yet they were all said to represent proletarian interests. Secondly, the Party claimed that there was no necessary conflict between its claim to represent both the proletariat and the vast majority of the people. According to this syllogism, because the majority of Chinese are workers and farmers, if the Party represents the interests of the majority of the people, they thereby represent the interests of workers and farmers. One conclusion from this was that the Party could maintain its proletarian class nature even if it recruited from other social strata. Even non-proletarians could allegedly have a proletarian outlook. According to a report from the National Defense University, the "party's class base [i.e. the proletariat] determines the class character of the party, and the party's mass foundation [i.e. the vast majority of the people] determines the party's extensive representativeness." But what if the other classes want to represent their own interests, or those of their professions? Membership in the Party will supposedly change those interests:

> Like a big furnace, the party can melt out all sorts of non-proletarian ideas and unify its whole thinking on Marxist theory and the party's program and line. Today, in admitting the outstanding elements from other social strata into the party, so long as we uphold the principle of building the party ideologically and require all party members to join the party ideologically, we will surely be able to preserve the ideological purity of the party members and the advanced nature of the party organizations.[23]

The "three represents" slogan recognizes that diverse interests now exist in China, but the rationale used to justify the slogan only legitimates proletarian interests.

A third theme of the "three represents" propaganda campaign was that the Party's claim to represent the interests of the majority of the Chinese people was allegedly nothing new. Numerous commentators pointed out that the Party passed a resolution asserting that it was the vanguard of both the proletariat and the whole nation at the Wayabao conference in 1935. This is a very weak precedent, however, because it ignores the next 65 years of the Party's history, and also ignores the historical context of that resolution: the Party's appeal to nationalism in the face of Japanese invasion. And despite the claims that the CCP always represented the interests of most Chinese, the media also emphasized the need to conduct extensive education and training of incumbent cadres and the selection of new cadres on the basis of these claims. Apparently, this Party tradition was not clear to all.[24]

Commentators were also careful to distinguish Jiang's call to recruit "the outstanding elements from all social strata into the party" from the reviled concept of a party of the whole people (*quanmindang*) first advanced by Nikita Khrushchev. The distinction is that not all people in each stratum deserve to join the Party, just the truly outstanding ones who also meet the other criteria of Party membership. Wang Changjiang of the Central Party School focused on this point in several articles. In *Liaowang*, he argued:

> When the party expands its social foundation to various social strata and groups, it doesn't mean that all the people in these strata and groups can join the party ... What we want to absorb are the outstanding elements of these strata and groups. Possessing the political consciousness of the working class and willingness to fight for the party's program constitutes the common characteristics of these outstanding elements and also the qualifications they must meet in order to join the party ... There is no connection between this kind of party and the so-called "party of all the people."[25]

In a journal for Party cadres, he argued that "since the elements [i.e. Party members] influence the nature of the party *to some extent*, we cannot just throw open the doors of the party and welcome everyone ... Allowing entrepreneurs into the party is not the same as saying that any entrepreneur can join the party."[26] Other Party media repeated this warning. According to *People's Daily*, "We allow the worthy people in the new social strata to join the party. However, this does not mean that we keep our doors wide open in an unprincipled manner. Still less should we drag into the party all those who do not meet our requirements for party membership."[27] *Qiushi* advised against "using erroneous methods to measure the new criteria for party membership, such as admission based on economic strength, on the amount of donation to society, and on personal reputation."[28] These easily determined criteria – as opposed to the more abstract considerations of supporting the Party's program and "standing the test of time" – were undoubtedly the ones used by many local committees in recruiting from the new social strata.

Although *People's Daily* claimed the "three represents" slogan had joined the pantheon of Mao Zedong Thought and Deng Xiaoping Theory as hallmarks of the "sinicization" of Marxism, not all in the Party were so enamored by it.[29] *Strategy and Management* (*Zhanlue yu Guanli*) criticized the notion of the "interests of the whole body of the people" as illusory because interest groups need to be checked and balanced in order to avoid "many calamities and difficulties."[30] The Party's orthodox leftists used a series of open letters to rebuke Jiang's proposal to admit entrepreneurs into the Party. Not only did they challenge the ideological propriety of admitting capitalists into a communist party, they also attacked the personal leadership style of Jiang Zemin. They accused him of violating Party discipline by making such a significant recommendation without getting formal approval from the Party's Central Committee or Politburo. They even compared him to Mikhail Gorbachev and Lee Teng-hui, leaders who are widely criticized in China for betraying their parties' interests.[31] These personal attacks led Jiang Zemin to order the closing of the leftist journals *Zhenli de zhuiqiu* and *Zhongliu*. Resistance to Jiang's proposal did not end there, however, witnessed by the failure of the Central Committee to endorse it at its fall 2001 plenum. Informal reports indicate the lack of consensus among local Party officials. While some have been actively co-opting entrepreneurs into the Party for years, even in violation of the Party's ban, others remain opposed to lifting the ban. Perhaps to acknowledge the controversy surrounding the "three represents" slogan, published reports on Jiang's speech to the Party School in May 2002 made no mention of his recommendation to recruit entrepreneurs and other new social strata into the Party.[32]

In a more oblique critique of the "three represents," the Chinese Academy of Social Sciences (CASS) published a lengthy report on China's social strata in December 2001.[33] It was reportedly prepared at the behest of CASS president Li Tieying, widely seen as skeptical toward economic reforms and their political implications. This report may have been a response to Jiang's 1 July speech and the subsequent campaign extolling the "three represents." It noted the inevitable choice of the CCP to tilt toward the new social strata, especially management, technical personnel, and private entrepreneurs, to promote the Party's economic development goals. But the consequence was a weakening of the workers and farmers in the Party's social base. A commentary on this report in *Strategy and Management* focused on the polarization and corruption caused by 20 years of reform, which would lead to a crisis of legitimacy if not corrected. Furthermore, it accused private entrepreneurs of buying political power: "While the new capital stratum is rising into becoming a vested interest group in the reform, it goes further in buying the power-holders with cash so as to consolidate and strengthen its position." Including such people in the CCP would only further undermine the already corrupt political system.[34] Because of the potentially embarrassing and inflammatory content of the CASS report, it was quickly withdrawn from circulation.

Despite these admonitions, the 16th Party Congress adopted the "three represents" slogan as a basic doctrine and revised the Party constitution accordingly. This symbolized the Party's embrace of the new social strata and the Party's pro-business orientation. As noted above, however, after the Party Congress, the new leaders eased away from Jiang's focus on "advanced productive forces" and emphasized the need to represent the "fundamental interests of the overwhelming majority of the Chinese people." In the grand tradition of Chinese politics, the new leaders used an existing slogan to justify a change, specifically a concern for the general welfare lest the Party be overwhelmed by the rising demands of a restive society.

The continued exclusion of unsanctioned claims

As noted above, the CCP makes several claims to legitimate its continued status as China's ruling party. Its ability to promote prosperity, raise living standards, guard against instability, and champion nationalistic aspirations is the basis of its claim to represent the common interests of most Chinese and define "truth, benevolence, and glory." But legitimacy alone cannot preserve the CCP's hold on power. In particular, basing its legitimacy on economic performance is risky; the inevitable economic downturn would threaten to de-legitimate it, and its claim to rule would be jeopardized. In addition, as Adam Przeworski has noted, it is not legitimacy that keeps an authoritarian regime in power, but the absence of a preferable (and, we should add, viable) alternative.[35] Following that rationale, the CCP also strives to prevent the emergence of a viable alternative, whether that be autonomous unions, an opposition party (see Teresa Wright's chapter in the present volume), or an organized dissident movement. The CCP's implicit strategy is to increase the cost of collective action by arresting political and labor activists and keeping most social organizations dependent on the state for their survival and success. In the process, it aims to prevent the emergence of a "critical realm" of civil society and prevent it from making claims on the state.[36]

The success of this strategy is seen by the nature of protest in China. Rural protests are typically parochial in nature, directed against immediate grievances without demands for political change or attempts at coordination with neighboring communities.[37] As the research of Kevin O'Brien and Lianjiang Li has shown, rural protests can be successful if they are limited to "rightful resistance," that is to challenging the local implementation of policy, but not the propriety of the policy itself.[38] Complaints against excessive taxes and fees, unpaid IOU's for grain purchases by the state, uncompensated land seizures, and cadre corruption can often be successful if they are framed as violations of central policy, not simply unjust, and if they can get the attention of higher-level officials or the media. But even as it addresses specific complaints, the CCP is reluctant to let its concessions in one incident become a precedent for others.

Those engaged in labor protests are normally careful not to be well organized, lest their leaders be identified and arrested. In most cases, protests are limited to bread-and-butter issues: unpaid wages, stolen pensions, harsh working conditions, etc. Rarely do they venture into political issues, such as demanding a change of leaders or the creation of new unions. To do so would doom them to immediate failure and often harsh punishment.[39] Large-scale labor unrest in the spring of 2002 in several industrial cities was an exception to this rule, and those who broke the rule paid a heavy price. In Liaoyang, workers called for the ousting of the city's leader. In both Daqing and Liaoyang, workers chosen as leaders of the protest were quickly identified, isolated, and arrested. Local leaders resolved the conflicts with a combination of carrots and sticks, recognizing the legitimate nature of the economic demands but ignoring the political issues and punishing the workers who played a leadership role.[40] While in custody, some of the labor leaders reportedly betrayed their fellow prisoners in order to protect themselves or their families. After their release, the solidarity that led tens of thousands of workers to protest in the streets turned to suspicion.[41] From the state's perspective, this resolution was generally positive. The protests were ended with minimal violence, the costs of the settlement would likely be compensated by the central government, and the atmosphere of mistrust among the workers would make future collective action less likely. This episode demonstrates the elements that make sustained social movements, as opposed to sporadic local protests, so difficult in China: the coercive power of the state, the absence of autonomous organizations, the difficulty of protestors to communicate and coordinate effectively, and low levels of interpersonal trust, especially as the stakes begin to rise.

Similarly, even activists on non-political issues are reluctant to organize themselves to engage in collective action lest they arouse the insecurities of the state and risk repression. A case in point is the environmental movement. Most people recognize that pollution of all types – air, water, land, noise, light – is a severe and growing problem in China, and yet non-governmental environmental organizations are largely limited to public education on the importance of a clean environment rather than advocacy of tighter regulations and improved implementation.[42] A movement on college campuses to ban the use of disposable chopsticks faced the dilemma of how to succeed in this collective action without suffering retaliation for being too well organized. As a consequence, its actions on various campuses were largely informal and uncoordinated.[43]

Conclusion

Although economic modernization has not yet changed China's political system, it may be changing the Party. The diversification of classes and the fluidity of China's social structure is leading the Party to change who it recruits and who it claims to represent. This is not quite equivalent to pluralism, because the Party does not allow fully autonomous interest groups or opposition parties. The CCP still retains its political monopoly, but tries to be more inclusive and therefore more representative. But the idea that the Party can represent the vast majority of the people may expose it to even greater criticism and cynicism. The notion that a single party can properly represent the diverse social forces in China is odd, especially from a Western perspective of a society made up of diverse interests. These interests need not be incompatible, but they normally desire, even demand, their own organization to represent their interests to the state and not grant that responsibility to a vanguard party.

One key to the Party's survival is its Leninist foundation. The CCP is monolithic neither in its relationship with society nor in its attitude toward adaptation. Instead, it has forged multidimensional relationships, depending on the sector of the society, and how it fits into the Party's modernization strategy. Even though the Party has abandoned its efforts to monitor and control all of society, it still protects its monopoly on legitimate political organization. Not all interests are able to organize themselves, and some groups, such as farmers, are not allowed any organizations at all, not even officially sponsored mass organizations like the Women's Federation or the All-China Federation of Trade Unions.

The merits and logic of this multidimensional relationship have also been contested within the Party. Some argue it is necessary to preserve the Party's right to rule and promote its economic program. Others argue it is a betrayal of the Party's traditions and *raison d'être*. Rather than bolstering the Party's legitimacy, critics allege that the Party's policies of inclusion will undermine the Party's authority, both by abandoning its traditional bases of support and by admitting new members who are likely to further divert the Party from its original mission and dilute its organizational coherence.

Nevertheless, the CCP is confronted with numerous challenges from an increasingly restive society. Its *gaige kaifang* policies have achieved dramatic and sustained growth rates, but for many the benefits of growth have been offset by a host of problems. The seemingly unstoppable spread of corruption serves to de-legitimate the Party. In some areas, local Party and government officials are seen as in cahoots with organized crime, or indistinguishable from it. Throughout the post-Mao era, but especially in the 1990s and into the early 21st century, rapid growth has been accompanied by rising inequality. Privatization of the economy has created vast numbers of newly unemployed workers, many too old and lacking the requisite skills to find new jobs in the private sector. Laid off from their old jobs and without the benefits of a welfare system, they rightly feel betrayed by a system that formerly promised them lifetime security. Decollectivization of agriculture and the decline of incomes in the countryside have compelled tens of millions of rural workers to migrate to the cities in search of work. The spread of modern values, international influences, and the logic of the marketplace undermine the Party's ability to define "truth, benevolence, and glory" for the nation at large. The Party's limited policies of corporatism and co-optation are unlikely to meet these challenges successfully, and the "three represents" slogan is equally unlikely to provide a suitable response. Whether Hu Jintao, Wen Jiabao, and others in the so-called "fourth generation" of leaders are able to devise a workable strategy will be a test of their leadership and their ability to preserve the political system they inherited from Jiang Zemin and the third generation until the fifth generation takes the stage.

Notes

1 This is a revised and expanded version of an essay that was first published in *American Asian Review* 21(1) (Spring 2003): 1–24. I would like to thank the journal's editors for granting permission to use material in the original essay for this chapter.

2 This distinction between economic and political demands is derived from Yanqi Tong, and Gordon White, Jude Howell, and Shang Xiaoyuan, who make similar distinctions about the different dynamics and sectors of civil society. See Tong, "State, society, and political change in China and Hungary," *Comparative Politics* 26(3) (April 1994): 333–353, and White *et al.*, *In Search of Civil Society: Market Reform and Social Change in Contemporary China* (Oxford: Oxford University Press, 1996).

3 Jowitt, "Inclusion," in *New World Disorder: The Leninist Extinction* (Berkeley: University of California Press, 1992), pp. 88–120.

4 Alfred C. Stepan, *The State and Society: Peru in Comparative Perspective* (Princeton: Princeton University Press, 1978).

5 Andrew G. Walder, "The decline of communist power: elements of a theory of institutional change," *Theory and Society* 23(2) (April 1994): 297–323.

6 Sidney Tarrow, *Power in Movement: Social Movements and Contentious Politics*, 2nd edn (NY: Cambridge University Press, 1998).

7 Bruce J. Dickson, *Democratization in China and Taiwan: The Adaptability of Leninist Parties* (Oxford and New York: Oxford University Press, 1997).

8 Andrew G. Walder, "Career mobility and the communist political order," *American Sociological Review* 60(3) (June 1995): 309–328; Bruce J. Dickson and Maria Rost Rublee, "Membership has its privileges: the socioeconomic characteristics of Communist Party members in urban China," *Comparative Political Studies* 33(1) (February 2000): 87–112; Andrew G. Walder, Bobai Li, and Donald J. Treiman, "Politics and life chances in a state socialist regime: dual career paths into the urban Chinese elite, 1949 to 1996," *American Sociological Review* 65(2) (April 2000): 191–209.

9 Hong Yung Lee, *From Revolutionary Cadres to Party Technocrats in Socialist China* (Berkeley: University of California Press, 1991); Melanie Manion, *Retirement of Revolutionaries in China: Public Policies, Social Norms, Private Interests* (Princeton: Princeton University Press, 1993).

10 The changing characteristics of Party elites are drawn from Dickson, *Democratization in China and Taiwan*, pp. 135 and 147; Cheng Li, *China's Leaders: The New Generation* (Lanham, MD: Rowman and Littlefield, 2001), p. 41; and Xinhua, 12 June 2002, in Foreign Broadcast Information Service (FBIS), 13 June 2002.

11 Lee, *From Revolutionary Cadres to Party Technocrats*, p. 56; Dickson, *Democratization in China and Taiwan*, p. 152; Xinhua, 1 September 2002.

12 The following analysis is based on my *Red Capitalists in China: The Party, Private Entrepreneurs, and Prospects for Political Change* (New York: Cambridge University Press, 2003).

13 Minxin Pei, "Chinese civic associations: an empirical analysis," *Modern China* 24(3) (July 1998): 285–318; Tony Saich, "Negotiating the state: the development of social organizations in China," *China Quarterly* 161 (March 2000): 124–141.

14 *Renmin ribao*, 12 September 2000, p. 11.

15 You Dehai, "The background of the launch of the 'three represents,'" *Xuexi yu shijian* (Wuhan), September 2000, pp. 18–20, 45; the author was president of the Party School in Wuhan. See also Xinhua, 25 February 2000, in FBIS, 29 February 2000.

16 Xinhua, 1 July 2001, in FBIS, 2 July 2001.

17 Lin Yanzhi, "How the Communist Party should 'lead' the capitalist class," *Shehui Kexue Zhanxian* (*Social Science Battlefront*), 20 June 2001, translated in FBIS, 14 July 2001. This article, written by a deputy Party secretary of the Jilin Provincial Party Committee, was originally published in the May issue of *Zhenli de zhuiqiu*.

18 *Renmin ribao*, 17 September 2001, in FBIS, 17 September 2001.

19 "Reviewing the 'three points' of Deng Xiaoping," *Liaowang*, 12 November 2001, in FBIS, 20 November 2001.

20 Kyodo News International, 15 January 2001.

21 Jiang's speech was carried by Xinhua, 1 July 2001, in FBIS, 1 July 2001. See also John Pomfret, "China allows its capitalists to join Party: communists recognize rise of private business," *Washington Post*, 2 July 2001, and Craig S. Smith, "China's leader urges opening Communist Party to capitalists," *New York Times*, 2 July 2001.

22 *Qiushi*, 16 November 2001, in FBIS, 29 November 2001.

23 *Jiefangjun bao*, 15 August 2001, in FBIS, 15 August 2001.

24 See, for example, *Qiushi*, 1 June 2001, and *Renmin ribao*, 2 December 2001, p. 1, in FBIS, 3 December 2001.

25 *Liaowang*, 13 August 2001, in FBIS, 22 August 2001.

26 *Zhongguo Dangzheng Ganbu Luntan* (Beijing), 6 January 2002, in FBIS, 4 February 2002; emphasis added.

27 *Renmin ribao*, 17 September 2001, in FBIS, 17 September 2001.

28 *Qiushi*, 16 November 2001, in FBIS, 29 November 2001.

29 *Renmin ribao*, 8 November 2001, p. 9, in FBIS, 8 November 2001.
30 *Zhanlue yu Guanli*, 30 April 2002, in FBIS, 7 June 2002.
31 A text of the letter identified with Deng Liqun was translated by FBIS, 2 August 2001.
32 Xinhua, 31 May 2002, in FBIS, 31 May 2002.
33 Lu Xueyi (general ed.), *Dangdai zhongguo shehui jieceng yanjiu baogao* (*Research Report on the Social Stratification of Contemporary China*) (Beijing: Shehui kexue wenxian chubanshe, 2002).
34 *Zhanlue yu Guanli*, 30 April 2002, in FBIS, 7 June 2002.
35 Adam Przeworski, "Some problems in the transition to democracy," in Guillermo O'Donnell, Philippe C. Schmitter, and Laurence Whitehead (eds) *Transitions from Authoritarian Rule, Volume 3: Comparative Perspectives* (Baltimore: Johns Hopkins University Press, 1986).
36 "Critical realm" is Yanqi Tong's term to describe the political or dissident portion of civil society which poses a threat to the state, in contrast to the "non-critical realm" which refers to economic and professional activities that do not necessarily threaten the state and may even be welcomed and encouraged by it. White *et al.* make a similar distinction between the "political dynamic" and "market dynamic" of civil society. See Tong, "State, society, and political change in China and Hungary," and White *et al.*, *In Search of Civil Society*.
37 Thomas P. Bernstein and Xiaobo Lu, "Taxation without representation: peasants, the central and the local states in reform China," *China Quarterly* 163 (September 2000): 742–763; Thomas P. Bernstein, "Instability in rural China," in David Shambaugh (ed.) *Is China Unstable?* (Armonk, NY: M.E. Sharpe, 2000).
38 Kevin J. O'Brien, "Rightful resistance," *World Politics* 49(1) (October 1996): 31–55; Lianjiang Li and Kevin J. O'Brien, "Villagers and popular resistance in contemporary China," *Modern China* 22(1) (January 1996): 28–61; Kevin J. O'Brien and Lianjiang Li, "The politics of lodging complaints in rural China," *China Quarterly* 143 (September 1995): 756–783.
39 See Ching Kwan Lee, "Pathways of labor insurgency," in Elizabeth J. Perry and Mark Selden (eds) *Chinese Society: Change, Conflict, and Resistance* (London and New York: Routledge, 2001), pp. 41–61.
40 Michael A. Lev, "7,000 Chinese workers unite in daring protest," *Chicago Tribune*, 13 March 2002; John Pomfret, "Chinese oil country simmers as workers protest cost-cutting: thousands laid off, benefits reduced," *Washington Post*, 17 March 2002, and "China cracks down on worker protests; leaders detained as 2 cities face continued unrest," *Washington Post*, 21 March 2002; Philip P. Pan, "'High tide' of labor unrest in China: striking workers risk arrest to protest pay cuts, corruption," *Washington Post*, 21 January 2002.
41 Philip P. Pan, "Three Chinese workers: jail, betrayal, and fear," *Washington Post*, 28 December 2002.
42 Carlos Wing Hung Lo and Sai Wing Leung, "Environmental agency and public opinion in China: the limits of a popular approach to environmental governance," *China Quarterly* 163 (September 2000): 677–704.
43 Philip P. Pan, "China's chopsticks crusade," *Washington Post*, 6 February 2001.

8 The state of youth/youth and the state in early 21st-century China

The triumph of the urban rich?

Stanley Rosen

How will China's youth respond to the state's claims to legitimacy at the dawn of the 21st century? In his recent book on state–society relations and the 1989 Beijing student movement, Dingxin Zhao notes that in the post-1989 environment, and in the absence within society of any real belief in communism, the state can only base its legitimacy on moral and economic performance. In part because older Chinese remember the chaotic times and poverty that marked the Maoist period, the regime currently seems to enjoy a high level of performance legitimation. What will happen, Zhao asks, after 20 years, when those with first-hand experience of the Cultural Revolution have aged, and affluence and stability are taken for granted? Since performance legitimation is "intrinsically unstable," how can the regime adjust and establish new and long-term bases of legitimation that will bind state and society together?[1] This chapter seeks to address this question, albeit at times indirectly, by examining the attitudes and behavior of China's younger generation, precisely those to whom the regime must appeal to maintain long-term legitimacy.

Particularly since Deng Xiaoping's 1992 "Southern Inspection Tour," the Chinese government has "internationalized" China, opening the country to a wide variety of international economic and cultural forces.[2] This is part of a concerted effort to make China rich, raise the standard of living of the population, and offer a more varied cultural life. An important component of this strategy is an enhancement of the social and political status of a new moneyed urban middle class, particularly white-collar professionals and private entrepreneurs, thus tying the regime's legitimacy – and its fate – to this rising elite. Indeed, a recent study of the "new middle classes" in Beijing concluded that "it is the CCP-controlled system which has created this new middle class ... [and they] will use all their means to support the CCP system to protect their new situation."[3]

In many ways, this strategy has been remarkably successful. In contrast to Chinese youth of the 1980s, who were often "searching for life's meaning," contemporary youth are "success-oriented," and openly seek "the good life."[4] Chinese society has been substantially transformed. A recent State Statistical Bureau ten-province survey of those with income levels above

60,000 yuan a year revealed that the largest cluster was in the 30–40-year-old age bracket[5] – China's yuppies. They have become the new role models, not "model workers" unselfishly serving the Party and the state. The newly affluent have enthusiastically embraced and become eager consumers in the global market place, and that has become a core aspiration of China's urban youth.

In the following pages, I discuss the effects of the regime's emphasis on performance and material success as a source of legitimation – including the acceptance of growing social stratification – and the effects of this on attitudes. I argue that "value," in a material sense, has become a key indicator of worth. In the sphere of social relations, upwardly mobile people are reluctant to interact with those from lower strata, for fear that such contact will tarnish their image. Money has also become essential for success across generations, by way of an increasingly commercialized educational system where access to schooling has become increasingly dependent on one's family's wealth. Strikingly, the regime is openly encouraging, or at least not discouraging, these changes. Parallel to this reshaping of regime norms, individuals are now much more willing to acknowledge their selfish motivations, and even more the selfish motivations of others.

Stratification, pragmatism, and materialism

Although they were already engaged in extensive surveys on the topic, social scientists in China a decade ago were generally restricted from openly publishing revealing details on the increasing stratification of Chinese society. As administrators at the Chinese Academy of Social Sciences (CASS) told me at the time, such public discussion was not considered conducive to social stability. In the last few years, however, there has been a virtual cottage industry of books and articles precisely on the new strata that make up Chinese society, replete with extensive statistical, survey, and public opinion data. A particularly prominent theme has been the rise of the middle class, especially those in white-collar professions.[6] In addition to the academic press, popular magazines have widely reported on the new stratification patterns, usually with an emphasis on the incomes and lifestyles of the wealthiest strata and individuals.[7] Some scholars, having conducted content analyses of the media, have railed against the extensive coverage of CEOs and general managers of companies on the one hand, and film stars, singers, and sports stars on the other, with an almost complete lack of concern for the common people.[8] Some prominent Chinese sociologists and social critics have gone further, warning that increasing inequalities and skewed patterns of stratification have already begun to produce a "fractured" (*duanlie*) society, in which people in the same country live in different technological ages.[9]

This open discussion of stratification patterns, which now includes an authoritative list of the different strata making up Chinese society and their characteristics, has been reflected in the more openly expressed attitudes and behavior of upwardly mobile Chinese youth. As I will show below, in key areas of political and social life, such as recruitment into the CCP, finding a job, obtaining and valuing wealth, and choosing schools, youth have become less reluctant to openly acknowledge that instrumental, success-oriented values take precedence. Although the reality is of course more complex, and "nationalistic" impulses will rise to the forefront when it is perceived that China is insulted or threatened, it seems clear that professional and economic concerns are paramount.[10]

The increasing importance of money as a value

Surveys, academic and media reports, and interviews all concur on the increasing roles that money and a moneyed lifestyle play in urban Chinese aspirations.[11] The surveys are of particular interest because they reveal the open willingness to acknowledge the rising value of money, in comparison to other cherished values.

A survey conducted by the Communist Youth League (CYL) and the National Student Federation in the cities of Shenzhen and Zhuhai in Guangdong Province asked 1,780 students about their aspirations. The first choice was to be a billionaire; the second choice was to be the boss of a multinational corporation; the third choice was to be a provincial or municipal leader.[12] In feature films as well, the importance of money in governing interactions, even in the most backward rural areas of China, has become a major and, at times, humorous theme.[13]

The media have played their part in legitimating wealth as a highly positive value, often lionizing the country's wealthiest citizens. One recent book profiles the fifty richest people in China.[14] One of the most widely circulated popular magazines devoted a cover story and lengthy articles to the report of the first official survey of the richest individuals in ten provinces, with details on age, educational background, annual income, investment strategies, professions, and so forth.[15] Another popular magazine provided thumbnail sketches of the ten richest and poorest "professions" in which to make money, providing annual income figures.[16]

Recently, there has been a government backlash against the open flaunting of wealth, with several high-profile celebrities – most notably the actress turned entrepreneur Liu Xiaoqing – arrested and convicted of tax evasion.[17] Wealthy entrepreneurs have begun to blanch when they find themselves among those ranked in *Forbes*, with one saying he was "disgusted" by his listing, and another protesting that *Forbes* had exaggerated his assets by eightfold.[18] Indeed, the treatment of the rich in the Chinese media has become a contentious issue. In early 2003, after three leading private entrepreneurs were murdered within three weeks of each other, and the media began to speculate on "revenge against the rich" and "politics among the rich" as motives, as well as whether the government should provide "special protection" to the newly rich, the internal journal of the Central Committee's Propaganda Department, acknowledging the glaring inequalities still existing in China, suggested that such reporting was damaging to social stability. The media were urged instead to offer positive accounts of, for instance, how the newly rich were helping the poor to become rich themselves.[19]

Nevertheless, even in youth magazines intended as socialization agents for middle and high school students, the subject of money – and how to get it – is not uncommon. *Shandong Youth* organized a discussion forum in February 2002 entitled "Men, women and money" in which students were asked the different means by which men and women could make money, and the relationship between money and bad behavior. The opening comment by the convener of the forum is helpful to understand the nature of the ensuing "debate":

> At present there's a popular saying: men with money become bad; women who become bad can get money. Does money really have such lethal power? More and more modern people are becoming slaves to money. Every person is linked to money in a thousand and one ways.[20]

The responses in this and other discussion forums revealed why money has become such a hot topic for discussion: it has become essential for success in virtually every key area of social life, including schooling, employment, marriage, and health care.

A large number of surveys deal with the new generation of university students – the next generation of China's professional middle class. One such survey was conducted among 918 university students in Shandong Province from March to June 1995. One question asked whether the ability to make money had become a factor in determining the value of a person in contemporary China. While only 6 per cent claimed that it was now the *only* standard, another 71 per cent felt that it was at least *one* of the standards for judgment. When asked about the importance of money in social, economic, and personal life, only 3 per cent said that it was not significant, while 86 per cent said that it had great importance and a further 11 per cent claimed that it was all-powerful, enough to "make a ghost turn a millstone" (*shigui tuimo*). In addition, close to 50 per cent felt that money was either as important as or more important than friendship, and just over 50 per cent felt that money was either as important as or more important than ideals.[21]

A more recent survey, with 465 respondents at South China Normal University, asked students their views on a series of value statements. The statement that drew by far the greatest support (83 per cent) was the following: "Modern man must be able to make money." Only 7 per cent disagreed. In the same survey, 53 per cent found it difficult to agree or disagree when asked whether competition should take into account issues of conscience or morality.[22]

Given such views, the results of a worldwide behavioral study commissioned by *Reader's Digest* (US) in 2001 are perhaps not so surprising. Originally conducted in large cities and small towns in the United States, and later extended to countries on every continent, the experiment placed a "lost wallet" containing $50, along with a name and a phone number, in such public places as parking lots, office buildings, phone booths, and so forth. The surveyors were close by observing, seeking to discover how many of those who found the wallet would make the effort to return it. The results ranged from the high of Norway, where 100 per cent tried to return the wallet, to the low of Mexico, where 21 per cent and virtually no one in the large cities did so. China was the second lowest in terms of return rate, with 30 per cent returning the wallet, just below Italy's rate of 35 per cent.[23]

The issue of morality in relation to success or wealth has come up frequently in other surveys, and is of interest because it reveals the complex patterns of youth attitudes and behavior in a partially reformed system. One fairly comprehensive study exploring contradictions in youth attitudes was conducted among urban and rural youth in various parts of Shanxi Province from March–April 2001. Informants were sampled from enterprises (*qiye*), offices (*jiguan*), and schools. Perhaps the most consistent finding was that youth in all sectors and locales were ambitious, impatient, and dissatisfied with the pace of reform and its lack of positive effect on their own lives. Rural youth wanted to find non-agricultural jobs; school graduates and dropouts were seeking meaningful employment; and everyone was demanding higher salaries, an opportunity to develop their skills, and a higher social status. Thus, while 79.6 per cent of those surveyed thought that improving the socio-economic status of youth in the province was important, 68.4 per cent were not very satisfied with their own status. This overriding desire for economic success and status, combined with a general dissatisfaction with current conditions – attitudes which the surveyors termed "realistic and pragmatic" – also influenced their views on morality. Thus, although the students were adamant in their opposition to official corruption and bribery, when asked if they themselves would give a bribe if it would solve an urgent need, 54 per cent said that they "most certainly would" or "they would decide based on the situation."[24] A recent survey of college students found that only 15 per cent would choose not to offer a bribe if they needed someone's help; another 14 per cent were undecided; but 71 per cent would go ahead and make the offer.[25] This attitude is reflective of elite and popular discourse in China. As Richard Levy has pointed out, corruption in China is defined in terms of bribe-taking by officials, not bribe-giving by people seeking official favors or seeking to avoid legal restrictions. When Levy asked a lower-level official about punishing bribe-givers as well as bribe-takers, the official answered that the law does not call for arresting bribe-givers and, anyway, if they were all arrested, there would be no one left.[26]

The publisher of the popular Chinese magazine *iLook* and the Chinese edition of *Seventeen* recently argued that even if Chinese youth have traded in their character for commercialism, it was not necessarily a bad thing. As she put it in a provocative article, it was good for the Chinese people to indulge in the material world; in fact, a healthy dose of selfishness would be beneficial in helping to change the thinking of future Chinese generations. "These days, no one can persuade the Chinese people to trade their search for a better life for a political cause."[27]

Money and education

In contrast to previous generations, China's young university aspirants and their parents are pragmatic and individualistic – even self-centered – in their values and strategies. As only children, their parents are ambitious for them. The most successful book in 2001 was *Harvard Girl Liu Yiting*, in which proud parents tell how they scientifically prepared their daughter from birth to get into America's most prestigious university. Liu Yiting's acceptance into Harvard and three other prestigious American universities in 1999 at the age of 18 made the book required reading and her parents' strategy a frequent topic on Chinese talk shows and in the media.[28] Provincial education departments organized forums for parents on how to learn from Liu's example. This was followed by *Harvard Boy, Cambridge Girl, Tokyo University Boy*, and similar imitations. When a literary editor, fed up with the adulation accorded to the obsession with education for material success, published a rebuttal entitled *I'm Mediocre and I'm Happy* on how he raised his talented daughter to seek happiness above conventional success as defined by society, the book sold only 20,000 copies (in contrast to the 1.1 million-plus sales of *Harvard Girl*), and he was roundly vilified by parents and educators.[29]

As parents strive to maneuver their children successfully up through the ladder of education and, through this, into secure high-paying jobs, an extensive use of money has penetrated the educational system at every level, from kindergarten on through the Ph.D. and beyond. The government has encouraged this. Universities were given the right to determine their own fee structures in 1992, and in 1993 the government issued a major policy document stating that higher education should move gradually from a system under which the government guaranteed education and employment to a system in which students were held responsible for both. As a result, fewer academically qualified students from non-prosperous homes were admitted. Tuition costs today vary widely depending on location, specialization, whether or not the student is in a degree program, and so forth, but one common factor has been increasing fees; the average annual tuition is currently around 4,000–5,000 yuan.[30]

Once in the university, students need a substantial amount of money just to survive. One study in Beijing in 1999 found that university students spent

5,000–9,000 yuan per year, with 80 per cent coming from parents, relatives, or friends. Taking an average of 7,300 yuan, the study found that tuition made up about 30 per cent, meals about 40 per cent, housing about 6 per cent, transportation and communications about 7 per cent, cultural activities and entertainment about 9 per cent, with the remainder spent on miscellaneous expenses.[31] A 2000 study suggested that the average expense for a university student was between 8,000 and 10,000 yuan. As the report noted, if one adds the cost to the parents of primary and secondary education, the financial burden of seeing a child through to university graduation in Shanghai, Beijing, or Guangzhou is on average 100,000 yuan.[32]

Highly competitive specializations, like the graduate MBA degree, are far more costly. For example, at Beijing University, tuition for an MBA degree had reached 70,000 yuan by 2001.[33] The Chinese media has helped fuel the MBA fever, with books and articles on the wealth accumulated by graduates of MBA programs in the United States, accounts of Chinese students who have received MBA degrees at leading American universities, and extensive coverage of Chinese programs which have prestigious foreign partners.[34]

If the high flyers receiving MBAs and joining multinational corporations at high salaries represent one end of the spectrum, somewhere further down are those who have not been able to enter university. There are cautionary tales of swindlers preying on parents desperate to find university places for their children. One exposé published in a widely circulated youth magazine under the title "'Just give me money and I can find a way to get your child into university' – do you believe this?" reported on one swindler who offered places at a junior college for 5,000 yuan and places at a four-year college for 10,000 yuan.[35]

Money has entered the educational system at the lower levels as well. In the past, the standard route to success for the brightest and most ambitious students included entrance to a key high school (and perhaps a key primary school as well), followed by entrance to a key university. Upon graduation, the fortunate student would be allocated a job in the state sector of the economy in a major city, and would spend the rest of his/her life with an "iron rice bowl." In recent years, because of the differential effects of economic reforms on different localities, there is no longer a "standard route" up the educational ladder. The diversity of the educational system has required parents and students to formulate diverse strategies depending on the locality. For example, in less developed areas of the country, the most intense competition is often over entrance to a technical school, not a key academic high school that prepares the student for university. Since the number of senior highs is limited, and only a small number will go on to university anyway – with the cost of university tuition prohibitive for many families – it is much more practical to seek education which ensures employment, and to do so as early in one's educational career as possible.[36] Indeed, one survey of junior-high students and their parents in the rural areas of Hunan Province found that students were dropping out in large numbers because of family finances, and that 65 per cent saw migrant labor, not further study, as their "ideal career choice."[37]

In large cities like Beijing, by contrast, the competition to enter the best schools is most intense at the lower levels, which are popularly seen as essential stepping stones into the most prestigious universities and professions. The government has sought, through public policy, to reduce the competitive fires by abolishing key schools below the senior-high level and compelling parents to send their children to primary and junior high schools based on neighborhood patterns. The result, particularly since 1993, has been a virtually complete flouting of the law.[38] Money, in the form of "tuition donations," has become the standard method by which – and often the only way – parents can get their children into the schools of their choice. Tuition costs vary considerably depending on a student's marks, the quality of the school, the connections the parents have to a school, and so forth. By the mid-1990s, these costs already ranged from about 10,000–60,000 yuan per year for a top school.

The growing inequalities in basic education and the resultant phenomenon of "selecting schools" is now so widespread that it is openly discussed in academic journals and the popular press. In addition to extensive surveys reporting on the inequalities, the costs of selecting schools in various cities have been regularized – and published – to make it easier for parents to calculate educational expenses. However, schools routinely ask for far more than the published fee. In Taiyuan, Shanxi Province, the Provincial Education Commission has sought to guarantee that every primary-school graduate can get a free junior-high education at their neighborhood school. In reality, fewer than 10 per cent are able to do so.[39] At some of the best primary schools in Guangzhou, only half the students in some classrooms come from the neighborhood.[40] With expanded enrollment also occurring at lower levels, key primary and secondary schools may recruit a few classes of top-notch students and fill the remaining classes with students paying high fees. In this "buyer's market" (*maifang shichang*), educators have been concerned that the distinction between key and ordinary schools has become blurred.[41]

In less-developed western China, which has been under pressure to achieve nine-year compulsory education and provide more educational opportunities for rural youth, an intriguing pattern has developed in which the educational authorities meet their responsibilities while still disadvantaging the rural areas and the urban poor. Chongqing is a particularly interesting and well-publicized case, attracting attention because of the city's high rate of promotion from senior high to university. In 2002, this promotion rate surpassed 85 per cent, which was 15 percentage points higher than Beijing and 5 percentage points higher than Shanghai. They were able to do this by limiting the number of senior highs and placing the large majority in the main centers of the city. Thus, most districts and counties had only one or two senior highs. Chongqing *had* expanded schooling at the lower levels, but then closed it off for most beyond junior high.[42] Such limited opportunities fueled the competition to enter even lower quality senior highs, with each school providing set charges depending on the school's quality, requiring still higher fees from those below the school's minimum admission score.[43]

The increasing recognition that these educational costs are an "investment" in one's future has begun to have a major impact on the more traditional function of the schools, i.e. to socialize the young by imparting appropriate state-sanctioned values. One prominent case brought this issue to public discussion and revealed the dilemma of a state increasingly basing its legitimacy on the rise of a middle class, while still clinging to "socialist values." A language teacher in Zhuzhou City, Hunan Province, named Yin offered his entering students the following motivation for studying:

> Why are you going to school? Why would you apply to university? In the final analysis, what's the reason? ... I want to tell you clearly, studying and applying to university is for you, not for anyone else. Studying will improve your capabilities, so that in the future you can get a good job and have a wonderful personal life. For example, you'll be happy; your life will be enriched, you'll have a great future with a splendid job, and even find a beautiful wife and have an intelligent child. It's for these reasons that I stress that going to school is for you.[44]

Yin then wrote up an outline of these and other comments to the entering students, winning a second-level prize from the municipal education research institute. When Yin's "going to school for the purpose of making money and marrying a beautiful woman" view was picked up by the media in Beijing, he became famous overnight. The Zhuzhou Municipal Education Commission was not pleased, dismissing Yin from his position and notifying all schools in the five counties and towns under its control not to hire Yin. Although Yin sued in court and won his right to be reinstated, he found that no one would hire him. In a survey on the *Renmin* website, 60 per cent of respondents agreed that "going to school is for the purpose of making money and marrying a beautiful woman," while only 30 per cent disagreed. Moreover, 81 per cent did not think Yin should have been fired or have his employment opportunities restricted.[45]

Money has also become important in finding employment in an increasingly competitive job market under which the individual is often dependent on his or her own initiatives. Entrepreneurial skills are particularly helpful. For example, to be successful, an applicant commonly is compelled to make a large number of phone calls, hence the purchase of a cell phone, and to send many faxes. Indeed, the Chinese press reports that 2,000–3,000 yuan is the average expense for college graduates looking for employment.[46] These expenses will only increase because of an ever-tightening job market. As a result of the expansion of university enrollment in 1999, the first of the enlarged graduating classes began to look for work in 2003. Thus, there were 2,122,000 graduating students that year, a whopping 46.2 per cent increase over 2002. The employment rate was expected to be around 70 per cent, so that 640,000 university graduates would be unable to find jobs. Approximately 2,500,000 graduates are expected in 2004, with the pressure on graduating students remaining well into the future. This issue was a dominant theme in the Chinese media in 2003, although there was some debate on whether enrollment expansion was the major cause of the problem.[47]

Political pragmatism and Party recruitment

Surveys have commonly shown the decline of interest in politics among Chinese citizens, with the level of interest in politics varying directly with age. The older the citizen the more interested (s)he is in politics.[48] In similar fashion, a recent survey in five districts of Ji'nan, the capital of Shandong Province, found a very high correlation between age and interpersonal trust. At every age level, the older the age cohort, the more the respondents trusted other people. Those over 50 were most trusting; those under 20 were least trusting.[49] In addition, surveys have shown that young and middle-aged Party members have little interest in doing "Party work" *(dangwu gongzuo)*.[50]

Given such problems, it might be expected that the CCP would have trouble recruiting among the cream of the young. In fact, however, the situation is apparently just the reverse. There is increasing interest among upwardly mobile educated young people in joining the Party.[51] According to data released by the State Education Commission (now the Ministry of Education), as of 1990, 0.8 per cent of university students were CCP members; by the end of 2000, 3.8 per cent (210,000) of China's undergraduates were Party members. Among graduate students, 28.2 per cent (77,000) were Party members.[52] It should be clear, however, that these aggregate figures conceal important variations. Party membership is concentrated at key universities and in specific departments.[53]

This in turn reflects the Party's decision to concentrate its recruitment efforts on the young and the well educated. As the careful study on Party-sponsored mobility into the administrative elite by Bobai Li and Andrew Walder concluded, in the late reform period (1988–96 in their study), there was "a dramatic shift toward a 'technocratic' pattern, in which individuals from red households are abandoned in favor of young college graduates."[54] This trend has been documented in many local studies, revealing that workers and peasants – even among the young – have not been interested and/or have not been cultivated as Party recruitment targets. Thus, an internal report on Party recruitment among the young in Heilongjiang Province noted that province-wide, the number of "activists" *(jiji fenzi)* declined from 595,000 in 1995 to 427,000 in 1999, a decline of 28.2 per cent; the decline was particularly prominent among young workers and peasants.

The average age of peasant Party members in the province was 48.7 years old, with only 19.2 per cent 35 years old or younger.[55] Thus, despite the well-documented increase in young Party members in college, particularly among those at elite schools, there has been a slight overall decline of Party members 35 years old or younger over the last few years. In 1998, such members constituted 23.1 per cent of the Party; in 1999, the equivalent figure was 22.5 per cent; and by the end of 2000, the figure had dropped further to 22.3 per cent, suggesting the losses came from the less favored, less educated classes. Indeed, the Chinese press has proudly reported in detail on the increasingly impressive educational credentials of Party members.[56]

The seeming paradox – a declining interest in politics and trust coupled with a greater desire to enter the CCP – can be explained by looking more closely at motivations for joining. Fortunately, Chinese authorities also have an interest in this issue, and have conducted a number of surveys, particularly on the link between Party membership and employment prospects. One university surveyed Party members who were students or intellectuals and discovered that close to half of them had joined because it would help them find a good job. A very popular slogan among them was: "Before you enter the Party you're sweating all over; after you enter the Party you can relax. Before you enter the Party you're full of revolution; after you enter the Party you meld into the crowd."[57] According to this report, Party membership was also popular because companies with foreign investment sought out such individuals to recruit. They reasoned that students who had joined the Party must have been on good terms with their instructors, which meant they were likely to be team players.

Another survey found that 40 per cent of students expressed interest in joining the Party, with the number increasing to 50 per cent for new students. When those who had already joined were asked why they sought membership, 30 per cent admitted that it would enable them to find a good job after graduation. They were also asked their opinion of the following statement: "Entering the Party is a bargaining chip that can increase one's chances in the competition to find a good job." A total of 70.1 per cent chose the following response: "It's not completely accurate, but it's definitely reasonable [to think that]."[58]

One imaginative study surveyed newly graduated students who had already signed employment contracts with their work units, and recent graduates with around five years of work experience behind them, to determine what the graduates felt were the key factors that enabled them to obtain their jobs. Of the ten factors studied, Party membership came in sixth, although 93.9 per cent felt that it was either of great importance (34.7 per cent) or of some importance (59.2 per cent). In the overall rankings, the factors considered more important than Party membership were, in order, academic specialization, study achievements, the reputation of the university attended, prizes awarded at school, and the oral exam with the employer.[59] Interviewees, however, noted that the value of Party membership was far from constant. For some jobs, such as in the sensitive area of media, it was essential; for others, it was unnecessary. For example, at Fudan University's Graduate School of Journalism, about 70 per cent of the (mostly female) students were Party members.[60]

Hong Kong magazines, quoting from classified mainland sources, have reported minimal interest in communist ideals. In one survey of over 800 graduating Party and CYL members at 16 universities in Beijing, reportedly only 38 students expressed a belief in communism. One political education instructor at Beijing University, interviewed by the magazine, said he had never met a student who really believed in communism.[61] Despite the apparent lack of belief in such ideals, some studies have found a strong desire to become an official (*dang guan*). For example, a CASS survey of 2,599 individuals in 63 cities who were 16 years of age or older asked respondents to rank 69 professions in order of job preference. The most favored choice was mayor, followed by government minister, university professor, computer/Internet engineer, judge, public prosecutor, lawyer, high-technology enterprise engineer, leading official in the Party or government, and natural scientist. Revealingly, the lowest-ranked job was migrant construction worker, followed by domestic maid (*baomu*) and employee of an individually owned business (*getihu gugong*).[62] As the next section will show, this low ranking for jobs associated with migrant workers is also reflected in attitudes toward personal relationships across social strata.

The social implications of new stratification patterns

The Party has long taught that the working class is to be admired. But the new stratum of upwardly mobile urban Chinese who have become the role models for society do not share this view – even apparently among those who enter the Party. The new viewpoint can be examined by way of a discussion forum that was carried in *Zhongguo qingnian* (*China Youth*), the widely circulated journal published by the CYL. Established initially in October 1923, just two years after the founding of the CCP, the magazine has long represented the appropriate values the regime sought to instill in the country's youth. For those among us who remember the ideological ortho-doxy of the Maoist period, when children of the pre-1949 upper classes carried the burden of their "bad family background," the discussion forum in *Zhongguo qingnian* in mid-2002 may perhaps seem a bit shocking. Arguably, it demonstrated the regime's recognition and acceptance of the implications of China's emerging stratification for human relationships.

The subject of the forum – "Can friendship transcend stratum?" – was introduced with an editorial note enquiring into the basis of friendship. The editor asked what the outcome would be if two close friends were suddenly separated by changing lifestyles and different mobility paths. Could friend-ship continue if one of the friends "entered" a higher social stratum (*shehui jieceng*) than the other? The answer was no.

This opening salvo in the discussion – as is common in such forums – was provocative and intended to elicit responses from the magazine's readers.[63] In his open letter to the magazine, "Young Bo" detailed the history of his relationship with his closest friend, Li Xijun, from his senior year in high school in Gansu Province. Even after Bo was accepted at a key university in Xi'an and his classmate failed the university entrance examination, the two friends swore that they would remain like brothers for the rest of their lives. After graduation, Bo was able to find a good job in Beijing, but his friend remained at home as an ordinary worker. Inviting Li to Beijing and sneaking him in to live in the unit's housing, they tried several ways to arrange for Li to find a steady job in the city, including an unsuccessful attempt to purchase a bogus college degree. Bo also began to realize that Li was not sufficiently educated to appreciate the work that Bo was doing. They were drifting further apart and, though still living together, hardly speaking at all. When Bo's supervisor discovered Li's presence, Bo was faced with a tough choice: his continued career in the organization depended on his friend's departure. Li was able to find very inexpensive housing in a county outside Beijing, but with no heat or electricity. Although he provided some material support, more and more Bo would find excuses to avoid meeting Li. In the end, Li felt that he could not make it in Beijing and went home to work in the fields. Thus, in spite of his best efforts, Bo felt that the relationship could not last. The concluding sentence of the letter was the crucial one for the forthcoming "debate." Bo agonized over whether the friendship foundered because of a personality flaw of his own, or because *society* prevented the friendship from continuing.[64]

The next three issues of the magazine contained twenty-five published responses to this opening contribution. Most were from the rising urban middle class. Those who felt that friendship across strata could not be maintained based this conclusion largely on changing economic and living conditions, arguing that individuals from different strata were no longer able to exchange thoughts and feelings successfully. As they are no longer classmates and in effect have no common interests or topics to share and discuss, the friendship must end. At best, they should cherish the memory of this formerly close friendship. A middle-school teacher, for example, felt that he could not have any relationship with a member of the *nouveaux riches*.

One participant in the discussion, a reporter for a Beijing newspaper, offered a particularly graphic response in arguing against friendships across widely divergent socio-economic strata, "at least in today's China," as he put it. He noted that a newspaper in Qingdao had written that some people proposed that a separate section of public transportation be set aside for the migrant workers (*min gong*) since the "neat and tidy" citizens could not tolerate the smell of these outsiders. This proposal, he felt, suggested that China was becoming worse than the United States in terms of discrimination. If people feel this way, how could one possibly make friends with these migrants? He also noted that many of his friends felt that they could have cross-strata friendships, until he pressed them and then they changed their minds. In an exchange with a chatroom friend who felt that he could be friends with a migrant worker, the reporter responded: "I don't believe you! Do you mean you wouldn't be put off by the bad body odor, the shabby clothes, or the diminished image you would have walking next to such a person?" The chatroom friend reluctantly agreed, suggesting that not only could he not be friends with a migrant worker, but that if his classmates or friends dressed badly or smelled badly, he wouldn't spend time with them either.[65]

Those more optimistic also agreed that the major impediment to friendship was China's increasing stratification, but felt that a person should not be bound by his or her social role and status. With sincerity and enthusiasm, individuals could transcend social distinctions and status. It was important to recognize, of course, that social roles are changing and that this will require a reassessment of the relationships one has, but for a psychologically healthy person there should be a rational way to solve these problems without abandoning former friends (there seemed much less likelihood of making *new* friends across strata).

Indeed, there is a saying that students on university campuses are divided into "five big tribes" (*wu da buluo*), based on wealth, consumption patterns, and housing. The poorest students live in shabby dorms; the richest students occupy the new apartments on campus. As one student told a *China Youth Daily* reporter, "We only hang out with friends in our circle. If a member of our group went looking for romance with an apartment dweller, (s)he would be mocked for 'trying to climb above their station' [*pan gao zhi*]."[66]

Conclusion

There had already been abundant evidence prior to the events of the spring/summer of 1989 that the state had lost its ideological legitimacy in the eyes of Chinese youth. What Beijing Spring revealed, with its massive support for the students from a broad section of society, was that this loss of legitimacy extended beyond ideology to include performance. Post-1989, the regime (and more specifically the CCP) recognized that old appeals to a discredited ideology had become counter-productive, and that a renewal of popular support required goals that could only be assessed using criteria based on performance. The competence of the leadership would be demonstrated through policies that were appealing on both the individual and the collective levels. Individually, citizens were offered the prospects of a higher standard of living economically and a more varied private life culturally. Collectively, the CCP committed itself to the creation of a rich and powerful China, fully able to take its rightful place among the leading nations of the world.

The first initiative – at the individual level – has been markedly successful, albeit primarily for those urban youth in the coastal regions best placed to benefit. China has begun to produce an upwardly mobile white-collar stratum of yuppies, and surveys have revealed important distinctions that differentiate this group in such areas as mate choice, reading habits, values, and friendships. As the market economy began to develop, it gave rise to a society very different from the pre-reform model. A well-defined route to success no longer existed. In the past, education had been relatively inexpensive, and talented youth and their parents had reason to hope that diligence would be rewarded with good prospects for upward mobility, even for the poor. However, changing public policies and the differential effects of economic reforms on different localities have led to a far more diversified educational and employment system, requiring diverse strategies for success. Parents with the ability to pay can virtually ensure places for their children in elite schools; graduates must be entrepreneurial in tracking down good jobs. Those without money and connections have found it difficult to compete.

How much of this new materialism has in fact been driven by public policies, as the state moved away from earlier models of socialism and in the direction of a capitalist market economy? How much has come from the bottom up, with state initiatives largely a response to popular demands and pressures? There are clearly elements of both purposeful state policies – particularly in response to the loss of public support following the events of 1989 – and the resurgence of long-suppressed desires on the part of the populace.[67]

In her perceptive discussion of what she labels "the post-communist personality," Xiaoying Wang notes how the powerful societal reaction against the "extreme asceticization" of Chinese life under Mao combined with the CCP's orchestrated ideological campaign to redirect individual and societal energy toward the post-communist struggle for wealth and pleasure. While the regime's intention was to promote a competitive ethos and develop a market economy that would promote rapid economic development, an unintended consequence – in the absence of a comprehensive, internally consistent ideology – has been the burning desire to get rich, linked to a suspicion of all moral values.[68]

To be sure, the CCP has sought to temper the rampant materialist impulses described in this paper in a number of ways, and to address the second initiative: the promotion of collectivist goals. One obvious measure has been the appeal to patriotism (read nationalism) as a core value that would unite Chinese youth who have been privileged, as well as those excluded under the first initiative, in a common mission. While the long-term effects of this strategy are unclear and are a subject of much debate, there is at least some preliminary evidence that such appeals have thus far had only short-term success, despite such dramatic events as the American bombing of the Chinese Embassy in Yugoslavia in May 1999 and the spy plane collision of April 2001 (see below, n. 10).

There is also the familiar emphasis on promoting "spiritual civilization." However, since this emphasis is of necessity tied to official, albeit discredited, socialist or communist values – including periodic reappearances of such hoary communist icons as Lei Feng – spiritual civilization campaigns have had little resonance among the populace.[69] In the spring of 2000, as Bruce Dickson's chapter (Chapter 7) notes, Jiang Zemin introduced the "three represents" slogan, an attempt to redefine the CCP's relationship to society. The CCP now represents the advanced productive forces (i.e. the growing middle class), the promotion of advanced culture (in contrast to rampant materialism, as well as "feudal" culture), and the interests of the majority of the Chinese people. However, this slogan has been associated with and used to justify the recruitment of private entrepreneurs into the CCP. Thus, rather than tempering materialist pursuits, the "three represents" initiative is far more likely to exacerbate them, while further calling attention to the gulf between a "communist" Party and the increasingly capitalistic economic order. So long as the economy continues to grow at a reasonably high rate, the disjuncture between politics and economics and state and society is not likely to produce an unmanageable crisis for the regime in the near term. In the long run, however, there are obvious dangers if the CCP increasingly embraces money-making elites yet is unable to harness the focus on materialist values to a new and acceptable moral discourse.

Notes

1 Dingxin Zhao, *The Power of Tiananmen: State–Society Relations and the 1989 Beijing Student Movement* (Chicago: University of Chicago Press, 2001), p. 345.
2 David Zweig, *Internationalizing China: Domestic Interests and Global Linkages* (Ithaca: Cornell University Press, 2002).
3 Li Jian and Niu Xiaohan, "The new middle class(es) in Peking: a case study," *China Perspectives* 45 (January–February 2003): 17.
4 On 1980s youth, see Luo Xu, *Searching for Life's Meaning: Changes and Tensions in the Worldviews of Chinese Youth in the 1980s* (Ann Arbor: University of Michigan Press, 2002).
5 *Gaige neican* (Inside Information on Economic Reform) No. 20, 2001, p. 45.
6 The most authoritative study of social stratification is the one supervised by the Chinese Academy of Social Sciences. See Lu Xueyi *et al.* (eds), *Dangdai zhongguo shehui jieceng yanjiu baogao* (*A Research Report on Social Stratification in Contemporary China*) (Beijing: Zhongguo shehui kexue wenxian chubanshe, 2001). For a good recent overview of the subject in English, see "Social stratification in contemporary China," *Social Sciences in China*, Special Issue, XXIII(1) (Spring 2002): 42–134.
7 See, for example, the special section entitled "The enigma of stratification" in *Xin zhou kan* (*New Weekly*), 1 January 2002, pp. 30–51, which tries to help readers understand where they fit among the various strata, and *Nanfang zhoumo* (*Southern Weekend*), 20 December 2001, p. 1, which offers a full-page lead story on the CASS report, sorting out the "five major social levels" and the "ten major social strata."
8 Ding Wang and Mou Jianqiu, "Everyone's ignoring the lower rungs," *Gaige neican* (*Inside Information on Economic Reform*) 2, 20 January 2002, pp. 2–5.
9 Sun Liping, "Are we beginning to confront a fractured society?" *Zhanlue yu guanli* 2 (2002): 9–15; Sun Liping, "Fracture: a new change in Chinese society," *Nanfang zhoumo* (*Southern Weekend*), 16 May 2002, p. A11; Anthony Kuhn,

"The myth of China's middle class," *Los Angeles Times*, 8 December 2002, p. A11.

10 In previous work, I have focused more on the contradictions and tensions between international influences, pragmatism, and the rise of popular nationalism among Chinese youth. While rising nationalism remains an important element in the attitudes and behavior of youth, and serves as a potential threat to the regime, the argument here is that pragmatism and the pursuit of the good life has made popular nationalism, at least in the short term, less of a threat. See Stanley Rosen, "Chinese media and youth: attitudes toward nationalism and internationalism," in Chin-Chuan Lee (ed.) *National and Global: Chinese Media Discourses* (London and New York: RoutledgeCurzon, 2003), pp. 97–118, and Joseph Fewsmith and Stanley Rosen, "The domestic context of Chinese foreign policy: does 'public opinion' matter?" in David M. Lampton (ed.) *The Making of Chinese Foreign and Security Policy in the Era of Reform* (Stanford: Stanford University Press, 2001), pp. 151–187. This has also been documented both in interviews and formal surveys, most tellingly after the May 1999 NATO bombing of the Chinese Embassy in Belgrade, Yugoslavia. For example, Dingxin Zhao's survey of 1,211 students and interviews with 62 informants conducted at three elite universities in Beijing four months after the bombing revealed that the anger expressed toward the United States, while genuine, was more of a "momentary outrage" than an enduring and popular anti-US nationalism. Respondents considered "to counteract US hegemony" the least important among eight national goal statements that were provided. Indeed, as this and other surveys and interviews demonstrated, personal interests in the form of career opportunities – including the taking of TOEFL and GRE exams needed to attend American universities – came to the forefront even while anger against the United States persisted. See Dingxin Zhao, "An angle on nationalism in China today: attitudes among Beijing students after Belgrade 1999," *China Quarterly* 172 (December 2002): 885–905. On the ambivalence toward the United States and the contradictions between positive views of US society and culture and negative views of US foreign policy, see Chen Shengluo, "Two Americas: the views of Chinese university students toward the United States," *Qingnian yanjiu* (*Youth Studies*) 6 (June 2002): 1–8. See also Deng Lilan, *Meiguo! Meiguo? Meiguo ...: shiji zhi jiao zhongguo daxuesheng de meiguo guan* (*America! America? America ...: Attitudes of Chinese University Students Toward the United States at the Turn of the Century*) (Shenyang: Liaoning renmin chubanshe, 2001).

11 See, for example, the cover story and the survey of seven cities entitled "What is money?" *Xin zhou kan* (*New Weekly*), 15 September 1999, pp. 52–57.

12 *Zhengming* (*Contention*) (Hong Kong) 8 (August 2000): 27. The original source was listed as Xinhua's Internal Reference, 15 July 2000.

13 For examples, see Zhang Yimou's *Yige dou buneng shao* (*Not One Less*) (1999), Zhang's *Qiu Ju da guansi* (*The Story of Qiu Ju*) (1993), and Zhou Xiaowen's *Ermo* (*Ermo*) (1994).

14 Jin Dan and Li Chunlin (eds), *Zhongguo: shei zui fu* (*China: Who's the Wealthiest?*) (Beijing: Qiye guanli chubanshe, 2001).

15 "Who are the richest people: China's first official investigation from ten provinces and cities," *Sanlian shenghuo zhoukan* (*Sanlian Life Weekly*), 19 March 2001, pp. 16–30.

16 *Baike zhishi* (*Encyclopedic Knowledge*) 5 (May 2000): 49. "Profession" is used rather loosely since the "small number of business people who violate the law" and "the extremely small number of corrupt officials" place at numbers nine and ten on the list. One internally reported study noted that 5 per cent of the population held about 50 per cent of the bank deposits. See *Jingji da cankao* (*Major Reference on the Economy*) 18 (July 2000): 23–24.

17 Liu Xiaoqing's arrest on charges of tax evasion was the subject of several quickie books, special issues of magazines, and extensive press coverage. See Xiao Xiao (ed.), *Beiqing yinghou – Liu Xiaoqing: cong yiwan fujie dao yindang ruyu* (*Post-movie Career Sorrow – Liu Xiaoqing: From Hundreds of Millions to Blocked Assets and Prison*) (Beijing: Xin shijie chubanshe, 2002), and "The braggart Liu Xiaoqing: a film star and her era," *Nanfang zhoumo* (*Southern Weekend*), 8 August 2002, p. 1. She was ordered to pay US$700,000 in fines and nearly US$2 million in back taxes. *New York Times*, 21 December 2002, p. A6.

18 "Forbes listing upsets some Chinese tycoons," China News Digest online, 27 October 2002, originally published in *Yangcheng wanbao*.

19 *Neibu tongxin* (*Internal Communications*) 7, 5 April 2003, pp. 11–13. For an example of such reporting, focusing on the uneasiness of the rich, see the series of reports on the murders and their implications in *Xinwen zhoukan* (*Newsweek*) 8, 10 March 2003, pp. 22–29.

20 Song Haifeng, "Men, women and money," *Shandong qingnian* (*Shandong Youth*) 2 (February 2002): 52–54.

21 Zhang Shenxia, "An analysis and categorization of the attitude toward money of university students in Shandong," *Qingnian gongzuo luntan* (*Forum on Youth Work*) 1 (1997): 33–37.

22 Liu Yongqin, "The ideological and political condition of contemporary university students and our countermeasures," *Sixiang zhengzhi jiaoyu* (*Ideological and Political Education*) 10 (October 2001): 83.

23 Xun Jianli, "When you pick up a wallet," *Shehui* (*Society*) 12 (December 2001): 43–44. The survey found Singapore in second place at 90 per cent, followed by Australia and Japan (70 per cent), the United States (67 per cent), England (65 per cent), France (60 per cent), the Netherlands (50 per cent), Germany (45 per cent), Russia (43 per cent), and the Philippines (40 per cent).

24 Han Yongqing, "An investigation and research on the countermeasures required to address the contradictions in the needs of contemporary Shanxi Youth," *Shanxi gaodeng xuexiao shehui kexue xuebao* (*Social Science Journal of the Shanxi Province Higher Education School*) 2 (2002): 88–90.

25 Zhang Chi, "Research into the contradictions in the moral choices of university students," *Qingnian yanjiu* (*Youth Studies*) 6 (June 2003): 23–31.

26 Richard Levy, "Corruption in popular culture," in *Popular China: Unofficial Culture in a Globalizing Society* (Lanham, MD: Rowman and Littlefield, 2002), p. 51.

27 Hung Huang, "Safety in shopping," *Enterprise Newsweek*, 28 October 2002, p. 44N.

28 Zhang Xinwu and Liu Weihua (eds), *Hafo nuhai Liu Yiting: suzhi peiyang jishi* (*Harvard Girl Liu Yiting: The True Story of Her Training*) (Beijing: Zhongguo qingnian chubanshe, 2000).

29 Zhou Hong, *Wo pingyong, wo kuaile* (*I'm Mediocre and I'm Happy*) (Taipei: Gaofu guoji wenhua gufen youxian gongsi, 2002; original edition published by Guangdong jiaoyu chubanshe). On the controversy generated by this book, see *Nanfang zhoumo* (*Southern Weekend*), 18 July 2002, p. D28, and Erik Eckholm, "A Chinese dad in defense of the average child," *New York Times*, 8 June 2002, p. A4. For the official document calling for the Guangdong forum, entitled "*Harvard Girl* and quality education," go to www.gzqg.net.cn/hdhf/szjy.

30 See the official *Xinbian gaoxiao zhaosheng luqu ji tianbiao zhiyuan zhinan* (*New Edition of the Guide to Higher Education Recruitment and How to Fill Out Application Forms*) (Beijing: Huayu jiaoxue chubanshe, 2001), p. 78, and Zhongguo qingnian yanjiu (China Youth Study) 3 (2003): 90.

31 *Lingdao juece xinxi* (*Decisive Information for Leaders*) 49 (December 1999): 30. For more details on the expenses of university students, see Zhang Zhixiang,

"The characteristics and trends in consumption by university students," *Zhongguo qingnian yanjiu* (*China Youth Study*) 5 (2002): 33–36.

32 In smaller cities such as Zhengzhou in Henan Province it would be 70,000 yuan; in Ji'nan in Shandong Province it would be 60,000 yuan. See Huang Zhijian, "Five major trends in consumption patterns of youth," *Liaowang xinwen zhoukan* (*Outlook Weekly*) 35, 27 August 2001, pp. 38–40. A more recent report from Zhejiang Province put the cost at 126,000 yuan. See *Qianshao* (*Frontline*) (Hong Kong) 2 (February 2003): 140, citing *Zhongguo xinxi bao*.

33 *Gaige neican* (*Inside Information on Economic Reform*) 23 (2001): 47.

34 For example, see Wu Yijun, "MBA meets the Internet economy," *Shehui* (*Society*) 8 (August 2000): 25–27, and *Hafo MBA: zhongguo ren ziji de gushi* (*Harvard MBA: Chinese People Tell their Own Stories*) (Beijing: Zhongguo jingji chubanshe, 1999), a collective effort by members of the 1999 Harvard MBA class.

35 *Shandong qingnian* (*Shandong Youth*) 3 (March 2002): 42–44.

36 Stanley Rosen, "Education and economic reform," in Christopher Hudson (ed.) *The China Handbook: Prospects Onto the 21st Century* (Chicago: Fitzroy Dearborn Publishers, 1997), pp. 250–261.

37 *Xinhua meiri dianxun*, reported in *Qianshao yuekan* (*Frontline Monthly*) (Hong Kong) 10 (October 2002): 140.

38 Rosen, "Education and economic reform," pp. 256–259.

39 *Neibu canyue* (*Internal Reference*) 49, 27 December 2002, pp. 30–31.

40 *Nanfang zhoumo* (*Southern Weekend*), 12 June 2003, p. A7.

41 *Gaige neican* (*Inside Information on Economic Reform*) 17, 5 September 2002, p. 48.

42 *Gaige neican* (*Inside Information on Economic Reform*) 12, 20 April 2003, p. 48, citing *Zhongguo jingji shibao*.

43 I have addressed the Chongqing case in more detail, including specific charges for different category schools, in Stanley Rosen, "The victory of materialism: aspirations to join China's moneyed classes and the corruption of education," *China Journal* (January 2004).

44 Zhou Langming, "A teacher with 'strange views' wins a lawsuit over the education commission," *Nanfang zhoumo* (*Southern Weekend*), 15 August 2002, p. 1.

45 Zhou Langming, "For whom are we studying? The court decides," *Xinwen zhoukan* (*Newsweek*) 18, 8 July 2002, pp. 42–43.

46 From *Yangzi wanbao* (*Yangzi Evening News*), reprinted in *Qianshao yuekan* (*Frontline Monthly*) (Hong Kong) 2 (February 2002): 140.

47 By 20 June 2003, only about 50 per cent of the graduates had found jobs, leaving about 1 million unemployed. While 80 per cent of postgraduate degree-holders had signed employment contracts, the rates for those with undergraduate degrees (60 per cent) and junior college degrees (30 per cent) lagged behind. Among many sources, see *Liaowang xinwen zhoukan* (*Liaowang News Weekly*) 23, 9 June 2003, pp. 12–15; *Jiaoyu fazhan yanjiu* (*Exploring Education Development*) 6 (June 2003): 8–12; *Nanfang zhoumo* (*Southern Weekend*), 3 July 2003, pp. A1–2; and the cover story in *Xinwen zhoukan* (*Newsweek*) 25, 14 July 2003, pp. 18–28.

48 Yu Guoming, "Survey of Beijing citizens' attitudes toward politics," *Zhongguo qingnian bao*, 28 September 1996, translated in Foreign Broadcast Information Service (FBIS) Daily Report 97–004, 8 January 1997.

49 Cheng Shengli, "Research on interpersonal trust among contemporary urbanites," *Shehui* (*Society*) 1 (January 2002): 29–30.

50 "The tendency of some young and middle-aged cadres to look down on Party work has become serious," *Neibu canyue* (*Internal Reference*) 3, 21 January 1998, p. 22.

51 Bruce Dickson, *Red Capitalists in China: The Party, Private Entrepreneurs, and Prospects for Political Change* (Cambridge: Cambridge University Press, 2003); Bruce J. Dickson and Maria Rost Rublee, "Membership has its privileges: the socioeconomic characteristics of Communist Party members in urban China," *Comparative Political Studies* 33(1) (February 2000): 87–112. For earlier data on Party recruitment among the young, see Stanley Rosen, "The Chinese Communist Party and Chinese society: popular attitudes toward Party membership and the Party's image," *Australian Journal of Chinese Affairs* 24 (June 1990): 51–92.

52 Almost one-third of university students were applying for membership. By the end of 2001, reportedly as many as 8 per cent of university students had entered the Party. See Duan Xinxing, "A perspective on what is 'hot' among university students," *Qingnian tansuo* (*Youth Studies*) (Guangzhou) 3 (1997): 32–34; Xinhua News Agency online, 1 and 5 June 2001; and *Zhongguo jiaoyu bao* (*China Education News*), 31 December 2001, p. 1.

53 Wu Bangjiang, "Why university students are now joining the Party," *Xin shiji* (*New Century*) 11 (November 1997): 54–57. At Qinghua University in Beijing, more than one-third of the students have expressed an interest in joining the Party. By mid-2002, 12 per cent of undergraduates and 30 per cent of graduate students there were Party members. See Erik Eckholm, "As China's economy shines, the Party line loses luster," *New York Times*, 5 November 2002, pp. A1, 12.

54 Bobai Li and Andrew G. Walder, "Career advancement as Party patronage: sponsored mobility into the Chinese administrative elite, 1949–1996," *American Journal of Sociology* 106(5) (March 2001): 1371–1408. They also note the increased recruitment of those still in college.

55 Han Guizhi, "It is necessary to cultivate and recruit youth into the Party," *Lilun dongtai* (*Theoretical Trends*) 1524, 20 April 2001, pp. 17–23.

56 The figures for 1998 are from *People's Daily Online*, 28 June 1999; for 1999, see *Dangjian wenhui* (*Collection of Materials on Party Construction*) 8 (2000): 43; for 2000, see *Dangjian wenhui* 7 (2001): 7. For statistics on the changing educational level of Party members from 1956–2000, see Cao Wenzhong and Feng Yincheng, "The level of formal schooling of Party members has been rising every year," *Beijing qingnian bao* (*Beijing Youth Daily*), 30 June 2001, p. 2.

57 Duan Xinxing, " A perspective on what is 'hot' among university students."

58 Pan Duola, "More on 'motivations for joining the Party,' " *Nanfang zhoumo* (*Southern Weekend*), 27 September 1996, reprinted in Wang Huaqiao (ed.), *Zhenshi de yanshuo: touguo 'Nanfang Zhoumo' kan zhongguo* (*The Truth in Words: Looking into China by Penetrating 'Southern Weekend'*) (Beijing: Zhongguo chengshi chubanshe, 1998), pp. 104–105.

59 Zhang Shujiang, Wang Kaiye, and Liu Guanghui, "Universities need to take an active part in paving the way for student employment," *Zhongguo daxuesheng jiuye* (*China University Students Career Guide*) 2–3 (2002): 21–22.

60 Interviews in Shanghai, November 2002.

61 For the first survey, see *Dongxiang* (*Trend*) 7 (July 2000): 27; for the second survey, see *Kaifang yuekan* (*Open Monthly*) 8 (August 2000): 22.

62 "Residents of urban China would most like to 'become officials,'" *Qianshao yuekan* (*Frontline Monthly*) (Hong Kong) 1 (January 2001): 131; originally published in *Henan ribao* (*Henan Daily*).

63 "Can friendship transcend stratum?" *Zhongguo qingnian* (*China Youth*) 9 (2002): 48–49; 10 (2002): 48–50; 11 (2002): 44–46; and 12 (2002): 38–40.

64 Emphasis added. "A lost friendship I'll regret forever," *Zhongguo qingnian* (*China Youth*) 9 (2002): 48–49. It is interesting to note that *Zhongguo qingnian* itself is a victim of the market economy. It has seen its circulation drop from more than 4

million in 1982 to less than 300,000 by 1994, with a corresponding decline in profits. In 2003, it went to a full-color magazine and a greater emphasis on popular culture to increase circulation. See *Meijie* (*Media*), December 2002, pp. 17–21.

65 Wang Chong, "New friendships cannot be established with those from different strata," *Zhongguo qingnian* (*China Youth*) 11 (2002): 44–45. Reports in the Chinese media on discrimination against rural migrants are common. For examples, see *Banyuetan neibuban* (*Semi-monthly Talks, Internal Edition*) 6 (June 2002): 8–11, and *Zhongguo qingnian yanjiu* (*China Youth Study*) 5 (2002): 56–59. For an example of university students playing a practical joke on gullible migrant workers seeking to make some money, see *Qianshao yuekan* (*Frontline Monthly*) 4 (April 2003): 61; original report in *Zhongguo qingnian bao*.

66 Wang Hui, "Idealism vs. new mankind," *Zhongguo qingnian bao*, 26 December 2002, p. 7. "*Pan gao zhi*" literally means "climbing to a higher branch of a tree."

67 Examples of popular urban desires include the wave of nostalgia in China's large cosmopolitan cities, such as Beijing, Guangzhou, and Shanghai. We have seen the return of elaborate weddings, with photos taken in traditional costumes; mothers have purchased pre-revolution feminine dresses such as the elegant *qipao* for their daughters; advertisers have appealed to the growing desire for privacy and luxury housing; and the popular media provide lurid thrills recounting the fascinating and deviant lifestyles of the *nouveaux riches*. In interviews, young women have suggested that their parents – particularly their mothers – have sought to compensate for the many years of personal privation they themselves had faced in Mao's China, offering their daughters opportunities for the "good life" they had been denied. In addition to interviews, also see Deborah Davis (ed.), *The Consumer Revolution in Urban China* (Berkeley and Los Angeles: University of California Press, 2000): virtually every chapter speaks to these changes, but see particularly David Fraser, "Inventing oasis: luxury housing advertisements and reconfiguring domestic space in Shanghai," pp. 25–53. On the changing trends in love and marriage from 1979–99, see *Aiqing ye liuxing* (*Love in Fashion*) (Beijing: Zhongguo qingnian chubanshe, 2001). On the new tabloid literature, see, for example, Yin Dou, *Bailing jieceng de yinmi shenghuo* (*The Hidden Life of the White-Collar Stratum*) (Haerbin: Heilongjiang renmin chubanshe, 2001).

68 Xiaoying Wang, "The post-communist personality: the spectre of China's capitalist market reforms," *China Journal* 47 (January 2002): 1–17.

69 *Ibid.*, pp. 15–17.

9 Popular nationalism and state legitimation in China[1]

Peter Hays Gries

In his thoughtful 1995 exploration of China's war with Japan, *Wailing at the Heavens*, People's Liberation Army (PLA) writer Jin Hui breaks new ground. Unlike the majority of 50th anniversary commemorative volumes published in 1995 China, Jin resists the temptation to either valorize Chinese victories or righteously condemn Japanese atrocities. Instead, Jin engages in sincere soul-searching, asking, for example, why so many Chinese were "as meek as lambs at the slaughterhouse" (*ren ren xing ge*) during the war: "Men are not lambs. But it seems like many of those slaughtered were even more obedient than lambs ... Why didn't they resist when faced with death?" This enquiry leads Jin into a probing examination of why the Chinese, like a "sheet of loose sand" (*yipan sansha*), lacked courage and unity in fighting the Japanese.[2]

As part of an official series commemorating the "War of Resistance against Japan," *Wailing at the Heavens* underwent rigorous editing at the PLA Literature and Arts Press. General Zhang Zhen wrote the book's Preface, further testifying to the book's official status. General Zhang cites Deng Xiaoping on how "Only socialism can save China" to make the standard Chinese Communist Party (CCP) argument that "In modern China, patriotism is tied to socialism." In the book itself, however, Jin Hui unties that knot, underscoring the "separation of the Chinese concepts of state [*guojia*] and motherland [*zuguo*]," and arguing that "there are 'two Chinas': the Chinese people's 'motherland', and the rulers' 'state.' "[3] Jin thus radically undermines the idea of a monolithic Party-state with complete hegemony over nationalist discourse.

The CCP, this chapter contends, is losing control over nationalist discourse. Under Mao, the Party claimed that because it had successfully led the revolutionary masses during the War of Resistance and the Civil War, the Party and the nation were fused into an inseparable whole. Only communists, in other words, could be genuine Chinese nationalists. Under Jiang Zemin and now Hu Jintao, however, the CCP's nationalist claims are increasingly falling on deaf ears. Popular nationalists like Jin Hui now speak regularly of the "Motherland" (*zuguo*) and the "Chinese race" (*Zhonghua minzu*) – without reference to the Party. And they care so deeply about the fate of the Chinese nation that they are demanding a say in nationalist politics. Nationalism is a grammar that potential challengers can use to contest the CCP's right to rule. Because regime legitimacy is at stake, nationalism may be an element in the future demise of the People's Republic.

That is not to say that nationalism is the only or most important source of CCP legitimacy. As the chapters of this volume demonstrate, the CCP makes a wide variety of claims to legitimate rule – and regime opponents counter with a wide variety of claims of their own. Rather than seek a single lodestone of PRC legitimacy, analysts should focus on context: certain events make certain claims salient at certain times. When Falun Gong practitioners stage silent protests in the streets of the nation's capital, state claims to possession of the truth are challenged. When a corruption scandal breaks out, state claims to benevolence are questioned. When rural elections are rigged or the China Democratic Party is suppressed, counterclaims about the importance of procedural legitimacy are raised. When the United States bombs the Chinese embassy in Belgrade, state claims to upholding China's national dignity come under scrutiny. This chapter focuses on the latter: contestation over nationalist legitimacy in China today. However, the relative importance of nationalism in (de)stabilizing the 21st-century PRC is a highly contingent matter.

Contesting nationalism in China

Nationalism, like all social movements, involves both leaders *and* followers. A myopic focus on one group at the expense of the other distorts our understanding of nationalist politics. Because regime legitimacy is at stake, a better understanding of how the Party and the Chinese people interact in Chinese nationalism is urgently needed.[4]

Chinese nationalist politics today exhibits the claim–response dynamic central to the negotiation of legitimacy in all political systems.[5] Popular nationalists both *support* and *challenge* the state's claims to legitimacy – and issue their own rival nationalist claims. And the Party both *suppresses* and *responds* to challenges to its nationalist credentials. The suppression of legitimate nationalist claims, however, causes the Party to lose *face* and authority before the Chinese people.[6] Such a suppression signals a reversion to coercive forms of power, undermining regime stability. Successful responses to popular nationalist demands, by contrast, allow the Party to gain *face* before nationalist audiences, solidifying regime legitimacy.

The thirty-something "Fourth Generation" producers of popular Chinese nationalist discourse today may support *or* challenge the state's foreign policies.[7] As Xu Ben has recently noted, "Nationalism in China is … a junction and node of contradiction, interaction, and integration between state and society."[8] For instance, in the 1997 bestseller *The Plot to Demonize China*, Pennsylvania State University's Liu Kang asserts that the US government, big business, and the media conspire to make China lose *face* before the people of the world. He complains, for instance, that there are "no Edgar Snows [i.e. friends of China] in America today."[9] *The Plot* clearly seeks to *support* the Party, and Liu is said to have connections among the Party elite. Another anti-American tract, 1996's *China Can Say No*, also supported the Party's America policy.[10]

Other products of popular nationalism, however, *challenge* the Party's legitimacy, claiming it has failed to maintain China's national *face*. In an open letter sent to the Party leadership in February 1998, for instance, Chinese dissident Lin Xinshu argued that Li Peng should not be given Qiao Shi's job as chairman of the National People's Congress. His argument, significantly, was not just Li's "incompetence," but also that Li – tainted by his role in the Tiananmen Massacre – would be a blight on "China's image in the world."[11] Li would be unable, in other words, to maintain *face* for China.

The elite both *suppress* and *respond* to such assaults on its status. Following the April 2001 spy plane collision, for example, the *People's Daily* sought to *censor* extreme nationalist postings on its Strong Country Forum (*qiangguo luntan*) online chatroom. Many Chinese cyber-nationalists responded by moving to chatrooms at private sites like sina.com, where they fervently decried the state's suppression of their nationalist views.

But the story does not, as the Western media so frequently suggests, end with censorship and repression. The elite also *responds* to popular nationalists by seeking to gain *face* for China. It has begun, for example, an active campaign of promoting Chinese culture abroad. In 1998, the New China News Agency announced an official website that will promote China's cultural image: it will "introduce China's 5,000-year-old culture on the Internet, promoting commercial performances and exhibitions … Cultural activities that might degrade the country's dignity, however, will be banned."[12] Similarly, responding to *The Plot to Demonize China* and other popular nationalists' concerns that the American media makes China lose *face* before international opinion, in September 2000 the Chinese government organized a nine-city tour of the United States to introduce Chinese culture to ordinary Americans.[13] Their real audience, however, was likely on the other side of the Pacific: by plugging Chinese culture and upholding China's dignity, the Party is making a claim to nationalist legitimacy. Such actions demonstrate its belief that crude repression is not enough: the Party must gain *face* for China before international society to earn the support of nationalist audiences at home.

The Chinese people and the Communist Party are both central to nationalist politics in China today. How do they interact? Regime legitimacy hinges on the combination of strategies that each side chooses during their encounters – and how these evolve over time. During three separate waves of nationalism in late 1990s China – the Diaoyu Islands protests of 1996, the *China Can Say No* sensation of 1996–97, and the Belgrade bombing protests of May 1999 – the CCP responded to each with a different combination of suppression and co-optation, largely suppressing Diaoyu protestors, seeking to co-opt and utilize the *China Can Say No* fever, and striving just to respond to the demands of angry Belgrade bombing demonstrators. This movement away from suppression and towards co-optation suggests the emergence of a popular nationalism that is increasingly challenging the Party-state. Struggling to keep up with popular nationalist demands, the Party appears to be losing its hegemony over Chinese nationalism.

State suppression: the Diaoyu Islands protests, 1996

The Diaoyu, or Senkaku, Islands are eight desolate rocks lying in the East China Sea between Taiwan and Okinawa, and are claimed by China, Taiwan, and Japan. "Diaoyu" and "Senkaku" are the Chinese and Japanese names for the Islands. Each implicitly embodies a sovereignty claim. I use the Chinese "Diaoyu" because I approach the issue from a Chinese perspective, not to take China's side in the quarrel.

The sovereignty dispute is long and complex. Chinese claims (mainland and Taiwan) are based upon historical records dating back to the Ming Dynasty (1368–1644), the 1943 Cairo Declaration stipulation that Japan return all Chinese territory it had annexed, and a "natural prolongation" of the continental shelf argument in international maritime law. Japan's claims are based on the 1895 Treaty of Shimonoseki, which formally ceded Taiwan "and its surrounding islands" to Japan, the US return of "administrative rights" over the Islands to Japan along with Okinawa in 1972, and a "median line" division of the continental shelf argument in international maritime law.

The first major protests over the Islands occurred in 1971, after a September 1970 incident in which the Japanese navy evicted reporters raising Taipei's flag on one of the islands. Large and vocal anti-Japanese protests were organized in Hong Kong and Taiwan and among Chinese in the United States. Normalization of relations between China and Japan in 1972, however, included an agreement between Beijing and Tokyo to shelve the dispute for future resolution.

The next major flare-up in the controversy transpired in the summer and fall of 1996. On 14 July, a group of nationalists from the Japan Youth Federation erected a jerry-built lighthouse on the islands to bolster Japanese sovereignty claims. On 28 August 1996, the Japanese foreign minister reasserted Japan's position: "The Senkaku Islands have always been Japan's territory; Japan already effectively governs the islands, so the territorial issue does not exist." The Chinese Ministry of Foreign Affairs spokesman promptly condemned the Japanese comments as "irresponsible": "as far as the issue of sovereignty is concerned, the Chinese government cannot make any compromise."[14]

Anti-Japanese demonstrations in Hong Kong and Taiwan gained momentum in September 1996. On 24 September, Chinese Foreign Minister Qian Qichen met with the Japanese foreign minister at the United Nations in New York, seeking to prevent nationalists from escalating the dispute. Two days later, however, Hong Konger David Chan drowned during an attempt to land on one of the Islands. Chan's death spurred even larger demonstrations in Hong Kong and Taiwan.

Authorities in mainland China, meanwhile, suppressed anti-Japanese demonstrations. Nationalist sentiments were instead expressed in print and cyberspace. Chinese protests thus have to be *read*, and usually in Chinese. It is perhaps partially for this reason that Western journalists and academics have tended to discount their significance in comparison to the more *visible* and easily understood demonstrations that occurred in Hong Kong and Taiwan. A reading of these Chinese writings, however, reveals the existence of a dynamic discourse that challenged the Communist Party's control over nationalism.

Numerous popular mainland books and articles discuss the Diaoyu Islands controversy. The authors of *China Can Say No*, which was published in the summer of 1996, issued a sequel in the fall entitled *China Can Still Say No*. The reason, they explain, is that "Quite a few Chinese took issue with *Say No* ... saying 'Why were you so polite to Japan? ... Don't you see that Japan is even more wicked than America?'" The authors thus resolved to attack Japan in their new book. Maintaining that "China has been too warm and accommodating towards Japan," the authors itch for a fight: "To the majority of contemporary Chinese, the mission of containing Japan has already begun; the final battle of the Western Pacific – Protecting Diaoyu – has already become imminent." They have few qualms about preaching spite: "Chinese 'hatred of Japan' is not necessarily a bad thing." The authors advocate a more forceful Japan policy and implicitly condemn the government for suppressing popular anti-Japanese protests.[15]

1997's *Be Vigilant Against Japanese Militarism!* also contains a chapter on the Diaoyu Islands controversy. Authors Zi Shui and Xiao Shi have a sinister view of Japanese intentions: "Japan does not seek to 'return to Asia' as an equal partner [*pingdeng huoban*], but seeks to become the master [*jiazhang*] ... Confronted by the Japan threat, China cannot give an inch." Their message to Party policy-makers is equally blunt: "No Chinese should be willing or dare to relinquish sovereignty over Chinese territory, leaving a name to be cursed for generations" (*wanshi maming*).[16] If the Party does not take a firm enough stand against Japan, Zi and Xiao imply, the Chinese people will revolt.

The Communist Party sought both to suppress and to co-opt popular Diaoyu activism. The framework for suppression was contained within a National Educational Commission circular. According to Hong Kong's *Xin Bao*, the directive contained the following points:

- patriotic actions require guidance;
- the public must be dissuaded and prevented from organizing spontaneous meetings, demonstrations, and protests;
- the publicizing of activities by printing or distributing documents, or using various communications means, is prohibited.

The vice-minister of foreign affairs even went to Beijing University personally to ensure that students remained calm.[17] *China Can Still Say No*, which had been critical of the Ministry of Foreign Affairs' Japan policy, was banned a month after its release. By contrast, the authors' first book, *China Can Say No*, had supported the Party's America policy and remained in bookstalls for years. Internet protest within mainland China was also suppressed. The Party denied students web access for ten days, and banished a prominent online activist to Qinghai in China's far north west.[18] On a small scale, such crude coercion could be an effective policy tool.

But the Party also *responded* to the claims of popular nationalism by attempting to co-opt it. The propaganda apparatus utilized Chinese- and English-language print media to publish arguments for Chinese sovereignty and condemnations of Japanese actions. Liu Jiangyong of the International Relations Institute published a lengthy study of Chinese historical records documenting Chinese sovereignty claims in the Chinese Academy of Social Sciences' *Japanese Studies*. Significantly, the study pleaded with its readers that the issue "be handled through cool government to government deliberations."[19] Popular nationalists, in other words, should cool it. The *People's Daily* had earlier published a scathing front-page editorial condemning Japanese actions entitled "Japan, do not do stupid things." The editorial clearly sought to champion anti-Japanese anger. The adoption of the phrase "Do not do stupid things" by several popular anti-Japanese diatribes suggests that the editorial was largely successful in co-opting popular sentiments.[20] Lengthy English-language articles in the *China Daily* and the *Beijing Review* also made the case for Chinese sovereignty over the Islands. Their purpose was likely twofold: to marshal Western opinion against Japan, and, perhaps more importantly, to assuage domestic critics by appearing to champion Chinese nationalism on the international stage.

This brief account of the 1996 Diaoyu controversy suggests that even when it chooses a strategy of suppression, the Chinese state does not have the monopoly over nationalism that Western accounts suggest. And because popular nationalism can threaten the Party's legitimacy, it is an increasingly significant constraint on China's Japan policy.

Co-optation and control: the *China Can Say No* sensation, 1996–97

The role of popular nationalism is even more apparent in the 1996–97 *China Can Say No* sensation. If books like *China Can Say No* were simply "propaganda tracts," as former American Ambassador to China James Lilley and numerous Western journalists have asserted,[21] why did the Party need to do a public about-face on the issue? The Party first praised *China Can Say No* as "fully reflecting popular opinion," but then criticized the book as an "irresponsible" interference with the state's conduct of foreign policy.[22] Conversely, if the "say no" fever was purely popular, as the Party initially claimed, how could it have been so widely endorsed by Chinese newspapers tightly controlled by the Party's own Propaganda Department?

The "say no" sensation involved a complex and dynamic interplay between state and popular actors. The Chinese state sought to use "say no" nationalists, but "say no" authors also used the Chinese state. Although the content of official and popular anti-Americanism was largely the same, regime legitimacy was jeopardized as the state lost control of nationalist writings.[23] The hyphen in "nation-state" lost its strength as popular nationalist writings, unlike official discourse, did not link the fate of the nation to the fate of the Party-state. When the Party realized that it was being marginalized in popular writings, it promptly curbed the circulation of select "say no" books.

The Party elite clearly sought to use popular "say no" nationalism. Beijing-based "free writer" Wang Lixiong correctly blames both Beijing and the Western media for inflaming "say no" nationalism. He argues that by "playing with fire" (*wanhuo*), Beijing undermined the national interest. Wang faults the Ministry of Foreign Affairs' endorsement of *China Can Say No* at a press conference. After stating that the book was "popular," and did not represent the official view, a Chinese spokesman added the line: "It is because the American government is opposing China that the Chinese people have expressed their righteous indignation [*fenkai*]." Beijing, Wang explains, sought to utilize Chinese popular opinion as a "bargaining chip" (*chouma*) in its America policy, sparking the nationalist fire. Wang also, however, directs his ire at the Western press, which, fed by "self-created delusional fears" (*beigong sheying*), mistook appearances for reality and "made a watermelon out of a sesame seed" (*ba zhima dangcheng xigua*). The resulting media snowballing, Wang laments, made China lose *face* on the international stage.[24]

The producers of "say no" discourse were no mere pawns of the state, however; they had goals of their own and utilized the state to achieve them. At a personal level, they sought to vent their anger, curry favor with the Party elite, and make some money. They used the Party's propaganda apparatus to achieve these goals. *Guangming Daily* journalist Chen Xiyan explains how the "commoners" (*xiao renwu*) who wrote "say no" texts "manipulated" (*caozong*) China's official media. By writing in a vulgar street slang designed to arouse the interest of their readers, *China Can Say No*'s authors received sufficient popular attention to attract official notice. Because the substance of their argument was in line with the state's interests, both as a foreign policy chip and as a way to redirect domestic discontent, the state was bound to endorse it. Once the Foreign Ministry and the New China News Agency did so, other news organizations felt safe in disseminating "say no" stories nationally. The commercial success of *China Can Say No* was then assured: "Once grasped," Chen writes, "the strict rules of the official media ... can be used to convert tiny costs into huge profits."[25]

Having secured official approval and, in effect, put the Party's censorship apparatus to work for them, "say no" authors were able to dominate popular nationalist discourse. Critical reviews of "say no" books were quashed domestically and forced abroad. For instance, a sharply critical *Readers Daily* review of *China Can Say No* was replaced with one that defended it.[26] Similarly, a magazine editor asked journalist Chen Xiyan to review *China Can Say No* for a special issue criticizing it, but the project was aborted two weeks later.[27] While glowing reviews were published widely in China during the height of the "say no" fever in 1996, critical reviews could only be published in places like Hong Kong and Taiwan.[28]

"Mutual exploitation," to borrow a phrase from Chen Xiyan, was thus clearly at play in the "say no" sensation. The Party sought to use "popular opinion," and "say no" authors sought to make money. But regime legitimacy was also at stake. As the "say no" authors staked a claim to represent "popular opinion," the state's hegemony over nationalist discourse was challenged, threatening its legitimacy.

The Chinese Communist Party has long rooted its legitimacy in its nationalist credentials. In 1996, however, popular "say no" nationalists issued a rival claim: they were the true representatives of Chinese popular opinion. Accused by their critics of being Party pawns, "say no" writers and their defenders proclaimed their independence from the state. One glowing review, for instance, declared *China Can Say No* "a pure individual action," written from the authors' own volition.[29] "Say no" authors also argued that they – not the Party – represented genuine popular opinion. In an emotional, grandiose speech, "A declaration to the world," given at Beijing's Politics and Law University in December 1996, Song Qiang defended *China Can Say No* against its critics: "We're respecting popular opinion, not misleading it." Song even attempts to include himself and his co-authors within popular opinion, arguing that "Some say we have aroused popular opinion. It would be better to say that popular opinion aroused us."[30] In their follow-up tract, *China Can Still Say No*, Song and his co-authors contend that the state should not seek to suppress popular nationalists like themselves: "the primary responsibility of diplomacy is to protect national interests ... mass movements should be seen as normal, and protected, 'people's diplomacy.'"[31] They also, notably, insinuate that the state is failing to protect the national interest. Xu Ben is certainly right that "While [popular nationalists] direct their attack explicitly against foreigners, the present government is held implicitly to account for yielding too readily to foreign political and commercial demands and for surrendering China's national dignity in the process."[32]

The Party responded with both suppression and persuasion. At the December 1996 6th Plenary Session of the 14th CCP Central Committee, Party participants decided that *China Can Say No* had violated the Party policy that foreign policy is not to be arbitrarily criticized.[33] Losing control over its ability to autonomously construct foreign policy, the Party clamped down on "say no" writings, quickly banning the more critical *China Can Still Say No* and other new books and writings. Party elites realized both that "say no" discourse was not receiving good press abroad and that the Party stood accused of making China lose national *face* before international audiences. The CCP's reversal on the "say no" sensation reflected its effort to maintain its legitimacy before domestic audiences.

But the Party also responded by co-opting popular nationalism, seeking both to moderate extreme views and to persuade the people to let the Party maintain its leading role in Chinese nationalism and foreign policy-making. For instance, Shen Jiru's 1998 *China Should Not Play 'Mr. No'* seeks to counter the parochial nationalism of the "say no" sensation with a more moderate nationalism. Chinese Academy of Social Sciences Vice-President Liu Ji wrote the Foreword to Shen's book, and *China Should Not Play 'Mr. No'* is arguably an official response to the popular *China Can Say No* books.[34] Shen is clearly a nationalist – "As a great nation, China should participate in constructing a new post-Cold War order" – and he praises the "righteous anger" (*yifen*) of Fourth Generation popular nationalists. But he rejects the extremism of many naysayers in favor of a more mature attitude toward foreign policy: "China's 21st century international strategy must not be a parochial nationalist, uncooperative stream of 'nos' ... 21st century China and the world require understanding, reconciliation, and cooperation – not antagonism." Shen wields the specter of the former Soviet Union as an admonition against those who advocate confrontation: "The Soviets were nicknamed 'Mr. No' for using their veto in the UN Security Council all the time. We do not need to play a second 'Mr. No.'" He then asks: "Is daring to say 'no' the only way that Chinese can prove their independence and strength?" Shen admonishes popular nationalists that "emotion cannot substitute for policy." It is the elite, in other words, who must coolly construct China's foreign policy. But that elite, Shen recognizes, must also be sensitive to popular opinion: "Those who lose the support of the people will fall from power" (*shi ren xinzhe, shi tianxia*).[35] The Beijing leadership would carefully heed Shen's advice just a year later.

Crashing the Party: the Belgrade bombing demonstrations, 1999

During the Belgrade bombing protests of May 1999, the Western media repeatedly hammered home the argument that the CCP was manipulating Chinese protestors to its own ends. In "Calculating Beijing seeks to harness popular outrage," the *Financial Times*'s James Kynge paints a top-down picture of the protests: "Beijing [i.e. the communist elite] has succeeded in converting popular outrage at NATO's bombing of the Chinese embassy in Belgrade into a swelling tide of nationalism." Kynge describes the "cool realpolitik" driving the Beijing elite's "delicately calibrated" reactions to the bombing: "the fuelling of nationalism provides a unifying force at a time when China's communist ideology is dying."[36]

This top-down "party propaganda" spin on the protests tells us more about ourselves (our fears of communist "tyranny," denials that the common Chinese people might be genuinely angry with us, and so on) than it does about what actually happened in China in May 1999. The protests were actually an overwhelmingly *bottom-up* phenomenon; the Party had its hands full simply responding to the demands of popular nationalists. Like the Diaoyu Islands and *China Can Say No* sensations of 1996 and 1996–97, the Belgrade bombing protests involved a complex interplay of top-down and bottom-up pressures. In 1999, however, the CCP was forced to make a pronounced strategic shift from suppression to accommodation. Far from coolly manipulating the protestors as the Western media frequently suggested, the Party was in for the ride of its life. As Minister Wei Zhen famously said to Tang Dynasty Emperor Li Shiming over a millennia ago, "Water can support a boat, but it can also flip it" (*shui ke zai zhou, yi ke fu zhou*).

During the Belgrade bombing protests, popular nationalists increasingly shifted from supporting the CCP to making demands of it. For instance, in "An open letter from a Chinese university student to Premier Zhu" posted on the website of the Chinese electronic journal *China and the World*, He Yu of the Computer Department at China Engineering College asks: "How could they dare to bomb our embassy?" He Yu's sarcastic response reveals his frustration: "The [Americans] know that our government policy is one of merely lodging 'fierce protests' [*qianglie kangyi*]." He then warns: "Premier Zhu ... Our government's weak stance has created a distance between itself and the people ... You are so capable ... and we need you ... But without the 'people's confidence' [*minxin*], how can you lead China's economic construction!"[37] He Yu clearly fears that the government's weak response to the bombing is undermining its legitimacy.

The Belgrade bombing protests were remarkably widespread. There were street demonstrations in over 100 Chinese cities, and Chinese of all generations and walks of life participated in protest activities. Many protestors demanded that their government take a tougher stand toward the United States. In a letter signed by thirty-five "hot blooded youth from Hunan," the line "We support the Chinese government's just stand!!!" reads more like a demand than an acceptance of CCP leadership. An e-mail from Wuxi, Jiangsu Province, similarly places a burden upon the Party-state: "I hope that the Chinese government will take the necessary measures to show the world that China will not be insulted."[38] As "We support" and "I hope" suggest, supporting the government is perceived to be a voluntary, not coerced, decision. It is, furthermore, a choice dependent upon the government fulfilling its nationalist obligation to "restore justice" for the Chinese people.

Unable to suppress the protestors, authorities were forced to plead with them for calm. In a nationally televised speech on 9 May, Vice-President Hu Jintao urged workers to work, and students to study. The Propaganda Department then set out to persuade the Chinese people of the wisdom of Hu's words. The *People's Daily* issued a photograph entitled "Beijing workers study Hu Jintao's speech" with the caption: "The workers expressed a desire to work hard, promote economic development, and increase our national strength."[39] A New China News Agency report on the same subject, "Workers turning anger into motivation," began: "For the last few days, workers in all localities have resolutely supported the important televised speech delivered by Comrade Hu Jintao." It concluded with an example: "Gu Yongmei, a female worker at the third steel-melting workshop of Xining Special Steel Group, said that we must turn righteous indignation into power, do our own jobs well, and exert ourselves for the prosperity and strength of the motherland."[40] The next day, the New China News Agency issued a similar report – "Students turn indignation into motivation": "All the classrooms at Beijing University were filled with students craving knowledge ... Jian Yi, a student of the International Relations Institute, said ... 'Although I am still filled with indignation, I think the best way to love my country is by getting back to the classroom.' "[41]

Pleading with protestors to go back to their work or studies was a risky strategy: what if they did not listen? If history was a guide, the protestors might not. During the 1930s, Nationalist Party officials repeatedly urged students to study calmly in order to "strengthen the nation," while communist activists urged them to take to the streets. The communists eventually won that argument, as large numbers of students joined the revolution. It is thus ironic that the communist elite was now taking on the role of its former adversaries.

The Party elite's choice of then Vice-President Hu Jintao to deliver the state's televised reaction to the bombing suggests that they were well aware of the risks that they were taking. Jiang Zemin, Zhu Rongji, Li Peng, and other high leaders were not willing to issue a message pleading for restraint. Jiang had been criticized after the bombing for being too weak with his "constructive, strategic partnership" America policy, and Zhu was under attack for giving away too much at WTO talks during a recent trip to the United States. Seeking to co-opt popular nationalism on the one hand while appealing for calm on the other would be no easy task. The senior leaders decided to pass this hot potato to Hu Jintao, who could take the fall if the Chinese people perceived the CCP's response to be too weak. As it turns out, Hu passed the test, and he is now chairman of the CCP and president of the PRC.

The Party also sought to co-opt popular nationalism by championing the Chinese cause. Besides repeatedly and eloquently condemning the bombing, the Propaganda Department sought to convey to domestic nationalists the impression that the CCP had won "international opinion" to China's side. The China Internet Information Center, an English-language government website, organized an extensive Belgrade bombing site, which included a page entitled "International community responses." It contained links to 159 documents in which prominent foreigners were said to condemn the bombing. Although the site was in English and sought to shame America and NATO, its audience likely also included nationalists back home. The Party, it suggested, was winning the battle for international popular opinion, gaining *face* for China at America's expense.

In sum, the Belgrade bombing protests were not, as most Western observers insisted, an exclusively top-down Party affair. Popular nationalists were outraged, and Party elites were barely able to control popular anger. Suppressing them was not an option available to the Party leadership. To maintain nationalist legitimacy, the CCP needed to appease the protestors. Regime stability was at stake.

Conclusion

This chapter has argued that the 1990s witnessed the emergence of a genuinely popular nationalism in China that should not be conflated with state or official nationalism. During three separate waves of nationalism in late 1990s China – the Diaoyu Islands protests of 1996, the *China Can Say No* sensation of 1996–97, and the Belgrade bombing protests of May 1999 – the CCP responded to each with a different combination of suppression and co-optation, largely suppressing Diaoyu protestors, seeking to co-opt and utilize the *China Can Say No* fever, and striving just to respond to the demands of angry Belgrade bombing demonstrators. While three cases cannot form a pattern, this movement away from suppression and toward co-optation suggests the emergence of a popular nationalism that is increasingly challenging the CCP's claims to nationalist legitimacy.

Although the anti-foreign substance of popular nationalism is often congruent with that of state nationalism in China, its independent existence undermines the Communist Party's hegemony over nationalist discourse. This development threatens the CCP's nationalist legitimacy in two ways. First, popular nationalists do not automatically accept the CCP's nationalist claims. Indeed, popular nationalists increasingly ignore or reject CCP claims that only the CCP can lead China to national glory. Secondly, popular nationalists have begun issuing their own nationalist counterclaims, which are frequently based on racial, and not party, identity. This creates space for the emergence of rival political forces.

And popular nationalism is not just a long-term threat to regime legitimacy; it is already having an impact on a variety of political practices. For instance, until recently, a pop-up appeared on the main page of the Ministry of Foreign Affairs' (MFA) Chinese-language website. It solicited the opinions of ordinary Chinese, linking the reader to a page where he or she could e-mail the MFA and read the transcripts of electronic chats now held regularly between senior MFA officials and concerned Chinese "netizens."[42] The MFA, it seems, does not just direct its attention at the international community; it also has an eye on the demands of domestic nationalists. Aware that popular nationalists now command a large following, the MFA is actively seeking to appease them. Indeed, one reason that the Sino-American "apology diplomacy" following the April 2001 spy plane collision near Hainan Island was so difficult was that MFA negotiators felt that popular nationalists would only be satisfied with an abject American apology.[43] Western analysts would be wise to recognize the emerging role of popular nationalism in constraining Chinese policy-makers.

Notes

1 My thanks to Stan Rosen, Jon Unger, Anita Chan, Ed Friedman, and several anonymous reviewers for their thoughtful comments.
2 Jin Hui, *Tongwen cangzang: Rijun qinhua baoxing beiwanglu* (*Wailing at the Heavens: The Violence of the Japanese Invasion of China*) (Beijing: Jiefangjun wenyi chubanshe, 1995), pp. 231, 234. Unless otherwise noted, all translations from the original Chinese are my own.
3 Jin Hui, *Tongwen cangzang*, pp. 4 (Preface), 465.
4 The following draws heavily from Ch. 7 of Peter Hays Gries, *China's New Nationalism: Pride, Politics, and Diplomacy* (Berkeley: University of California Press, 2004).
5 Reinhard Bendix, *Nation-building and Citizenship: Studies of Our Changing Social Order* (Berkeley: University of California Press, 1977); Max Weber, *The Theory of Social and Economic Organization* (New York: The Free Press, 1964).
6 The figurative *face* is the self revealed to others. *Face* is neither uniquely Oriental nor used as a pejorative. It may therefore be useful for the Western reader to think of it in the more value-neutral language of honor.
7 In China, youth and leadership generations are delineated differently. The first generation of revolutionary youth endured the hardships of the anti-fascist and civil wars of the 1930s and 1940s. The second generation suffered during the Anti-rightist Campaign and the Great Leap Forward of the late 1950s. And the third generation of Red Guards was sent down to the countryside during the Cultural Revolution of the late 1960s and 1970s. The fourth generation of PRC youth, by contrast, grew up with relative material prosperity under reform in the 1980s and 1990s. This categorization of Chinese youth generations conflicts with the delineation of generations of political leadership. To distance himself from Mao, leader of the "First Generation," Deng declared himself leader of the "Second Generation," despite the fact that they both participated in the Long March and the War of Resistance. Hence, Jiang is of the "Third Generation," and Hu Jintao leads the new "Fourth Generation" of technocratic leadership.
8 Xu Ben, "Chinese populist nationalism: its intellectual politics and moral dilemma," *Representations* 76(1) (2001): 120–140.
9 Li Xiguang and Liu Kang, *Yaomohua Zhongguo de beihou* (*The Plot to Demonize China*) (Beijing: Zhongguo shehui kexue chubanshe, 1996), p. 5.
10 *China Can Say No* was the single most popular book in 1990s China. See Kang Xiaoguang, Wu Yulun, Liu Dehuan, and Sun Hui, *Zhongguo dushu toushi: 1978–1998 dazhong dushu shenghuo bianqian diaocha* (*A Perspective on the Reading Habits of the Chinese: An Investigation of the Changes in the Reading*

Habits of the Masses from 1978 to 1998) (Nanning: Guangxi jiaoyu chubanshe, 1998), pp. 52–59. My thanks to Stan Rosen for this reference.

11 Wu Fang and Ray Zhang, "Dissident called the Chinese premier 'incompetent,'"*China News Digest*, 13 February 1998.

12 "China gets wired as cultural blitz planned," *China News Digest*, 2 February 1998. This state project also suggests that the Internet in China is not the realm of a civil society set against the state. The Internet is instead another site for political contestation, with actors both for and against the state vying for authority.

13 See, for example, David Briscoe, "China trying to improve image with ordinary Americans, still wary of government," *Associated Press*, 30 August 2000.

14 Quoted in Erica Strecker Downs and Phillip C. Saunders, "Legitimacy and the limits of nationalism: China and the Diaoyu Islands," *International Security* 23(3) (1998/99): 134, 35.

15 Song Qiang *et al.*, *Zhongguo haishi neng shuobu* (*China Can Still Say No*) (Beijing: Zhongguo wenlian chubanshe, 1996), pp. 101, 88, 89.

16 Zi Shui and Xiao Shi, *Jingti Riben diguo zhuyi!* (*Be Vigilant against Japanese Militarism!*) (Beijing: Jincheng Press, 1997), pp. 279–280, 78.

17 See Norihiro Sasaki, "Chinese policy toward Hong Kong and Taiwan: present and future," in Yasuo Onishi (ed.) *One Country, Two Systems: China's Dilemma* (Tokyo: Institute of Developing Economies, 1997), p. 27.

18 Gérémie Barmé and Sang Ye, "The great firewall of China," *Wired*, June 1997, p. 176.

19 Liu Jiangyong, "What lies behind the Japanese attempt to beautify its history of aggression?" *Xiandai guoji guanxi* (*Contemporary International Relations*) 9 (1996): 27.

20 See, for example, the section entitled "Japanese shouldn't do Stupid Things," in Zi Shui and Xiao Shi, *Jingti Riben Diguo Zhuyi*, pp. 278–279.

21 James R. Lilley, "The 'Fu Manchu' problem," *Newsweek*, 24 February 1997.

22 "Beijing about-turn, says 'no' to US-bashing bestseller," *Straits Times*, 12 December 1996.

23 Unlike Chen Xiaomei's findings in her analysis of Occidentalism in 1980s China, pitting "official" against "anti-official" nationalisms during the "say no" sensation of 1996 would obscure a basic similarity in the substance of state and popular nationalism. Like Chen's findings, however, both elite and popular Chinese actors sought to utilize images of America for distinct purposes. See Chen Xiaomei, *Occidentalism: A Theory of Counter-discourse in Post-Mao China* (New York: Oxford University Press, 1995).

24 Wang Lixiong, "China has already lost the foundation for establishing a 'doctrine,'" in Xiao Pang (ed.) *Zhongguo Ruhe Miandui Xifang* (*How China Faces the West*) (Hong Kong: Mirror Books, 1997).

25 Chen Xiyan, "The mutual exploitation of the official media and commercial stir-fried works," in *ibid.*, pp. 271–272.

26 "Why can't we say no?" *Zhonghua dushubao* (*Readers Daily*), 4 September 1996.

27 Chen Xiyan, "The mutual exploitation," p. 268.

28 See Xiao Pang (ed.), *Zhongguo Ruhe Miandui Xifang*.

29 Liang Minwei, "The story of the publication of *China Can Say No*," *Lianhe zaobao*, 20 August 1996. Reprinted in Jia Qingguo, *Zhongguo bu jinjin shuobu* (*China Should Not Just Say No*) (Beijing: Zhonghua gongshang lianhe chubanshe, 1996), pp. 251–253.

30 Song Qiang et al., *Disidairen de jingshen: Xiandai Zhongguoren de jiushi qingjie* (*The Spirit of the Fourth Generation: The Savior Complex of Modern Chinese*) (Lanzhou: Gansu wenhua chubanshe, 1997), pp. 88, 86.

31 Song Qiang *et al.*, *Zhongguo haishi neng shuobu*, p. 92.

32 Xu Ben, "Chinese populist nationalism," p. 133.

33 Cheng Yue-ching, "Chinese authorities criticize book *China Can Say No*," *Mingbao*, 10 December 1996. Translated in BBC, 13 December.

34 For a concurring interpretation of the official nature of *China Should Not Play 'Mr. No,'* see Joseph Fewsmith, "Historical echoes and Chinese politics: can China leave the twentieth century behind?" in Tyrene White (ed.) *China Briefing 2000: The Continuing Transformation* (Armonk, NY: M.E. Sharpe, 2000), p. 21.

35 Shen Jiru, *Zhongguo budang 'bu xiansheng' – Dangdai Zhongguo de guoji zhanlue wenti* (*China Should Not Play 'Mr. No': The Problem of China's Contemporary International Strategy*) (Beijing: Jinri Zhongguo chubanshe, 1998), pp. 56, 2–3, 57, 22.

36 James Kynge, "Calculating Beijing seeks to harness popular outrage," *Financial Times*, 17 May 1999.

37 He Yu, "An open letter from a Chinese university student to Premier Zhu," online at www.chinabulletin.com/luntan/58/heyu.gb. Accessed 1999. Domain now for sale.

38 *Guangming Daily*, "Martyrs Xu Xinghu and Zhu Ying will live forever in our hearts!", online at www.gmdaily.com.cn/2_zhuanti/jinian/jnzj/jnzj.htm. Last accessed 5 September 2003.

39 Online at http://web1.peopledaily.com.cn/item/kangyi/tpxw/051102.html. Accessed December 1999.

40 Xinhua, "Workers turning anger into motivation," *Xinhua*, 10 May 1999.

41 Xinhua, "Students turn indignation into motivation," *Xinhua*, 11 May 1999.

42 See the MFA's Chinese-language website at www.fmprc.gov.cn/chn/. The pop-up led to an interactive bulletin board service (BBS), http://bbs.fmprc.gov.cn/index.jsp. The English-language site is at www.fmprc.gov.cn/eng/. All sites accessed 19 August 2002. The pop-up no longer appeared on 15 August 2003, but the interactive BBS page remained.

43 John Keefe, who was special assistant to US Ambassador to China Joseph Prueher during the April 2001 spy plane incident, later related that during the negotiations in Beijing, American diplomats "saw a Chinese government acutely sensitive to Chinese public opinion." See John Keefe, "Anatomy of the EP-3 incident" (Alexandria, VA: Center for Naval Analysis, April 2001).

10 When legitimacy resides in beautiful objects

Repatriating Beijing's looted Zodiac animal heads

Richard Kraus

Political legitimacy is a kind of public illusion, a shared and often fragile understanding that a regime is somehow appropriate, fitting, and in some vague sense a part of the natural order of things. Because legitimacy is ultimately a cultural concept, it is understandable that its claims often center upon specific cultural objects. These are art works whose history may be imagined to represent the nation's, and which are surrounded by an aura that may extend its magic to the possessor of the art.[1]

Students of Chinese politics can easily identify moments when the magic of legitimacy was questioned or refashioned around some object which might be famous or otherwise remain obscure: peasant rebels who raid the costume trunks of opera troupes for the "imperial gown" which will make a rebel resemble an emperor; Cultural Revolutionary struggles over physical possession of a bureaucratic seal, believed to be the talisman of office; Tang Taizong's decision to take to his grave China's most celebrated piece of calligraphy – Wang Xizhi's *Orchid Pavilion Preface*; Hua Guofeng's praise of the oil painting of Mao Zedong assuring him that *With You in Charge, I Am at Ease*. In none of these instances can one specify how much "legitimacy" was conveyed by the cultural object in question, yet political actors certainly behave as if legitimacy is at stake.

Political legitimacy must be won on two fronts. Not only must domestic populations believe in their rulers' right to occupy office, but foreign states must recognize these same rulers' authority through diplomacy, if the nation is to participate fully and conventionally in international affairs.

When political legitimacy is imagined to derive from objects which reside outside the nation, a peculiar combination of politics arises. Internally, the object becomes the subject of the nationalist politics of popular indignation, yet externally, the object is associated with the far more refined elite political world of fine arts and diplomacy. For instance, after the Second World War, the United States was in possession of Hungary's Crown of St. Stephen. A gift from the pope to Hungary's king a thousand years earlier, the crown was the nation's most visible emblem of national continuity and political legitimacy. By refusing to return it to Hungary, the United States withheld a key symbol of legitimacy from a communist government with which it had otherwise normal relations. Émigrés who understood the meaning of the crown protested President Carter's decision to transfer the crown from Fort Knox to Budapest, even as the communist government celebrated in the crown's recovery.

Art stolen from China during the long era of imperialist plunder arouses indignant patriotism in China, yet while it evokes little concern to most foreigners, it is of great interest to the elite world of fine arts. I will use one such act of plunder, the 1860 sack of Beijing's *Yuanming Yuan*, as a starting point for exploring China's relationship to its purloined past. In brief, the story is about the use of state power to return a set of statues to China. But this success in overcoming the national shame of imperialist plunder is eroded by China's continuing position as an exporter of newly plundered art treasures for foreign collectors. It is impossible to consider the question of plunder and repatriation without considering China's simultaneous position in an international system of production and distribution of art objects. While China's successful repatriation of one set of statues may have some legitimizing symbolism within China, the international politics of using art to buttress legitimacy are considerably more difficult.

The Zodiac statues of the Garden of Perfect Brightness

The 1860 sack of the *Yuanming Yuan* (Garden of Perfect Brightness) stands out among the many contemptuous gestures of European imperialism toward a weakened China. Located some five miles to the north-west of Beijing, this elaborate garden was constructed over several decades beginning in 1709 as a retreat for China's Manchu rulers.[2] The *Yuanming Yuan* is often known in English as the "Old Summer Palace," to distinguish it from the present Summer Palace, which was imagined to have been built as its replacement. In fact, the "new" Summer Palace (the *Yihe Yuan*) began as a part of the older garden, and the *Yuanming Yuan* was never a summer palace, but the favored residence and political center for the Qing emperors.

The Garden of Perfect Brightness featured many architectural delights modeled upon the styles of the wealthy and sophisticated lower Yangzi region. The cosmopolitan Qianlong emperor added several European-style buildings in this garden, under the supervision of the Italian émigré artist Giuseppe Castiglione. Castiglione, well known in China as "Lang Shining," was a Jesuit who worked in China from 1715 until his death in 1766. As painter and architect, he introduced Sinified Western styles to Chinese court circles.[3]

For the *Yuanming Yuan*, Castiglione worked under the inspiration of Versailles, fashioning elaborate stone buildings set amid colorful walkways. In front of a large building known as the *Haiyantang* (Seafood Banquet Hall), he designed an elaborate fountain. Twelve animal heads, representing the figures of the Chinese Zodiac, were cast from bronze and placed atop life-size human bodies which were arranged alongside a pool of water. Every two hours a different animal spouted water, so that the fountain served also as a clock. At noon, all twelve animals joined in an expectorating ensemble. The complex mechanism broke down in 1786, never to be repaired.

In October 1860, French and British troops laid waste to the *Yuanming Yuan* as punishment for Chinese recalcitrance in settling the Second Opium War. The immediate rationalization was the claim that Chinese had killed European prisoners, but the broader political purpose was to press a reluctant Chinese government to accept European terms. The British took the lead in destruction, putting wooden structures to the torch, demolishing as much of the stone structures as they could, and, of course, seizing as much loot as they could carry. According to Captain Charles ("Chinese") Gordon, later famous as imperialism's martyred general in Sudan, "Everyone was wild for plunder." "You can scarcely imagine the beauty and magnificence of the places we burnt. It made one's heart sore to burn them; in fact, these palaces were so large, and we were so pressed for time, that we could not plunder them carefully."[4]

The British leader was the 8th Earl of Elgin, son of the notorious thief of the Parthenon Marbles (known in London as the Elgin Marbles, but not in Greece).[5] Perhaps it was a family tradition, or a genetic disorder (*his* son, the 9th Earl, was Viceroy of India from 1895–99, and no doubt also managed to take some nice things home to Britain). China had declined sharply from its power and prosperity of the previous century, and was unable to repel the European forces. The first Opium War (1838–42) began a long cycle of humiliation at the hands of European armies whose military superiority only increased with each year. At the same time, China was torn by the massive disruption of the Taiping Rebellion, a civil war which cost some 20 million lives over two decades.

The *Yuanming Yuan* was rich in symbolic potential; it was there in 1793 that the British emissary Macartney was received by the Qianlong emperor, causing a crisis when he refused to kowtow.[6] But the British commanders seemed unaware of the coincidence, although they took back to England several cannon which had been presented to the emperor by George III.[7]

Among the treasures looted by the European soldiers were the decapitated animals of Castiglione's Zodiac Fountain. Their plunder included other work with a distinctive international character, such as a set of engravings of Qing military victories over the Western Mongols. Sketches from the field in the 18th century had been turned into paintings, which were sent to France to be engraved on copper plates from 1766 to 1775. The Qianlong emperor had later inscribed poems upon the engravings.[8]

As cultural property, the loot from the *Yuanming Yuan* is awash in symbolism. European usurpation of the emperor's treasures and destruction of his palaces denoted a new stage in relations in which Chinese were forced to confront their defeat and humiliation. That these were the emperor's personal belongings heightened the injury to China's sovereignty.[9]

The *Yuanming Yuan* remained a shattered ruin for many years, a visible scar in Beijing to remind all Chinese of their government's weakness and of the West's might. While before 1860 the garden had been a private pleasure palace for the emperor, after its sack it became a public spot, with contending interpretations inscribed upon its ruins.

When reformers such as Kang Youwei and Liang Qiqiao saw objects looted from the imperial garden on public display in Paris and New York, they were humiliated at their nation's weakness, and strengthened in their resolve to overthrow its tottering Qing dynasty.[10] It was not until after the dynasty's fall in 1911 that the radical May 4th Movement began to spread a popular awareness of national shame from the West's plunder of Chinese art. In response to growing nationalist resentment, in 1930 the Kuomintang government legislated to limit the participation of foreigners in archeological digs and from purchasing relics.[11]

In the People's Republic, the grounds of the former imperial garden have been turned into a public park, with the ruins a major center of attention, where young people pose to have their photos taken with scenic fractured columns in the background. The government displays these relics in a rather subdued manner. Instead of indignant displays on the history of their destruction, a long signboard reproduces in their entirety the unequal treaties forced upon China by Britain, France, the United States, Russia, Japan, Germany, and lesser imperialist powers, joined by a simple notice urging visitors to "never forget national humiliation."

A semi-official compendium for Overseas Chinese of the basic elements of Chinese culture includes the *Yuanming Yuan*, focusing on its role as seeking to synthesize Chinese and Western architecture. The implication is clear, that the 1860 destruction of the palace by European imperialists demonstrated that such a synthesis was difficult, and premature.[12]

Today, the *Yuanming Yuan* is being partially restored; a stone gazebo, situated at the heart of a maze, was the first to be rebuilt in 1999. One developer has proposed to restore the site, beginning with the Chinese palaces, to be fitted out with ethnic restaurants.[13] But even if it were possible to reconstruct the entire collection of buildings, walks, fountains, and waterways that constituted the palace in its days of glory, one imagines that the government would be averse to give up such a potent symbol of victimhood.[14] Yet this victimhood is often missed by non-Chinese: a group of American university students who visited the *Yuanming Yuan* in 1987 believed the ruins to be the result of the Cultural Revolution's infamous Red Guard vandalism. For Europeans, the booty's symbolism has been malleable. As memories of war faded, looted objects became heirlooms only loosely associated with some ancestor's Eastern service. Crusted with a vague imperial nostalgia, the pieces became commodities, or offered up for sale as curiosities, rather than as art.[15] Some of the loot never even left China, but was auctioned off in Beijing immediately after the sack of the palace.

Among the pieces which did leave China were several of the Zodiac statues (or rather, the heads of these statues, which are the only parts to survive). The monkey and pig were auctioned in October 1987 in New

York. In London, in June 1989, Sotheby's sold the tiger, horse, and ox. Three of the Zodiac heads ended up in private Taiwan collections late in the 20th century. Five of the dozen bronze heads are missing. The rabbit and rat are said to be in France, the pig in the United States, and the horse in Taiwan.[16]

In the spring of 2000, the tiger, ox, and monkey heads were offered yet again at twin auctions in Hong Kong by the leading international art dealers Christies (monkey and ox) and Sotheby's (tiger).[17] Sotheby's also sold a large hexagonal vase which was looted from the *Yuanming Yuan*, but this piece attracted much less attention than the Zodiac sculptures.[18] The companies did not deny that the art was looted, and marked the pieces as coming from the *Yuanming Yuan*. The Chinese government was appalled, and urged the auction houses to hold the sales elsewhere, rather than embarrass China by a public reminder on its own territory of its century of shame.[19] The Ministry of Culture's Cultural Relics Bureau claimed that it would be "insulting and deeply painful to the Chinese people to have these things sold before their eyes."[20] The two auction houses denied that the sale would violate any treaty or law, and announced that the sale of the offending items would go on, despite growing unease among Hong Kong Chinese. The crisis left a Cultural Relics Bureau official to mutter, "We will take measures soon. We will not leave the matter as it is."[21]

The Chinese army rescues monkey, tiger, and ox

The successful bidder for the three heads was the Poly Group, a Beijing company which operates a small museum, and which is intimately connected to the People's Liberation Army. The Poly Art Museum describes its purchase (for US$4 million) as a patriotic adventure:

> Half an hour before the sale, the leaders of the China Poly Group felt profoundly that control was about to be lost over these treasures of the nation, that they might once again suffer calamity and be carried away, and that the sale by auction in Hong Kong of national treasures was a great blow to the interests of the nation, not only impinging on a century of national sentiment on the part of the Chinese people, but further bearing on the prosperity and stability of Hong Kong. As a state-owned enterprise, it is naturally right that the thoughts and concerns of the state should also be our thoughts and concerns. Whilst seeking direction from the relevant state organs and those of the Beijing municipality, the leaders of the Poly Group thereupon instructed the Hong Kong representative of the Poly Art Museum to attend the auction and rescue the national treasures.[22]

Of special interest are the role of the Chinese army and the assertion that the three Zodiac heads are "national treasures."

The highest bidder for the three Zodiac statues at both auctions was Yi Suhao, the Poly Group's representative.[23] The Poly Group is a state-owned corporation with many financial ventures, but its wealth is rooted in arms exports. Given its specialized business, it is not surprising that the leadership of the corporation is intimately connected to top army leadership, including its general manager, He Ping, who is Deng Xiaoping's son-in-law. The corporation has become wealthy through the international arms trade, much like its US counterparts General Dynamics, Rockwell, or General Motors. And like these counterparts, Poly has lots of former military officers on its staff, and prides itself on its patriotism. The English name "Poly" may refer to its diversified holdings in real estate, high technology, and arms. But it also is homophonous with the Chinese name "*Baoli*," which means "protect interests."

There is a nice historical symmetry to art plundered by British troops being repatriated by the cash of China's army, and the quotation above certainly suggests that the People's Liberation Army wants to present itself as the heroic rescuer, undoing the shame of a Qing dynasty army which lost the art to foreign troops. It is clear that Poly's purchase was closely coordinated with top national leaders. The regime which won their return claims a kind of legitimacy in its act of restoring trophies to a place of honor in their nation of origin.

The recovered statues will be exhibited in Beijing's Poly Museum, established in 1998, and headed by a former director of Beijing's Palace Museum. One might imagine that an army art collection would feature grandiose oil paintings of heroic battle scenes. But the Poly Museum has none of these. Instead, the three Zodiac heads will join a small but select collection which otherwise features only two types of objects. One gallery displays perhaps a hundred bronzes from the Shang, Zhou, and Han dynasties. A second gallery features a collection of forty exquisite Buddhist figures, from the Northern Wei through the Tang dynasties. The objects appear to be of very high quality, and are very effectively displayed by overhead spotlighting.[24] The Poly Museum apparently also has an unexhibited collection of paintings.

In a Chinese context, the army's role is a little less odd than it might be in the West. China's armed forces have long been involved in arts and entertainment. There are many military ensembles which perform popular music, as well as military opera troupes, literary magazines, publishers, and an arts school. The Poly Museum is on the second floor of the popular Poly Theater building. The lobby of the Poly Theater advertises concerts of chamber works with harpsichord, and the "Trovatore Bar" invites guests, as does a small bookshop, whose titles included expected works on Napoleon and the German army, but also books on courtesy (including Browning's *Lord Chesterfield*), fiction (including "literary" novels by such contemporary authors as Su Tong), a guide to raising dogs, and, most surprisingly, a study of politically persecuted poets.[25]

But the Poly Art Museum does not merely add a layer of refinement to the tough core of the Chinese army. It also responded to a state directive in 1999, when the fifty-three top state-owned enterprises were instructed to set aside funds for culture, in order to prepare for an onslaught from Western cultural industries after membership in the World Trade Organization.[26] With its museum, Poly was already well positioned to help be a bastion for national art. And with the national treasures under its control, Poly was also able to exhibit them to promote its real-estate subsidiary in Shenzhen.[27]

The mystique of national treasures

The Zodiac statues were repatriated as "national treasures." The concept of national treasures is borrowed from Japan, apparently via Taiwan. In Japanese practice, the term denotes a specially protected category of art works. In 1998, Japan had 1,048 works designated as national treasures which cannot be exported.[28] In China, on the other hand, "national treasure" is not an official category, but a subjective one, applied to works that someone believes to be essential to defining China's national spirit.[29]

The animals' heads are prized as "national" treasures for political, not aesthetic, reasons. The legitimacy of the ruling Communist Party is rooted in ending a "century of humiliation, blood and tears," and the return of the plundered heads does symbolize the success of the revolution in winning international status.[30]

There is no strong argument to be made for the Zodiac heads on aesthetic grounds. One art historian has likened them to garden ornaments, of no special interest even to the Qianlong emperor. They were certainly not the best art plundered from the *Yuanming Yuan* by Lord Elgin's troops.[31] And the failure of Chinese budgets for arts conservation and the simplest protection against looters and thieves to keep pace with growing national prosperity suggests that this flamboyant purchase may not have been the best way to spend money in support of Chinese culture.

Are the Zodiac heads really Chinese at all? They were executed by Chinese craftsmen in accord with the rather Westernized conceptions of an Italian artist who was honestly attempting to satisfy his Chinese patron. One of the heads, a tiger, looks remarkably like a bear. The bear is not in the Chinese Zodiac, and one imagines that Castiglione had little experience with tigers as he was completing the fountain.

As symbols, the three heads are not ideal emblems of a rising China overcoming a decaying Western imperialism. It might be more aesthetically and politically satisfying if the auction houses had tried to peddle a more unambiguously Chinese and universally respected piece of plunder. But symbols cannot be matched ideally with their causes, and objects often become symbolic by happenstance.

Yet the Zodiac statues have some advantages as emblems. They are easily recognizable by the artistically unsophisticated, in contrast to many ink paintings which might well be better appreciated by connoisseurs. Indeed, a 1982 Chinese film, *The Burning of the Imperial Palace*, uses a quick view of a (reconstructed) Zodiac fountain to signal that the action had moved to the *Yuanming Yuan*, so sure was its director that his audience would recognize these figures as emblems of the garden's impending destruction.[32] The Zodiac animals' status as "national treasures" is enhanced by the monumentality of bronze, perhaps strengthening the impact of statuary, which is not the most prestigious of pre-modern Chinese art forms.

Moreover, the bronze statues are relatively sturdy, making it easier for their new owners to move them around the nation for patriotic display. The Chinese state quickly exploited the return of its long-lost objects to spur nationalist sentiment. The three heads were sent around the nation on tour. Immediately after the purchase, a large crowd came to inspect them in the Hong Kong Art Museum. They were also put on display to large and enthusiastic crowds in Shenzhen, Guangzhou, Chongqing, Chengdu, Tianjin, and Beijing. The whole episode of the Zodiac statues is scripted to bolster the legitimacy of the regime which repurchased the statuary. From their 1860 plunder, through 140 years during which the statues wander abroad like a set of homeless ghosts, to their army-backed purchase, and finally their triumphant display across China, the narrative reads like an example of art as an instrument of statecraft.

An unspoken background for the Zodiac statue drama was the collection of art housed in Taipei at the National Palace Museum. This superb collection of art, once owned by China's emperors, is a much better candidate than the Zodiac heads to be the emblem of political legitimacy.

Revolutions are often occasions for massive transfers of art objects. Cromwell sold many of the paintings assembled by Charles I, and the Louvre was founded on the art collection of the late Bourbon ruling family. The Soviet Union quietly disposed of many pieces from the czar's collection, selling some to Andrew Mellon, who set them up in the United States National Gallery of Art. The Chinese revolutionary century has been no different in reminding us of the mobility and liquidity of fine art objects.

The emperors of China included many connoisseurs, and the imperial collections of art were unrivaled. When the empire collapsed, the last emperor, Pu Yi, treated the collection as his personal property, despite efforts by various republican regimes to claim the art as national patrimony. Aware of the controversy, the young Pu Yi slipped pieces out by his brother to sell for money. When Pu Yi became Japan's puppet ruler of Manchukuo, he hauled more art treasure with him to the north-east.[33]

Amid this drainage by the emperor, Chiang Kai-shek's new national government moved the remaining pieces to the new capital in Nanjing. But with the approach of Japanese invaders, Chiang divided and concealed the collection. It was not reassembled at the end of the war, but much was shipped, with American help, to Taiwan along with the retreating Kuomintang army.[34]

As seen from Beijing, Taiwan is an art-poor and culturally marginal province which was for fifty years a Japanese colony; yet it has possession of the deepest cultural symbols of political legitimacy. For Chiang Kai-shek, the possession of these treasures was a marker of the viability of his claim to rule the entire nation. For the Kuomintang, possession of the imperial art collection denoted right to rule, even from temporary quarters in Taiwan. The Kuomintang government also deployed objects from the imperial collection in its diplomatic rivalry with the mainland. Items from the National Palace Museum were exhibited in the early 1960s in Washington and elsewhere, without controversy in Taiwan. But when some 400 pieces were sent on exhibition to the United States in 1996, 500 people sat in for two days in front of the museum, demanding that the government reduce the scale of the tour in order to protect the objects. One banner demanded: "Museum is no Foreign Ministry, don't take top art treasure to work for national diplomacy."[35]

What had changed was US recognition of the People's Republic of China, coupled with the rise of Taiwan's new Democratic Progressive Party (DPP), many of whose supporters want Taiwan independence. For the DPP, Taiwan is home, the National Palace Museum is another bastion of mainlander power, and its art is a sometimes awkward symbol. Indeed, when Chen Shui-bian was elected president in 2000, he made three symbolic gestures to reassure Taiwan's mainlander population: he placed flowers at the Chiang Kai-shek Memorial Hall, he visited Chiang Ching-kuo's widow, Faina Chiang, and he visited the National Palace Museum in suburban Taipei. But there was discussion in Taiwan of splitting the collection, establishing a new museum in southern Taiwan, the base of DPP support.[36] A government decision to build a branch in Chiayi was accompanied by discussion of changing the museum's name, leading the Kuomintang to complain that the government was seeking to remove cultural symbols that are not Taiwanese.[37] One can imagine the collection becoming a bargaining chip as Taiwan and the mainland work out their relationship.

The Zodiac heads have a role to play in Taiwan–mainland relations. At the end of 2001, following a visit to Taiwan by Poly Group head He Ping, the Zodiac statues went to Taipei, as part of a three-month exhibit of over 100 pieces from the Poly Museum collection.[38] The repatriation of imperialist plunder provides a medium by which all Chinese, not only the citizens of the People's Republic, can be proud of their improved status in the world.

New plunder replaces the old

The story of the army rescuing national treasures from the clutches of foreign collectors may be read with many meanings. The appeal to Chinese national pride is obvious enough, as is the Communist Party's desire to be seen as the inheritor of a revolutionary tradition of standing up to foreign exploitation. But this drama was also staged for the benefit of foreign arts firms in Hong Kong. Patriotic bravado helped China deal with its embarrassment that Hong Kong continues to be a center for the sale of artistic plunder from China, while it put the Hong Kong art market on notice that China expected its activities to be low-key, at least superficially legal, and to avoid causing public awkwardness for China's rulers.

The fact that two foreign auction companies offered these works for sale in Hong Kong was problematic. The Zodiac statues came to Hong Kong soon after China regained sovereignty over the city in 1997. They became one of a series of contests by which Hong Kong and Beijing are working out how Chinese sovereignty should apply to the former British colony.[39] Beijing has generally tried to rule with a light hand through its formula of "one country, two systems." Despite (some might say because of) a steady stream of alarms from the neo-colonial Hong Kong elite, and a barrage of Western press accounts warning of the loss of Hong Kong's "autonomy," Beijing has generally treated Hong Kong quite loosely. In this instance, as in most, Hong Kong law prevailed over the frustrated State Cultural Relics Bureau.

Perhaps some in Beijing fantasized about simply sending the army in to seize the controversial fountain heads. After all, Hong Kong is a city which still honors the looter of the emperor's garden with the name of Elgin Street. But Beijing has generally been patient with Hong Kong, resisting any temptation to fill the former colony's map with "People's Avenues" and "May First Squares" to replace markers of British imperialism. To put the matter more sharply, Hong Kong itself was repatriated imperialist booty.[40]

Nevertheless, it might have been prudent for Christies and Sotheby's to put obviously stolen works for sale in another country. But they did not, and China's use of troops armed with money (Hong Kong's weapon of choice) to recover the art by purchasing it enabled Beijing to claim the moral high ground.

One reason for the auction houses to disregard Beijing's warnings is that these are companies with long traditions of arrogance toward China. Christies first sold loot from the *Yuanming Yuan* in May 1861, and has been profitably churning this stock for 140 years.[41] Why should it stop, or even alter its plans, after such a long run of success?

A second reason is commercial, and even more compelling. A Hong Kong sale promised greater publicity and higher prices than other venues.

As China has prospered, an indigenous class of collectors has re-emerged after many decades, and Christies and Sotheby's want to profit from its new purchasing power and cultural interest. Christies and Sotheby's handled 90 per cent of the world art business in the 1990s, when both firms opened offices in China. They employed relatives of high officials to promote sales mostly held outside of China.[42] New Chinese auction houses have also arisen, with close ties to families from the political elite. Late President Liu Shaoqi's daughter, Liu Tingting, headed the Sungari International Auction Company, while former Party head Zhao Ziyang's daughter, Wang Yannan, was vice-president of the Guardian Auction Company.[43] On the eve of the

Zodiac statues auction, Sotheby's was trying to stimulate similar interest in art auctions among younger members of Hong Kong's wealthy. The firm organized a "practice" auction for charity, in order to familiarize Hong Kong's golden youth with the conventions of the fine arts auction. Often educated abroad, the young rich of Hong Kong typically cannot read calligraphy, or understand the poetry in a painting's inscription. Sotheby's sought to institutionalize the provision of expertise to meet such deficiencies.[44]

An expanding global art market, eager to recruit wealthy Chinese into its embrace, needed Hong Kong in 2000. Hong Kong remains the prime site where mainland, Hong Kong, and Southeast Asian collectors of Chinese fine arts can conveniently assemble. It is not surprising that this trend in the sales of Chinese art led to a clash with a self-consciously ascending Chinese state.

The clash was made more likely by Hong Kong's role in the supply of new plunder for the world market. Hong Kong's prosperity rests on its role as commercial intermediary between the People's Republic and the outside world. In the fine arts, this has made Hong Kong a major center for the distribution of freshly plundered art objects. China is unable to control art theft, despite ample criminal penalties. Grave robbing is an ancient profession in China, which is littered with unexplored underground burial sites. Many peasants find it more profitable to "harvest" items from tombs than from their own fields. And many officials have been caught selling objects from museum collections. Massive corruption smooths the way to market. The most desirable items end up for sale in an export market, for which Hong Kong remains a central point for smuggling, a position it has held since the establishment of the People's Republic. Increased Chinese shipping from other ports facilitates smuggling from other cities, but Hong Kong is likely to remain important for some time.

State efforts to combat archeological plunder are so inadequate that the failures have elicited protests from legislators. The site of Zhejiang's Liangzhu culture has been particularly hard hit. Although China designated the area for special protection in 1996, there have since been at least 57 instances of robbery, leaving a residue of 127 pits dug by robbers. Moreover, this archeological site shared its "protected zone" with 23 rock quarries. In June 2000, nearly 100 members of Zhejiang's Political Consultative Conference visited the site to demand stronger measures by the state.[45] Further evidence of the political frustration with the art-theft problem is found in the serious penalties which befall those who are apprehended. Zhang Guohua, leader of a gang which blasted its way into a tomb of the Western Han dynasty (206 BCE to 24CE), was sentenced to death in Henan Province.[46]

The Zodiac rescue alarmed many in the Hong Kong fine arts world, who fear restrictions on their ability to export freshly plundered art. Many Hong Kong collectors were understandably concerned that they could not document the origin of each piece in their collections. In some cases, the art has been obtained from dubious sources. The Hong Kong legislature considered amending local law to restrict the sale of smuggled goods, but decided this would be disruptive to the local arts market.

The role played by Sotheby's and Christies is not particularly noble. A price-fixing scandal forced resignations from the leadership of both companies (and the 2001 conviction of former Sotheby's chairman Alfred Taubman), suggesting that they conspired to form an international criminal organization.[47] Despite the social register connotations of the international arts trade, this business depends upon stirring up customer demand with the titillation of new goods, which it then sends agents to find. This can mean casting an indifferent eye at the origins of the goods they sell.[48] A 1997 article criticized Chinese auction firms for "unprofessional and unethical behaviour" which limits "the Chinese art market's bid for international respectability."[49] However accurate the assessment, the point seems ill-placed in light of the New York conviction of Taubman and the agreement to restore half a billion dollars to the customers he cheated.

As the Zodiac statue controversy escalated, and China's seriousness began to become evident, Beijing's claims began to be treated with more seriousness. Hong Kong's chief English-language newspaper, for instance, stopped putting "looted" art in ironic quotation marks. Anthony Lin of Christies warned that pressure from China might lead to Hong Kong art sales moving to other venues.[50] But such defiant responses were replaced by calmer words, as the auction houses were reported shaken by Beijing's tough attitude. An aide to Hong Kong Chief Executive Tung Chee-hua characterized the double sale as a "commercial activity that could not be more stupid." But he said there was no need for new legislation to ban such sales (as Beijing had demanded), because the auction houses would not do it again.[51]

The Zodiac heads controversy thus led to no legal changes for Hong Kong's fine arts economy. Although Beijing participates in the 1970 UNESCO convention against illegal export and transfer of cultural property, the Basic Law which governs Hong Kong does not allow its application in Hong Kong. However, the Zodiac rescue mission was more than symbolic, to the extent that it raised consciousness of China's position in an international distribution of fine arts. In 1997, when China joined the Unidroit Convention to help repatriate lost art, Beijing announced that it did not give up its right to claim art stolen prior to signing the treaty.[52] On 21 May 2000, at the height of the controversy, China announced the formation of a recovery team to lead the effort to repatriate more of the nation's plundered national treasures.

The international distribution of art objects as a measure of global inequality

While many citizens of the West deplore the sale of stolen art objects, wealthy nations tend to resist measures to remedy it, taking the view that countries such as China should limit the supply, instead of having Britain, the United States, or Japan limit demand. At one level, the situation is of course scandalous, with art-importing nations blaming their suppliers and victims as they try to sustain a status quo which permits easy smuggling and lower prices for collectors and museums. There is a parallel in approaches to the drug trade, with wealthy importing nations seeking to regulate supply, while poorer, supplying nations often argue that European and North American governments should control their domestic consumers.

From a somewhat colder perspective, the trade may be seen as an unavoidable leakage, by which China participates in the international cultural economy. National wealth and power are manifest in several dimensions. Military might and quality of health care are two quite different indicators of international standing. Another, less frequently noticed measure is the international distribution of art objects. Items of beauty, at least a beauty recognized in global markets, tend to flow from poorer to richer nations.

The fact that the distribution of beautiful objects is rather more uneven indicates that we do not take very seriously our own rhetoric about art as the common heritage of all humanity. In a more equal world, there would not only be pre-Columbian statues in New York, but American abstract impressionist paintings in Peru and Guatemala. There would be Cambodian Buddhist sculptures in Paris and canvases by Delacroix and Manet in Phnom Penh, batik in Argentina and totem poles in Senegal. However, this is not what happens. Not only is the art unevenly distributed in terms of economic value, but it is difficult to "exchange" art among Africa, Asia, and Latin America without the mediation of wealthy nations. For instance, in 1999, Shanghai displayed seventeen cases of antiquities from ancient Egypt. Yet the art came from Britain, not Egypt. The items were from the British Museum, sent on tour to Asia during its recent remodeling.[53] Egypt cannot easily afford to mount such a show, and when it can, the art is typically shown in wealthy nations which have helped finance the exhibition.

A crude classification misses out on subtleties, but suggests an underlying dynamic in the international cultural economy. Some nations are unusually art-rich, often because they occupy land where their ancestors (or someone else's ancestors) left abundant architectural and monumental artifacts. Other lands are art-poor, often because they were never the locations for great civilizations of the past, or because fewer artifacts have survived, or because indigenous arts have not been discovered by the international market. Italy, China, Peru, and Turkey are examples of art-rich nations, while the United States, New Zealand, Namibia, and the Dominican Republic are relatively art-poor.

Some of the art-rich nations are also economically wealthy, such as Italy, Japan, or France, but others are not. And some of the art-poor nations are also economically prosperous (see Table 10.1). The United States, for instance, has used its wealth to make itself an international center for contemporary art. But pre-modern art treasures must be acquired from other nations. The historic pattern has been for the American robber baron to decorate Cleveland or St. Louis with renaissance oils purchased from downwardly mobile Italian aristocracy.

Table 10.1 Comparison of countries in terms of economic and cultural wealth

	Art-rich	**Art-poor**
Economically rich	Italy, Japan, France	Australia, New Zealand, United States, Norway, Switzerland
Economically poor	China, Peru, Mexico, Egypt, Cambodia, Turkey	Namibia, Paraguay, Timor

How art-rich is China? China has been losing art for longer than many nations have made it.[54] The Liang dynasty's Yuandi (r. 552–554) assembled 240,000 scrolls of paintings, books, and calligraphy in his palace collection. As Western Wei armies attacked the capital, he burned the lot, of which only 4,000 scrolls survived. Sui Yangdi's achievements as emperor (r. 605–617) included the Grand Canal and a fine art collection. When the emperor traveled on these canals with a spectacular flotilla, he liked to carry his pieces of calligraphy and painting with him. On one of these journeys, a boat loaded with art treasures capsized and sank. Through this accident, the greater part of the imperial collection was lost. The Emperor Taizong of the Tang dynasty was crazy for the calligraphy of Wang Xizhi, collecting 2,290 pieces in the imperial palace collection; none survives, except as copies. This is not to justify foreign plunder by arguing that the Chinese have been beastly toward their own art, but to remind us that China has been producing phenomenal amounts of art for millennia.

The point is not that it is immoral for Americans to have collections of Chinese art, but that there is an asymmetry in our exchange by which few Chinese citizens have access to American or other Western art. The present distribution of art objects, like the distribution of brain surgeons, ballistic missiles, and top-rate universities, is uneven.

The maldistribution of art is rarely regarded as an issue in wealthy nations.[55] But it is an issue for poor countries, where artists and art students are deprived of opportunities to understand the techniques behind entire genres. The history of oil painting in China, for instance, is partly a history of limited access. There are no great Western oils in China; traveling shows have brought some paintings, but often of a very inferior quality. Lack of Western art in Third World nations is not a trivial issue. China not only has no great Western paintings, but it is even difficult to find books with first-class reproductions of Western paintings. This scarcity made it easier to shut off access altogether during the Cultural Revolution. It is striking how the modern history of oil painting in China gives such a prominent role to key individuals who helped introduce techniques, such as the Russian expert Maximov in the 1950s, or who arranged exhibitions of actual Western paintings, such as the American tycoon Armand Hammer in the 1980s.

No one would argue that the citizens of poor nations are about to riot for a more just redistribution of objects of beauty ("Dozens hurt as Karachi mob demands impressionist paintings and Toltec carvings"). But when art works become associated with all the emotions of nationalism, people do get excited, as did the angry crowd in Hong Kong outside the Zodiac heads auction.

Arguments against the current international distribution come most frequently from those nations who have been plundered. The classic case is Greece's persistent demands that the British return the Parthenon marbles. In 1799, the 7th Lord Elgin was British Ambassador to Turkey. Caught up in a craze for Greek things, Elgin took along his architect, with an eye to redecorating his mansion in Scotland. Elgin set his heart on Athens' Parthenon. Greece was not yet independent of Turkish rule, and British influence in the Eastern Mediterranean was high after Nelson's victory over the French at the Battle of the Nile. The Turks permitted Elgin to remove any sculptures which did not interfere with the walls of the Parthenon. By 1806, Elgin had shipped 200 crates of Greek national heritage to Scotland aboard British warships.

Byron and others demanded that the statues be returned to the Greeks. When Greece gained independence in 1832, the refurbishing of the Parthenon as national symbol began a long and still unsuccessful campaign to repatriate the marbles. Elgin eventually sold the statuary at great loss to the British government. They now reside in London's British Museum, where they are known as the "Elgin Marbles," to give an edge to British claims of legitimate ownership.

The Parthenon Marbles case is of interest to any nation which has lost art through plunder and hopes to regain possession. The British responses to Greece set the pattern for all plunder cases.[56]

First is the argument to legal ownership. British claims that the Turkish government approved Elgin's removal of the Parthenon friezes are not very convincing to Greece. But plunder-hosts utilize the complexity of international law to sow confusion about counterclaims to art whose acquisition has come under question. Such art can include items which were purchased in perfectly straightforward and honorable sales, those which were stolen outright, and those extracted under unfair conditions, which can in no way be called free exchange.

Second is the argument about care and protection, that the marbles would have suffered physical loss, if not destruction, if it hadn't been for the watchful care of the British Museum, which is protecting the art on behalf of all humanity. Similar arguments have been made about Chinese art in foreign collections: at least they were protected against Red Guard violence. The argument has lost appeal, however, in light of information that the

British Museum damaged the marbles in the 1930s, and has covered it up until recently. One might also point to the German "protection" of Dunhuang treasures lost to bombing in the Second World War.[57]

A third argument looks with horror at the purported implications of returning the marbles. This is deemed likely to initiate a ceaseless demand for restoration of artworks to their nations of origin. And who would want to see a world in which the only Greek art were in Greece, and the only Chinese art in China? This would be culturally damaging to us all. This is of course a red herring, as return of a specific piece of art does not require creating a global harmonization of nationalities and art.[58] Indeed, the growing "world heritage" movement, which draws moneyed tourists to view restored art and architecture in its national setting, offers an alternative path to the status quo.

Unsurprisingly, Western legal scholars interested in the trade in cultural objects have developed a neo-liberal critique of the state-centered approach favored by China and some other Third World nations.[59] Self-styled "cultural internationalists" argue that China and similar states need to expand, not restrict, the trade in cultural artifacts. There should be fewer restrictions, which are said to encourage theft and black markets. For poor nations, old objects must be desacralized and newly regarded as secular items which can be sold by peasants for economic advantage as the objects "pass from the cultural to the economic sphere."[60]

Neo-liberals say that China should have a process of judicious selection that may result in the export of all but the most culturally significant items. "The developing art-rich nations should treat cultural property as an exploitable national resource, not to be hoarded absolutely, but to be 'mined' as a source of income." Funding would somehow thus be assured for preservation efforts. In one optimistic projection, "scientists would replace thieves."[61]

These arguments resemble a brief for Western museums and art dealers. Murphy's informative book on China dismisses much protection out of hand: "the 'protected' resources are very often unowned – indeed, unexcavated – relics rather than identifiable owned objects." Murphy tarnishes those who favor tighter regulations by associating them with takers of bribes who seek "to protect the illicit income."[62] A country's comparative poverty becomes an argument against, rather than for, stricter national controls. In general, the approach is to blame the victims, who may not choose to regard artifacts of their cultures as objects to be mined. "Mining" art from the ground devalues the objects into the rawest export commodities, rather than allowing value to be added by the nation of origin. As art works are turned into export commodities through illicit excavation, the plunderers destroy invaluable evidence needed to understand the context in which the objects were found, and, by extension, adding to knowledge of life and beliefs in ancient China.

The Western fine arts world is inevitably intertwined with the world of big money and high finance. For instance, the invaluable Internet resource artnewspaper.com announces that it is available on Bloomberg terminals, which exist chiefly to convey stock market figures and other information for investors. Sotheby's and Christies may recently have been administered by scoundrels, but the auction houses are inevitably drawn into the realm of international commerce.[63] At the same time, in nations which have been plundered, the recovery issue is likely to fall in the political arena, with a risk that it will become the realm of political adventurers, manipulating patriotic appeals for career advantage.

The Zodiac heads controversy pitted Western dealers who regarded the heads as fine arts commodities against a Chinese state which was not yet willing to see them "pass from the cultural to the economic sphere." In addition to helping buttress the Communist Party's claim that its authority is just, the Zodiac statues helped provide a practical focus for energetic and potentially disruptive nationalist emotion throughout China. In addition, they also provided Hong Kong citizens an opportunity to display their own rather tentative patriotic sentiments.

Of course, much art has been returned to China. For example, the National Gallery of Canada recently returned a plundered arhat which was first sold outside China by Sotheby's in 1970.[64] And a Japanese museum returned a piece stolen in 1994.[65] China and other Asian nations may take some encouragement from the recent turn of respectable opinion in the West about art plundered by the Nazis. Much has been found to have been resold to private collectors or museums after the war, fueling a movement to restore art works to the heirs of their owners, many of whom were Jews killed by Germany.[66] But slow as this restoration has been, it has been eased by the fact that it is primarily an intra-Western phenomenon, and does not require the dispatch of art from one culture to another.

The movement to restore Nazi art plunder did not discourage Sotheby's and Christies from selling the Zodiac heads in Hong Kong. After that sale, China announced the formation of a special team to work on retrieving plundered art. Xie Zhenzhen of the Cultural Relics Bureau declared that over 1 million high-quality Chinese cultural artifacts lie in the collections of 200 museums in 47 nations. The New York Metropolitan Museum has the most paintings, but the British Museum has the finest. Japan has the most oracle bones, and France has the best ceramics.[67] Xie's assessment is debatable, and lumps plundered art with works of clearer provenance, but it reveals a conscious effort by the Chinese state to track cultural treasures. China may think it knows where to go to find the art, but it must have a realistic notion of how difficult it would be to obtain even a small part.

Of course, the restoration of national glory must ultimately rest upon more solid accomplishments: economic prosperity, military might, and the encouragement of vibrant new cultural works are all likely to contribute more importantly to political legitimacy than the recovery of plundered art works. Episodes such as the Zodiac heads can only be a small current in a much broader national effort. The particular circumstances of their partial recovery are unlikely to reappear, resting upon the coincidence of Hong Kong's return to China and the stubborn arrogance of Western auction houses. Yet the Zodiac heads episode also reminds us that the Chinese state needs evidence that it is overturning China's past shame. In an era in which nationalist protest can easily move faster than the state desires, art recovery presents itself as a virtuous and controllable nationalist project that appeals to Chinese patriotism in the broadest manner.

The Zodiac statues temporarily cloud the pride that many Chinese feel at finding their nation's art to be admired, coveted, and displayed abroad. The search for domestic legitimacy through repatriating lost art thus may pull China away from greater international acceptance. Just as many in the West regard China as a difficult rising power in economic and military affairs, the politics of art repatriation may be used by some as a high art example of Chinese truculence in the existing international aesthetic order.

Notes

1　I thank Ellen J. Laing for helpful comments on this piece.
2　A recent study of the *Yangming Yuan* is Young-tsu Wong, *Paradise Lost: The Imperial Garden Yuanming Yuan* (Honolulu: University of Hawaii Press, 2001).
3　See Cécile and Michel Beurdeley, *Giuseppe Castiglione: A Jesuit Painter at the Court of the Chinese Emperors* (Rutland, VT: Charles E. Tuttle Company, 1971).
4　Quoted in Young-tsu Wong, *Paradise Lost*, p. 149.
5　See Christopher Hitchens, *The Elgin Marbles: Should They be Returned to Greece?* (New York: Verso, 1998), and Russell Chamberlin, *Loot! The Heritage of Plunder* (New York: Facts on File, 1983).
6　See James L. Hevia, *Cherishing Men from Afar: Qing Guest Ritual and the Macartney Embassy of 1793* (Durham: Duke University Press, 1995), and Alain Peyrefitte, *The Immobile Empire* (New York: Alfred A. Knopf, 1992), pp. 135–151.
7　James L. Hevia, "Loot's fate: the economy of plunder and the moral life of objects 'from the Summer Palace of the Emperor of China,'" *History and Anthropology* 6(4) (1994): 319.
8　The engravings were returned to Asia when put up for sale in Singapore auction in 1997. Associated Press, "Rare imperial engravings on sale," *South China Morning Post*, 2 October 1997.
9　See Hevia, "Loot's fate," pp. 319–345. Hevia reminds us that the bulk of the "British" troops were in fact Indian, which adds a piquant complexity to the event.
10　Hevia, "Loot's fate," p. 336.
11　J. David Murphy, *Plunder and Preservation: Cultural Property Law and Practice in the People's Republic of China* (Hong Kong: Oxford University Press, 1995), p. 183.
12　See *Zhongguo wenhua changshi* (General Knowledge of Chinese Culture) (Hong Kong: Shijie jiechu huaren jijinhui, 2000), p. 52.
13　Eric Eckholm, "A glorious ruin and a face-life furor," *New York Times*, 10 August 1999.
14　A scaled-down replica of the pre-looted *Yuanming Yuan* has been built as a tourist attraction in Zhuhai, Guangdong, complete with fountain.
15　James Hevia, "Looting Beijing: 1860, 1900," in Lydia H. Liu (ed.) *Tokens of Exchange: The Problem of Translation in Global Circulations* (Durham: Duke University Press, 1999), pp. 192–213.

16 Stella Lee, "Looted bronze head on offer," *South China Morning Post*, 25 May 2000.

17 The Christies auction was on 31 April, the Sotheby's on 2 May 2000.

18 The Beijing Cultural Relics Company, owned by the Beijing Municipal Government, bought the vase from Sotheby's. General manager Qin Gong collapsed and died shortly thereafter, apparently from the stress of the deal. "Buyer of looted vase 'killed by stress of sale,'" *South China Morning Post*, 12 May 2000.

19 Mark Landler, "China asks auction houses to withdraw 4 relics," *South China Morning Post*, 29 April 2000.

20 Mark Landler, "Christie's auctions relics despite China's objection," *South China Morning Post*, 1 May 2000.

21 Stella Lee and Niall Fraser, "Beijing threatens auction houses," *South China Morning Post*, 29 April 2000.

22 The Poly Museum tells this story on a set of commemorative postcards: "*Guobao huigui tezhan*" ("Special exhibition of repatriated national treasures").

23 On Yi, see Wu Huan, "The mystery man of the 'seizing national treasures' incident," *Mingbao yuekan* 414 (June 2000): 36–39.

24 When I visited the Poly Art Museum on a Saturday afternoon in April 2001, the absence of other visitors assured close, yet polite, surveillance by guards and a staff member. The museum has prepared many volumes illustrating its collection, including *Baoli yishu bowuguan cang shike fojiao zaoxiang jingpin* (*Selected Works of Sculpture in the Poly Art Museum*) (Beijing: Baoli yishu bowuguan, 2000).

25 Ni Sha *et al.* (eds) *Shi shiren pipan shu* (*The Denunciations of Ten Poets*) (Changchun: Mingdai chubanshe, 2001). The poets include two victims of Guomindang criticism (Guo Moruo and Xu Zhimo), but the others have all done battle with the communist state (such as Shu Ting, Bei Dao, and the chief editor, Ni Sha).

26 Oliver Chou, "Sold (to the soldier at the back)," *South China Morning Post*, 22 November 2000.

27 Josephine Ma, "Bronze heads are priceless: buyer," *South China Morning Post*, 19 October 2000.

28 Of these, 839 were pieces of fine and applied arts, while the remaining 209 were architectural works. See the website of the Japanese Ministry of Education, Science, Sports, and Culture at www.monbu.go.jp/aramashi/1998eng/e602.html.

29 The Chinese National Artifacts Bureau classifies art objects into "valuable" and "ordinary" categories. There are three grades of valuable art objects. See Wang Hongjun (ed.), *Zhongguo bowuguanxue jichu* (*The Basis of Chinese Museology*) (Shanghai: Shanghai guji chubanshe, 2001), pp. 148–157.

30 "*Guobao huigui tezhan*" ("Special exhibition of repatriated national treasures").

31 I am indebted to Professor Puay-peng Ho of the Chinese University of Hong Kong for his informative lecture "Heads or tails? The flip side of Chinese national treasures," Hong Kong Anthropological Society, 20 March 2001.

32 *Huoshao Yuanming Yuan*, directed by Li Hanxiang. Bai Hua was one of the script-writers for this patriotic epic. The scene with the fountain ignores the fact that it had not worked since 1786.

33 See Yang Renkai, *Guobao Chenfu Lu* (*The Rise and Fall of National Treasures*) (Shanghai: Shanghai renmin chuban she, 1991), and Liu Jinku, *Guobao Liushi Lu* (*The Drain of National Treasures*) (Shenyang: Liaohai chubanshe, 1999).

34 A recent popular account is Dou Yingtai, *Wenwu da qianxi* (The Great Migration of the Artifacts) (Zhengzhou: Henan wenyi chubanshe, 2001).

35 See "Hundreds protest at art tour," *South China Morning Post*, 8 January 1996, and "Imperial treasures on move again," *South China Morning Post*, 16 January 1996.

36 Zhang Yang, "Should the National Palace Museum establish a branch in the south?" *Mingbao yuekan* 425 (May 2001): 114.

37 Sandy Huang, "Stop mixing culture with politics, KMT warns," *Taipei Times*, 16 January 2003, available online at www.taipeitimes.com/News/taiwan/archives/2003/01/16/191185.

38 Fong Tak-ho, "Approval sought to exhibit art in Taipei," *South China Morning Post*, 11 July 2001; "National treasures to be displayed in Taiwan," *People's Daily Online*, 28 November 2001.

39 Other issues by which the meanings of Chinese sovereignty and Hong Kong autonomy have been tested are immigration rights for Chinese relatives of Hong Kong residents, the importance of English-language instruction in schools, and the visa status of a Chinese-American convicted of espionage in a mainland trial.

40 The same phrase, "*huigui,*" was used to refer to the return or repatriation of both Hong Kong and the Zodiac statues.

41 In 1864, one of the many Christies sales of *Yuanming Yuan* plunder included the "skull of Confucius" made into a drinking cup. Hevia, "Loot's fate," p. 330.

42 Kari Huus, "Do I hear three?" *Far Eastern Economic Review*, 12 May 1994, pp. 69–70.

43 Pamela Yatsko, "Seducing China's rich," *Far Eastern Economic Review*, 27 March 1997; "Liu widow to sell rare antiques," *South China Morning Post*, 2 November 1996.

44 Gwyneth Roberts, "Sotheby's bidding to stimulate interest in future generations," *South China Morning Post*, 8 April 2000.

45 "'Liangzhu' culture faces destruction," *Renmin ribao (Huadong xinwen)*, 19 June 2000.

46 Associated Press, "Chinese tomb robber gets death," 12 June 2001.

47 Sotheby's and its former executive Diane ("Dede") Brooks have confessed to collusion with Christies; the chairmen of both firms have been indicted; but the Christies executive has hidden behind British law, which protects him against extradition to the United States. See Douglas Frantz, "Secret partners: the unraveling of a conspiracy," *New York Times*, 8 October 2000; Carol Vogel, "Indictment names two ex-chairmen of auction houses," *New York Times*, 3 May 2001; and Ralph Blumenthal and Carol Vogel, "Ex-chief of Sotheby's is convicted of price fixing," *New York Times*, 6 December 2001.

48 Christies recently attempted to auction a marble panel from the 10th-century tomb of Wang Chuzhi in Hebei Province, stolen in 1994, even characterizing it as similar to the Wang Chuzhi tomb. See Julian E. Barnes, "Alleging theft, U.S. demands rare sculpture go back to China," *New York Times*, 30 March 2000; Victoria Button and Cheung Chi-fai, "US to return panel looted from old tomb," *South China Morning Post*, 10 March 2001; and Cheung Chi-fai, "Dealer denies knowing marble panel looted. Antique's origins 'unknown' before it was sent to US for auction," *South China Morning Post*, 10 March 2001. Carelessness about origins is of course not limited to Chinese art. Robert D. McFadden, "Long after Napoleon's conquests, a tale of intrigue leads to court," *New York Times*, 6 April 2001, describes a case in which Sotheby's offered for sale a copy of the 1814 Treaty of Fontainebleau which had been reported stolen from the French National Archives in 1988.

49 Yatsko, "Seducing China's rich."

50 Cheung Chi-fai, "Disputed bronzes go for $16m," *South China Morning Post*, 1 May 2000.

51 Chris Yeung, "Sale of looted relics 'stupid,'" *South China Morning Post*, 3 May 2000.

52 "International help sought to recover relics," *South China Morning Post*, 25 July 1997.

53 "Egyptian treasures arrive in Shanghai," *Jiefang ribao*, 6 August 1999.
54 The following examples are all found in Lothar Ledderose, *Mi Fu and the Classical Tradition of Chinese Calligraphy* (Princeton: Princeton University Press, 1979), pp. 42, 24–25, 13.
55 On this point, see Rosemary J. Coombe, *The Cultural Life of Intellectual Properties: Authorship, Appropriation, and the Law* (Durham: Duke University Press, 1998), 222.
56 Among others, see Jeanette Greenfield, *The Return of Cultural Treasures*, 2nd edn (Cambridge: Cambridge University Press, 1966), and Hitchens, *The Elgin Marbles*.
57 When Afghanistan's Taliban demolished the 4th-century Buddhist statues at Bamiyan in 2000, some in the West revived the care argument, yet it retains a nasty core that the poor cannot be trusted to maintain pretty things.
58 On plunder and illegal art sales, see Pernille Askerud and Etienne Clement, *Preventing the Illicit Traffic in Cultural Property: A Resource Handbook for the Implementation of the 1970 UNESCO Convention* (Paris: UNESCO, 1997); Harrie Leyten (ed.), *Illicit Traffic in Cultural Property – Museums Against Pillage* (Amsterdam: Royal Tropical Institute in collaboration with Musée National du Mali, Bamako, 1995); Roderick J. McIntosh and Peter Schmidt (eds), *Plundering Africa's Past* (Bloomington: Indiana University Press, 1996); Kathryn W. Tub (ed.), *Antiquities Trade or Betrayed: Legal, Ethical and Conservation Issues* (London, Archetype Publications, 1995); and Neil Brodie, Jenny Dhole, and Peter Watson, *Stealing History: The Illicit Trade in Cultural Material* (Cambridge: McDonald Institute for Archaeological Research, 2000).
59 For example, Murphy, *Plunder and Preservation*; Paul M. Bator, *The International Trade in Art* (Chicago: University of Chicago Press, 1983); and John H. Merryman, "The retention of cultural property," *University of California Davis Law Review* 21 (1988): 477.
60 Murphy, *Plunder and Preservation*, p. 4.
61 *Ibid.*, p. 157.
62 *Ibid.*, p. 155.
63 For recent anthropological work on the art–money link, see George E. Marcus and Fred R. Myers (eds), *The Traffic in Art and Culture* (Berkeley: University of California Press, 1995).
64 "Canada returns stolen art to China," *Ottawa Citizen*, 12 April 2001. I cannot resist pointing out that the Canadian museum in question was, in 1970, located on yet another Elgin Street.
65 Eric Prideaux, "Japanese museum to return stolen statue," *Cleveland Plain Dealer*, 19 April 2001.
66 Recent books examining the issue of restoring art plundered during the Second World War include Lynn H. Nicholas, *The Rape of Europa: The Fate of Europe's Treasures in the Third Reich and the Second World War* (New York: Knopf, 1994); Caroline Moorhead, *Lost and Found: The 9,000 Treasures of Troy* (New York: Penguin Books, 1994); Hector Feliciano, *The Lost Museum: The Nazi Conspiracy to Steal the World's Greatest Works of Art* (New York: Basic Books, 1997); and Richard Z. Chesnoff, *Pack of Thieves: How Hitler and Europe Plundered the Jews and Committed the Greatest Theft in History* (London: Weidenfeld and Nicolson, 2000).
67 "Our country is to set up an organ for 'recovering national treasures' from abroad," *Gongren ribao*, 21 May 2000.

11 What is China? Who is Chinese?

Han–minority relations, legitimacy, and the state

Colin Mackerras

> I am Yi first and Chinese second. Lolo is the traditional name of my people. The meaning of the name was originally good until the Han turned it into a pejorative name. I want to show people that to be a Lolo is respectable and that we also have a culture.[1]

The speaker is a musician who calls himself "Lolo," after a traditional name for his south-west China ethnic group that the Chinese state had renamed "Yi." Lolo and many other Lolo/Yi do not regard it as legitimate for the Chinese state to have changed their name. With a population of 7,762,272 according to the census of November 2000,[2] they have a strong and probably growing sense of ethnic identity and are strongly resistant to any attempts to assimilate them.

Lolo still calls himself Chinese, though for him that is secondary to being Lolo/Yi, implying greater loyalty to his own ethnic group than to the Chinese state. Unlike several other ethnic groups to be considered in this chapter, the Yi have never shown any sign of wanting to secede from China.[3] Admittedly, they are not especially near a national border. Yet they are striking among China's ethnic minorities in the combination of the strength of their ethnic identity but weakness of separatist tendencies among them. The musician who calls himself Lolo shows one side of a very complex problem in China: what does Chineseness mean for the ethnic minorities, how do they relate to the majority Han, and where does state legitimacy fit itself into ethnic matters?

In China, every person belongs to a *minzu*, which means a nationality or nation.[4] In the Preamble to its Constitution, the PRC defines itself as "a unitary multinational State built up jointly by the people of all its nationalities."[5] The PRC follows Stalin in defining a "nation" as "a historically constituted, stable community of people, having a common language, a common territory, a common economic life and a common psychological makeup, which expresses itself in a common culture."[6] Ethnicity is rubbery at the best of times, but one significant point of silence in this definition is the idea of consciousness, which most scholars nowadays regard as a necessary attribute of an ethnic group.[7]

The census of November 2000 put the majority *minzu* in China, called the Han, at 91.59 per cent of the total population of 1,265,830,000, or about 1.159 billion people. The remaining 8.41 per cent of China's total population, or just over 106 million people, belong to fifty-five state-recognized "minority nationalities" (*shaoshu minzu*). By far the most populous of the minorities is the Zhuang, with 16,178,811 people.[8]

Although the minorities are a tiny proportion of China's total population, they take up about five-eighths of China's total territory, including almost the whole of the western half and many of its south-western regions, including provinces like Yunnan and Guizhou. This lends them an importance politically and socially out of all proportion to their population. It is true that over the centuries and especially under the PRC, Han migration to the minority areas has been ongoing and extensive. What is the basis for the claim that the minority areas should belong to China? What is "China," and which territories should it include? Are the minorities really "Chinese"?

What is China? History and territory

Both the Republic of China (ROC) and the PRC based their territorial claims upon the greatest extent of China as it had become under the Qing dynasty (1644–1911). There are two points of great interest about this empire:

1   China was very much larger under the Qing than under the preceding Ming dynasty (1368–1644), having taken varying degrees of control over the Tibetan, Mongolian, Turkic Muslim, and Manchurian territories to the south-west, west, north-west, and north-east.
2   The ruling family of the Qing dynasty belonged to the Manchus, an ethnic group that was to integrate itself into the Han Chinese majority to the extent that most of the markers of its ethnicity like language declined greatly during its reign.

Some suggest that it was "Qing imperialism" that led to the enlargement of China under the Manchus.[9] Yet Western and Japanese imperialism exonerated the Manchu dynasty from the taint of imperialism from the early 1840s onwards by their own onslaughts onto the decaying empire that was China. It is hardly surprising that the ROC was not interested in giving up over half its territory. Countries do not behave like that unless some force compels them to do so. When there is a major change of regime, such as the overthrow of the monarchy in China in 1911, what happens is that regimes take over the same territory as the predecessor, frequently adding claims over unfairly lost regions, such as Hong Kong to Britain in the case of Qing China. Yet it is extremely striking that the *Manchus*, who were not part of the Han Chinese majority, took over this foreign country, doubled its territorial size, and then were removed from power in favor of a *Han Chinese* regime, which chose to hold on to the enlarged territories as far as it could.

The western areas of the Qing empire did not necessarily share the enthusiasm of successor regimes that they should be part of the ROC. No sooner
had the Qing dynasty fallen than both Tibet and Mongolia declared independence from China, and in 1913 actually established diplomatic relations
with each other. The ROC refused to recognize the independence of either
territory, even though its actual control of them was negligible. As it turned
out, half of Mongolia did achieve lasting independence, while the other did
not, the single overwhelmingly important reason having to do with external
military power.

In the case of what the Chinese called "Outer Mongolia," the northern
part of Mongolia more distant from the Chinese heartland, Soviet troops
intervened to get rid of White Russian troops they found threatening. It was
not Mongolia that interested them but the Soviet Union. They initially
restored the *ancien régime*, but in 1924 put in power a socialist government
led by a Marxist–Leninist party, which led to the founding of a state calling
itself the Mongolian People's Republic (MPR). The ROC refused to recognize this state until after it signed a treaty of friendship with the Soviet
Union in 1945. Indeed, when the ROC troops and government were forced
out of the mainland late in 1949, the ROC on Taiwan reverted to its old
position, with the result that for decades it refused to recognize the independence of Mongolia.

The Chinese Communist Party (CCP), however, had never been in any
doubt about recognition of the MPR. Because it had been Soviet troops that
had intervened to bring about Mongolian independence, the CCP accepted
this reality from the start. On 16 October 1949, the new Chinese government
cabled recognition of the MPR, and despite occasional, and unconfirmed,
reports that China would like to take Mongolia back, that has remained its
formal position ever since.[10]

In the case of Tibet, the ROC never recognized independence, even
though Chinese control over most Tibetan areas was very weak or even non-
existent.[11] The British, who were in control of India, had interests in Tibet,
but nothing occurred remotely corresponding to the Soviet occupation of
Mongolia. One Tibetan scholar suggests that, even though Britain never
formally recognized Tibetan independence, British India functioned "as the
informal protector" of the Tibetan state during this time.[12] Tibet continued
to consider itself independent, or at least the western part further from the
Chinese heartland, while Chinese governments continued to regard Tibet as
part of China. In any case, the ROC had overwhelming concerns closer to
home, relegating Tibet to a very low place on its list of priorities.

In Xinjiang to the north-west, a succession of Han regimes followed the
collapse of the Manchu dynasty, the most important of which lasted from
1933 to 1944 under the leadership of a Han from Manchuria called Sheng
Shicai.[13] There were numerous rebellions against Han Chinese rule from the
Turkic Islamic minorities, who could not see why they should be part of
China. The neighboring Soviet Union was heavily involved in Xinjiang

affairs, and Sheng Shicai even joined the Soviet Communist Party. In 1944, local Uygurs and other minorities declared an independent East Turkestan Republic, but it proved impermanent.[14] There was no repetition of the situation in Mongolia, where Soviet occupation had led to independence.

Finally, we may note that the heartland of the former Manchu rulers to the north-east became very Sinicized after restrictions against Han migration there were totally lifted at the end of the 19th century. There was a spectacular rise in the population from about 10 million at the turn of the 20th century to just over 30 million in 1932, the year Japan set up its puppet state of Manchukoku, most of the increase being due to Chinese immigration.[15] The irony here is that the expanding Sinicization coincided with the time Japan took the territory over and formally proclaimed it an independent Manchu state under the protection of Japanese bayonets. With Japan's defeat in 1945, there was no doubt that the territory would return to China.

So what does this history tell us about what China is and about its legitimacy? The answer is that it depends on how strongly the past weighs upon the present. PRC governments have always insisted that the minority areas are legitimately part of China because the PRC state inherited these territories from earlier governments, making them "integral parts of China." For all Chinese governments, the unity of China – defined as the China enlarged by the Qing conquerors with the exception of Outer Mongolia – has ranked at or near the top of their priorities, and that includes the ethnic territories. However, even the cursory glance offered above shows that the inheritance of the ethnic territories is uneven in legitimacy. During the republican period, Chinese control over its territories was uneven at the best of times, but weaker over Xinjiang than Inner Mongolia, and weak to negligible over Tibet. Over Manchuria, it was non-existent from 1931 to 1945, but the sections of the international community that won the Second World War had never been happy with the fact of Japanese rule, and were more than happy to see the territory return to Chinese sovereignty after the war. The defeat of Japan in 1945 obliterated any semblance of legitimacy it had ever enjoyed in controlling parts of China in the view of any power. All those territories Japan had taken over from China since the end of the 19th century, including Manchuria and Taiwan, reverted to China at the end of the Second World War, and were claimed as "China" by the incoming PRC government in 1949.

Foreign governments have generally accepted Chinese claims over its minority areas, because it would be virtually impossible to redefine a country's territory every time it underwent a change of regime. Redefining territory leads to instability and even warfare. Moreover, if we went back in history to allocate territorial boundaries, the decision of which period was most appropriate would cause endless troubles. If the boundaries of the Qing were considered illegitimate, why should it go back to the much smaller Ming in preference to the quite extensive Tang dynasty boundaries? What would prevent Turkey reclaiming the boundaries of the Ottoman empire at its largest extent? Of course, one major exception to such a pattern is Israel, which was re-established in 1948 after a hiatus of more than two millennia, but this is very much a special case and shows the amount of trouble restorations of old states and boundaries can cause the international community. So it comes as no surprise that the international community continues to recognize the ethnic areas of China as part of the country.

The general principle that a nation has the right to inherit its territorial boundaries from its predecessor is a legitimate one. So it appears unnecessary to challenge the legitimacy of the Chinese boundaries in terms of the minority areas. I see little merit in the suggestion put forward by some scholars that China might well return to its Ming size,[16] because it can only be problematic to decide on which period's boundaries are legitimate if not those of the predecessor regime.

The most controversial and problematic of all those territories the current Chinese government claims as part of China, and the most likely to cause conflict, is Taiwan. However, it is outside the scope of the present chapter, because the legitimacy of the various claims concerning its status has little to do with Han–minority relations.

History is an important criterion for the legitimacy of a state's intervention in ethnic areas. However, history can be subject to differing points of view. Moreover, history is not the only criterion to establish legitimacy. A regime may be legitimate in the eyes of the international community, but not in the eyes of its own ethnic minorities. It is also possible that ethnic relations may deteriorate to such an extent as to affect legitimacy. If relations with the majority deteriorate to the point where rebellions break out, or dissatisfaction becomes extreme, then the legitimacy of Han rule is again called into question.

Who is Chinese? Ethnic identity and Han–minority relations

"What is China?" raises another question: "Who is Chinese?" Are all those people who live within the borders of "China" equally "Chinese"?

The second sentence of the 1982 PRC Constitution, which remains in force as the 21st century begins, says that "The people of all nationalities in China have jointly created a splendid culture and have a glorious revolutionary tradition." Article 4 states that all the nationalities are equal; it bans any action that might undermine "the unity of the nationalities" or instigate their secession.[17] This inclusiveness suggests that all citizens of China regardless of ethnicity are indeed equally Chinese, but that any attempt to secede from China's family of nationalities will be firmly suppressed.

Part of this policy toward minority nationalities is a system of autonomy. In essence, this means that the government establishes "autonomous" areas in places where there are concentrated communities of minority ethnic groups and allows them a limited degree of autonomy. This includes the need for the government head of the autonomous place to belong to the nationality exercising autonomy, although this privilege does not extend to the CCP, which holds the real power. It also includes the right of the minority group to use their own language in the government and elsewhere, to follow their own customs and religion, provided there is no threat to the state, and to exercise some control over the local budget.[18] In reality, practice has not always corresponded to theory, and some ethnic languages have recently declined in use, including in government.

Also involved in "autonomy" is a system of "preferential policies" (*youhui zhengce*), such as exemption from the one-child-per-couple policy, preferential access to higher education, such as the ability to enter university with lower marks than comparable Han students, and favorable treatment for entry into the job market.[19] The primary aim of these policies is to allow the minorities to "catch up" with the Han. The implication is clear: minorities are inferior to the Han. In general, minorities are poorer than the Han; but not all minorities are economically behind the Han. Affirmative action policies of one sort or another have now become commonplace in a great many countries throughout the world, even if they are under challenge.

Many people have drawn attention to a haughty, even racist, streak in Chinese culture. One scholar argues that the concept of "Chinese nation" (*Zhonghua minzu*) is "deeply inflected by racism" because as an inclusive concept it presumes the Han as its core.[20] My own personal observations over many years in China lead me to think that many Chinese care little for minorities, let alone their cultures, and tend to look down on them. Racism is not a weakness exclusive to China, nor is it particularly dominant there. But it is certainly quite strong enough to cause serious resentments among those who suffer from it.

In the period of reform, there have been contrary tendencies concerning ethnic identity. In some cases, ethnic consciousness is extremely weak and probably getting weaker. One scholar researched Tujia and Miao communities in the far north-west of Hunan and came to the conclusion that ethnicity had no clear meaning to them, their accepted identity as Tujia and Miao being nothing more than a classification imposed from outside.[21] Another scholar, focusing attention on a Hubei prefecture classified as Tujia-Miao, also found that many people consider themselves Han, even though legally classified as Tujia.[22] Both scholars agree that people whom outsiders classified as Tujia have little or no sense of ethnic consciousness as Tujia.

On the other hand, many of China's ethnic minorities have indeed experienced an *increase* in ethnic identity. One example is the Yao people of Guangxi and other parts of south-west China (population 2,637,421 in 2000). Ralph Litzinger concluded from field research in the late 1980s and early 1990s that Yao identity was undergoing a strengthening process. Indeed, he found that "elite members of the Yao nationality" had been "active agents in the making of a modern socialist and, more recently, postsocialist Yao identity."[23] It is noteworthy that Litzinger calls his book

Other Chinas and uses the term "national belonging" in the subtitle, suggesting that the Yao are "another China" along with the Han.

Another nationality of interest is the Hui, usually identified as Chinese Muslims. The 2000 census put their population at 9,816,805. Dru Gladney's intensive study of the Hui suggests a significant rise in their self-identification by the late 1980s. He concluded that this identity was ethnic, not merely religious, with Islam being only one of the markers of ethnic identity.[24] What is striking about this finding is that the Hui are among the very few ethnic minorities in China who lack their own language. They are culturally very similar indeed to the Han, except for their Islam. It is evident that the revival both of Hui identity and of Islam gathered momentum strongly during the 1990s and beyond.[25] I have heard credible reports that the revival of Islam is beginning to exercise a negative effect on relations between Hui and Han in some places, and that the Islamic clergy has even managed to gain influence and power in some Hui villages at the expense of the CCP.

One ethnic group in a rather special category is the Koreans, whose population the 2000 census put at 1,923,842. The Koreans have a very specific language and culture, and, despite living in China, remain very close culturally to their co-nationals in Korea. There is a strong sense of identity among the Koreans, and it appears to have grown stronger during the 1990s.[26] On the other hand, Korean identity poses no threat to the Chinese state or to the CCP, and relations between Han and Korean appear to be comparatively free of serious tensions. The reasons for this favorable situation are highly complex, but might include the following:

- The Koreans on the other side of the border (in North Korea) do not in any sense constitute a model that could inspire co-nationals in China to wish to secede.
- The Koreans in China have done remarkably well economically and socially, with a standard of living just as high or higher than that of their Han counterparts.
- Historically, Chinese influence over Korea was heavy, including sharing Confucianism-based culture. Koreans in China are far better disposed to the CCP than almost any other major ethnic minority in China, partly because they shared a strong hostility and resistance to Japanese imperialism in the first half of the 20th century.
- Religion is not a factor in Han–Korean relations.

China is diverse. And so are China's minorities. Even within minority communities there is a great deal of difference, just as there is among the Han and indeed other communities worldwide. At the same time, there are quite a few commonalities as well. All the minorities have been affected by the broad outlines of CCP policy. So, during the Cultural Revolution, traditional cultures and religions suffered persecution all over China, though it is true that the *extent* of pressure was not uniform everywhere. The thrust toward modernization that began in the late 1970s has also had a major impact just about everywhere in China, although again the *extent* of influence has varied greatly. In general, the cities have modernized much more quickly than the countryside, and Han areas more quickly than minority areas.

Yet it appears that many minority members are quite keen to participate in the economic benefits that go together with modernization. Many perceive more tangible and stronger advantages in the integration of their people into the Han Chinese economy, even if it means a decline in those special features that set their nationality apart. They may remain proud of belonging to their own ethnic group, but that does not mean they have to disavow being Chinese, or isolate themselves from China's economic rise. A very good example of this process is China's most populous nationality, the Zhuang. One scholar claims that many Zhuang villagers, who might never have even heard the name "Zhuang" in 1949, "today boast of their membership in China's large minority nationality." At the same time, she states that these same people, whose villages were once remote and isolated, "have now begun to participate in a modernizing integrated market economy."[27]

Modernization presents minorities with a challenge. As Stevan Harrell notes of the Nuosu, the name applied to the Sichuanese part of the state-recognized ethnic group called Yi, with which the chapter began:

> The challenge now for Nuosu who have some knowledge of the wider world (and they are still a minority) is to manage wisely the tension between cultural survival and economic development. It would be a great loss for the Nuosu if development passed them by, for Nimu [a Nuosu area in Sichuan] is still a poor, unhealthy, and often brutal environment, despite its natural and cultural beauty. It would be an equally great loss for the Nuosu and for the world if development and consumer culture finally smeared out the exquisite mountain patterns that have survived the efforts of so many regimes to tame them and have regenerated themselves so spectacularly after the dark years of the Cultural Revolution.[28]

Harrell's argument applies equally well to many minority communities.

During the "dark years" of the Cultural Revolution, the CCP tried quite consciously to stamp out ethnic cultures, including those of the Han. It was following a clearly assimilative policy, determined by the needs of the class struggle, as Mao Zedong (1893–1976) interpreted it. In the period of reform, on the other hand, we see a range of processes pointing in different directions. On the one hand, traditional cultures have revived. On the other, modernization processes are whittling away differences as globalization gathers momentum.

What follows from this material is that most members of minority ethnic groups are reasonably well integrated with the Han majority and enjoy relations with them that are not necessarily any more rancorous than those the Han have with one another. They are keener to take advantage of economic progress and a rise in the standard of living than to assert their national status by breaking free of China. Some care nothing for their ethnic identity, even when it is offered. That suggests that there is no crisis of legitimacy on the grounds of ethnicity in most of the ethnic areas. It is likely that most members of ethnic minorities are quite happy to consider themselves Chinese, even if they do have a sense of ethnic consciousness that has strengthened over the years.

The Tibetans

In terms of legitimacy, by far the most problematic of the minority areas is the Tibetan heartland. I suggested above that China's claim to sovereignty over Tibet was less well grounded historically than its claims over other ethnic areas currently part of the country, in part because of the weakness of central government influence in Tibet during the republican era. China sent troops into Tibet in 1950, and the following year its representatives signed an agreement with the Tibetan authorities under which Tibet would become part of the PRC but remain autonomous within it, including enjoying freedom of religion. However, in March 1959, a rebellion broke out, which the Chinese suppressed quickly and brutally. The head of the Tibetan government, the 14th Dalai Lama, fled to India and set up a government-in-exile there, while in Tibet itself both sides went back on the 1951 agreement. During the Cultural Revolution of 1966–76, radical Han and Tibetan Red Guards made active attempts to stamp out traditional Tibetan culture and religion. However, the early 1980s saw a drastic change in policy, with a consequent revival of Tibetan culture. Great improvements in conditions did not prevent large-scale demonstrations for independence from 1987 to 1989. The Chinese authorities suppressed these firmly, and imposed martial law from March 1989 to May 1990. They also implemented policies promoting rapid economic development, coupled with some degree of freedom of religion, but zero tolerance for separatism or any religious activities with the potential to promote it.[29]

Even though China's claim over Tibet is not as strong on historical grounds as its claims over its other territories, countries that establish diplomatic relations with the PRC all recognize Tibet as part of China. In the sense that international recognition of territory is one criterion of legitimacy, then China's claim may actually have strengthened under the PRC. On the other hand, international criticism of China for human rights abuses in Tibet reduces at least the perception of legitimacy. In the United States and elsewhere, there are movements that advocate Tibetan independence, some of them enjoying support in the high echelons of power. In 1989, the Dalai Lama won the Nobel Peace Prize, which greatly raised his already high prestige. Since that time, his trips abroad have multiplied in frequency and he has become an icon of the new spirituality that is so widespread in Western countries. However, although governments have mostly welcomed him, none has moved towards granting him diplomatic recognition. Criticism of Chinese policy and actions in Tibet has mainly stayed at the level of condemning human rights abuses, few challenging that Tibet is part of China.[30]

Since the disturbances of the late 1980s, Tibet has been reasonably stable. There has been no repetition of the large-scale disturbances of the late 1980s. There were no serious disturbances during the March 1999 40th anniversary of the 1959 uprising and 10th anniversary of the 1989 demonstrations that led to the imposition of martial law. And state-organized celebrations in 2001 commemorating the 50th anniversary of the 1951 agreement passed without incident.

The Tibetan standard of living has risen greatly, especially in the cities. I visited Tibet in 1990, 1997, and 2002 and found economic conditions improving dramatically each time, with people better dressed, better educated, and apparently in better health. It is true that this rise in living standards is uneven. A study of development at the end of the 20th century in Tibet came to the conclusion that "an extreme form of 'urban bias' skews development in Tibet, stratifying society across the ethnic divide and disparately benefiting the Han population mainly because it is urban."[31] The main site of disparities is urban/rural, not ethnic.

According to the 1990 and 2000 Chinese censuses, the Han population in the Tibet Autonomous Region rose from 81,217, or 3.68 per cent of the total, in 1990 to 155,300, or 5.9 per cent of the total, in 2000.[32] These figures are open to debate. For instance, they do not include the army or the short-term floating population, both of which are overwhelmingly Han. However, there seems little doubt that there was an acceleration of Han migration to Tibet in the last decade of the 20th century. The floaters are mostly Han from other parts of China seeking employment in cities, especially the capital Lhasa.

As the 21st century dawns, Tibetan culture is alive and in no danger of dying out. Tibetans are still overwhelmingly dedicated to traditional Tibetan Buddhism, with no shortage of young men keen to enter the monastic life. One writer's reference to "dozens of robed novices, many no older than 12" amid 300 monks in a Tibetan monastery in Sichuan province early in 2003 accords with my own findings both in Tibet itself and in other Tibetan areas of China.[33] In mid-2002, the Tibetan government actually issued regulations promoting the study, use, and development of the Tibetan language.[34]

At the same time, modernization is exercising a weakening effect on Tibetan traditions, as it tends to do everywhere. According to a Tibetan college student, "The more money we Tibetans have, the higher our living standard is, the more we forget our own culture. And with or without the Chinese, I think that would be happening."[35] Tibetan language is tending to decline in use in favor of Chinese, because it opens more doors toward a good career and prosperity.[36] And religious persecution persists. At the end of 2002, two Tibetan monks were tried for allegedly being accomplices in bombings and separatist activities. The younger monk was executed in January 2003.[37] Although the Chinese government no longer suppresses Tibetan culture unless it perceives it as a threat to CCP rule, the Chinese authorities keep an eagle eye out for "dangerous" activities, and may be quite happy to see traditions weakening among the people.

What does all this tell us about Han–Tibetan relations? The political protests of the late 1980s suggest that relations reached a low ebb at that time. Since then, however, economic development has to a large extent relieved tensions. But the very strong Han presence in the cities appears to me still (again, from random interviews I have undertaken) to arouse strong resentments. Moreover, Chinese authorities can hardly expect the Tibetan population to approve crackdowns on Buddhism and monks, who still enjoy great respect and affection among the Tibetan people.

On the other hand, according to one survey, relations may not have been as bad in the mid- to late 1990s as most in the West believed. Covering 586 families from various Tibetan areas, it was carried out in 1996 by a team of eighteen people led by Herbert Yee (Yu Zhen) of Hong Kong's Baptist College and including four Tibetans.[38] In answer to one question relating to Tibetan integration into China, 546 people responded to the statement that the Han were honest and reliable, 12.5 per cent strongly agreeing, 62.5 per cent agreeing, 9.7 per cent disagreeing, and 1.3 per cent disagreeing strongly, the remaining 14.1 per cent holding no opinion.[39] Surprisingly, the survey also found strong support for intermarriage between Han and Tibetans.[40]

The Uygurs

The Uygurs are a Turkic people, and the great majority believe in Islam. Their language, culture, and lifestyle are closer to the Turkic peoples further west than to the Han Chinese. According to the November 2000 census, their total population at that time was 8,399,393, almost all living in Xinjiang.

In the early 21st century, Han relations with the Uygurs are worse than with any other ethnic minority in China, including the Tibetans. Since 1990, there have been repeated violent political disturbances. And since 2001, the war against terrorism has compounded the problem.

In April 1990, a small-scale rebellion erupted in Baren Township, Akto County, in the south-west of Xinjiang. Inspired by the Islamic doctrine of the "holy war" (*jihad*), it gained some support but was quickly suppressed by the Chinese state. Yet the 1990s saw a series of violent incidents aimed against Chinese rule, all of them suppressed by the authorities. Amnesty International was among worldwide human rights organizations that accused the Chinese authorities of serious abuses. In a long April 1999 report, Amnesty International charged, among other serious abuses, that torture was systematically used against Xinjiang's Uygur separatists.[41]

Several studies have suggested that Han–Uygur relations in Xinjiang deteriorated over the 1990s.[42] A major reason for this deterioration is increasing Han immigration into Xinjiang. This is not a new phenomenon, but appears to have gathered momentum in the 1990s. One study found a distinction in Uygur attitudes toward the original Han settlers who came in the early decades after 1949 and the new Han immigrants. Uygurs are not so badly disposed toward the old settlers, but hate the new ones intensely. The reason is that many of the "original settlers" were prepared to learn Uygur and adopt Uygur customs like giving up pork, while the new ones behave like colonial masters, adopting "great Han chauvinist attitudes."[43]

Despite "preferential policies" and rising living standards among virtually all people, including ethnic minorities, Uygurs feel a growing marginalization in education and work. Han immigrants tend to get the better jobs, while Uygurs "end up doing blue-collar jobs or remain in traditional agricultural roles." In the cities, the presence of more prosperous Han gives the Uygurs something to compare themselves with, adding to resentments.[44]

The war against terrorism that followed the 11 September 2001 attacks on the World Trade Center and the Pentagon has also affected Han–Uygur relations. As in many other countries, the war has increased mutual fear and mistrust among the Han and Muslim populations. Since the early 1990s, Muslim extremists have indeed occasionally targeted civilians. On the same day as the funeral service for Deng Xiaoping, 25 February 1997, terrorists planted four bombs in buses in the Xinjiang capital of Ürümqi, killing at least nine people and wounding numerous others, mostly children on their way home from school.

With the war against terrorism, the Chinese authorities were quick to claim connections between the al-Qaeda network and Uygur and Muslim separatists and extremists. At first, the United States was cautious in accepting the link, continuing to condemn PRC crackdowns as human rights abuses. However, in August 2002, both the United States and the United Nations formally listed the most important of the Uygur separatist organizations, usually known as the East Turkestan Islamic Movement, as "terrorist." Uygur diasporic groups denounced the move, but won little international support.

The deterioration of Han–Uygur relations, combined with the fact that the Uygurs direct greater hatred toward the newly arrived Han than toward those of longer residence, suggests strongly that the legitimacy of Chinese rule in Xinjiang has suffered as far as the Uygurs are concerned. However, for its part, the Chinese state seems more determined than ever to maintain stability in Xinjiang, irrespective of the cost in terms of Uygur resentment. The international attitude, as expressed by the UN and US labeling of the East Turkestan Islamic Movement as terrorist, suggests that the war against terrorism may actually have improved China's claim to legitimate rule in Xinjiang.

The Mongolians

Inner Mongolia (or Southern Mongolia) has always remained part of China. Indeed, there are still far more Mongolians in Inner Mongolia than there are in the Republic of Mongolia. Censuses taken in China and Mongolia in 2000 showed 5,813,947 Mongolians in Inner Mongolia and 1,877,410 in Mongolia.[45] The 2000 Chinese census had the total population of Inner Mongolia at 23.76 million, Han outnumbering Mongolians four to one.

Of all ethnic minority leaders, it was a Mongolian, Ulanhu (1906–88), who reached the highest leadership positions in China. He not only led the Inner Mongolian Autonomous Region from its foundation in 1947, even before the PRC itself was established, to 1966, but was a member of the CCP's Politburo from 1977 to 1985. Ulanhu was personally involved in drafting the Nationalities Autonomy Law of 1984. He became an icon of loyalty both to the Chinese state and to the Mongolian people, a remarkable achievement. His son Buhe to some extent inherited his status (though never his power), calling in 1997 for extension of the provisions of the 1984 Autonomy Law.[46]

However, the Mongols of Inner Mongolia enjoyed more rights during Ulanhu's rule than at the turn of the 21st century.[47] Uradyn Bulag argues that despite Buhe's 1997 efforts, autonomy has actually *declined* since the 1990s, due to a combination of economic development and suppression of Mongolian dissent.[48] However, like other ethnic minorities, the Mongols have been enthusiastic and successful in making money. Increasing numbers learn Chinese to advance their job and career opportunities. A Mongolian incarnate lama I met told me that although he taught Mongolian in a secondary school because he felt passionately about its survival, he believed it was a language with very limited use or potential in the modern world, and that he was pessimistic about its future in Inner Mongolia.

Separatism and state legitimation

The Tibetans, Uygurs, and Mongolians are the three minorities that history has shown to have the greatest potential for separatism from China. Were they to secede from China, the Mongolians would doubtless join up with the Republic of Mongolia, while the Tibetans and Uygurs would form their own independent states. However, the likelihood of this occurring seems slighter in all cases at the beginning of the 21st century than it was in the early 1990s. The Chinese have won over enough members of the economic and political elite and the power of the Chinese army is such that successful secession today is more or less out of the question.

Because of the large Han population in Xinjiang and Inner Mongolia, ethnic conflict might be worse in an independent East Turkestan Republic and united Mongolia than at present. A united Mongolia including Inner

Mongolia would have far more Han than Mongolians, a prospect no Mongolian leader could welcome.

Separation of any territory from China would require:

• the collapse of the Chinese state; and/or
• armed foreign intervention.

By the collapse of the Chinese state, I mean more than the overthrow of the CCP; rather, a disintegration involving social, political, and economic turmoil, and probably civil war. The imminent collapse of China has indeed been predicted, but seems unlikely as long as the economy continues to grow.[49] Long-term economic downturn could trigger social instability and political fragmentation. However, the model of Indonesia suggests that one case of successful secession need not necessarily lead to national disintegration.

At present, the likelihood of foreign intervention to assist any separatist movement in China seems remote. The war against terrorism has made such an eventuality in China less likely than ever, because the most likely candidate for intervention – the United States – is much more interested in keeping China as an ally in the struggle against terrorism than in turning it into an outright enemy through provocations that affect its vital interests. Neither the United States nor any other power has any interest in intervening militarily in China.

Tibetan independence enjoys a great deal of support in the West, including the United States, but supporters of an independent East Turkestan and united Mongolia are still comparatively few and not well organized. The Free Tibet lobby may wish for American diplomatic recognition of the government-in-exile and later an independent Tibet, but hardly for armed intervention. American recognition of Tibetan independence would most certainly arouse fury in Beijing, and in the foreseeable future is most unlikely to be a cause worth the trouble that would undoubtedly result in Washington and elsewhere.

A farmer begins a fascinating autobiography by observing: "I am, of course, Chinese; however, I should like to add one more word: I am Bai Chinese. I belong not to the great Hans of Central China but to the Bai National Minority."[50] For him, being Chinese comes *before* being Bai. At the beginning of the chapter, we discussed the case of Lolo, a Lolo/Yi musician who said, in contrast to the Bai farmer, that he was Lolo/Yi first and Chinese only second.

What this shows is that members of different ethnic groups frequently have different attitudes toward being Chinese. There are most certainly quite a few Tibetans and Uygurs, and doubtless members of other minorities in China, who would deny being Chinese altogether. And among the same ethnic group, not all people hold the same view of their identity.

In the period of reform, the Chinese state has responded to the minorities in large part according to their loyalty to the Chinese state. It has reserved coercive responses for those ethnic groups with separatist tendencies, and violence has been sharpest when separatism flared into open rebellion, such as the Tibetans in the late 1980s and the Uygurs throughout most of the 1990s. Methods used toward other ethnic minorities have generally been more in line with what most would regard as legitimate. One thinks of ethnic groups like the Yi or Koreans, both with very strong ethnic consciousness but no separatist movements. Though these two peoples are extremely different in their histories, cultures, and economic levels, the Chinese state has been able to handle them without provoking excessive hostility. Indeed, the Koreans are a "model" ethnic minority in terms of economic development, literacy, and lack of opposition to the Chinese state, despite their strong culture and language, including their own script.

I have argued that the Chinese state has some legitimacy in its territorial claims, with Tibet being much more doubtful than any of the other ethnic territories. But the question remains: to what extent are the members of the ethnic minorities challenging the legitimacy of the CCP and the current Chinese state? The answer to that question is that the situation varies greatly from ethnic group to ethnic group and within ethnic groups themselves. The revival of Islam that several scholars have noted in the Hui, the Uygurs, and several other ethnic groups cannot fail to reduce their sense of CCP legitimacy, because of the strength of monotheistic belief among Muslims.

For members of ethnic minorities, ethnicity *may* be the most important issue in determining CCP legitimacy but it is not *necessarily* so. Among ethnic groups that have experienced separatist movements, notably the Uygurs and Tibetans, ethnicity is bound to weigh more heavily than among those better integrated into the Chinese state, such as the Zhuang or Tujia. Ethnicity counts far more in determining how Tibetans or Uygurs feel about the legitimacy of the CCP than it does among the Koreans or Zhuang, because their sense of identity is stronger and based more solidly on resentments against injustice.

Class analysis may not be the same among ethnic minorities as it is among the Han. There may be as many Korean intellectuals and workers proportionately as Han, but among the Tibetans, rural people are even more numerous, as a percentage of their total population, than among the Han. One class that has gained a considerable amount of press in China at the turn of the 21st century is the entrepreneurs. As Bruce Dickson's chapter of the present volume (Chapter 7) notes, Jiang Zemin showed himself very keen to introduce them into the CCP in the late days of his formal rule, and actually had the CCP Constitution changed at the 16th CCP Congress in November 2002 to encourage their entry. The question that arises is: are there enough entrepreneurs among the minorities to form a class substantial enough to affect how the minorities view CCP legitimacy?

My answer is that this varies from place to place, but overall it will indeed make some difference. We do not yet know how entrepreneurship will affect CCP legitimacy among the Han, let alone the minorities. But, as Harley

Balzer notes (see Chapter 12), it is likely that entrepreneurs, plus others prosperous enough that they could be said to make up a new "middle class," will become more important in Chinese politics. Already there is beginning to be a significant body of private entrepreneurs among virtually all the most populous minorities. Some may find it in their interests to join the CCP and exercise some impact on its direction.

With China's accession to the World Trade Organization at the end of 2001, China is increasingly becoming part of the globalized world. This does not necessarily mean the end of ethnic cultures. Indeed, there are cases where globalization provokes localization as a form of resistance. I do not see the imminent demise of Yao or Miao culture in China, let alone Tibetan or Uygur. But the overall impact of the globalization of markets, consumer practices, communications, and tourism is to reduce the differences between cultures. Among the tensions operating in China and intensified by globalization is that between the CCP's Marxist–Leninist ideology and the non- or anti-Marxist tendencies in society. This cannot fail to weaken the legitimacy of the CCP overall, among both the Han and the ethnic minorities.

Notes

1 Nimrod Baranovitch, "Between alterity and identity, new voices of minority people in China," *Modern China* 27(3) (July 2001): 378.
2 National Bureau of Statistics of China (comp.), *Zhongguo tongji nianjian 2002 (China Statistical Yearbook 2002)* (Beijing: Zhongguo tongji chubanshe, 2002), p. 97. This is the source for populations of all specific ethnic groups cited in this chapter.
3 See, for instance, Thomas Heberer, "Nationalities conflict and ethnicity in the People's Republic of China, with special reference to the Yi in the Liangshan Yi Autonomous Prefecture," in Stevan Harrell (ed.) *Perspectives on the Yi of Southwest China* (Berkeley: University of California Press, 2001), p. 232.
4 The terms "*min*," or "people," and "*zu*," or "tribe" or "race," have existed in the Chinese language for millennia. However, the combination "*minzu*" in the modern sense of nation was first used by Liang Qichao in 1899. See Wu Shimin and Wang Ping *et al.*, *Minzu wenti gailun* (Chengdu: Sichuan Renmin chubanshe, 1999), p. 6.
5 "The Constitution of PRC," in *People's Republic of China Yearbook 2000* (Beijing: PRC Yearbook, 2000), p. 2.
6 According to Wu Shimin and Wang Ping (*Minzu wenti gailun*, p. 7), Stalin's definition "summarizes the essential features of a nationality quite completely."
7 In his definition of an "ethnic group," Richard Schermerhorn includes the following: "A necessary accompaniment is some consciousness of kind among members of the group." See "Ethnicity and minority groups," in John Hutchinson and Anthony D. Smith (eds) *Ethnicity* (Oxford: Oxford University Press, 1996), p. 17. Cited from *Comparative Ethnic Relations* (New York: Random House, 1970).
8 The figures given here do not include Taiwan, Hong Kong, or Macau. They come from *Zhongguo tongji nianjian 2002*, pp. 95, 97.
9 See, for instance, James A. Millward, *Beyond the Pass: Economy, Ethnicity, and Empire in Qing Central Asia, 1759–1864* (Stanford: Stanford University Press, 1998), pp. 15–18.

10 For an excellent narrative sympathetic to the independence of Mongolia, see C.R. Bawden, *The Modern History of Mongolia* (London: Weidenfeld & Nicolson, 1968).

11 For an excellent history of Tibet at this period, see Melvyn C. Goldstein, *A History of Modern Tibet 1913–1951: The Demise of the Lamaist State* (Berkeley: University of California Press, 1989).

12 Dawa Norbu, *China's Tibet Policy* (Richmond: Curzon, 2001), p. 175.

13 Excellent coverage of this period in Xinjiang comes from Andrew D.W. Forbes, *Warlords and Muslims in Chinese Central Asia: A Political History of Republican Sinkiang, 1911–1949* (Cambridge: Cambridge University Press, 1986).

14 David D. Wang, *Under the Soviet Shadow: The Yining Incident, Ethnic Conflicts and International Rivalry in Xinjiang 1944–1949* (Hong Kong: Chinese University Press, 1999) argues that the East Turkestan Republic was more or less a Soviet creation. In her *The Ili Rebellion: The Moslem Challenge to Chinese Authority in Xinjiang 1944–1949* (Armonk, NY: M.E. Sharpe, 1990), Linda Benson claims much more initiative from local Islamic peoples (see p. 178).

15 See Colin Mackerras, *China's Minorities: Integration and Modernization in the Twentieth Century* (Hong Kong: Oxford University Press, 1994), pp. 120–121.

16 See, for instance, Ross Terrill, *The New Chinese Empire And What It Means for the United States* (New York: Basic Books, 2003), pp. 249–252.

17 "The Constitution of PRC," pp. 1, 3.

18 For a detailed treatment of policy from 1949 to the early 1990s, see Colin Mackerras, *China's Minorities*, pp. 139–166, and for the period from 1989 to 2002, see Colin Mackerras, *China's Ethnic Minorities and Globalisation* (London and New York: RoutledgeCurzon, 2003), pp. 37–55.

19 See Barry Sautman, "Expanding access to higher education for China's national minorities: policies of preferential admissions," in Gerard A. Postiglione, *China's National Minority Education: Culture, Schooling, and Development* (New York and London: Falmer Press, 1999), pp. 173–210.

20 Uradyn E. Bulag, *The Mongols at China's Edge: History and the Politics of National Unity* (Lanham, MD: Rowman & Littlefield, 2002), pp. 17–18.

21 Chih-yu Shih, "Ethnicity as policy expedience: clan Confucianism in ethnic Tujia-Miao Yongshun," *Asian Ethnicity* 2(1) (2001): 88. According to the 2000 census, the total Tujia population in China was 8,028,133, while that of the Miao was 8,940,116. See *Zhongguo tongji nianjian 2002*, p. 97.

22 Melissa J. Brown, "Ethnic classification and culture: the case of the Tujia in Hubei, China," *Asian Ethnicity* 2(1) (2001): 56.

23 Ralph A. Litzinger, *Other Chinas: The Yao and the Politics of National Belonging* (Durham: Duke University Press, 2000), p. xx.

24 See Dru C. Gladney, *Muslim Chinese: Ethnic Nationalism in the People's Republic* (Cambridge, MA: Council on East Asian Studies, Harvard University, distributed by the Harvard University Press, 1991), esp. p. 323.

25 See Dru C. Gladney, *Ethnic Identity in China: The Making of a Muslim Minority Nationality* (Stanford: Harcourt Brace, 1998), and Raphael Israeli, *Islam in China: Religion, Ethnicity, Culture and Politics* (Oxford: Lexington Books, 2002).

26 See also Bernard Vincent Olivier, *The Implementation of China's Nationality Policy in the Northeastern Provinces* (San Francisco: Mellen Research University Press, 1993), esp. p. 262.

27 Katherine Palmer Kaup, *Creating the Zhuang: Ethnic Politics in China* (Boulder: Lynne Rienner, 2000), p. 171.

28 Stevan Harrell, "The survival of Nuosu culture," in Stevan Harrell, Bamo Qubumo, and Ma Erzi, *Mountain Patterns: The Survival of Nuosu Culture in China* (Seattle: University of Washington Press, 2000), p. 9.

29 The best history of Tibet under the PRC is Tsering Shakya, *The Dragon in the Land of Snows: A History of Modern Tibet Since 1947* (London: Pimlico, 1999). Another excellent study is A. Tom Grunfeld, *The Making of Modern Tibet*, rev. edn (Armonk, NY: M.E. Sharpe, 1996).

30 For an interesting discussion of American government attitudes toward Tibet in the 1990s, see Melvyn Goldstein, *The Snow Lion and the Dragon: China, Tibet, and the Dalai Lama* (Berkeley: University of California Press, 1997), pp. 117–125.

31 Barry Sautman and Irene Eng, "Tibet: development for whom?" *China Information: A Journal on Contemporary China Studies* 15(2) (2001): 21.

32 The 1990 figure, from the census of that year, is given in Population Census Office of Xizang Autonomous Region (comp.), *Xizang zizhiqu 1990 nian renkou pucha ziliao: dianzi jisuanji huizong (Tabulation on the 1990 Population Census of Xizang Autonomous Region: Computer Tabulation)* (Lhasa: Xizang Publishing House, 1992), p. 38. The 2000 figure is from *Renmin ribao (People's Daily)*, 3 April 2001, p. 1.

33 Erik Eckholm, "From a Chinese cell, a lama's influence remains undimmed," *New York Times*, 23 February 2003, online version.

34 See Nicolas Tournadre, "The dynamics of Tibetan–Chinese bilingualism: the current situation and future prospects," *China Perspectives* 45 (January–February 2003): 30.

35 Quoted in Sautman and Eng, "Tibet: development for whom?" p. 74.

36 Tournadre, "The dynamics of Tibetan–Chinese bilingualism," p. 35.

37 Eckholm, "From a Chinese cell."

38 Yu Zhen and Guo Zhenglin, "Xizang, Sichuan Gansu Zangqu shehui fazhan diaocha baogao" ("Report of a social survey in the Tibetan areas of Tibet, Sichuan and Gansu"), in Yu Zhen and Guo Zhenglin (eds) *Zhongguo Zangqu xiandaihua, lilun, shijian, zhengce (The Modernization of China's Tibetan Regions, Theory, Practice, Policy)* (Beijing: Zhongyang minzu daxue chubanshe, 1999), pp. 35–36.

39 Yu and Guo, "Xizang," p. 81.

40 *Ibid.*, p. 82.

41 Amnesty International, *Gross Human Rights Violations in the Xinjiang Uighur Autonomous Region* (London: Amnesty International Publications, 1999), online version.

42 There are quite a few studies of the situation in Xinjiang during the 1990s, with some reference or a focus on Han–Uygur relations. The main ones include Nicolas Becquelin, "Xinjiang in the nineties," *China Journal* 44 (July 2000): 65–90, and Gardner Bovingdon, "The not-so-silent majority: Uyghur resistance to Han rule in Xinjiang," *Modern China* 28(1) (January 2002): 39–78.

43 See Joanne N. Smith, "'Making culture matter': symbolic, spatial and social boundaries between Uyghurs and Han Chinese," *Asian Ethnicity* 3(2) (September 2002): esp. Conclusion, pp. 172–174.

44 Smith, "'Making culture matter,'" p. 173. The point about job discrimination looms large in other accounts, such as Amnesty International, *Gross Human Rights Violations*.

45 For the number of Mongolians in China according to the 2000 census, see *Zhongguo tongji nianjian 2002*, p. 97. According to the provisional figure for the 2000 census in the Republic of Mongolia, the total population was 2,392,500, of whom 78.8 per cent were Mongolian peoples, i.e. 1,877,410. See Barry Turner (ed.), *The Statesman's Yearbook: The Politics, Cultures and Economies of the World 2003* (Houndmills and Basingstoke: Palgrave Macmillan, 2002), p. 1140.

46 See June Teufel Dreyer, "The potential for instability in minority regions," in David Shambaugh (ed.) *Is China Unstable? Assessing the Factors* (Armonk, NY: M.E. Sharpe, 2000), p. 137.

47 Bulag, *The Mongols at China's Edge*, p. 234.
48 Uradyn E. Bulag, "Ethnic resistance with socialist characteristics," in Elizabeth J. Perry and Mark Selden (eds) *Chinese Society: Change, Conflict and Resistance* (London and New York: Routledge, 2000), pp. 189–192.
49 See Gordon G. Chang, *The Coming Collapse of China* (New York: Random House, 2001).
50 He Liyi, with Claire Anne Chik, *Mr China's Son: A Villager's Life* (Boulder: Westview Press, 1993), p. 3.

12 State and society in transitions from communism

China in comparative perspective[1]

Harley Balzer

How might the accumulated knowledge about state–society relations in transitions from communism in the former Soviet Union and Eastern Europe inform our understanding of China? Sinologists focus overwhelmingly on whether the Chinese Communist Party (CCP) will be able to rule an increasingly diverse China, one ever more integrated into the global economy. Can the Party maintain its monopoly of political power? Or will the Party be compelled to liberalize, creating an opening that could lead to the end of its monopoly on political activity? Can the CCP maintain stability, and what are the costs and benefits of that stability?

Drawing on insights offered in the preceding chapters, this chapter offers a comparative perspective on evolving state–society relations in China today. It begins with a discussion of the essential condition for a reciprocal state–society relationship, the development of "civic society." The next section describes the evolving regimes in Russia and China, a system I call "managed pluralism," and the ways those regimes seek to both co-opt and constrain civic society. Assuming that elites do not willingly divest themselves of wealth and power, the potential counterweight to managed pluralism is contestation, and in the third section I explore the diverse forms of social and political contention evolving in China in a comparative context. This is followed by a discussion of the potential for political change, focusing in particular on the role of business and the middle classes. Communist ideology and charismatic authority (for now) have been discredited as bases for regime legitimacy. This leaves economic success (the Mandate of Mammon), stability, some form of nationalism/national greatness, or democracy as potential bases for legitimacy. These sources of legitimacy are mutually contradictory. Rapid economic development and the requirements of World Trade Organization membership involve structural changes that threaten stability; integration with the global economy requires muting nationalist rhetoric; while democracy, which may be the only long-term solution, is perceived by China's leaders to undermine both stability and national greatness, as well as their own power.

Civic society after communism

The communist extrication has further confused the already vague concept of "civil society." Western scholars studying repressive societies tend to become enthralled when the repression becomes less severe. In Central and Eastern Europe, not to mention the USSR, just about any group engaged in activities the communist regime prohibited was heralded as a harbinger of civil society. This included not only social and political opposition, but also a wide-ranging counter-culture including youth cults, alternative music ensembles, a range of artists from the crazed to the brilliant (sometimes a fine distinction), and some religious groups.[2]

Communist regimes demobilized independent social organizations while demanding participation in state-sponsored collectives, leaving populations both atomized and wary of organized social and political activity.[3] The social networks that developed to provide mutual assistance under communism were often dense, but they were also narrowly focused and highly distrustful of outsiders. This helps explain why the explosion of social movements in 1988–89 was followed by rapid demobilization once Soviet control ended.[4] Emphasis on the "return of civil society" diverted attention from the vital issue of political integration.[5] Much of the activity considered indicative of civil society consists of "expressive politics" rather than institution-building. Lone opponents of the forces of bloated and anonymous bureaucratic power form a transnational community of conscience that helps to undermine dictatorships. This is, however, quite different from developing a balanced relationship between social forces and the structures of government.

Dichotomies generally obscure as much as they reveal. The state–society relationship might better be formulated in tripartite terms: as state–private–civic. Markets and professions make this clearly apparent. Even (and perhaps especially) in a globalized economy, markets depend on the state. Societies transiting from communism have (re)discovered that modern markets require a developed legal system, mechanisms for contract enforcement, and myriad other institutions that cannot exist independent of the state.[6] In a similar vein, professional groups do not wish merely to be independent of the state; they seek, rather, to achieve autonomy while utilizing the state's power, including its coercive power, to enforce ethical codes and limitations on membership. The true key to "civic society" is a relationship with the state in which the public and private spheres are not only demarcated but also interdependent, with the state performing crucial intermediating roles. Unfortunately, in the extrication from communism, it is civil society, implying independence from and resistance to the state, rather than civic society, implying an interrelationship, that has most often been in vogue.[7]

It is *partnership with the state*, rather than independence from the state, that is the hallmark of civic society. Several scholars offer a valuable corrective to the emphasis on opposition between civil society and the state,[8] while scholars examining state–society relations in a context of mutual dependencies and the potential for mutual empowerment have offered useful guidelines for viewing this problem.[9] A repressive state is not the only danger; a state too weak to be a partner cannot support civic society. A plethora of "independent" social organizations existing in a political vacuum does not empower civic society; it invites corruption and chaos, often leading to authoritarianism in the name of stability.

In China, the discourse on civil society has been heavily influenced by Leninist ideas transmitted through Mao and others. This is clearly evident in Michael Frolic's description of China's "state-led civil society."[10] Many analysts are groping for a "uniquely Chinese path" that might permit the regime to change over time through accommodation with society. "Seeds of democracy," "inklings of democracy," "intellectual rethinking," and other harbingers of political diversity are important indicators of the potential for change, but none points in an inexorable direction.[11]

Debates about civil society among Chinese intellectuals and political scientists in the 1980s and 1990s often resemble discussions among Russian analysts during the Gorbachev era, involving a search for a definition of civil society suited to the particular political conditions, history, and unique culture of the society.[12] Like markets and democracy, civil society may well have Chinese, Cyrillic, Latin, or Arabic "character(s)," but the importance of the distinction between civil society and civic society persists regardless of the (trans)script. Communist regimes never accepted the civic relationship. The rules, boundaries, and character of the relationship are an arena of ongoing contention in any civic society, but in democratic societies the legitimacy of the relationship itself is not open to renegotiation.[13] This is the crucial distinction between civic society and various forms of hybrid regimes.[14] Corporatist or managed pluralist regimes may appear to be closer to the civic model than dictatorships, but they limit the players to those acceptable to the regime and delimit the agenda of issues open to public participation.

Managed pluralism

The political systems emerging in both Russia and China may be described as "managed pluralism," an evolving variant of hybrid regime tailored to the information-age global economy. Despite important differences, there are striking political similarities between the regime Vladimir Putin is establishing in Russia and Chinese political life in the era of Jiang Zemin and now Hu Jintao. Managed pluralism is an alternative to democracy or authoritarianism with adjectives, like illiberal democracy or competitive authoritarianism. Both hyphenated democracy and modified authoritarianism imply their own teleologies; pluralism with adjectives, in contrast, leaves the direction of change open.[15]

Managed pluralism is similar to Juan Linz's "limited pluralism." But Linz views limited pluralism as a feature of most authoritarian regimes, rather than as a regime type, and he wrote before the Third Wave of democratization led to a proliferation of modified democracies. Regimes with regular elections that are moderately free, even if not always fair, and in which rulers tolerate electoral reversals and encourage some degree of social and political diversity, would seem to constitute a special case.[16]

Managed pluralist regimes differ from authoritarianism in that the leaders endeavor simultaneously to encourage and also to place limits on cultural and political diversity. These leaders appear to understand that global economic and information interdependence makes it impossible to govern complex societies through monolithic structures. While having no choice but to "open up" to outside influences, leaders attempt to impose limits on diversity, often in the name of "national traditions." The regime fosters social groups (civil but not civic society), while constraining their activity. These efforts are self-serving, abetting elites' preservation of power, yet may mesh quite well with popular reactions to the unsettling consequences of globalization, increased speed and volume of information flows, and immigration with its resulting cultural diversity.

In some European nations, elements of managed pluralism are appearing in policies involving culture, religion, and immigration. One element of managed pluralism is manifested in Russia, France, and Germany all adopting legislation to limit the activity of "non-traditional" religious groups, though none has resorted to the level of violence China has used against Falun Gong. In his work on Russia's law on religion, Nickolas Gvosdev suggests that Russia and China share the ethos/mythology that national unity is essential to survival, and that periods of disunity correspond to periods of weakness and subjugation. In this view, ideological pluralism is bad because it divides the community.[17]

In Putin's Russia, managed pluralism extends well beyond religion. It is applied to the media, political parties, trade unions, associations of entrepreneurs, and civil society. Independent broadcast media have been sharply curtailed. Those who would restore Soviet-era censorship have not been successful (thus far), but the regime reserves the right to interdict expression that it finds undesirable.[18] A new law on political parties seriously raises the bar to entry, and effectively precludes regional or ethnic-based parties. The regime fosters trade union and entrepreneurial organizations that advocate top-down organizing.[19]

Russia's increasingly restricted multi-party system and China's greater diversity within the CCP are hardly identical. Yet managed pluralism resembles Frolic's "state-led civil society," and fits with Andrew Nathan's recent description of China's orderly and rule-bound succession. The "three represents" Bruce Dickson describes (see Chapter 7 of the present volume) implies the need to include a broader representation of society in political life while maintaining control over precisely which individuals and groups are included. One clear principle is that the Party must select the new players; those who insist on putting themselves forward on their own are not acceptable, not least because they might have independent bases of power. The Party is co-opting capitalists from the "non-critical" realm, but has imposed limitations on what may be discussed – most notably the "three unmentionables" of political reform, constitutional change, and the interpretation of Tiananmen.[20]

If the broad spectrum of interests Teresa Wright describes as constituting the China Democratic Party (CDP) (see Chapter 6) are not permitted to organize independently, can the CCP represent these interests? Elizabeth Perry and Mark Selden discuss the fate of "China's reform-minded Communist Party." But precisely what does this mean? Are China's leaders committed reformers, or are they self-interested elites seeking to preserve their power and increase their wealth? Most likely the answer is both, and the dual motives may manifest themselves not only in differences between groups in the leadership, but also as dualities in the motivations of individuals. This makes "unpacking" the state, as Kevin O'Brien argues (see Chapter 5), increasingly important.[21] Despite growing – in some regions stunning – social and cultural diversity, China's leaders have not accepted untutored pluralism. The Party shows no sign of surrendering its monopoly over political power. Yet the "three represents" does imply an effort to include a broader range of interests within the political leadership, while the use of elections and the legal system to impose constraints on local officials also points to reliance on new mechanisms to address problems before they lead to uncontrolled political expression.

Contestation

Discussions of contestation have become, perhaps inevitably, highly contentious.[22] Compared to China in the decade after 1993, the former Soviet bloc has been remarkably docile, especially in view of the enormous social dislocation accompanying economic change. Meanwhile, China appears to be a cauldron of social movements, with strikes and protests taking place almost daily.

Some analysts see the lack of protest in the former Soviet Union as a serious problem; rather than indicating that everything is going well, it suggests a disturbing absence of collective action, with few organized interests. The landscape of protest in the former Soviet bloc changed dramatically from 1986, when the first perestroika-era public actions took place, to the late 1990s. Between 1988 and 1991, the region experienced widespread strikes, the burgeoning of strong ecology movements that in many instances evolved into popular fronts, and frequent protests and instances of civil disobedience. The ultimate manifestations of this phenomenon came in late 1989 in Central Europe and in resistance to the coup attempt in Russia in August 1991. But as is so often the case, stunningly rapid mobilization was succeeded by even more rapid demobilization. Patterns of protest in Russia since 1993 reflect the difference between the

Soviet-era neo-traditionalist economy and new private businesses. Unprofitable state-owned enterprises (SOEs) cannot pay workers a living wage, but agreements with local governments preclude reducing the workforce. State employees, who have not received their pay, stage strikes in collusion with regional officials to extract additional resources from the federal government. Russian labor protest in the 1990s rarely reflected a demand for higher wages or a reaction against lay-offs. In the private sector, those with jobs do not risk their livelihood by instigating labor conflicts. Four out of ten strikes involved teachers.[23] Some indications of a change in the Russian patterns emerged in early 2003. Air traffic controllers, and employees at Norilsk Nikel, Aeroflot, and a few other firms, began to demand higher wages and greater transparency in the firms' accounting practices so that they could gauge whether their wages represent a fair assessment of the value they are adding. There is likely to be more activism as large state monopolies (railroads, electric power) shed workers to improve their economic performance.

In China, the strikes have been far more numerous and widespread. Chinese SOEs have been shedding workers since the late 1980s, and in large numbers since 1995. The result, as Dorothy Solinger puts it (see Chapter 2), is "a searing dread on both sides." Solinger notes that labor unions are practically unknown in the new factories, where many employers explicitly forbid labor organizations. New organizations are being formed by "retrenched" workers, not by those in new enterprises. Labor organizers often focus on abuses in foreign-owned plants, a reasonable strategy on several levels: exploitation by foreigners remains a hot political issue (as Peter Gries reminds us in Chapter 9), and an international non-governmental organization (NGO) community, not to mention a horde of anti-globalization activists, remain ready to champion the cause of workers laboring for transnational corporations. Attacking abuses at foreign-owned firms also gives officials opportunities to extort bribes.[24] In both Russia and China, the working class has been toppled from ideological primacy and economic security.

In demographic terms, Chinese workers may be in a far worse position than workers in the former Soviet Union. The Chinese private manufacturing sector in township and village enterprises (TVEs) and special economic zones (SEZs) has created many (relatively) desirable jobs, but job growth cannot continue at a rate that will absorb both redundant SOE workers and the excess rural population. As manufacturers are increasingly forced to compete with each other and in international markets, they are looking for ways to reduce their costs. The search for higher productivity exerts downward pressure on wages and the number of workers.[25] Timothy Weston (Chapter 3) notes that some Chinese workers seek to use Maoist pro-worker propaganda against Party leaders, and have found support among the Red Guard generation.[26] But economic and demographic trends suggest that this will almost certainly be a losing strategy in the long term.

Like the communists in Russia, neo-Maoists represent social and economic groups that are in decline economically and shrinking numerically. The victims of economic reform do not constitute a stable power base.

Rural protest is widespread in China but practically non-existent in Russia. This reflects the radically different starting points of the two transitions: Russia's population was 80 per cent urban, China's 80 per cent rural.[27] As the chapters by Patricia Thornton (Chapter 4) and O'Brien (Chapter 5) reveal, the majority of rural protest in China is directed against corruption and abuses by local officials, and at the TVEs. Many TVEs are run by owners in collusion with local officials (often relatives). As their initial development spurt gives way to a more saturated market and increasing competition from other producers, many TVEs have been forced to cut costs, increasing tensions. As the state divests itself of direct responsibility for the economy, it is able to tolerate economic (as opposed to political) strikes, and may even be able to use labor protest to calibrate economic reforms.[28] But links between entrepreneurs and local officials inevitably also create instances where the coercive power of the state is placed at the service of owners or managers. Weston's account of large urban protest movements illustrates this sort of political involvement, and a familiar pattern of accommodating demands while punishing the leaders. The character of protest and collective action varies in different local settings. Broad differences between TVEs, SOEs, and SEZs do not capture the relative capacity and honesty of local governments and the degree of trust established by local officials. If corruption continues to spread, it may create a situation similar to what Vadim Volkov has described in Russia, where the state security services, private security firms, and criminals make common cause.[29]

Strikes and public protests are hardly the only forms of contestation. One of the intriguing developments in both Russia and China is a growing resort to the legal system. In both countries, reliance on lawsuits and judicial processes has reached a level that surprises many observers. Why do peasants, workers, and businessmen go to the trouble and expense of extended legal processes when they doubt the impartiality of the judiciary and when the courts lack mechanisms to enforce judgments in favor of the plaintiffs? Minxin Pei attributes a growing "rights consciousness" among Chinese dissidents to the interrelated factors of a decline in repression, constraints on the leadership stemming from increased participation in international organizations and commitments to international norms, and legal reforms within China.[30] David Zweig's account of rural cases is somewhat more ambiguous: village cadres often pay off the entire "food chain" up to the municipal level; petitions frequently fail unless backed up by collective action because the middle-level authorities support their subordinates or, as Kevin O'Brien demonstrates, higher-level officials are not able to alter the behavior of village officials.[31] Winning a case may prove dangerous to the health of the victor. Yet, as Li Lianjiang and O'Brien note, both rural and suburban dwellers increasingly resorted to formal petitions in the 1990s.[32]

Is this a matter of a "shotgun" strategy, trying everything in the hope that something will work? Or does the legal process provide some "cover" for subsequent collective action? Given the crucial role played by the media in bringing disputes to public attention, it may be easier (and safer) for a journalist to cover a judicial proceeding that leaves a paper trail than to attempt investigative journalism.

Stanley Rosen (Chapter 8) and Richard Kraus (Chapter 10) raise the issue of cultural contestation. Culture is *always* contested. Do alternative cultural movements necessarily imply political dissent? Rosen's rich portrait of China's evolving youth culture focuses overwhelmingly on the yuppies. The youth he describes are concerned with success – not politics or ideology. They are experiencing the same reordering of friendships that took place in Central Europe and the former Soviet Union. While the regime expresses concern about growing economic stratification, it also seems powerless to do much about it. Rosen's data show that one of the most highly valued attributes in Chinese society, education, is now heavily dependent on one's ability to pay. The students benefiting from the evolving system value membership in the CCP for its help in their careers – not because they have an interest in politics or a commitment to public service. This poses two dangers. One is that a system based on affluence rather than talent does not make optimal use of human resources. The second (related) danger is that the losers may not remain quiescent – especially if they include individuals with talent. One wonders if there are any emerging blue-collar culture heroes who might provide a focal point for protest or collective action.

Rosen's "fifth generation" youth are avid consumers in the global marketplace. Does consumption provide an identity? Communist regimes severely suppressed consumption. Studying its revival has become a cottage industry, part of a boom not limited to post-communist venues.[33] This literature needs to be tempered with an understanding of the political, psychological, and health effects of increased stratification. Surveys indicate that upwardly mobile consumers are neither happier nor more liberal in their politics than the "losers."

Intellectuals are the group most likely to focus on growing inequality. They are also a group that traditionally has been the most significant in creating initial political openings. Archie Brown's comment about the Soviet Union is pertinent: "Perhaps the most important development of all in the years between 1953 and 1985 in preparing the way for what followed was the growth of privacy and the development of free discussion in small and informal groups."[34] China's intellectuals are the focus of much attention.[35] But they should be viewed with some perspective on the culture of dissent and the effects it has on political life. One of the lessons of the Central European and Soviet deconstructions was that the qualities it took to be a dissident in a communist regime – steadfast resistance, uncompromising moral values, and utter certainty of one's own rightness – are *not* the qualities needed in the give-and-take compromise politics of democratic systems.[36]

Elections are a crucial form of contestation in democratic polities, and Kevin O'Brien's chapter raises the intriguing issue of elections in a one-party regime. In the absence of competing parties, are these elections harbingers of democracy? Or are they simply a mechanism that the central authorities can use to discipline local cadres while also making them (or making them appear) more accountable to local interests? Using elections to discipline local cadres was something Gorbachev tried, and it sometimes produced shocking results. It is one answer to the seemingly intractable problem of inducing local officials to carry out central policies and to work for the good of their locales rather than ignoring the wishes of the central government and feathering their nests. While it is clear that Chinese leaders are concerned with the problem, no communist or authoritarian regime has solved it: discipline, rotation, and execution all have drawbacks.

The type of local activism O'Brien describes is just as likely to be system-preserving as it is to lead to serious change. As Vivienne Shue (Chapter 1) notes, by providing a safety valve for local discontent, drawing in the activists and opinion leaders, and in some instances providing adequate redress to keep people coming back to try again, this sort of game may be an alternative to more fundamental political change. Yet as Gorbachev discovered, exposing local Party leaders to electoral competition can have unintended consequences. Gorbachev badly underestimated the legitimacy that accrues to elected leaders, and never became one himself. Local election activity was the beginning of democratic development in Taiwan.[37] One place where the literature on sequencing in transitions provides important lessons is the negative effect of conducting elections without permitting independent opposition parties to compete. Movements do not provide aggregation or articulation of interests.

Are any organized agents promoting the integration of the diverse forms of contestation in China? Teresa Wright challenges the view that the CDP was easily repressed, suggesting that a "true opposition political party" bringing together workers with students and intellectuals has developed in China. Although sharing the fate of other groups that have been subjected to severe regime repression, Wright argues that the CDP represents something qualitatively new. China's intellectuals have become more professionalized and less isolated from workers and other ordinary citizens, and they have acted without first securing patrons in the CCP leadership. Wright sees these developments in large part as a result of the ongoing transition to a market economic system and connections to the global economy, and due in particular to the burgeoning of information technologies that may render elites incapable of maintaining control. Thus far, the CDP is neither strong enough nor influential enough to force a change in the CCP's monopoly. But if Chinese society does eventually insist on an end to that monopoly, the existence of at least one coherent alternative political party will be of help. It is important on occasion to contemplate the unthinkable.

Once the unthinkable happens, no one is as surprised when it happens again. O'Brien touches on this point when he emphasizes the *dynamics* of boundary-spanning contention, suggesting a focus on *trajectories*: "Zeroing in on acts that share some of the advantages of transgression (surprise, uncertainty, and novelty) and some of the benefits of contained contention (accepted, familiar, and easy to employ) can cast light on those critical moments in the evolution of a repertoire of contention when what is forbidden one year, is tolerated the next, and is readily accepted the third" (pp. 113–114). Implicit in O'Brien's account is the fluid nature of the boundaries. They are constantly shifting, and will vary not only over time but over space – different local officials will interpret the rules and situations in different ways, and the same officials may interpret them differently at different times.

The players on some of those local chessboards are not all Han. Colin Mackerras (Chapter 11) notes that the minority peoples of China constitute less than 10 per cent of the country's population, but some of them occupy large, strategically located regions with relatively sparse populations, making their loyalty an important issue for the regime. Mackerras notes that ethnic groups' self-perceptions do not always conform to the image of these groups prevailing among leaders or the dominant ethnic group (the Han), yet he does not see the minorities as representing a serious threat to the regime. Certainly, there have been no instances of nationalist mobilization corresponding to what took place in the last years of the USSR.[38] But Islam could prove to be the exception. Mackerras does note that local mullahs play an important role in some Hui communities, a development paralleling the revival of sharia law in the North Caucasus and Central Asia in the 1970s and 1980s. Xinjiang Uygurs in China's north-west may be an even more difficult problem. Uygur residents of Ürümqi do not set their clocks to Beijing time, suggesting that Han legitimacy is in serious question. The Bush administration policy of accepting China's claim that Uygur groups are linked to international Islamic terrorist groups may turn out to be a self-fulfilling prophecy, as it did in Chechnya. It sends China a signal that their performance in human rights is less important than the common struggle against al-Qaeda.

The limits of contention

Despite the diverse forms of contention in China and the potential for evolution over time, this section concludes with a cautionary note. The portion of the population involved in protest, the lack of common purpose among the diverse social movements, and the limited reach of the Internet all suggest that the "correlation of forces" favors the regime. Thus far, the CCP has expanded the boundaries of acceptable activity in a way that keeps pace with boundary-spanning contention, permitting targeted protests but prohibiting independent organizations in a pattern characteristic of managed pluralism. No rival political force is capable of compelling change.

China has developed a generation of intellectuals, artists, entrepreneurs, yuppies, and a youth culture that in important ways resemble social groups in Eastern Europe and the Soviet Union in the 1980s. But as a proportion of the total Chinese population, these groups are still minuscule.[39] In some respects, they resemble the Russian intelligentsia in the 19th century, caught between the oppressive state and (what they thought was) an inert but potentially violent mass of peasants. The intellectuals wanted to help the peasants, but also feared them. In this context, the state played off the educated population's demands for a role in political life against the threat of social revolution. At the same time that we note the changing (and growing) varieties of contestation, we should remember that even in periods of intense political activity, a majority of people in post-communist societies devote far more of their effort to simply coping. This is particularly true of women.[40]

Analysts who look at the enormous challenges to stability in China and conclude that together these various forms of political contestation represent a substantial threat run the risk of two errors: assuming that these diverse forms of opposition are capable of uniting to achieve a common goal, or assuming that a regime change would produce democracy.[41] Wright is hardly alone in asserting that the Internet enormously complicates the task of controlling information. But the Internet and information technologies are not a panacea – they are more likely to undermine hierarchies in the workplace than in the political system. Despite the important role it has played in the development of the CDP and other groups, the Internet is exaggerated as a spur to political change, at least in the short run. Sophisticated users can circumvent government obstacles, but their numbers are not large. Internet use is common among less than 1 per cent of the Chinese population (in Russia, it is 4–6 per cent; in the United States, 62 per cent). Only 10 per cent of Chinese have telephones. Even if the mobile phone boom continues and this doubles to 20 per cent by 2010, it should be compared to South Korea, where over 70 per cent of the population is online, and in 2002 more than 20 per cent used broadband. It is impossible, furthermore, to gauge what proportion of Chinese Internet users are downloading MP3 files compared to the number accessing CDP or other opposition materials. Since 1995, there has been a game between the users and the regime, with the regime attempting to maintain control over the content and use of information technologies and the opposition seeking to circumvent those controls. Thus far, the regime seems to be able to keep both usage and content within non-threatening limits.[42]

Yet Chinese authorities would not be expending so much energy if there were not profound social changes emanating from the Internet revolution. As Peter Gries notes, the Internet facilitated an outpouring of inconvenient nationalist expression following the American bombing of the Chinese Embassy in Belgrade. Internet policy is a realm where talking about "the regime" can be misleading. There is inevitably a range of opinions within the leadership, with some in favor of limiting all forms of expression, others willing to risk some increase in communication, and an important group weighing the dangers of unrestricted information against the need for openness in modern economic life.[43]

It is not clear that participation in the global economy will significantly alter the equation. The effects cut in multiple directions. International norms of behavior, supported by a dense web of international organizations, can have a serious impact on governments over time, as can demonstration effects resulting from greater knowledge of the outside world.[44] Opening capital markets makes it possible for foreign direct investment (FDI) to replace import substitution industrialization (ISI) or primitive accumulation.[45] Integration allows leaders to blame "them" (foreigners, international financial institutions, etc.), while arguing that they have no other choice but to do the things that promote participation in the global economy.

The forms of contestation visible thus far suggest either isolated outbreaks that the regime can co-opt or control, or a potential volcano.[46] There is little here promising an evolutionary path to a more open political system. The renewal or decay discussion is eerily reminiscent of the "transformation or degeneration" debate about the USSR in the Brezhnev era.[47] Yet the debate about change or decay in the Soviet system missed both the powerful impulse for the Central European satellites to rejoin Europe and the way the multi-ethnic character of the USSR brought about its fragmentation along national lines. Despite all the attention paid to China's fourth and fifth generations, the Chinese elite has not put competitive politics on the national agenda. What might change this equation?

Business and the middle classes

Absent independent social and political organizations, business interests and the middle classes have the strongest claims on the political system. In both Russia and China, the commercial middle classes are developing in an environment where it is difficult to avoid enlisting official protectors or paying significant bribes. David Goodman portrays China's middle class as overwhelmingly symbiotic with the Party elite.[48] Yet there are also indications that corruption and accommodation are not the entire story. Bruce Gilley sees rural entrepreneurs potentially demanding genuine village elections, arguing that they may force the CCP to extend elections despite the unease this creates among local officials. Margaret Pearson, focusing on the managerial elite in foreign-owned firms, suggests that they may eventually provide the basis for a pro-democracy middle class, but thus far the evidence is at best ambiguous. Doug Guthrie's profile of managers in the state sector finds them to be genuine innovators, yet he also finds their behavior heavily conditioned by experience in the command economy, the models of joint venture firms, and the demands of the state bureaucracy. They often perceive the state to be demanding that they privilege stability over profitability. His account closely corresponds to descriptions of managers at many Russian enterprises, including many factories that have been privatized but are still under the strong influence of local officials.[49] Taken together, these studies do not seriously undermine Goodman's conclusions. But they do provide additional benchmarks to watch as China's economy develops. The Korean middle class initially supported authoritarian regimes. It was only over time, as it grew in size, felt more secure, and found its economic interests undermined by the behavior of the authoritarian state, that it joined those demanding democracy.[50]

Rosen's discussion of the middle class and education points to the danger of a simple correlation between economic and educational modernization and political development.[51] The political consequences of downward mobility for educated professionals in Germany and Central Europe in the 1930s demonstrate this lesson. And the Soviet Union achieved universal literacy and educated 40 million specialists, yet Russia now has the best-educated impoverished population in the world. Education alone is not enough to guarantee either economic development or greater democracy.[52] The commercial middle classes rarely provide the leadership for broad democracy movements. This is more typically the role of professionals and the intelligentsia. Post-communist societies help us to remember that the middle classes are not the same thing as the bourgeoisie or entrepreneurs. Professionals often outnumber merchants.[53] Professionals in both Russia and China are endeavoring to re-establish or reinvent communities repressed under communist rule. They face a new set of challenges, as new locations of employment influence their political as well as economic and status concerns. Steven Brint suggests that the purported "liberalism" of professionals in America was tied more to their employment in government and the non-profit sector than to their association with intellectual activity. Brint's distinction between social trustee professionalism and a market-value model is highly pertinent in the post-communist context. Breaking with the intelligentsia emphasis on community stewardship and cultural authority, an inevitable consequence of market relationships, is a source of great pain and vocal protest.[54]

The communist-era intelligentsia is being declassed. Teachers, scientists, engineers, and other highly educated specialists often find that the transition to a market economy not only undermines their prestige, but threatens their livelihood. Many find that their skills do not transfer easily to the market system. Those who depend on the public sector learn that governments unable to pay pensions on time are hardly likely to support education, culture, and science at the unrealistic levels of the communist era.[55]

The declassing of communist professionals raises a serious danger of their not merely becoming less liberal, but turning to authoritarian alternatives. Scenarios outlining a "Weimar Russia" future remain quite popular. While most of these focus on workers and pensioners as the "fodder" for fascist movements, recent research on Germany suggests that the middle classes and professional groups played an important role in the Nazi party. Downward social mobility led many professionals not only to abandon liberalism and accept discriminatory policies, but also to embrace political extremes.[56]

Thus far, China's government has continued to pay state salaries to scientists, educators, and cultural workers. But increasingly, these salaries diverge from what people can earn in the private sector. In the best of worlds, individuals might have a choice between the security of state employment and the greater risks but potentially higher rewards of the non-state sector.[57] This depends on the government's capacity to continue paying reasonable salaries to state knowledge and cultural workers. Even if they are able to do this, many intellectuals are likely to object to the higher earnings "popular" writers, performers, and others are able to derive from mass culture.

Merle Goldman's discussions of opposition among intellectuals and the potential for intellectuals and workers to make common cause posit a world in which the intellectuals join with workers out of a sense of moral or ideological responsibility.[58] If the Chinese government goes further with its reforms and begins to shed redundant intellectual workers, or if success in the private sector continues to exert a "wealth effect" on the living standards of teachers, doctors, and other salaried professionals, there may be a qualitatively different type of protest by intellectuals, one defending their own interests rather than linked to other social groups. An even more serious form of "downward mobility" is occurring in the frustrated expectations of young people who took advantage of expanded opportunities for higher education and now cannot find employment. The number of university students almost doubled between 1998 and 2002. The first graduates of the expanded higher education programs entered the labor market in 2003, and the experience for many has been disappointing.[59] Radical political movements are more often fostered by educated groups who cannot find jobs corresponding to their skills than by the poor. China's success in expanding educational opportunities could turn sour quite quickly if the economy does not provide enough good jobs for the growing number of graduates.

What role will the middle classes play in China's political development? Three hypotheses should be examined through further comparative research. One is that the middle class will support political opening only when it is convinced that extending the franchise will not empower a disadvantaged population likely to demand significant income redistribution. Authoritarian governments are often perceived as being more capable of dealing with the "surplus population" than are democracies. Secondly, the middle class will become an active agent of change only when it both achieves "critical mass" and also judges its economic interests to be threatened by the inevitable cronyism of the authoritarian regime. Thirdly, professionals experiencing downward social mobility are not likely to provide leadership for liberal political movements.

Middle-class "revolution" is almost a contradiction in terms, and its political meaning is debased by analyses equating McDonalds and consumption with serious political movements.[60] Michael Kennedy and Padraic Kenney describe the successful Central European revolutions of 1989 as carnivalistic events in which protestors used irony and the media to bring down communist regimes.[61] Successful middle-class revolutions in the 21st century may require a middle class capable of irony. The war on terrorism following 11 September 2001 is likely to make this more difficult, at least in the short term.[62]

The evidence presented in this volume hardly adds up to a warning of impending revolution, but rather to a more complex set of challenges for China's leadership. Through most of China's history, stability has been intricately linked with legitimacy. What does the new emphasis on economic performance mean for legitimacy?

Legitimation: from the Mandate of Heaven to the Mandate of Mammon?

The task of scholars is not to predict the future, but to identify trends and markers of potential change. Taken together, the essays in this volume enable us to appreciate the multiple sources of legitimacy for the Chinese regime – economic development, national greatness, moral authority, and the exercise of power to preserve stability. We should be wary about taking any one of these as the sole basis for the regime's staying power. Yet each is double-edged. Change is likely when the CCP is threatened on most or all of these fronts, rather than on just one of them.[63]

Peter Gries argues for a view of Chinese nationalism that accounts for the dynamic reciprocal relationships between leaders and the general population. He concludes that Party legitimacy now depends on meeting the expectations of nationalists, suggesting an evolution of regime responses from repression to toleration to co-optation of popular nationalism.[64] The Diaoyu (Senkaku) Islands protests in 1996 (primarily in writing) were suppressed. The reaction to the *China Can Say No* sensation in 1996–97 was different, with some in the regime seeking to utilize it for their own purposes. Even when the regime cracked down on later phases of the phenomenon, like *China Can Still Say No*, they sought to co-opt popular nationalism. Following the bombing of China's embassy in Belgrade in 1999, the government had to accommodate popular protests, which were "diverse" and "widespread." This resembles O'Brien's description of the evolution of "the permissible," and in both examples we see the regime attempting to co-opt popular activity and resentment for its own purposes. This is always an attractive but also potentially dangerous game.

Vivienne Shue argues that popular religious practice has traditionally been and continues to be a major source of threat to the Chinese regime, and the seriousness of the challenge provokes severe state repression. But

Shue goes further, suggesting that syncretic religious sects have repeatedly appeared in China due to the logic of state legitimation: by claiming knowledge of ultimate ethical truths, the state turns almost any popular religion into a challenge to authority, thereby guaranteeing a cycle of challenge and repression. Shue reminds us that there have been "numerous episodes of popular protest" in China since 1989, "but no major social movements," and no serious opposition movement until Falun Gong.

Shue is skeptical of the descriptions of Chinese legitimacy based solely on economic performance, suggesting that the Chinese state is trying to take credit for simply getting out of the way. Performance-based legitimacy that depends on continued economic growth is always a risky long-term strategy, and not only due to business cycles. We need to ask if "To be rich is glorious" inevitably translates into "Greed is good." Many China specialists are so caught up in what Charlotte Ikels termed "The Return of the God of Wealth" that they seem to think that wealth is *the* new religion, rather than one god among many. There are lots of new religions out there, as Shue's chapter demonstrates.[65] The burgeoning literature on consumption tends to obscure our memory of the counter-culture movements that arise to question excessively materialist values. MP3 files and McDonalds may not be the dominant icons of global youth culture a decade from now. America's postwar materialism brought forth a counter-culture; Europe is portrayed as pervaded by post-materialist values.[66] China's young consumers may eventually formulate their own variant of "post-dialectical-materialist values."

Stability, economic growth, national greatness, and moral authority are all interconnected, and the definition of each shifts over time. Excessive stability can produce stagnation. Economic growth in and of itself may not produce equitable distributions of wealth (and the definition of "equitable" is also a realm of constant contention). National greatness may be perceived in terms of "hard" or "soft" power, and in economic or military terms. Moral authority is always subjective. Sustainable legitimacy derives not from solving problems, but from creating an environment in which they can be solved in ways that people consider just. The Chinese Communist Party will be able to retain its hold on power only if it is able to successfully shift from the former to the latter, something few authoritarian regimes have managed to sustain.

Notes

1 The author is grateful to Victor Cha, Mary Gallagher, Merle Goldman, Peter Gries, Stan Rosen, Mark Selden, and several anonymous reviewers for comments on earlier versions of this chapter. None of them is responsible for errors that remain.

2 S. Frederick Starr, "A civil society," *Foreign Policy* 70 (Spring 1988); cf. Thane Gustafson, "A civil society in the Soviet Union," *Sovset' News* (online newsletter) 5(4) (2 October 1989). On rock music and culture, see Timothy Ryback, *Rock Around the Bloc: A History of Rock Music in Eastern Europe and the Soviet Union* (New York: Oxford University Press, 1990); cf. Robert Efird, "Rock in a

hard place: music and the market in nineties Beijing," in Nancy N. Chen, Constance D. Clark, Suzanne Z. Gottschang, and Lyn Jeffery (eds) *China Urban: Ethnographies of Contemporary Culture* (Durham: Duke University Press, 2001), pp. 67–86.

3 Marc Morjé Howard, *The Weakness of Civil Society in Post-communist Europe* (Cambridge: Cambridge University Press, 2003), and "Postcommunist Civil Society in Comparative Perspective," *Demokratizatsiya* 10(3) (Summer 2002): 285–305.

4 M. Steven Fish, *Democracy from Scratch: Opposition and Regime in the New Russian Revolution* (Princeton: Princeton University Press, 1995). This was also the pattern in many non-communist transitions. See Guillermo O'Donnell and Philippe C. Schmitter, *Transitions from Authoritarian Rule: Tentative Conclusions about Uncertain Democracies* (Baltimore: Johns Hopkins University Press, 1986).

5 This is not just a post-Soviet issue: Alfred Stepan, "State power and the strength of civil society in the southern cone of Latin America," in Peter B. Evans, Dietrich Rueschemeyer, and Theda Skocpol (eds) *Bringing the State Back In* (Cambridge: Cambridge University Press, 1985), pp. 317–346, esp. 318; and Augustus Richard Norton (ed.), *Civil Society in the Middle East* (Leiden: E.J. Brill, 1995).

6 Charles E. Lindblom, *Politics and Markets: The World's Political-Economic Systems* (New York: Basic Books, 1977); Peter Evans, "The state as problem and solution: predation, embedded autonomy, and structural change," in Stephan Haggard and Robert R. Kaufman (eds) *The Politics of Economic Adjustment* (Princeton: Princeton University Press, 1992), pp. 139–181.

7 Jurgen Habermas, *The Structural Transformation of the Public Sphere: An Inquiry into a Category of Bourgeois Society* (Cambridge, MA: MIT Press, 1989). For a more extended discussion, see Harley D. Balzer, "Conclusion: the missing middle class," in Harley D. Balzer (ed.) *Russia's Missing Middle Class: The Professions in Russian History* (Armonk, NY: M.E. Sharpe, 1996), pp. 300–303.

8 See Fish, *Democracy from Scratch*, and Victor M. Perez-Diaz, *The Return of Civil Society: The Emergence of Democratic Spain* (Cambridge, MA: Harvard University Press, 1993).

9 Peter B. Evans *et al.*, *Bringing the State Back In*. The "contingent" approach is presented in Joel S. Migdal, Atul Kohli, and Vivienne Shue (eds) *State Power and Social Forces: Domination and Transformation in the Third World* (Cambridge: Cambridge University Press, 1994), and extended in Joel S. Migdal, *State in Society: Studying How States and Societies Transform and Constitute One Another* (Cambridge: Cambridge University Press, 2001).

10 B. Michael Frolic, "State-led civil society," in Timothy Brook and B. Michael Frolic (eds) *Civil Society in China* (Armonk, NY: M.E. Sharpe, 1997), pp. 46–67. On the Chinese debate, see Yijiang Ding, *Chinese Democracy After Tiananmen* (New York: Columbia University Press, 2001).

11 Merle Goldman, *Sowing the Seeds of Democracy in China: Political Reform in the Deng Xiaoping Era* (Cambridge, MA: Harvard University Press, 1994); Suzanne Ogden, *Inklings of Democracy in China*, Harvard East Asian Monograph Series No. 210 (Cambridge, MA: Harvard University Press, 2002); Ding, *Chinese Democracy After Tiananmen*.

12 Again, Ding provides a good summary of the Chinese debate and its evolution over time in *Chinese Democracy After Tiananmen*. See also Minxin Pei, "The growth of civil society in China," in Jim Dorn (ed.) *Economic Reform in the New Millennium* (Washington DC: Cato Institute Press, 1998). For a comprehensive treatment of the Russian discussion of civil society, see Alfred B. Evans, Jr., "Recent assessments of social organizations in Russia," *Demokratizatsiya* 10(3) (Summer 2002): 322–342. For an account closer to the mainstream Chinese definition, see Henry E. Hale,

"Civil society from above? Statist and liberal models of state-building in Russia," *Demokratizatsiya* 10(3) (Summer 2002): 306–321.

13 Guillermo O'Donnell and Philippe C. Schmitter, *Transitions from Authoritarian Rule: Tentative Conclusions about Uncertain Democracies* (Baltimore: Johns Hopkins University Press, 1986), pp. 66–69.

14 David Collier and Steve Levitsky, "Democracy with adjectives: conceptual innovation in comparative research," *World Politics* 49(3) (April 1997): 430–451; Larry Diamond, "Thinking about hybrid regimes," *Journal of Democracy* 13(2) (April 2002): 21–35; Steven Levitsky and Lucan A. Way, "The rise of competitive authoritarianism," *Journal of Democracy* 13(2) (April 2002): 51–65.

15 The most obvious differences are that the CCP retains a monopoly on political activity and relies on greater use of repression. Nonetheless, the "three represents" implies broader involvement in China, while Russia's political space is becoming more restricted. The key in both countries is the leadership tolerating some diversity, but determining which forms of diversity are acceptable.

16 Juan J. Linz, *Totalitarian and Authoritarian Regimes* (Boulder, CO: Lynne Rienner, 2000), p. 161.

17 "Throughout Eurasia, governments and societies appear to be moving towards a consensus as to how to deal with ideological pluralism: rather than imposing a single philosophical-spiritual system upon the entire population, the state instead presents a menu of acceptable 'choices' from which the population is free to choose. 'Managed pluralism' allows competing and diverse ideologies to be filtered and vetted for compatibility with the ethos of society." Nikolas K. Gvosdev, "'Managed pluralism' and civil religion in post-Soviet Russia," in Christopher Marsh and Nikolas K. Gvosdev (eds) *Civil Society and the Search for Justice in Russia* (Lanham, MD: Lexington Books, 2002), pp. 78–79.

18 One of the important differences between Russia and China is that Chinese media have achieved some degree of financial autonomy, even if they are not free from political interference. This could have important implications in the future.

19 For a full discussion of managed pluralism in Russia, see Harley Balzer, "Managed pluralism: Vladimir Putin's emerging regime," *Post-Soviet Affairs* 18(3) (July–September 2003).

20 B. Michael Frolic, "State-led civil society"; Andrew J. Nathan, "Authoritarian resilience," *Journal of Democracy* 14(1) (January 2003): 6–17. See also Ding, *Chinese Democracy After Tiananmen*; Robert A. Scalapino, "Current trends and future prospects," *Journal of Democracy* 9(1) (January 1998): 35–40; and Bruce J. Dickson, *Red Capitalists in China: The Party, Private Entrepreneurs, and Prospects for Political Change* (Cambridge: Cambridge University Press, 2003), p. 169. On the "three unmentionables," see John Pomfret, "China orders halt to debate on reforms," *Washington Post*, 27 August 2003, p. A1.

21 Elizabeth Perry and Mark Selden, "Introduction: reform and resistance in contemporary China," in Elizabeth Perry and Mark Selden (eds) *Chinese Society: Change, Conflict and Resistance* (London and New York: Routledge, 2000), p. 10; Migdal, *State in Society*.

22 The emphasis is on comparison, at a minimum across time if not across borders, to provide some perspective beyond the story of individual actors and movements. See Sidney Tarrow, "Social movements in contentious politics: a review article," *American Political Science Review* 90(4) (December 1996): 874–883. See also Sidney Tarrow, *Power in Movement: Social Movements and Contentious Politics*, 2nd edn. (Cambridge: Cambridge University Press, 1998); Doug McAdam, Sidney Tarrow, and Charles Tilley, *Dynamics of Contention* (Cambridge: Cambridge University Press, 2001); Hanspeter Kriesi, Ruud Koopmans, Jan Willem Dyvendak, and Marco G. Giugni, *New Social Movements in Western Europe* (Minneapolis: University of Minnesota Press,

1995); and Marco Giugni, Doug McAdam, and Charles Tilly (eds) *How Social Movements Matter* (Minneapolis: University of Minnesota Press, 1999).

23 Graeme B. Robertson, "Who's complaining? Regions, politics and protest waves in post-communist Russia," unpublished ms., Columbia University, 2002.

24 On township and village enterprises and foreign-owned factories, see Anita Chan, "The changing rural elite and political opposition in China," in Garry Rodan (ed.) *Political Oppositions in Industrializing Asia* (London and New York: Routledge, 1996), pp. 161–187. If scholars do not write about these movements in the same article, it suggests that they really are separate realms of activity.

25 Thomas G. Moore, *China in the World Market: Chinese Industry and International Sources of Reform in the Post-Mao Era* (Cambridge: Cambridge University Press, 2002); Nicholas R. Lardy, *Integrating China into the Global Economy* (Washington DC: Brookings Institution, 2002); David Zweig, *Internationalizing China: Domestic Interests and Global Linkages* (Ithaca: Cornell University Press, 2002).

26 Merle Goldman, "The potential for instability among alienated intellectuals and students in post-Mao China," in David Shambaugh (ed.) *Is China Unstable?* (Armonk, NY: M.E. Sharpe, 2000), pp. 112–124.

27 While half of Russians report relying on privately grown food supplies, there is a significant difference between Chinese peasants and Russian urban dwellers engaged in coping strategies.

28 Perry and Selden, "Introduction," pp. 10, 17.

29 Vadim Volkov, "Violent entrepreneurship in post-communist Russia," *Europe-Asia Studies* 51(5) (July 1999): 741–754, and *Violent Entrepreneurs: The Use of Force in the Making of Russian Capitalism* (Ithaca: Cornell University Press, 2002). Cf. Elizabeth J. Perry, "Crime, corruption and contention," in Merle Goldman and Roderick MacFarquhar (eds) *The Paradox of China's Post-Mao Reforms* (Cambridge, MA: Harvard University Press, 1999), pp. 308–329.

30 David Zweig, "The externalities of development: can new political institutions manage rural conflict?" in Perry and Selden, *Chinese Society*, pp. 120–142; Minxin Pei, "Rights and resistance: the changing contexts of the dissident movement," in Perry and Selden, *Chinese Society*, pp. 20–40. Cf. Kathryn Hendley, "Suing the state in Russia," *Post-Soviet Affairs* 18(2) (April–June 2002): 122–147, and "Legal development in post-Soviet Russia," *Post-Soviet Affairs* 13(3) (July–September 1997): 228–251; and Robert Sharlet, "Putin and the politics of law in Russia," *Post-Soviet Affairs* 17(3) (July–September 2001): 195–234.

31 Zweig, "The externalities of development." Cf. Akhil Gupta, "Blurred boundaries: the discourse of corruption, the culture of politics, and the imagined state," *American Ethnologist* 22(2) (May 1995): 375–402.

32 Lianjiang Li and Kevin J. O'Brien, "The struggle over village elections," in Goldman and MacFarquhar, *The Paradox of China's Post-Mao Reforms*, pp. 129–144.

33 Louisa Schein, "Urbanity, cosmopolitanism, consumption," in Chen *et al.*, *China Urban*, pp. 225–241; Charlotte Ikels, *The Return of the God of Wealth: The Transition to a Market Economy in Urban China* (Stanford: Stanford University Press, 1996); Chengze Simon Fan, "Economic development and the changing patterns of consumption in urban China," in Chua Beng-Huat (ed.) *Consumption in Asia: Lifestyles and Identities* (London and New York: Routledge, 2000), pp. 82–97; cf. Adele Barker (ed.) *Consuming Russia: Popular Culture, Sex and Society Since Gorbachev* (Durham: Duke University Press, 1999).

34 Archie Brown, *The Gorbachev Factor* (Oxford: Oxford University Press, 1996), p. 18.

35 Merle Goldman, *China's Intellectuals: Advise and Dissent* (Cambridge, MA: Harvard University Press, 1981); "The potential for instability among alienated

intellectuals and students in post-Mao China," in Shambaugh, *Is China Unstable?*, pp. 112–124; and "The emergence of politically independent intellectuals," in Goldman and MacFarquhar, *The Paradox of China's Post-Mao Reforms*, pp. 283–307. Cf. András Bozóki (ed.), *Intellectuals and Politics in Central Europe* (Budapest: Central European University Press, 1999).

36 Steve Fish describes the ways that the KGB sought to demoralize democratic groups in the USSR in the late 1980s. Fish, *Democracy from Scratch*.

37 Linda Chao and Ramon H. Myers, "How elections promoted democracy in Taiwan under martial law," in Larry Diamond and Ramon H. Myers (eds) *Elections and Democracy in Greater China* (Oxford: Oxford University Press, 2000), pp. 23–45. I am grateful to Merle Goldman for calling this relationship to my attention.

38 Mark R. Beissinger, *Nationalist Mobilization and the Collapse of the Soviet State* (Cambridge: Cambridge University Press, 2002).

39 These groups are, of course, a larger share of the urban population, but the pressure for rural migration to cities will inevitably dilute their relative numbers.

40 Sarah Cook, "After the iron rice bowl: extending the safety net in China," IDS Discussion Paper 377 (Institute of Development Studies, 2000); cf. Michael Burowoy, Pavel Krotin, and Tatyana Lytkina, "Domestic involution: how women organize survival in a north Russian city," in Victoria E. Bonnell and George W. Breslauer (eds) *Russia in the New Century: Stability or Disorder?* (Boulder: Westview Press, 2001), pp. 231–261.

41 See, for example, Shambaugh, *Is China Unstable?*, and the ten short articles in *Journal of Democracy* 14(1) (January 2003).

42 Several recent studies found Chinese Internet restrictions the most obtrusive among the countries studied. See Shanthi Kalathil and Taylor C. Boas, *Open Networks, Closed Regimes: The Impact of the Internet on Authoritarian Rule* (2003), and William Foster and Seymour E. Goodman, *The Diffusion of the Internet in China* (Washington DC: CSIS, November 2000).

43 In September 2000, Vladimir Putin convened a closed meeting to discuss Russian information policy. The security ministries argued that the flow of information should be subject to monitoring, even if this slowed it down and exacted economic costs. Representatives of business, science, education, and the provider community argued for open networks, attempting to demonstrate that the costs of inhibited information flow would ripple through the entire economy and retard Russia's economic recovery. At the end of the session, Putin opted to keep monitoring technology in place but not implement its use. For now, at least, this is a victory for openness – or at least *some* openness. Personal communications, Moscow, September 2000.

44 John Gerard Ruggie (ed.), *Multilateralism Matters: The Theory and Praxis of an Institutional Form* (New York: Columbia University Press, 1993).

45 Mary E. Gallagher, "'Reform and openness': why China's economic reforms have delayed democracy," *World Politics* 54(3) (April 2002): 338–372.

46 Minxin Pei, "Contradictory trends and confusing signals," *Journal of Democracy* 14(1) (January 2003): 73–81.

47 *Ibid.*, p. 81. For the debate about transformation or degeneration in the USSR, see Zbigniew Brzezinski, "The Soviet political system: transformation or degeneration," in Zbigniew Brzezinski (ed.) *Dilemmas of Change in Soviet Politics* (New York: Columbia University Press, 1969), pp. 1–34; Jerry Hough, "The Soviet system: petrification or pluralism?" *Problems of Communism* (1972); and Mark R. Beissinger, "Transformation and degeneration: the CPSU under reform," in James R. Millar (ed.) *Cracks in the Monolith: Party Power in the Brezhnev Era* (Armonk, NY: M.E. Sharpe, 1992). There might well be a Gorbachev lurking in the Chinese leadership. But by 1983, some Sovietologists

had specifically identified Gorbachev and were predicting significant change in the USSR.

48 David S.G. Goodman, "The People's Republic of China: the Party-state, capitalist revolution and new entrepreneurs," in Richard Robison and David S.G. Goodman (eds) *The New Rich in Asia: Mobile Phones, McDonalds and Middle-class Revolution* (London and New York: Routledge, 1996), pp. 225–242, and "The new middle class," in Goldman and MacFarquhar, *The Paradox of China's Post-Mao Reforms*, pp. 241–261.

49 Victoria E. Bonnell and Thomas B. Gold (eds), *The New Entrepreneurs of Europe and Asia: Patterns of Business Development in Russia, Eastern Europe, and China* (Armonk, NY: M.E. Sharpe, 2001), contributions by Bruce Gilley, "The Yu Zuomin phenomenon: entrepreneurs and politics in rural China," pp. 66–82; Margaret M. Pearson, "Entrepreneurs and democratization in China's foreign sector," pp. 130–158; and Doug Guthrie, "Entrepreneurial action in the state sector: the economic decisions of Chinese managers," pp. 159–190.

50 Sunhyuk Kim, *The Politics of Democratization in Korea: The Role of Civil Society* (Pittsburgh: University of Pittsburgh Press, 2000); Denise P. Lett, *In Pursuit of Status: The Making of South Korea's "New" Urban Middle Class* (Cambridge, MA: Harvard University Press, 1998).

51 Tianjian Shi, "Cultural values and democracy in the People's Republic of China," in Diamond and Myers, *Elections and Democracy in Greater China*, pp. 176–196.

52 India demonstrates that a country with far higher levels of illiteracy can maintain democratic institutions.

53 Harley Balzer, "Russia's self-denying middle class in the global age," in Klaus Segbers (ed.), *Explaining Post-Soviet Patchworks, Volume I: Actors and Sectors between Accommodation and Resistance to Globalization* (Aldershot: Ashgate Publishing, 2001).

54 Stephen Brint, *In An Age of Experts: The Changing Role of Professionals in Politics and Public Life* (Princeton: Princeton University Press, 1994), pp. 14–15.

55 Yifei Sun, "China's national education system in transition," *Eurasian Geography and Economics* 43(6) (September 2002): 476–492; Cong Cao and Richard P. Suttmeier, "China's new scientific elite: distinguished young scientists, the research environment, and hopes for Chinese science," *China Quarterly* 168 (December 2001): 960–984.

56 Konrad Jaurausch, "The decline of Liberal professionalism: reflections on the social erosion of German Liberalism, 1867–1933," in Konrad Jaurausch and L.E. Jones (eds) *In Search of a Liberal Germany: Studies in the History of German Liberalism from 1789 to the Present* (New York: Berg, 1990), pp. 273–280, and *The Unfree Professions: German Lawyers, Teachers, and Engineers, 1900–1950* (New York: Oxford University Press, 1990), pp. 80ff.; Michael H. Kater, *The Nazi Party: A Social Profile of Members and Leaders 1919–1945* (Cambridge, MA: Harvard University Press, 1985). A similar analysis has been applied to Hungary. See Mária M. Kovács, *Liberal Professions and Illiberal Politics: Hungary from the Habsburgs to the Holocaust* (Oxford: Oxford University Press, 1994), esp. Ch. 2.

57 Wenfang Tang and William L. Parish, *Chinese Urban Life Under Reform: The Changing Social Contract* (Cambridge: Cambridge University Press, 2000), p. 33, and Cao and Suttmeier, "China's new scientific elite," pp. 975–977, discuss the ways differential material rewards are affecting scientific researchers.

58 Goldman, "The potential for instability among alienated intellectuals and students in post-Mao China," and "The emergence of politically independent intellectuals."

59 Peter S. Goodman, "College degrees lose their magic in China: graduates flood the job market," *Washington Post*, 19 August 2003, p. A01.

60 Robison and Goodman, *The New Rich in Asia*. Cf. Beng-Huat, *Consumption in Asia*, and Schein, "Urbanity, cosmopolitanism, consumption."

61 Padraic Kenney, *A Carnival of Revolution: Central Europe 1989* (Princeton: Princeton University Press, 2002); Michael D. Kennedy, *Cultural Formations of Post-communism: Emancipation, Transition, Nation, and War* (Minneapolis: University of Minnesota Press, 2002).

62 Larry Diamond, "Assessing global democratization a decade after the communist collapse," address to the Workshop on Democratization organized by the New Europe College and the Romanian Academic Society, 6 May 2002, Bucharest. Available online at www.stanford.edu/~ldiamond/papers/romania_speech.pdf.

63 The view that current forms of contestation will represent a serious threat to China's communist leadership only if their legitimacy is challenged on multiple "fronts" is shared by Perry, "Crime, corruption and contention," pp. 308–329.

64 Cf. Thomas Christensen, "Chinese realpolitik," *Foreign Affairs* 75(5) (September–October 1996): 37–52. See also Prasenjit Duara, "Historicizing national identity, or who imagines what and when," in Geoff Eley and Ronald Grigor Suny (eds) *Becoming National* (New York: Oxford University Press, 1996), pp. 151–177.

65 See also Stephan Feuchtwang, "Religion as resistance," in Perry and Selden, *Chinese Society*, pp. 161–177. Cf. Toby Lester, "Oh, gods!", *Atlantic Monthly* (February 2002). Available online at www.theatlantic.com/issues/2002/02/lester.htm.

66 Ikels, *The Return of the God of Wealth*; Theodore Rozak, *The Making of a Counter-culture* (New York: Doubleday, 1969); Ronald Inglehart, *Modernization and Postmodernization: Cultural, Economic and Political Change in 43 Societies* (Princeton: Princeton University Press, 1997).

Index